THE
LEFT HAND
of
GOD

THE
LEFT HAND
of
GOD

*Taking Back Our Country
from the Religious Right*

MICHAEL LERNER

HarperSanFrancisco
A Division of HarperCollinsPublishers

HarperCollins books may be purchased for educational, business, or sales promotional use. For information please write: Special Markets Department, HarperCollins Publishers, 10 East 53rd Street, New York, NY 10022.

HarperCollins Web site: http://www.harpercollins.com

HarperCollins®, ☙®, and HarperSanFrancisco™ are
trademarks of HarperCollins Publishers.

FIRST EDITION
Designed by Joseph Rutt

Library of Congress Cataloging-in-Publication Data
Lerner, Michael
The left hand of God : taking back our country from the religious right / Michael Lerner.
p. cm.
Includes bibliographical references and index.
ISBN-13: 978–0–06084247–5
ISBN-10: 0–06–084247–4
1. Christianity and politics—United States. 2. Religion and politics—United States.
3. Religious right—United States. 4. Democratic Party (U.S.) 5. Conservatism—Religious
aspects—Christianity. 6. Conservatism—Religious aspects. I. Title.
BR115.P7L37 2005
322'.1'0973—dc22 2005052510

05 06 07 08 09 RRD(H) 10 9 8 7 6 5 4 3 2 1

I dedicate this book to my grandchildren, Ellie Lyla Lerner and Jeremiah Jacob Lerner—may they move the world toward more love, kindness, compassion, generosity, peace, and social justice.

And to Trish and George Vradenburg in appreciation of all the support they give me to continue this work and in appreciation of their work as publishers of *Tikkun* and as champions of the need to put more of our society's resources into curing Alzheimer's disease, assisting its many victims, and supporting all the caregivers of those who suffer from the disease.

Contents

viii

Contents

Introduction

The unholy alliance of the political Right and Religious Right threatens to destroy the America we love. It also threatens to generate a popular revulsion against God and religion by identifying them with militarism, ecological irresponsibility, fundamentalist antagonism to science and rational thought, and insensitivity to the needs of the poor and the powerless.

In the following pages, I will explain how a progressive spiritual politics can help rescue this country from its current self-destructive course. By addressing the real spiritual and moral crisis in the daily lives of most Americans, a movement with a progressive spiritual vision would provide an alternate solution to both the intolerant and militarist politics of the Right and the current misguided, visionless, and often spiritually empty politics of the Left.

The first section of this book details the spiritual and psychological needs that the Right was able to address in ways that allowed it to grow powerful and that the Left ignored and misunderstood (thus precipitating its decline) over the past thirty years. In the second section, I'll present a Progressive Spiritual Covenant with America that could advance a progressive political revival in the coming years.

We live in a world in which a technocratic rationality has replaced an awareness of spirit, flattening the way we experience nature and each other. Social theorists from Max Weber to Zygmunt Bauman have described the disorientation and desperation that this has caused to people in the modern world. In the United States this process has reached its fullest development in the form of a bottom-line mentality that judges every activity, every institution, every social practice as rational, productive, or efficient only to the extent that it produces money or power.

This way of organizing our society promotes selfishness, materialism, and disconnection. We are encouraged to live on the surface of things, to deal with other human beings as though they were mere material objects to be manipulated for the sake of our own self-interest, and to relate to the physical universe as though it is nothing more than a resource to satisfy our personal needs. Nature becomes another commodity to be bought and sold. Human relationships become increasingly instrumental, utilitarian, and manipulative, as people learn to see each other through the frame of "How can other people be of use to me to serve my needs?"

Professions are no longer seen as vocations serving the common good or the God of the universe but become instead simply careers, opportunities for individuals to accumulate money and prestige for themselves.

Most of us have learned to accommodate to a world that has been flattened, made one-dimensional, disenchanted, despiritualized. And yet, we feel an abiding hunger because human beings are theotropic— they turn toward the sacred—and that dimension in us cannot be fully extinguished. People feel a near-desperate desire to reconnect to the sacred, to find some way to unite their lives with a higher meaning and purpose and in particular to that aspect of the sacred that is built upon the loving, kind, and generous energy in the universe that I describe as the "Left Hand of God." The Left Hand of God view encourages us to be like this loving God. As the Talmud teaches, "Just as He is filled with mercy, compassion, and loving-kindness, so should you live your life manifesting mercy, compassion, and loving-kindness to all whom you encounter." I will contrast that notion of God in this book with the "Right Hand of God," which sees the universe as a fundamentally scary place filled with evil forces. In this view God is the avenger, the big man in heaven who can be invoked to use violence to overcome those evil forces, either right now or in some future ultimate reckoning. Seen through the frame of the Right Hand of God, the world is filled with constant dangers and the rational way to live is to dominate and control others before they dominate and control us.

It is the search for meaning in a despiritualized world that leads many people to right-wing religious communities because these groups seem to be in touch with the sacred dimension of life. Many secularists imagine that people drawn to the Right are there solely because of some ethical or psychological malfunction. What they miss is that there are many very decent Americans who get attracted to the Religious Right because it is the only voice that they encounter that is willing to challenge the despiritualization of daily life, to call for a life that is driven by higher purpose than money, and to provide actual experiences of supportive community for those whose daily life is suffused with alienation and spiritual loneliness.

Many Americans have a powerful desire for loving connection, kindness, generosity, awe and wonder, and joyous celebration of the universe. These desires are frustrated by the way we organize our society today. A progessive movement or a Democratic Party that speaks to these desires in a genuine and spiritually deep way could win the popular support it needs to create a world of peace, social justice, ecological sanity, and human rights.

It may be hard to foresee today's Democratic Party becoming a champion of love or kindness or generosity or spiritual sensitivity to the grandeur of the universe. That party, at least as it exists in 2006, is so dominated by self-interested politicians who rely on the backing of the wealthy and legitimacy from a corporate-dominated media that they'd be unlikely to embrace a discourse of love or a practice of awe and wonder in response to the miracles of creation. Nevertheless, it's a mistake to get crystallized in the static. I remember how hard it was in 1968 to imagine that the Democrats would ever be responsive to the ideas being developed by the antiwar movement, the women's movement, and the gay rights movement. Yet much changed, and changed within a few decades. That can happen again. It is already happening in regard to the war in Iraq, and it can happen on the even more fundamental levels proposed in this book.

The Network of Spiritual Progressives can be for the Democrats and Greens what the Religious Right has been for the Republicans: a movement that energizes and provides intellectual, political, and spiritual inspiration for those in the party even while not being formally aligned when it comes to elections, a movement to which the party responds with serious attention, respect, and commitment to taking parts of its program and placing it at the center of the party's agenda. While a progressive spiritual politics is unlikely to move hard-core fundamentalists or those who have made an idolatry of their worship of the free market, there are millions of others who could be reached were they to experience the Democrats, Greens, and liberal/progressive movements as really challenging the ethos of selfishness and materialism in daily life.

As I watch the likely Democratic Party candidates for president in 2008 scramble to position themselves as mainstream, I am all too aware that taking this kind of spiritual politics seriously is going to require a huge leap for many of us. So in much of this book I'm going to talk to our most skeptical side and address the doubts that are certainly likely to be most prominent. I'll present a plan for how to structure a society that is humane, generous, peace-oriented, and ecologically responsible, and I'll challenge our depressive certainty that these kinds of changes are never going to happen.

Some Democrats think that they don't need these changes to win power, and they may be right in the short run. The current implosion of the Bush administration as it wallows in the aftermath of Hurricane Katrina, a failing war in Iraq, and scandal and indictments at the highest levels of government may be enough to provide Democrats with election victories in 2006 and 2008 (though Republican redistricting is likely to dampen the chance for a Democratic landslide in 2006, and electoral fraud has increasingly characterized American national elections where so much is at stake).

But Democrats have won elections, even the presidency, before—and yet the movement of intellectual and political energy keeps on sliding to the Right, and so Democrats in office often end up acting from the assumptions of the Right in order to show that they are "realistic" and "non-ideological."

I invite you to compare the Democratic Party agenda for 2006 with the Spiritual Covenant with America you'll find in the second part of this book. The Spiritual Covenant isn't just doing "more" or more radical versions of the Democrats' agenda—while incorporating many of the specifics of the Democrats' program. Rather, it represents a whole different way to think about human needs. It is my hope that spiritually or religiously grounded progressives among the Democrats, the Greens, and even the Republican party, and in the array of social change movements, will use these ideas to challenge the more mechanistic, materialistic, and selfishness-oriented assumptions that currently predominate and distort political discourse in America.

Nothing has been more dispiriting than to watch years in which Congressional Democrats continued to vote for tens of billions of dollars to fund the war in Iraq even after learning that the country had been lied to and manipulated into that war. Even after conservative Democratic congressman John Murtha called for immediate withdrawal from Iraq within six months in November 2005, the Democrats were unable to firmly endorse that courageous call. Without a larger spiritual vision, the Democrats too often develop their programs by poll data, reacting rather than leading. They may eventually oppose a specific war, but they are afraid to oppose war. They throw money to alleviate suffering from some particularly terrible social injustice, but they are afraid to envision and fight for an end to all social injustice. Spiritual progressives have to help them find their own inner strength, and in the Spiritual Covenant we will also provide them with a way of thinking that grounds their politics (not merely "reframing" it so that it will sell, but deepening it by giving it a spiritual dimension), and then draw them into programs such as "the Generosity strategy" for homeland security outlined in the Covenant.

Let me reassure you that the spiritual vision I present is not an attempt to recruit you to some particular religious community or spiritual trip. You do not have to become religious to embrace a spiritual politics or to learn from the wisdom of various spiritual practices.

I do not blame many secularists who resent the way that some in the Religious Right seek to shove a fundamentalist and intolerant religion down our throats. Almost every religion, like almost every political and intellectual movement, has people of that sort, and holy texts (both religious and secular) have voices that validate an oppressive, dominating, fearful way of seeing. Yet in most religions (just as in many secular social change movements and liberation ideologies) there are also voices of the Left Hand of God, voices that embrace compassion, love, generosity of spirit, kindness, peace, social justice, environmental sanity, and nonviolence. I invite secular liberals and progressives to momentarily suspend their cynicism and allow themselves to experience the world through the framework presented here, and I believe they'll encounter a way of thinking that could lead a progressive movement to winning a majority of Americans to a politics that is at once politically liberatory, economically progressive, emotionally satisfying and spiritually deep.

Meanwhile we face a Bush administration that remains deeply committed to using its remaining years in power to implement a right-wing agenda by sacking the common wealth of this country to enrich its allies in America's economic elite. The political Right is willing to deplete the educational system of its funding base, to dismantle Social Security benefits for the elderly and social services for the poor, to destroy forests and pave over farmlands and pour poisons in the air, to turn water into a private commodity to be sold, to eliminate fish and animal species, to lift restraints on putting dangerous chemical into the foods and products we consume, and to make war around the world. It fervently believes that the corporate America whose interests it serves will be able to create wealth and jobs that will benefit everyone if only government is sufficiently weakened, its most popular programs dismantled, its mandate to impose environmental and health-and-safety regulations dramatically curtailed.

This political Right achieved power by forging an alliance with a Religious Right that is willing to provide a sanctimonious religious veneer to the selfishness and materialism of the political Right in exchange for the political power it needs to impose parts of its religious agenda on America. Capitalizing on a very real and deep spiritual crisis engendered by living in a society that teaches "looking out for number one" as its highest value, the Religious Right has managed to mobilize tens of millions of people to vote for candidates who end up supporting the very economic arrangements and political ideas responsible for creating the spiritual crisis in the first place. With this alliance now propelling them into control of Congress, the presidency, and the judiciary, they have launched a cultural crusade against liberals, secularists, activist judges, homosexuals, feminists, and anyone who still believes in peace and social justice. The country received its strongest alert to the nature of the assault on the American tradition of religious tolerance when, in the spring of 2005, the Right began to talk openly about impeaching from the judiciary "activist judges" who were imposing "secular values" on the country, then managed to torpedo Bush's nominee to the Supreme Court (Harriet Miers) and encouraged him to appoint Samuel Alito, a sophisticated conservative ideologue.

But the assault of the Religious Right is taking place not only on the federal level. Reporting in the *New York Times* (December 13, 2004), Neela Banerjee outlined how "Christian Conservatives" are pushing their agenda on state and local levels, particularly on issues of same-sex marriage, public education, stem-cell research, and abortion. In some states legislation has been introduced to remove state requirements that all forms of contraception and their potential health effects be taught in schools, leaving the focus on abstinence. Other proposed state legislation would require publishers of biology textbooks to include at least one chapter devoted to alternative theories of evolution. Capturing a frequent formulation of the Religious Right, which prefers to see itself as a beleaguered minority despite the power it wields at all levels of government, Banerjee quoted Christian conservative legislator Representative Cynthia Davis of Missouri, who likened the liberals dominating the political agenda to the terrorists hijacking planes on September 11, 2001.

Though the Religious Right attracts political conservatives from the Jewish and Catholic world as well, its primary funding and organizational energies come from Protestants. Not all members of fundamentalist, Pentecostal, and charismatic churches support the Religious Right, of course, and many Christian leaders strongly oppose it. Nonetheless, its role in the Christian world and in American politics has grown dramatically over the past twenty years and has reached a new height in the second term of a president who talks at times as though he believes that he is receiving messages directly from God.

Although I do not share the goals of many leaders of the Religious Right—and in fact believe that they pose a huge danger to American society—I must admit some appreciation for their willingness to state their objectives clearly and honestly, a refreshing change from the diet of mush that often emerges from the Democratic Party. Paul Weyrich, one of the Right's most serious strategists, said it clearly in 1980: "We are talking about Christianizing America. We are talking about simply spreading the gospel in a political context." I was invited that same year to debate Weyrich at the Moral Majority's annual Family Forum and found him a powerful advocate for a frightening worldview that I hoped would remain marginal in America. But twenty-five years later, having followed the advice of Jerry Falwell, who famously said, "Get them saved, get them baptized, and get them registered," the Christian Right is now carrying out its agenda.

George Grant, who served as executive director of one of the many successful organizations of the Religious Right, the Coral Ridge Ministries, likewise hid nothing when he put forward a goal shared by many in his book *The Changing of the Guard: Biblical Principles for Political Action:* "Christians have an objective, a commission, a holy responsibility to reclaim the land for Jesus Christ—to have dominion in civil structures, just as in every other aspect of life and godliness. But it is dominion we are after. Not just a voice. It is dominion we are after. Not just influence. It is dominion we are after. Not just equal time. It is dominion we are after. World conquest. That's what Christ has commissioned us to accomplish. We must win the world with the power of the Gospel. And we must never settle for anything less.... Thus, Christian politics has as its primary intent the conquest of the land—of men, families, institutions, bureaucracies, courts and governments for the Kingdom of Christ" (pp. 50–51). Or as televangelist Pat Robertson put it more succinctly in 1986, the goal is to "rule the world for God."

I am very concerned to avoid the tendency of some on the Left to dismiss or demean people on the Right. It's no excuse that some on the Right talk and act in a demeaning fashion toward liberals and secular people. Though I strongly wish to diminish the political power of the Right, no worthwhile political goal justifies demeaning the humanity of and ignoring the spirit of God in those with whom we disagree.

It is perfectly legitimate to be alarmed at the growing power of those on the Right and the way they use it, to challenge their ideas forcefully, and to warn of the dangers should they succeed in their stated intentions. I will certainly do everything I can to prevent them from popularizing the notion that people have to be religious or believe in God to be moral and to challenge their particular understanding of what God wants of us.

What I will not do, and what I urge my friends in liberal and progressive movements not to do, is attribute evil motives to those on the Religious Right or to view them as cynical manipulators solely interested in power and self-aggrandizement. The Religious Right certainly has its share of power mongers and hypocrites. But the vast majority of those involved are people who are driven by principles and who want what is best for the world. We can strongly disagree with those principles, as I do, and we can argue, as I will, that they lead in a very dangerous direction, one that would actually increase the pain and suffering of humanity. But I do not doubt the sincerity or basic goodness of most of those who are involved.

Moreover, it is a mistake to portray people on the Religious Right as monolithic in their thinking or all sharing the views of their more extreme leaders, or to reduce the complexities in their thinking to a few slogans. As I'll discuss later in this book, many of the people who have been attracted to the Religious Right do not share the goal of Christianizing America. Many are people who have turned to the Religious Right to address legitimate spiritual needs that were not being addressed elsewhere.

However, many Religious Right activists and organizations *do* share this Christianizing goal, and even though many of their supporters may not intend this, their growing participation in politics and their support for the candidates of the Religious Right are in fact empowering some of the more extreme elements.

According to a report by Glenn Scherer in *Grist* magazine (October 27, 2004), a survey conducted in 2003 found that 45 senators and 186 representatives earned 80 to 100 percent approval ratings from the nation's three most influential Christian Right advocacy groups—the Christian Coalition, Eagle Forum, and the Family Resource Council. The seven highest-ranking Senate Republicans were each awarded a score of 100 percent by the Christian Coalition—whereas the League of Conservation Voters, a consortium of environmental groups, gave them a mere 0 to 8 percent. They are Bill Frist (Tenn.), Mitch McConnell (Ky.), Rick Santorum (Pa.), Bob Bennett (Utah), Kay Bailey Hutchison (Tex.), Jon Kyl (Ariz.), and George Allen (Va.) (reported on www.theocracy-watch.org). These are the people shaping American politics in the first decade of the twenty-first century.

Nor are the zealots content to control the more obvious branches of government. The armed services of the United States have been another target. On June 22, 2005, an Air Force panel sent to investigate charges of religious intimidation at the Air Force Academy in Colorado Springs found evidence that officers and faculty members periodically used their positions to promote their Christian beliefs and failed to accommodate the religious needs of non-Christians. The proselytizing of non-Christian cadets remains under investigation in the Air Force (primarily because a whistle-blower managed to receive national attention), but the behavior continues in other branches of the armed forces, and although media attention forced the top brass to describe the behavior as unacceptable, they also concluded that it was not "overt religious discrimination."

The Right is bulldozing the whole society toward a world that the majority never chose. Republican moderates worry that the policies being pursued by the Bush administration are undermining the long-term stability of the country and the Constitution yet find themselves under intense pressure to show absolute loyalty or else face the wrath of a Republican leadership that has increasingly adopted the agenda of the most extreme members of its party. Representative Christopher Shays (R-Conn.), said it clearly to the *New York Times* (March 23, 2005): "This Republican Party of Lincoln has become a party of theocracy." For ongoing coverage of this development, make frequent visits to the Web site of Theocracy Watch (www.theocracywatch.org), a group chronicling the rise of the Religious Right in the Republican Party.

The attempt by the Bush administration and the Religious Rightists in Congress to pack the federal judiciary with extremists has not only persisted but has been extremely successful. By threatening to eliminate the filibuster as a tactic, congressional supporters of the Religious Right maneuvered the Democrats into a "compromise" that pushed into the federal judiciary three judges who were far more extreme in their views than are most of those who support the Right. They then succeeded in confirming a new chief justice of the United States whose legal views would have been considered extremist before the Right dominated public discourse.

It's not just the packing of the courts but the intimidation of sitting judges that has taken the Religious Right way beyond the boundaries of respectful political discourse. Recognized leaders of the Religious Right charge repeatedly that decisions of the federal judiciary concerning civil liberties and the separation of church and state constitute an assault on Christianity by activist judges who are trying to impose their own secular religion on the society.

"As the liberal, anti-Christian dogma of the left has been repudiated in almost every recent election, the courts have become the last great bastion for liberalism," Tony Perkins, president of the Family Research Council and organizer of a telecast in April 2005 aimed at mobilizing opposition to liberal judges, wrote in a message on the group's Web site. "For years activist courts, aided by liberal interest groups like the A.C.L.U. have been quietly working under the veil of the judiciary, like thieves in the night, to rob us of our Christian heritage and our religious freedoms."

When the majority leader of the Senate, Republican Bill Frist, joined this telecast, it became clear that the Religious Rightists who are mobilizing this assault on the judiciary have powerful allies in Congress. Mr. Perkins stood by the characterization of the Democrats as hostile to faith. "What they have done is, they have targeted people for reasons of their faith or moral position," he said, referring to Democratic criticisms of nominees on the basis of their opinions on cases about abortion rights or separation of church and state.

In characterizing court decisions as an assault on Christianity or on people of faith, some powerful leaders of the Religious Right have sought to undermine the separation of church and state, calling it anti-Christian. Moreover, contrary to the Family Research Council's claims, court decisions have not resulted in the "banning of school prayer" and "the expulsion of the Ten Commandments from public spaces." As Melissa Rogers, a visiting professor of religion and public policy at Wake Forest University Divinity School, pointed out in the *Baltimore Sun* (April 22, 2005), courts have repeatedly recognized that students have every right to pray in public schools, as long as the school does not sponsor the prayer. Similarly, the Supreme Court has held that if public parks are generally open for community group rallies and signs, religious rallies and signs must be welcome too, so long as it's clear that the government itself isn't promoting religion. Many religious people support the principles underlying the separation of church and state precisely because they don't want the government secularizing the sacred and otherwise meddling in religion.

Yet President Bush has been very adept at infusing the agenda of the Religious Right into national politics. Bush introduced "faith-based funding," reassured the nation that he was not going to fund proselytizing, and then managed over the course of several years to move that funding increasingly into the hands of organizations that do in fact actively promote their particular version of Christianity. Bush, Frist, and the leadership of key elements of the Religious Right have shown the direction in which they hope to move the country, step by step, and it is a direction that would effectively create a theocracy, limiting civil liberties to a minimum and significantly undermining the separation of church and state.

Jim Wallis, in his important book *God's Politics,* did an outstanding and politically important job of showing how very far the Religious Right has wandered from the teachings of Jesus. Bill Press's provocative book *How the Republicans Stole Christmas* and Mark Lewis Taylor's *Religion, Politics and the Christian Right* have done an impressive job of showing how dangerous the Religious Right has become for our civil liberties, our moral compass, and our democratic values. In this book I don't spend much time going over the ground that Wallis, Press, and others have so effectively covered. I touch different ground, trying to understand what the Religious Right reached in people that makes them succeed and how a network of spiritual progressives might successfully counter them and take back our country.

So where are the Democrats, the liberals, and the progressive forces that have traditionally been able to provide a counterweight to corporate selfishness and have fought for separation of church and state?

For much of the past thirty years the Democrats have been more interested in showing how similar they are to the Right than how different. Faced with both a corporate takeover of the media that increasingly portrays liberal and progressive ideas as some form of extremism or "class warfare" and with a Religious Right that has managed to put secular people on the defensive, the Democratic Party and much of the liberal and progressive world (which for convenience I'll call the Left)* has contented itself with mild reforms. It tinkers with narrow policy goals instead of promoting an alternative vision and alternative values to those of the Right. Fearful of political isolation, Democrats listen to the wisdom preached by the media and by a bevy of corporate-friendly professional consultants who tell them to be "realistic" by accepting the contours of politics as defined by the Right. And the more they do so, the less anyone else sees these Democrats as a viable alternative. Democratic voters lose their enthusiasm. They go to the polls grudgingly, not because they believe that the Democrats have any solutions but rather to stave off the even worse consequences of Republican dominance. Many do not even bother voting, and millions of others look for vision elsewhere—and find it in the Religious Right.

Others take the approach of the "let's-move-further-to-the-left" section of the Left, insisting that the old formulas of the really radical Left, mixed with a repackaging of identity politics and presented as economic populism, would provide the magic formula, if only those Democrats would listen! But meanwhile, they can't explain why their candidates, running in Democratic primaries or as Greens, rarely manage to get significant support from American voters. But the "let's-get-closer-to-the-middle-of-the-road" mavens of Democratic leadership face that same

---

* Although I don't like being pushed into this Left/Right distinction, trying to list all the groups and capture all the nuances each time I refer to the array of forces involved in this political struggle is tedious and clumsy. For purposes of this book, when I talk about the Left, I'm referring to the Democratic Party, the Greens, the labor movement, the women's movement, environmental movements, the peace movement, and an array of NGOs, nonprofits, and social change movements seeking social justice, universal health care, disarmament, civil rights, civil liberties, and stricter rules for worker safety and health and for consumer protections. When I talk about the political Right, I'm talking about those groups that oppose the use of government to rectify social ills, believe that the capitalist market will solve most of our social problems if left alone, with only the barest minimum of regulations, and wish to see government restrict its major efforts to police work and military activity, to protecting the country from terrorism and other threats from abroad, and to government legislation and programs that support the infrastructure of the capitalist economy and assist corporations in becoming more profitable in the global economy.

challenge, since they've also tried the "let's-be-softer-and-gentler-born-again Republicans" strategy, and it too has failed.

We need to look deeper.

When the Democrats were up against the political Right alone, the arguments seemed easier. The Right was interested in advancing the interests of corporate power, claiming that others would benefit from trickle-down economics that would allow the rest of the country to benefit from the wealth at the top. The Left argued that not enough was trickling down and that government was needed to offset the worst consequences of the competitive marketplace. But when the Religious Right teamed up with the political Right, the dynamics began to turn. The Religious Right mobilized the deep spiritual yearnings of the American public, yearnings made more intense by the strengthening of an antispiritual reality in the daily lives of many people.

Liberals and progressives sometimes like to make fun of the Right by pointing out that it is precisely in the Red states of the Republican majority where abortions are most prevalent, where divorce is most rampant, where the power of corporate selfishness is most unrestrained by laws, where the malls have done most to uproot small businesses, and where materialism on the whole seems to be having its greatest field day. The same is true for many of the enclaves of Red-state consciousness in Blue states, such as the gated communities and mostly white valleys of Southern California or the suburban areas of many other Blue states. But that, of course, is just the point. It is precisely because people in the Red states are suffering most from the epidemic of uncontrolled me-firstism that so many residents of those states are so desperate to find a counterforce. They are the most susceptible to the appeals of a Religious Right that has become a champion for family values, tradition, the stability that is offered by authoritarian and patriarchal norms, and the real comfort that spiritual life offers through connection to something higher than money.

The point is that there is a *real* spiritual crisis in American society, and the Religious Right has managed to position itself as the articulator of the pain that crisis causes and as the caring force that will provide a spiritual solution. And then it takes the credibility that it has won in this way and associates itself with a political Right that is actually championing the very institutions and social arrangements that caused this problem in the first place. And with the power that each of these has gained by their alliance, they have become ever more arrogant in trying to impose their worldview on everyone else in society. Their alliance threatens to destroy the fragile balance between secular and religious people and to move the United States toward the very kind of theocracy that people originally came to this country to escape.

So, how could this happen?

It has happened because the political Left doesn't really have a clue about the spiritual crisis in American society and is thus unable to address it in any persuasive way. Witnessing the country give electoral victories to the Right, those on the Left are totally confused about why it's happening. They earnestly study poll data and then reposition themselves in ways that will not put them too far beyond where they imagine popular opinion is moving. It never occurs to them to be the shapers of this social energy instead of merely the responders. For much of the past twenty-five years, since the early days of the Reagan administration, the Democrats have explained their electoral losses by claiming that the country is just in a "conservative period," as though the political climate had fallen mysteriously from heaven and had nothing to do with the way liberals failed to develop mass support for a progressive worldview when they held political power. In this book I will provide you with an explanation of why we got into a conservative period and how that can be changed.

After the 2004 elections many Democrats read the exit-poll data and realized that some voters were motivated by "values." Since then the Democrats have been frantically looking for a magic bullet to win back the "values voters." But mostly their discussion has been about hype, not about substance.

If we, the American people, are going to win back our country from the Religious Right, we are going to have to reshape the Democratic Party and the Greens, or create some other party, to come to grips with the depth of alienation from liberal politics among the many people who continue to vote, unenthusiastically, for the Democrats as the only way to stop the Right.

As I'll show in this book, a reshaped Democratic Party, or a new party, must minimally:

Understand, acknowledge, and respond to the spiritual crisis in American society—and provide a progressive spiritual vision that is more attractive than the one currently offered by the Right. This book will show how that can be done.

Recognize that people hunger for a world that has meaning and love; for a sense of aliveness, energy, and authenticity; for a life embedded in a community in which they are valued for who they most deeply are, with all their warts and limitations, and feel genuinely seen and recognized; for a sense of contributing to the good; and for a life that is about something more than just money and accumulating material goods. It is to these needs that I refer when I speak about "meaning needs."

Reject the tendency to regard people who are not part of the liberal culture as stupid, demented, or evil. Instead, it must affirm the fundamental decency and goodness of people. When it finds people acting in ways that are hurtful or irrational or violent, it will look deeper to discover the legitimate needs that have been frustrated by some aspect of social or psychological reality and then find a respectful way to address those needs. Most people do not aspire to militarism, insensitivity to the poor, torture of prisoners, or denial of human rights. So if some set of needs has been manipulated in ways that get people to support politicians who advocate these policies, our task is to find the rational kernel in the need structure of these people and then move them in a less hurtful and destructive direction. That can never happen if the message being communicated is that we perceive them to be stupid or evil.

Fight for ideals that are not yet popular and be willing to stand for those ideals even if that means temporarily losing some elections. The respect generated by sticking to one's ideals even at the expense of one's short-term electoral ambitions is necessary for building trust. No party can hope to retain the enthusiasm of its own supporters, much less the interest of the undecideds, unless it can clearly articulate its own vision, require that vision to be shared by its candidates, and argue for that vision even before it is popular.

Unite secular people in a movement with "spiritual but not religious" people and join both of those groups with progressive religious people. Reject and combat the religion phobia that dominates important sectors of liberal and progressive culture. Make religious and spiritual people feel welcome and their practices respected. Just as the Democrats once made their party unwelcoming to those who were overtly racist, sexist, or homophobic, so it must be unwelcoming to those whose legitimate anger at oppressive forms of religion turns into a disdainful attitude toward all religions and all religious people. At the same time, it must insist on tolerance and respect from religious people toward those who do not believe in God and those who have a nontheistic form of spirituality.

Only a political party that can incorporate these goals at the center of its agenda can hope to win a majority, which would allow it to implement the other peace, justice, and ecological goals of the liberal and progressive agenda. I will show in this book that for many Americans, meaning needs are the most pressing issues in their lives. This hunger for meaning, mutual recognition, and a spiritual foundation for their lives—for a sense of aliveness to counter the emotional and spiritual deadness that people experience in work and on television—is just as significant as the hunger for material well-being. Hence these are not issues that can be addressed "later," after all the peace and justice and ecological issues have been solved. These needs lie at the center of many Americans' lives, and unless we address them powerfully and convincingly, the Democrats and the Left will continue to lose power.

Beyond Left and Right

Many people don't really care at all about the Left or the Right, are tired of political rhetoric and opportunistic politicians and of the endless divisiveness that this discourse generates.

We just want this planet to survive, and we see the growing craziness in government, and even the obsessive struggle between Left and Right, as part of the problem.

We feel a yearning for a whole different level of discourse, not something narrowly instrumental that is basically about winning an election.

We want to hear political leaders acknowledge that we today are the latest embodiments of the evolution of the consciousness of the universe, and we want to see the human race get over its petty struggles, its nationalism and wars, its racism and demeaning of others, and start pulling together as a global community so that together we can face the major challenge of the twenty-first century: repairing the life-support system of planet Earth.

That very yearning for a world based more on love than on domination over others, for a world in which people respond with awe and wonder rather than with a purely utilitarian attitude toward other human beings and toward nature, is the core of a religious and spiritual tradition that I call the Left Hand of God. Those who belong to this tradition see God as the Force in the universe that makes possible transformation from a world based on pain and cruelty to a world based on love and generosity, the Force that makes possible the transcendence of what Freud called the repetition compulsion (the tendency to pass on to others the pain that has been inflicted upon us), the Force that makes possible a world of nonviolence, peace, and social justice.

The Left Hand of God stands in marked contrast to the vision of God as the powerful avenger, the Force that will overthrow evil through superior power, the Force that seeks to exterminate enemies and suppress dissent. The vision of the Right Hand of God imagines that evil can be wiped out by one more war or by imposing rigid commandments about how to live and enforcing them through violence and punishment. It imagines that people can be coerced into goodness.

The human race needs and yearns for the Left Hand of God. It longs to be part of a world in which kindness, generosity, nonviolence, humility, inner and outer peace, love, and wonder at the grandeur of creation stand at the center of our political and economic systems and become the major realities of our daily life experience.

The spiritual consciousness that I call the Left Hand of God is not the exclusive property of any one party or movement. Although I'd like the political Left to adopt it, it certainly does not characterize all parts of the Left today. I've attended antiwar demonstrations where speakers played on people's fears or justified the violence of terrorists or talked in the kind of aggressive, militaristic language that is indistinguishable from the harsh and judgmental tone I frequently hear coming from the political Right. And I witnessed that same aggressive tone at the Democratic National Convention in 2004, though that time it was about the need to kill all the terrorists and be more militaristic than the Right.

I was worried that in naming this book *The Left Hand of God* I might appear to be just another of those who want to manipulate religious or spiritual truth so that it can be used to advance the needs of the Democrats or the Left. The truth is that the Democrats and the Left today are far from espousing the vision that I believe the world needs, a vision that would transcend both the existing Left and Right while incorporating some of what is good from both ends of the political spectrum. But to move in that direction, we have to start somewhere, and I think the most plausible place to start is by trying to move the tens of millions of people who support the Democrats, the Greens, or the social movements of the Left toward the Left Hand of God.

I pick the Left as the best potential embodiment of the Left Hand of God view because I believe that much of its current agenda (end the war, provide for the poor, save the environment, protect civil liberties, fight for social justice, respect the rights of minorities and groups that have faced discrimination or oppression in the past, end torture, respect human rights), no matter how poorly articulated, is consistent with the spiritual vision of the Left Hand of God. Moreover, my experience in social change movements has exposed me to many people who already hold a Left Hand of God sensibility, even though articulating that would be very difficult in the Left as currently constituted.

Moreover, many in the Left who think of themselves as secular are actually already spiritual in a deep way. Though they reject patriarchal and hierarchical visions of God (as do many of us who are involved in religious traditions), many of them have developed an acute awareness that the dominant materialist and scientistic worldview is not an adequate framework within which to understand their own ethical values, their own consciousness and ideas, or their own experience of love and awe. Many of them are what I call "spiritual but not religious" people. Yet in the context of their involvement with the Left, they tend to keep those sensibilities to themselves, aware that if they articulated them explicitly, they might face ridicule from the most militant secularists, who often shape the public discourse of the liberal and progressive world. When I critique the Left in this book, I'm referring to the most militant secularists; I am well aware that these criticisms don't apply to many spiritual people who are engaged in the Left but feel they need to keep a low profile. One of my goals for this book is to encourage liberals and progressives who identify with the Left Hand of God to come out of the closet and identify publicly as spiritual beings and claim their right to be heard and respected as spiritual people within the Democratic Party, the Greens, or any other liberal and progressive group.

However, I'm aware that the moment we begin to talk in this way about a world based on love and generosity or about awe and wonder, cynicism surfaces in most of us.

A close friend reading a draft of this book warned me: "You can talk about God, but you can't appear to be taking seriously the love and kindness messages of Torah, the Prophets, and the New Testament as though you are actually taking them as guides for action in the contemporary world. Stay away from any of that religious stuff suggesting that a world can be based on love and kindness, because you'll be dismissed as a naive utopian, New Age flake, or at best politically irrelevant."

This comment gets to the heart of the problem facing Democrats. If they try to win power by being copycats of the Republicans, they will face no critique from the media, because the values that they need to espouse when justifying an expanding American empire and preferential option for the needs of the rich (in the hopes that some of that wealth will then trickle down to the rest of us) are perceived not as utopian but as realistic. But if the Democrats try to chart an alternative path, one that builds on a recognition of the interdependence of all people on this planet and on our need for an ethos of generosity and caring—that is, if the Democrats take the Left Hand of God seriously—then they will immediately be dismissed by the powerful as naive or utopian.

Now this may seem unfair. How can the Religious Right get away with using religious language and even mentioning values like kindness and generosity and love, while those with a more progressive politics have to fear being marginalized if they take these same values seriously?

There's a certain perverse logic in this situation, because although the Right may talk about love or invoke God, what they have in mind is the

Right Hand of God. The Right Hand of God is the hand of power and domination, the vision of God in which love is presented as consistent with celebrating the pain inflicted on those who are perceived as evil. So, for example, some on the Christian Right may celebrate the baby Jesus and acknowledge the Sermon on the Mount, but many experience God through the frame taught to tens of millions of Americans who have made the books in Tim LaHaye's Left Behind series best sellers. The Jesus they think about is the God whose Second Coming to earth will violently wipe out enemies and punish sinners. And that view of God then fits neatly with a politics of militarism, xenophobic nationalism, and support for U.S. domination over other countries. It's this vision of a muscular religion, backed by a God of power, that ensures that no one will ever call them naive, because in their actual politics they are not siding with the powerless but cheerleading for the powerful.

This kind of religious triumphalism—"Our God will emerge as the real God at the end of history, and all the rest of you will get your deserved punishment"—is not confined to right-wing Christianity. It is as prevalent in some parts of Judaism, Islam, and many other religions. It was also an element in the eschatology of Marxism, with its secular vision of the triumph of the working class and the overthrow of the bourgeoisie. In part, this way of thinking is appealing because many people can't imagine how a world dominated by pain and cruelty will ever be overcome in any other way. God as the all-powerful savior provides an answer.

But there's another reason why the Right Hand of God has so many supporters: most people have never even been exposed to a coherent spiritual-political alternative. They've never encountered people who take seriously the path of love, generosity, and compassion as a realistic strategy for building a different kind of world. When they meet Democrats who claim to be for peace and justice, they rarely hear them defend their perspective by referring to the values of the Left Hand of God or by describing what a world based on love and kindness might look like. Rather, the moment the Democrats are challenged, they revert to protecting their own credibility by locating themselves in the discourse of the Right Hand of God. And what the rest of the population gets from this maneuver is clear: these Democrats don't really believe in what they are saying, so how can anyone feel safe backing their ideas and policies?

That is why it is important to be unequivocal rather than apologetic about championing a vision of love and generosity. So, yes, I do want to embrace the Left Hand of God and the teachings of Torah, the Prophets, Jesus, Muhammed, the Buddha, and the wisdom of most of the world's religious and spiritual traditions to the extent that they provide a foundation for the belief that a world of love, kindness, generosity, peace, and social justice really is possible.

The task of building an alternative to the dominance of tough-guy thinking, muscular religion, and domination-as-the-path-to-security is going to be challenging for precisely this reason: embracing the Left Hand of God will require us to get over our fear of the cynical realism that surrounds us and that resonates with the fear inside us. We need to learn how to give each other the confidence to affirm publicly what we most deeply yearn for privately and to stand up against those who seek to humiliate anyone who wants to build a society based on the loving and compassionate teachings in Torah, the Prophets, Jesus, Muhammed, the Buddha, and many other religious traditions.

And if we study the traditions of interpretation in each of these religions, we see that there has been in each a tension through the centuries between those whose life experiences, perceptions, emotional proclivities, and spiritual intuitions drew them to a patriarchal and punishing parent God whose primary resource was domination and power and those drawn more to a nurturing and loving God, a God of generosity and kindness who had more of the motherly and affirming qualities that have often been identified as feminine. Because most people have both voices inside themselves, we've often been tempted to work out a compromise in which we've seen God in both ways. But in the contemporary period, the Religious Right and fundamentalists have created a fundamental imbalance by giving priority to the Right Hand of God. As a result, many of us in the religious world see that there is a realignment across religious faiths among the punishing father God elements, so that the religious right-wingers in Israel who settle the West Bank have a conception of God that is far more compatible with that of Protestant, Catholic, and Islamic fundamentalists than it is with the view of a loving, kind, and generous God held by many other Jews, Protestants, Catholics, Muslims, and others.

The Right Hand of God people understand this realignment, and they have created the political underpinning for the ascendancy of their worldview. That's why Ariel Sharon meets with Christian fundamentalists more quickly than with the leaders of the Religious Action Center of Reform Judaism or the mystics of our Jewish Renewal movement. It's why I feel more deeply aligned with the progressive Christian evangelists Jim Wallis, Glen Stassen, and Tony Campolo or with Catholic Benedictine Sister Joan Chittister and the nonviolent activist Jesuit priest John Dear and the pope-silenced former priest Matthew Fox and some of the outspoken antiviolence voices in the Muslim world than I do with those Jews who think of God as a champion of violence who encourages us to wipe out His enemies (which conveniently turn out to be our political enemies). But while the champions of God's Right Hand have been actively organizing for several decades, questioning the legitimacy of the Left Hand of God interpretations of their traditions, the champions of the Left Hand of God have been trying to keep their particular denominations or religious groups united by playing down their differences with the voices of the Right and ignoring the potential strength of uniting across denominational and even religious lines with others (including "spiritual but not religious" others) who share their orientation toward a world of love, nonviolence, social justice, ecological responsibility, openheartedness, and generosity. It's time now for those Left Hand of God people to recognize each other and build a global network of mutual support.

Consider the situation facing the Democrats. The real choice they face is either to remain the minor-league champions of the Right Hand of God—a path that usually leads them to defeat, because people who are seeking champions of the Right Hand of God usually find the Republicans a more authentic representative—or to claim the Left Hand of God and face up to all the ridicule that a cynical corporate-guided media machine will heap upon them. Imagine how much stronger they would be if they could count on the public voice of a progressive interfaith religious and spiritual movement that was actively challenging the cynical realists and apologists for militarism.

This book will show you how to stand up for the Left Hand of God, how to develop a coherent approach that can not only win political victories but also take significant steps toward the world that most people already desire. But this is going to require sophistication, patience, and courage.

This book will also begin the process of forging a new political alliance among: (a) militantly secular leftists, (b) "spiritual but not religious" people who are equally uncomfortable with the antispiritual biases of the secularists and what they see as the dogmatism and rigidity of the religious world, and (c) progressive people in the religious world—people who pray regularly or attend religious services or engage in the rituals of a given religious community and who also have a strong commitment to social justice and peace. Each of these groups has important contributions to make.

Building this alliance is going to push many buttons in each of these groups. Repeatedly people are going to have to ask themselves: Would I rather see the political Right and its allies in the Religious Right continue to have the power to make war, escalate militarism, weaken the First Amendment separation of church and state, reduce taxes for the rich while eliminating social programs for the poor, dismantle environmental protections, lead campaigns against gays and lesbians, and pack the Supreme Court so that it could place new restrictions on women's right to choice? Or would I prefer to overcome my negative feelings about people who are in a different place than I am on religious issues and questions about God so that I could make common cause with them and create a Left that could speak to the spiritual hungers of the American people?

The progressive spiritual politics articulated in *The Left Hand of God* is a modest contribution to the discourse about what could become the new foundational philosophical framework for all those seeking progressive social change. It is framework for understanding how to successfully challenge the most destructive aspects of global capitalism, or, in my language, the most effective alternative to the globalization of selfishness. Although this book addresses the current realities of American politics and offers a strategy and program for how to change them, underlying the discussion here is a new social theory that is as much a challenge to the traditional Left as it is to the traditional Right. It is meant to be a modest contribution to the discourse that has, in the past, flourished among Marxists, Freudians, feminist theorists, liberation theologians, deconstructionists, critical theorists, and many others who have debated for more than a hundred years about what would be the central contradictions in the existing social reality that would enable human beings to overcome a globalizing capitalism that is perceived by some to be the most powerful, seductive, and seemingly intractable system of domination that the world has ever seen.

Globalized capital has accelerated the economic, communicative, and ecological interdependency of all people on the planet while simultaneously fostering social relations that heighten our mutual isolation and alienation from one another. It has fostered (or in some cases, brought into fuller focus previously underplayed) "radical needs" that it cannot satisfy: the need for a life that has higher meaning and purpose than a one-dimensional focus on economic security and accumulation of material goods; the need for work that contributes to the common good; the need for love and sanctity both in family life and in friendships; the need for privacy and protection from the invasiveness of new technologies; the need for a new relationship to nature that not only fosters ecological sustainability and a massive effort to repair of all the environmental damage we have done to the planet but also encourages awe and wonder and joyous celebration at the grandeur of creation; the need to experience and form a life that has a relationship to the spiritual dimension, that is, to those aspects of reality that cannot be measured or subjected to empirical verification; the need for a society that encourages kindness, generosity, compassion, nonviolence, peace, and social justice, and affirms pleasure and wisdom and rejects the manipulative, technocratic, reductionist thinking that today parades as "savvy" or "efficient."

It is these needs that cannot be met in the "flatland"of globalized capital, and it is these needs that form the foundation for a fundamental transformation of our world. And it is only when these needs are placed at the center of a progressive political agenda that secular, religious, and "spiritual but not religious" people will be able to proffer an emancipatory spiritual politics that speaks to the deepest hungers in human beings and enables us to overcome the cynicism, emotional depression, and despair that have paralyzed the best within us and empowered the worst.

The existence of these needs is a central part of what I seek to make plausible to you in the first section of this book, and then in the second section I'll show how we might develop a program and strategy that place these needs at the center of politics and, in so doing, empower people to acknowledge publicly the great spiritual hunger that has been systematically hidden from view except in the (in my view, distorted) form it has been given to date by the Religious Right. So please read this book with an eye not only toward the 2008 and 2012 elections, but with a sense of how it might provide a foundation for a whole new way of thinking about and doing liberal and progressive politics.

Of course, as a spiritual being who seeks to be aware of my own limitations, I'm all too conscious of the ways that my approach is likely to be flawed. Even if you disagree with some particulars of my application of this framework, or my specific suggestions on how to frame a spiritual program, I earnestly hope that you might nevertheless find that the framework I develop here could be a solid foundation for making your own spiritual analysis of contemporary politics or for developing your own spiritual platform.

For those who are unwilling to live in a world tranquilized by trivia and adrift in drivel—a world in which our fundamental humanity is constantly being undermined by ridiculing the visionary and instrumentalizing the sacred, by flattening and homogenizing our experience and forgetting our history, by insisting that we deaden ourselves to our own intuitions and ethical outrage at injustice and instead go along with the values of the society before us even at the expense of our integrity—the ideas presented here provide the foundation for a new way of being in the world. This new way is actually the ancient path of the Left Hand of God.

With the elections of 2008 and 2012 facing us, we will have two major chances to overcome the terrible splits in American society that have made so many people wonder about the sanity and moral goodness of their fellow Americans. For those of us on the Left, this opportunity is too important to botch as we did in 2004. The specter of a right-wing takeover of the judiciary, already in full swing as I write this book, a further consolidation of a militarist worldview and a politics of fear, the dismantling of Social Security and other programs designed to provide a minimum net of protections from the impact of the competitive marketplace—the possibility of all these policies actually becoming reality should motivate us to do some deep rethinking of the way we've been approaching politics.

Unfortunately, many on the Left have had no intellectual categories with which to understand their own spiritual foundations. They lack such understanding in part because they have become addicted to a narrowly technocratic pragmatism that blinds them to the spiritual hunger of the American people (including their own spiritual yearnings) and convinces them that the most important thing to do is to win power so that they can pass narrowly construed pieces of legislation designed to ameliorate the worst excesses of the global marketplace. Fearful that talk of any larger vision will make it easy for the political Right to tar them as communists or utopians or worse, the Left substitutes for vision a checklist of reforms. It imagines that by piecing together a coalition of disparate interests it can build an electoral force that will give it victory.

The Democratic Party is filled with people who are involved precisely because they have a deep moral and spiritual sensitivity, even if they are reluctant to label it as such. One of the goals of this book is to allay some of the fears and challenge some of the ideas that keep many on the Left from acknowledging to themselves or others that they actually *are* motivated by a deep spiritual sensibility. If they can free themselves from those ideas and fears, they will become a far more credible political force in American society.

Democrats are also limited by their fear that addressing spiritual issues will breach the wall of church-state separation. They are mistaken. The spiritual needs that the Religious Right addresses are real needs. There is a real spiritual crisis in this society, and it has everything to do with the way we organize our economic and political lives. For that very reason, it's not at all convincing to tell people that they should keep their spiritual concerns out of the public sphere. Our economic world massively reinforces an ethos of selfishness and materialism, and those values permeate and shape the rest of our lives. A civil libertarian approach calling for stronger boundaries between religion and the public sphere is valuable when it insists that no specific religion should become the established religion of the state. But separation doesn't reach the issue here: that there already are spiritual values built into the normal operations of the capitalist marketplace and that the only way to effectively challenge them is to introduce countervalues.

The Religious Right is onto something very important: there really are values in the society that need to be challenged, and the only way to do this is to promote an alternative set of values. If our response to this situation is to say, "Keep your religious values out of the public sphere," and if we have no alternative values with which to challenge the values of the marketplace, we fall right into the trap that the Religious Right has set for us, allowing right-wingers to say, in effect, "You people on the Left claim to have no values but merely to want a value-neutral public sphere, but actually your public sphere is already suffused with secular materialism and selfishness, which is what we've come to combat."

What the Religious Right does, in essence, is blame all liberals and progressives for the values of the capitalist marketplace. And they can get away with this tactic as long as the only answer most people hear from the Democrats and the Left is "Keep your values out of the public sphere, which should remain neutral."

Ironically, the liberal, value-free, nonideological discourse has been appropriated by the champions of global capitalism. They present capitalism as above mere politics and as simply seeking "progress" as it destroys local economies and cultures and puts in their place the mechanisms of a global system. Global capitalism always claims to be apolitical and to have no agenda except allowing people to buy whatever they want. Those who critique the logic of the market are portrayed as ideologues, whether they be from the Left or the fundamentalist Right.

A progressive spiritual politics agrees with the Religious Right that there is no such thing as a neutral public sphere. Our political institutions, our economic institutions, and our dominant culture are all suffused with values. And by and large today those values are rooted in an ethos of materialism and selfishness that is corrosive to human life, to community, and to religious and spiritual values.

So when the Religious Right orchestrates its campaign to pack the judiciary with people who share its worldview, it is unpersuasive for liberals to yelp about the need for judges who will be more "neutral" or "professional." There is little that is "neutral" or "value-free" or "professional" or "a matter of expertise" when the courts address issues of abortion, gay marriage, torture, reduction of civil liberties in order to fight terrorism, or the teaching of evolution or intelligent design in schools. Where a judge or an elected official or an academic teaching in a university stands on these issues reflects a worldview. Yet instead of liberals defending their own worldview and trying to convince others to share it, too often they hide behind procedural issues or issues of competence, expertise, or professionalism and then act shocked when the Right insists on championing its values. It would be far more honest for those on the Left to acknowledge that they have a worldview and that it is not any less partisan than the worldview of the Right, and then to explain to people why they think it is their worldview that will create a society benefiting the most people and most in accord with our highest moral intuitions.

The Right often uses this liberal obfuscation of its own value commitments as a reason to blame the liberals for contributing to the demise of values. Or it attacks secular people and claims that they, too, have rejected a values approach to life. This is largely unfair. Nobody in American society became convinced that they should be materialistic or selfish because there were people in their neighborhood or workplace or school who were liberal or didn't believe in God. Truth is, these liberals and nonbelievers are not one inch more materialistic or selfish as a group than those who do believe in God, attend church, or vote Republican.

A spiritual Left can protect the achievements of liberalism precisely because it is willing to take on what is correct in the Religious Right's critique of the society as constituted. At the same time, we can challenge the Religious Right to understand that the materialism and selfishness that it legitimately critiques are rooted not in secularism but in the values of the global marketplace, the very values the political Right is advancing around the world.

The Left Hand of God thus faces a struggle on two fronts. On one, it must challenge the values of the marketplace and call for a new bottom line of love and generosity to replace the ethos of selfishness and materialism. On the other, it must challenge the attempt by the Religious Right to impose its values on the society and its attempts to break down the separation between church and state. We can accomplish both of these tasks only by putting forward our own positive vision of the world we seek (which I do in the second part of this book).

That vision must be embodied and promoted by an interfaith spiritual movement that opposes any attempt to use government to mandate a belief in God or any particular religion but that is not shy about fighting for a *tikkun,* a healing and transformation, of our planet in accord with a new bottom line. It will draw upon the spiritual wisdom and experience of humanity and recognize that, at the most fundamental level, what is wrong with our world today has everything to do with the ways our economic, political, and social institutions undermine our love, generosity, kindness, compassion, nonviolence, humility, and joyfulness. It is our daily life experience in the institutions of our society that wither our capacities to respond to the universe with awe and wonder, or with what my teacher at the Jewish Theological Seminary, Abraham Joshua Heschel, liked to call "radical amazement" at the grandeur of creation.

The Religious Right Is Part of an Old Struggle Against God

There is a growing voice of spiritual and religious people in the United States who are critical of the political direction of the Religious Right and see their activities as a distortion of the religious traditions they purport to espouse. In alliance with the political Right, the Religious Right has brought to power and continues to champion an administration that has:

> Led the United States into an offensive military posture that is not only conducting a war that has killed tens of thousands of civilians but is also proclaiming the right to make unilateral preemptive strikes against other regimes that it deems potentially dangerous to American values or interests;

> Violated basic standards of human rights and engaged in the systematic torture of prisoners in Abu Ghraib and Guantanamo Bay as well as in dozens of other locations, some run directly by the American government, others by allies who willingly do America's dirty work;

> Stripped U.S. states and cities of badly needed revenues to fund education and social services—creating local struggles for resources between factions of the population who need funding for schools or for emergency hospital services or for the homeless or for police and fire services—in order to provide huge tax cuts to the rich and only mild tax cuts for the rest;

Fostered a selfishness that finds expression in ignoring the potentially disastrous consequences of current economic and ecological decisions to the well-being of future generations;

Sought to undermine Social Security and other key elements of the social safety net that were created to offset the worst impact on the poor and powerless of the economic inequalities and distortions that flow from the normal workings of the capitalist marketplace;

Dismantled ecological protections and promoted junk science to obscure the dangers of global warming—in order to provide a cover for corporate environmental irresponsibility and to justify U.S. opposition to global environmental accords. The devastation wrought by Hurricane Katrina was partly a product of American environmental irresponsibility, partly a product of misplaced priorities as funds to repair the levees were cut in order to fund the war in Iraq and to provide major tax reductions for the wealthy, and partly a reflection of government indifference to the plight of African Americans and the poor. Though both parties have participated in these sins, the particular crusade of the Right to undermine governmental services by reducing funding for projects like repair of bridges and levees was a direct cause of the massive flooding that took lives and monumentally damaged New Orleans. Their denial of the need to reorganize our society to stop global warming, and their popularizing of the notion that environmental reforms would necessarily undermine employment massively contributes to our continuing environmental destructiveness;

Imposed fundamentalist religious criteria on stem-cell research, thereby limiting funding for scientific work that might lead to a cure for or prevention of Alzheimer's and Parkinson's diseases;

Sought to weaken or dismantle protections for ordinary citizens against corporate violations of their health and safety needs, by weakening the mandate of agencies created to provide these protections, by pushing into the judiciary people who believe that such protective legislation is unconstitutional, by filling these agencies with people who are more sympathetic to corporate power than to the powerless the agencies were set up to protect, and by seeking to limit the right of individuals to use the courts to sue on behalf of those who have been injured by corporate irresponsibility.

In all religious traditions we find both the voice of hope and the voice of fear. Our religious texts, divinely inspired though they may have been, were composed and interpreted by human beings who heard both voices in their heads. At times they have responded more to one voice, at other times more to the other. And so, God's voice has sometimes been heard as more loving, compassionate, justice seeking, and generous and sometimes as more harsh, judgmental, power oriented, and domination seeking. Both voices are present in our religious traditions. Which one we give greater credence to then becomes our "true reading" of texts and traditions.

I'd like to think that, from the beginning, the more loving and compassionate vision of God, what I'm calling here the Left Hand of God, represents the healthy, hope-filled position of human beings, while the harsh and judgmental vision, what I'm calling the Right Hand of God, represents the situation of human beings who have not yet become healthy and are therefore filled with irrational fear. But this is an oversimplification, in that it misses the complexity of the historical realities within which our religious traditions developed. In my view, there were moments when holding to a vision of the Right Hand of God was a psychologically and spiritually healthy position, given the historical realities of oppression that people were facing. Sometimes the most brutalized people need to believe that their oppressors will be overthrown, and a Right Hand of God consciousness gives them the only picture they can imagine of how that might happen, given their perception that there are no other political options.

When Jews were enslaved by Egyptian imperial power, they were subjected to genocidal measures on the part of Pharaoh (who sought to kill all the male children), constant physical oppression, material deprivation, and religious repression. It was in this context that they responded to the death of the Egyptian army sinking into the waters of the sea by celebrating God as "a man of war" and proclaiming, "Your Right Hand O Lord, is Mighty in Power" (Exodus 15: 3–6).

Yet history often shows that this is a difficult balance to maintain, because once one justifies using violence and domination over others in some circumstances to overthrow oppressive rule, one can develop a psychological proclivity for using violence to solve one's pressing problems.

What the Prophets saw, and what has happened once again in contemporary Israel, is that the Torah tradition could be used to justify a social order that was in many respects the exact opposite of the loving message of God. When the message of the Right Hand of God, developed for the powerless, is adopted instead by the powerful, existing inequalities and systems of oppression are ignored and calls for social justice, peace, and nonviolence are dismissed as pretty thoughts about some future messianic era (for Jews) or a Second Coming (for Christians). Arguing that the "real world" is too dangerous for the demands of the Torah, the Prophets, and Jesus to be taken seriously, the powerful insist that the only path to peace and social justice is to impose their own religious vision on the whole world, and to accept cruelty and injustice as inevitable until that apocalyptic transformation has taken place. The purveyors of this distortion can always refer, as they always have, to external threats as evidence that the world is not yet ready for the transformative call of the Left Hand of God.

Jesus railed against the Jewish establishment of his day, like other prophets had done in their own time, and once again highlighted a commitment to the poor and the oppressed. Jesus insisted that people not duplicate Rome's oppressive rule in the way that they treated each other. His followers and many early Christians understood this message clearly—understood, as did the powerful in Rome, that it was a revolutionary message calling upon the faithful to reject the power of tyrants and embrace the power of love, which would ultimately be more forceful than anything Rome could deliver. Just as the message of Torah was tragically turned into its opposite by "the religious" and their establishment, so Christianity, taken over by Constantine, became its opposite, a system that provided justification for the powerful while ignoring or even actively subverting the needs of the poor and the powerless. For more on how this played out, I recommend James Carroll's monumental work, *Constantine's Sword,* as well as a powerful new study by Michael S. Northcott, *An Angel Directs the Storm: Apocalyptic Religion and American Empire.*

These perversions of Judaism and Christianity took place in the name of the original vision, drawing on the texts and the justifications that could be found there because at one point those triumphalist texts had provided needed empowerment for the poor and the downtrodden, and had been a psychologically necessary buttress against despair.

In the United States, the powerful have appropriated God and religion to justify imperial rule around the globe. They are not intent on using power to rectify the situation of the powerless. On the contrary, as their domestic moves make clear, they redistribute the wealth upward from the poor to the rich. The global system of capital that they have created has had that same impact, increasing the suffering of the powerless while empowering a small class within each society to act as the guardian of the interests of Western capital in third-world countries.

The Religious Right allies with and provides much of the ideological cover for this development. It allows the powerful to worship their own power and then, taking the work of their own hands, declare it the God to be worshiped by all. This is pure idolatry. It allows America, the most powerful and arrogant of all the arrogant and powerful nations that exist today, to identify itself in its own mind with the oppressed children of Israel and thus to imagine that its use of force is divinely sanctioned.

If this were the whole story, you might despair about whether it would ever be possible to win back our country from the Religious Right. But it is possible. As I'll show in this book, it is critical to distinguish between the hard core of the Religious Right, who may be temporarily unreachable and stuck on this misguided path, and millions of other very decent and loving Americans who have been attracted to the Right and sometimes vote for its candidates. Many in this latter group have become involved in the Religious Right because they seek a community that gives priority to spiritual aliveness and is affirming and loving. That is the experience they are looking for, and for that they are willing to hear God's voice in the way the Religious Right hears it.

You might ask, "Why not just give up the whole flawed enterprise of religion, which allows for these kinds of distortions?" That is the powerful challenge of many secularists, and it is certainly a legitimate question.

My answer is, first, that the religious traditions flourishing in Western societies offer powerful countervoices to the logic of global capital. The practice of Shabbat is one such element. Following the rules of the Jewish tradition, Sabbath observance mandates taking one day a week in which all work-related activity is abandoned, in which all acts of "getting it together" and catching up with errands, household chores, unanswered e-mail, shopping, fixing things, washing clothes, repairing the house, getting a jump on homework or next week's work assignments are completely suspended. Instead, the entire time is dedicated to celebration of the grandeur of the universe, community prayer and sharing of meals, sexual pleasure, communion with nature, singing, dancing, storytelling, reading, study (but with no goal other than the joy of the study), and rest. That kind of slowing down and detachment is achieved in other religious traditions through meditation, fasting, seclusion from the world, and so on. However it is achieved, though, such time apart provides a powerful countermessage to the constant "getting and spending" of the capitalist market.

So, too, is the focus on awe and wonder as a response to the universe. By insisting on seeing the universe in those terms, and not simply as a commodity, religious traditions, when taken seriously, put a brake on how much the market consciousness can permeate daily life.

The story of the liberation of the Jewish people from Egypt, along with many other religious stories, offers an instructive lesson to those who have been indoctrinated by the media and by our educational systems to think that the way people think and act today is the only possible way. The very insistence on history, and the changes in consciousness and power that sacred history witnesses, can provide the intellectual space that allows a person to realize that the way things are is not the only possible way things could be.

Still, you might protest, can't we have these stories without clinging to religious traditions that are so flawed?

Well, yes, but then understand that the flaws in religion are not flaws generated by religion itself but by the fears that are universal in human experience and that need to be healed. Recognize that there is no human enterprise that has not similarly been flawed. There is no system of thought or practice, and no "non-system" either, that cannot be taken and used in oppressive and hurtful ways.

And yet some secularists might still reasonably ask, "True, but why do you stick with religion and try to reclaim its potential goodness?" But get this: 95 percent of Americans say they believe in God, and 60 percent say they pray at least once a week. Our government stands at the center of the global empire, and its ability to function in hurtful ways is enabled by the distortions in religion that are currently dominant. So getting more energy into the Left Hand of God—with its religious/spiritual perspective that opposes war and oppression—can be an important counterforce, one that might even enable the Left to win elections and start reconstructing this society.

And there is a final reason. When you read the second part of this book, you will see that a transformative vision of society emerges from a spiritual foundation. I believe that this spiritually based vision, which is rooted in taking seriously the Left Hand of God, is not only a plausible way to defeat the political Right over the course of the next several decades but is also the path most likely to bring back into politics those whose souls yearn not only for justice and peace but also for connection to the deepest truths of the universe. The world is a mystery. Those who are absorbed in that mystery, responding with awe and radical amazement to the universe, can bring into our public life a dimension of wisdom we badly need.

Try giving the ideas in this book a chance. Particularly if you've never tried to see what the world might look like if you saw it through a compassionate spiritual framework, allow yourself to momentarily drop the cynicism we've all ingested in this society. If you do, you'll soon understand how badly America needs a progressive spiritual movement. Tens of millions of people already know this, but they don't know about each other and so many of them keep their spiritual yearnings to themselves. I'll show you why it's time for those people to come together and change and heal our world.

As I start this analysis, I pray for the well-being of our country and all people on our planet. And I ask for God's blessing not only for those who agree with me but also for those whose ideas and politics I will challenge in this book.

PART ONE

America's Spiritual Crisis

ONE

The Real World's Bottom Line

Before I became a rabbi, I was a social change activist and a psychotherapist. I had participated in sit-ins for civil rights, had organized teach-ins and demonstrations and nonviolent civil disobedience against the war in Vietnam, and had been involved in the early development of the environmental movement. Yet I felt uncomfortable with the way these movements at times seemed more interested in proving their own righteousness than in finding ways to attract and build an American majority that supports peace and social justice.

In the early 1970s I tried to convince my compatriots to link our movements with a critique of the prevailing tax structure, which placed a huge burden on middle-income working people, and so I proposed a ballot initiative to shift that burden onto the rich. But many of my comrades in the movement felt that the Left shouldn't be pandering to the "white-skin privilege" of white American working people, a decision many came to regret a few years later when a tax revolt led by right-wingers did indeed reduce the tax burden but only by cutting social services for the poor. Then, in 1976, I joined with Jeremy Rifkin in an effort to design a celebration of the country's bicentennial that would focus on what was positive in America's history. But again, I encountered considerable resistance from liberals and progressives whose anger over the war in Vietnam had obscured for them all that deserved to be honored about our past—the way the American people had successfully separated church and state and had fought against their own economic and political elites to expand democratic rights, to over-throw slavery, to eliminate property requirements for voting, and, more recently, to extend equal rights to women and minorities while em-powering working people to organize for a living wage and for health-and-safety standards in the workplace.

As a Jew, I have always been particularly grateful to America for providing my people a safe haven in a world that has too frequently murdered us. I felt blessed to be part of a generation of Jews that could look at this country not as a refuge but as a homeland. For that reason, I wanted the Left to let go of some of its angry rhetoric and its preoc-cupation with what had yet to be achieved in order to affirm more clearly all that had already been accomplished in America. Having ex-perienced some of that anger myself, I understood the appeal of this dichotomizing between the good guys and the bad guys, but as I grew beyond my own simplistic thinking and began to recognize that we in the social change movements needed more humility and compassion for those with whom we disagreed, I hoped that a movement could emerge that would embrace what was best in America and build a pro-gressive social change movement across class, race, and gender bound-aries.

I had hoped that making this case would be easier in post-Vietnam America. The war had been shown to be a disaster, the Nixon presi-dency had collapsed in disgrace, the Democratic Party had begun to listen to feminists and environmentalists. Surely, I thought, this would be a moment when liberal and progressive forces could consolidate power, end the cold war, and devote America's massive resources to promoting social and economic justice. Unfortunately, though, some-thing different was happening beneath the surface, at least among middle-income Americans. I detected the first inkling of a major shift away from the Democratic Party and the Left on the part of white working males—ironically, people whose economic interests were far better served by the Left than the Right.

I was puzzled by this phenomenon. So, after completing my PhD in psychology in 1977, I helped found the Institute for Labor and Mental Health to study the psychodynamics of American society. The psy-chotherapists, union activists, and social theorists who were working at the institute had one question we particularly wanted to answer: why is it that people whose economic interests would lead them to identify with the Left often actually end up voting for the Right?

The answer to that question lies at the heart of this book.

In an effort to discover why working people have increasingly turned to the Right we have spent the past twenty-eight years interviewing middle-income working people in the United States, Canada, England, and Israel. We began by recruiting subjects from the labor movement and by advertising on buses, billboards, and posters. We were seeking people who, apart from the normal tensions everyone faces in the workplace, were not experiencing excessive stress in their lives. In fact, we used standard measures to screen out and refer elsewhere people in need of psychotherapy as well as candidates for marriage or family therapy. We were interested in speaking to people who did not have any particular presenting problem and who would not have agreed to participate had they thought they were going to a therapy session. As part of our program, we ran groups that taught communications skills, stress reduction, and leadership skills. Most of those groups met once a week for a period of eight to ten weeks.

After that initial phase of research, institute researchers conducted follow-up studies using a wide variety of both quantitative and qualitative research instruments. Over two decades we've done phone interviews, one-time in-person interviews, and written questionnaires. In addition, as the political world has changed, we've continued to reassess the results of our observations.

What we have discovered, fundamentally, is that many people need what anthropologist Clifford Geertz once termed a "politics of meaning" and what I now call a spiritual politics—a spiritual framework that can lend meaning to their lives. They yearn for a purpose-driven life that will allow them to serve something beyond personal goals and economic self-interest. If they don't find this sense of purpose on the Left, they will look for it on the Right.

In fact, our research has led us to conclude that more than half the working people who vote for the Right do so because they are suffering from the spiritual crisis in American society. They are concerned about living in a society where values are eroding, families are unstable, sexuality is cheapened, and money and selfishness rule everything. These people have come to believe that the Right is the only political force that addresses this spiritual crisis in a systematic and public way. The alliance between the political Right and the Religious Right makes it easy for many Americans to believe that the Right is sensitive to their spiritual concerns.

Remarkably, the people with whom we have spoken do not necessarily believe that the Right's specific policies and programs will actually solve the spiritual problems that concern them. In fact, when asked, the people we interviewed often did not know much about specific policy proposals and, when these were described, often did not agree with them. And yet even though they sometimes disagree with its policies, they feel better understood by the Right because they believe at least the Right is trying to take seriously their concerns.

At first we were astounded by much of what we heard, to the point that we were tempted not to believe it. Most of the early activists at the institute in the late 1970s and the 1980s were people who felt that to be a progressive thinker was to approach religious or spiritual commitments with skepticism. And many on the staff who were trained in psychoanalysis suspected that anyone who followed a spiritual path did so in search of an authority figure—perhaps to compensate for inadequate parenting during their childhood—or out of some other pathological mind-set. Others were convinced that religion was little more than Marx's "opiate of the masses," a distortion in consciousness that had been inflicted upon the working class by a cleverly orchestrated set of social and cultural institutions aimed at lulling the American public into passivity.

Many of my colleagues changed their minds as they watched how the Left dealt with the election of Reagan in 1980 and his reelection in 1984. Those two elections should be studied by anyone who cares about the Left today, especially in the wake of the reelection of George W. Bush. Over and over again, both in the 1980s and I'm afraid even today, we hear the Left explain its defeat in terms that imply that anyone who voted for Reagan (or Bush) must be pathological, stupid, or hopelessly reactionary. Yet the vast majority of the thousands of Reagan supporters we got to know through our research were ordinary, sane, and reasonably smart people, as, in general, are the Bush supporters we have interviewed over the past five years. Nor can the people who fill the mega-churches of the Religious Right be dismissed as uneducated fools or illiterate fanatics; they are as often working people who have completed college and whose income puts them close to the middle of the economic range in America.

Far from being fools, we discovered, these people have needs that go beyond a narrow focus on the economy. People earning close to the median income in the United States told us that they wondered what their life was really about, what the purpose of living was, what they could tell their children they had achieved while living on this planet.

Many complained that their work did not offer them an opportunity to contribute in some way to the well-being of the human race. They told us that they wanted to feel that their work was about something more than just making a living, that it served some higher purpose. Some asked us, the group leaders, to tell them how we saw our own lives. Were we oriented toward serving something more than ourselves?

When people talked about "meaning" in their lives, they frequently specified that they felt their lives should have a spiritual goal, a focus that would provide what some called "justification for being on this planet." They saw it as quite peculiar that we would need to ask them to explain what they meant by their desire for "a meaningful life," and at least several thought that perhaps something had been missing in our education that made such an idea seem puzzling to us. Many reported that we—the liberal intellectuals, therapists, and social change activists leading these groups—were the first people they had ever met who didn't immediately know what they were talking about when they spoke of wanting a meaning for their lives that went beyond having money or power or fame or sexual conquests or fun at sports or pleasure in good food and pleasant vacations. "It's about something more, life is!" said one group member, and all nodded their heads—and, in one form or another, this was the message that most of the people we spoke to kept trying to tell us. As one interviewee told me in 2005, "If you psychologists haven't heard about the millions of copies of Rick Warren's book *The Purpose Driven Life* that have been sold since it was published in 2002, and don't understand why so many people feel excited to have their desire for meaningful life spelled out so clearly, maybe it's you so-called intellectuals who need to have your heads examined."

Americans hunger for a framework of meaning and purpose to their lives that transcends their own individual success and connects them to a community based on transcendent and enduring values. For a significant number of Americans, the major crisis in life is not lack of money but lack of meaning—and that is what I mean when I say we face a spiritual crisis. It is this spiritual crisis that the most visible forces of the Left have been unable to address, largely because they don't even recognize spiritual needs as a central reality of contemporary life.

The World of Work

Most adults in America spend the majority of their waking hours at work and in travel to and from it. Not surprisingly, then, the values they find in the workplace have a massive impact on the way they think about their lives in the hours that remain to them outside of work. Work becomes the "real world" in contrast to the ideas and ways of living they might encounter in other areas.

But what are the values of this "real world"? Whether they are autoworkers or high-tech industry professionals, lawyers or hotel workers, teachers or machinists, truck drivers or telephone operators, postal workers or dentists, people working in America tell a common set of stories about what the real world teaches them. In the simplest terms, Americans are told to focus on the economic bottom line, to value money and power above all else, and to see themselves primarily as rational maximizers of their own self-interest.

Marjorie Sanders (not her real name; all names have been changed and identities altered slightly for purposes of confidentiality), a telecom worker in Los Angeles, summed it up this way:

> I've worked as a secretary, I've worked as a waitress, I worked for years as an assistant to a producer in a movie production company, and I worked at a plant constructing airplanes, and I can tell you that they are all the same; they are all governed by one and only one thing: money. They are in business to make money, and your only worth to them is whether you can help them make money. And if you can't show them that what you are doing helps that along, well, you are out of there. It's just the way the world is,

and I'm smart enough to know that and play along, because it's the only game in town.

We interviewed Carlos Hernandez in the late 1990s. He described himself as being "at the top of [his] game" in his management position at a burgeoning Silicon Valley electronics firm. Here's what he told us:

I learned early that there was one thing you had to know to succeed in the world of business: know who you can count on to stay loyal and who will betray you in order to watch out for their own ass. Because it's really that way. Everyone pretends to be friendly and wants to know what's happening in your life and all that, and they really are friendly. But there's a limit, and you hit it pretty quick. Everyone knows that you have to show the top management that your unit is making them money, or that unit is going to be downsized or phased out. So you look at everyone else around and ask, "Who here can help me and who will?" and really you don't have time or energy for others, except to watch your back because you know that they are going to try to screw you if they can. And it's nothing personal, because some of these people are great—and I know because we had a baseball team we put together, and I can tell you that a lot of these people who work for this firm are great people, but that doesn't change the bottom line, and the bottom line is this: everyone is out for themselves, and everyone is going to get an advantage wherever they can and whenever they can, and that means don't trust anyone, because they are all going to do what they have to, to get ahead and make it for themselves. It's just how it is—and I don't blame anyone, but I know to keep my eyes open.

Or here is a report from Sandy Levin, a physician in Chicago who works for a large hospital chain:

I never imagined that medicine would turn out to be so bottom-line oriented. I went into medicine because I wanted to do something to help others. I was a teenager in the early 1970s, and I could feel the goodness of people who were engaged in trying to change the world, and I wanted to be part of that, but I also felt like I didn't want to have a life of poverty, because I had seen a lot of that around me after my own family had some big financial problems when I was a kid. So I picked medicine and had graduated med school by the mid-1980s and had a wonderful time doing medical work. But then, in the late 1980s, things started to change. The medical system was taken over by insurance companies, and suddenly I became an employee of some huge corporation whose only interest in health was that they could make a buck off of someone else's suffering.

So I have to operate by that bottom line today, and I don't really think I have much choice, although whenever I can I fight back by trying to give more care and more services than the insurance company wants. But I've come to realize that everyone goes along with this whole thing, and there's not much point of fighting it, because that's just the way it is.

What is hardest for me is that I wanted my life to be about serving some higher purpose. I thought medicine was a kind of calling to service for humanity. Now I have to resist treating my patients as objects. But it's like this everywhere I look—everything is reduced to material gain. The world used to be such a magical and enchanting place for me ... but now it all seems so flat, lifeless, even pointless. I feel like I've lost too much!

Finally, listen to Lucinda Jones, a midlevel government employee in Dallas:

I feel very secure in my job—it's civil service—and I never worry that I'm going to get fired. But, still, the people in my office act as though they were on a treadmill. People are always knifing each other in the back, so to speak. Everyone is trying to get the attention of the top management of our agency.

I asked someone about it once, and he told me that he wanted to move up the ladder, make more money, get more things for his kids. At first I thought, "He is just selfish and doesn't care about the rest of us," but then I realized that maybe he was kind of a good guy, worrying about his family, and the only way he could do it was to be pushy and aggressive here. So I asked him once again, and he told me, "Hey, this is the real world, everyone has to watch out for themselves." It kind of shocked me, because I thought he was a cool dude, but then I thought, "Yeah, everyone does have to look out for themselves, 'cause sure ain't no one else going to do that for you"—and I've tried to teach that to my kids, because I don't want them to get hurt in this world.

If we had heard this only a few hundred times, we probably would have dismissed them as unrepresentative. But we heard variations on this theme thousands of times, to the point that we finally became convinced that there is in fact a shared reality for those who participate in the economic life of this country. The reality goes something like this:

We live in a world of intense competition, and in order to stay in our jobs and succeed in them, we need to maximize the bottom line of money or power (or in some cases fame or prestige) flowing to those who run the institutions for which we work. To succeed in doing that, we need to learn to see others primarily in terms of "How can they be of use to us in our position in the marketplace?"

For people whose job is to sell, the question becomes, "How do I get this person to see things in such a way that they will buy my product?"

For self-employed professionals or for owners of small businesses, the question often takes the form of, "How do I get this person to see me as someone they'd trust enough to pay me for my services or buy from my company?" For those who work in corporate settings, the question is often more like, "How do I get my work group in this large corporation to be more successful than other groups in this same corporation, and what can I get from people in other work groups that will aid me in that quest?"

In short, "How can this person be of use to me?" becomes the guiding question, shaping many, not all, relationships in the world of work. All day long we are taught to see others in instrumental terms—to ask how they can be useful to us to advance our goals and interests. And we are also learning to see things from an external standpoint, to accept a technocratic rationality in which ethical and spiritual awareness is replaced by a manipulative and materialistic consciousness.

We also heard from thousands of people variants of another deep truth, namely, that it's hard not to think this same way when you get home from work. Because, after all, what you've learned to do at work is the "real world." and that's the world people have to learn to get along with because that's where the money for food and rent or mortgage comes from.

Many people talked about the missing element in terms of a cheapening of work itself—that once it had been separated from the idea of a higher mission or purpose, work became vulgar or debased. Some brought up the idea of work as holy enterprise; at least three different people quoted the commandment, "Six days shalt thou labor and do all thy work, and on the seventh day shall be a Sabbath" as reason to think that work itself should have a sacred dimension. Several mentioned the idea of work as a vocation, an opportunity to live out in life some higher purpose. As Sister Joan Chittister put it in her article "Work: Participation in Creation," work is a commitment to God's service:

> In Benedictine spirituality, work is what we do to continue what God wanted done. Work is co-creative.... It is not a time-filler or a money-maker or a necessary evil. We work because the world is unfinished and it is ours to develop.... The parable of the unproductive fig tree is a dramatic one. The fruit tree that does not do what it can and should do, Jesus curses. To have a gift that can nourish the community and to let it go to waste strikes at the very heart of community. I must be all that I can be or I can't possibly be anything to anyone else. God goes on creating through us. Consequently, a life spent serving God must be a life spent giving to others what we have been given.

Though no one in our groups put it so clearly, many people had the same basic intuition. They clearly felt a sense of loss that work was being transformed in ways that made it less and less an opportunity to serve God or an opportunity to build a vocation in life.

There was another dimension to the spiritual crisis that kept coming up in our groups. People repeatedly mentioned that work made them feel deadened inside. At first, we thought we had not adequately screened for depression, but after applying all the most advanced psychological testing techniques to exclude from our sample anyone who fit the traditional definition of depression, we began to think that there was a general psychological depression permeating the workforce that was better described in spiritual than in psychological terms. This spiritual depression is characterized by a sense of loneliness or alienation, a feeling that we are not really being recognized or dealt with in an authentic way, a feeling that our deepest life energies are being depleted or at best have been put to sleep temporarily, a loss of awareness of the beauty and holiness that surrounds us, a sense that our world is filled with meaningless activity and is lacking in love and joy, a sense that, rather than expressing our inner being, we and others are going through mechanical motions that have been imposed upon us by an outside force. Hillary Hunt, a shop steward for the AFSCME union representing government employees, captured this spiritual malaise in a way that was representative of much that we heard:

I know most of my fellow workers very well, and they are wonderful people. But many of us meet for a drink after work and talk about how dead we feel after a day in our offices. I sometimes remember what a lively little girl I was, how full of life and energy, and I wonder whatever happened to that girl. I actually miss myself the way I used to be before I grew up. It's almost as if growing up is "coming down" from a high. Here I am now in a life where everything seems so mechanized and out of control. Sometimes I feel like I'm a zombie surrounded by zombies—everyone doing their assigned role, trying to fit in and be the way they are supposed to be, and even in the way that people talk to each other, it's so unreal and forced.

I never realized how much I felt this way till I started going to an Assembly of God church. When I felt the juices flowing there, I thought maybe everyone had been drinking or taking drugs. But they weren't. They just seemed more alive. And then I was suddenly flooded with memories of how I used to be when I was younger, and I got sad for all that I had given up. Actually, I don't really believe in Jesus, and I didn't want to get brainwashed, so after a few times I stopped going to that church. But I have to tell you that I felt something there that reminded me of how empty I feel most of the rest of the time. And when I've mentioned that to friends, everyone knows exactly what I mean, because most of the people I know suffer from this same feeling of emptiness and deadness.

This deadness is yet another dimension of the spiritual crisis that people face in their daily lives, a crisis that some people on the Right have been able to exploit.

Here is where the spiritual crisis begins. Over and over again people told us that they felt that they had no alternative but to adjust to the "real world" in which competition for money, power, and recognition sets us against one another. Yet at the same time they told us how much they hated it, how they felt dirtied by being part of such a world and longed to escape it. We continued to hear people say that they wanted work that had some higher purpose than making money for the company's owners or for their immediate bosses or even for themselves. They wanted to feel that their lives had meaning because they contributed in some way to a world they could believe in. Yet, simultaneously, they sought to assure us that they knew that this was a crazy desire, that it was impossible given "the real world."

Another way to put this is that when you listen carefully to what people are saying, most seem to have two voices in their heads, the voice of fear and the voice of hope. The Right Hand and the Left Hand of God. The voice of fear tells them that the world is a place in which everyone is going to exercise power over you, dominate you, control you unless you dominate and control them first. The voice of hope, however, tells them that this fearful view isn't right, that this isn't who they were born to be, that there is something deeply screwed up about such a world. When they listen to the second voice, the people we talked to want to find a way to get out of a world ruled by the economic bottom line.

Hearing both voices, the people we interviewed ended up being passionately drawn to churches or other religious practices that rejected many of the "real world's" values yet did not ask them to try to change that world while they are in it. The most that the churches asked them to do was to back right-wing political candidates who supposedly shared their religious and spiritual values (who challenged abortion and homosexual marriage and identified themselves as pro-family) but who in the rest of the policies they supported actually rein-forced the very same "real world" values, the revulsion at which had led so many people into churches in the first place. But even the right-wing politicians who sing the praises of the marketplace sometimes admit privately that they'd love to live in another kind of world, but learned a long time ago to be realistic and to work to achieve the best that is possible in the world as it is given to us. So, despite the desire of many on the Left to dismiss them as hypocrites, the truth is that many of these right-wing politicians, just like many liberal politicians, are split between their more idealistic yearnings, which they can express in church, and the more "realistic" consciousness that leads them to fight for the interests of corporations. Given their certainty that the power of corporations can't be dislodged, many have concluded that the wis-est path is to make corporations feel enthusiastically supported lest corporate leaders stop investing or even move their companies to other countries (either of which will only cause the people they know great economic suffering). So they adjust to "reality" while keeping alive a different set of values in the way they treat each other within the reli-gious communities they create.

Because these two voices tend to operate below the surface of con-sciousness, people often are not fully aware of which voice they are re-sponding to at any given moment. Often they act in ways that seem on the surface contradictory, responding in one set of actions to the "real-ity" messages of domination, control, and manipulation, and in an-other set to the messages of hope and possibility for a world of greater caring. To the outsider, this behavior seems almost schizophrenic until you understand the way people have internalized both sets of mes-sages.

We also discovered that many people we interviewed blame them-selves for their sense of frustration or alienation. Many understood that their lack of fulfillment in their jobs was connected to the way that their workplace was structured, the powerlessness (in some jobs) or competitiveness (in other jobs) and the kind of "looking out for num-ber one" that they foster. Yet they blamed themselves for having that kind of a job in the first place. They imagined that if only they had worked harder when they were younger or been smarter or more attractive or more personable, they would have been out of this kind of a job and into a far more satisfying one. Instead of understanding that very few jobs with meaning exist in this society, they believed that it was only people who had messed up their lives who would be faced with a work life that seemed so at variance with their own beliefs.

Why did so many people think this? One reason is that the "real" world tells us that success in our society is based solely on merit. From childhood on, we hear that anyone can grow up to be president of the United States or get into any position of power if only we have the smarts and the willpower to do it. Or, to put it the other way around, if we don't succeed in looking out for number one, it's all our fault.

The fact is, of course, that most of us won't grow up to become president or even CEO of a major corporation. That's because success in the world is not in fact based solely on merit. Because of the way our society organizes work, there are simply not all that many fulfilling jobs in comparison to the number of smart, hardworking, and deserving people. As a result, thousands, possibly millions, of talented people are stuck in jobs that give them very little opportunity to use their intelligence and creativity.

Along with smarts and determination, it helps to be born into a wealthy family and to have connections to people in power. It also helps to be talented at showing those with real economic power how good you'd be at serving their interests. In fact, no matter how hard we try, many of us will never achieve the material wealth and social status we are led to believe could be ours if only we "merited" them. What could be an empowering message—"You can do anything you set your heart on"—turns into a destructive psychological rebuke: "If you haven't succeeded in getting a fulfilling life, then you have no one but yourself to blame. You had the opportunity, and you screwed it up."

The power of the social myth of meritocracy was explored by a team of *New York Times* reporters in a "Class Matters" series beginning May 15, 2005. The mobility that working Americans experienced during the 1950s and 1960s has, it turns out, largely disappeared. Although higher-end incomes are often tied to skills that could be interpreted in terms of merit, what is really being rewarded is increasingly a function of social class. As the *Times* explained: "Parents with money, education and connections cultivate in their children the habits that the meritocracy rewards. When their children then succeed, their success is seen as earned."

Of course, we all know people born poor who became rich, and this fantasy of transformation remains central in the minds of many Americans. Moreover, thanks to workers in other countries whose own economic circumstances leave them little choice but to work in factories producing goods that will appear for relatively cheap prices in the Wal-Marts, Costcos, and Targets of America, people in this country often have the sense that their standard of living is improving. So it may be easier to ignore the fact that actual mobility has been on the decline over the past several decades, while the gap between rich and poor has grown enormously.

As the *Times* reported: "The after-tax income of the top 1 percent of American households jumped 139 percent, to more than $700,000, from 1979 to 2001, according to the Congressional Budget Office, which adjusted its numbers to account for inflation. The income of the middle fifth rose by just 17 percent, to $43,700, and the income of the poorest fifth rose only 9 percent. The same report cited studies that seemed to show that fewer families experienced mobility in the 1980s than in the 1970s, and still fewer moved upward in the 1990s than in the 1980s.

Yet the power of the dominant story has not been altered by this reality. A *New York Times* poll on class found that 40 percent of Americans believe that the chance of moving up from one class to another has risen over the past years.

While it certainly remains true that some high achievers can make it out of their original class position, the fact is that family and the benefits that it can provide in terms of skills, educational opportunities, and networking remains the best predictor of future class position. While the sense of possibilities surrounding us may be enhanced by television shows that dramatize "extreme makeovers" that seem to promise unlimited possibilities, while moments like the tech boom of the late 1990s offer chances for some specially talented or lucky people to dramatically advance, and while more people of color now get opportunities to compete and land jobs serving the nation's elites, the belief in rags-to-riches possibilities has little empirical foundation for most Americans.

When, through participating in our groups, working people really came to understand that their chances of making it were dramatically limited by the circumstances of their birth, they began to blame themselves less for ending up in jobs that are alienating or at best uninteresting.

It was only when people in our groups began to listen to each other that they realized that they were blaming themselves for not having been more successful in getting more fulfilling jobs. They were hearing from people in different kinds of jobs that there really are very few such jobs. And they learned that while most jobs reward those who are best at manipulating others, very few jobs provide an opportunity to connect to meaning and purpose higher than "making it" financially.

Why is this psychological issue so important? Because how people feel about themselves has a direct relationship to the kind of politics they support. The self-blaming narratives that members of our groups had over the years embraced intensified their feelings of powerlessness. All our interviewees felt that the most they could hope for would be to find some place in their lives, like a church, where they could find a way of being with people other than the way encouraged in the world of work.

Instead of challenging the real world, many of the people we talked with sought to escape from the economic and psychological bottom line of the real world by joining a religious community. Unable to fulfill their spiritual selves in their everyday work, they sought out religion as psychic nourishment.

Let me be clear that in making this choice, the people we interviewed were not rejecting other options for addressing their spiritual need for higher meaning to their lives. Their unions had little understanding of their spiritual needs, the liberal political world never addressed their spiritual needs, and no social change movement was articulating this spiritual hunger while also challenging the belief that the dynamics of power and competition really can't be changed. People had turned to religious and spiritual communities because these were the only places where they heard their spiritual needs being addressed in an explicit way.

BUSINESS REPLY MAIL

FIRST CLASS MAIL   PERMIT NO. 92037   ESCONDIDO, CA

POSTAGE WILL BE PAID BY ADDRESSEE

TIKKUN
2342 SHATTUCK AVE.
BERKELEY, CA 94704-9914

GET CONNECTED with MICHAEL LERNER

The Left Hand of GOD
TAKING BACK OUR COUNTRY *from the* RELIGIOUS RIGHT

Michael Lerner

For decades leading up to *The Left Hand of God*, Michael Lerner has been advocating for a progressive spiritual politics through **Tikkun** magazine, and now through the interfaith organization the **Network of Spiritual Progressives**.

To receive FREE emails from Michael Lerner through both organizations, please mail us your completed information.

Name _____

Address _____

City/State/Zip _____

E-mail _____

Phone _____

Network of Spiritual Progressives
An interfaith movement (for spiritual but not religious people as well)
www.Tikkun.org • www.spiritualprogressives.org
MLBT LH   2342 Shattuck Ave, Suite 1200, Berkeley, California 94708

TIKKUN
THEOCRACY IN AMERICA
Hostile Takeover

If you join the Network, you get a free subscription to **TIKKUN**, plus you get to work with Michael Lerner in building a whole new approach to politics.

TWO

Signs of Crisis

Escaping into the embrace of a religious community does not stop the spiritual crisis from happening out in "the real world." No matter how affirming it feels to be part of a spiritual or religious community that speaks about the spiritual crisis, sooner or later people find themselves back in that same real-world situation. They may love the idea of a world based on sanctity and the notion that others are created in the image of God, but to keep their jobs they have to perform all week long in a situation where they are continually pushed to use others to advance themselves and to focus on "the bottom line" of money and power.

The disconnect between people's values and their actions, between what they truly need and what fulfillment is available, does not go away. Instead, the me-firstism that characterizes the so-called real world continues to manifest in ever more powerful ways. People bring home from work a set of views about how to treat others based on a message learned in the world of work. To be smart, you must maximize your self-interest; you must be on the lookout for every opportunity to use other people to advance your own cause; you must see people as the means to your ends. Further, what really counts is how much you have in the way of material goods and comforts and how much power you are able to exercise over others. Inner life, spiritual contemplation, the joy of grappling with the perennial questions, reading the great literature and poetry of the human experience are replaced with a focus on the externals, the accumulation of things or fame or sexual conquests or power over others.

Surrounded by selfishness and materialism, many people feel that they don't know whom they can trust. After all, everyone seems to have learned the same lesson: that you are foolish not to advance your own narrowly defined interests, even at the expense of others. Feelings of emptiness, disconnection from others, and isolation thus become common. Many people talk of feeling less alive or present in their own lives or of feeling numb or of going through their lives as observers of what is happening rather than as active participants and shapers of their experiences. This is the way the spiritual crisis is played out in personal life, in every realm and dimension of our lives.

Although signs of a spiritual crisis pervade our world, we tend to notice them first, and react to them most strongly, in children. We rightly believe that children reflect the values we teach them. So when children display qualities like selfishness, greed, and insensitivity to others, or when they bully others or seem unduly fearful, jealous, or angry, we get nervous. Especially when these children are our own children! How could our own kids not value what we value? We asked people, "Do your children seem to be 'getting' the values you've been trying to teach them?" The most frequent response we got was a set of variations on the following theme: "I try my best, and I've often tried to preach to my kids the values I hold and want them to believe in, but it just doesn't seem to be getting across. I send them to church (or synagogue or mosque or some other religious school), and sometimes I take them to political meetings about topics that should interest them, but frankly they seem to be dancing to a different tune. It must be the peer pressure on them, but I don't know how to counter that pressure."

Again and again, parents told us they were trying to teach their children the values of responsibility, respect, generosity, kindness, caring for others, and justice. Yet no matter how hard they tried, their children too often acted in ways that seemed selfish, possessive, rude, or mean-spirited.

We then pressed these parents to tell us more about what they themselves really believed about how best to live in the world. They told us that, when it came down to it, they basically believed that the "real world" is all about people learning how to look out for number one. They also admitted they had no alternative but to share that information with their children, whether explicitly or implicitly. In other words, even though they might have told their children that they valued kindness, generosity, and justice, what they *showed* their children was that they valued me-firstism and getting ahead.

As we neared the end of our sessions, we tested the suggestion that children might instead be taught a different lesson, namely, that the world could be based on kindness and generosity. The middle-income people responded with varying degrees of disbelief. They thought this showed our lack of understanding of how the world really is. As Sarah Jane Middlefield, from San Diego, put it: "I love my kids too much not to prepare them for what they are going to face out there. And they are already facing it on the school playground and in some of the ways other kids treat them at school. Everyone is out for themselves, and if you therapists running this group don't know that, well, you are too naïve to understand what I'm up against."

Similarly, James Howard, of Brooklyn, told us: "No one is going to help you unless you help yourself. So I teach my kids to be respectful of others, but always to ask, how can I get this guy to see things my way?"

Or as Lucinda Guerrega, of Miami, declared: "I'm not giving my kids teachings that are going to get them to look like they are dumb. And it's plain dumb not to know that people are going to screw you if they can."

What these parents are pointing to is a fundamental problem: that the message of me-firstism goes so deep into our culture that parents themselves can do little to prevent their children from picking it up even if the parents don't believe in that message. Just turn on a television or look at a video game and you'll get the idea: everyone is after power or money. Everyone is going to take advantage of you if you don't get them first. These are the background assumptions you need in order to make sense of what the culture throws at our children today. Without those assumptions, children would not be able to decipher the cartoons on TV, play video games, or understand pop music.

Try to teach children that they are supposed to turn the other cheek or that the highest goal of life is to be loving and caring toward others, and guess what? They're not going to buy it. Why should they when they know that their parents, their teachers, and all the other representatives of the larger society don't really believe that message and don't base their own lives on it.

In fact, it is this contradiction between what parents do as they live their lives and what they try to teach their children that the teenagers with whom we sought to discuss values repeatedly brought up. One after another would point to the difference between "what my parent does" and "what my parent says" as a major reason why they couldn't take their parents' lessons about values seriously.

Both for parents and for society as a whole the impact of this contradiction is deeply disturbing. More and more children grow up to be narcissistic and self-indulgent, believing that their highest mission on the planet is to accumulate as much money, power, and social status as possible and that it is perfectly acceptable to do so without regard for the consequences to others in their lives. These children don't need to be convinced of the reality of the marketplace because they are already there.

As one teenager put it to me bluntly, "I've seen through the bullshit, and I know that it's all about getting what one can when one can." He was the son of a Presbyterian minister. No amount of moral preaching is going to offset this deep acculturation to the dominant values of our economic life.

When you live in a society where most people learn that looking out for number one is the primary value you need to survive, you can expect that human relationships are going to have a very peculiar quality.

Friendships, courtships, marriages, and families begin to reflect this strange logic, so that, far from cherishing one another as embodiments of the holy, we increasingly see each other instrumentally—as tools for satisfying our own needs. Instead of taking an interest in finding out who someone is and how we might build a relationship with him or her, we spend our time figuring out how to manipulate the person to get whatever it is we want.

I don't want to romanticize previous periods in human history. Sadly, human society has not needed capitalist social relations to justify treating other human beings as mere means to an end. Slavery institutionalized that way of thinking in the ancient world, feudalism incorporated it into a legal order, patriarchy transmitted it into family life. Once some people feel the need or right to dominate others, they create a dynamic in which others begin to feel that they have no alternative but to protect themselves by dominating those who would otherwise dominate them.

In fact, the capitalist revolution made important strides in overcoming some forms of this misuse of others by dissolving feudal bonds of subordination. The triumph over feudalism was a major moment in the history of human liberation. Many who championed capitalism imagined that it would free human beings to use their intelligence, creativity, and initiative in the service of beauty. Yet there were others who thought that human life is fundamentally an ongoing struggle of all against all and that the marketplace could simply harness these energies to produce material goods, thereby increasing our wealth but not necessarily our moral wholeness. Few sought to structure the newly emerging competitive marketplace in ways that would end the struggle for domination and control: to do so would have robbed the market of its fuel. Rather, the marketplace began to reward those who were best at recognizing the need to advance themselves by getting the jump on others. Those who did not seek their own advantage were dismissed as fools, if they were citizens of the first industrializing societies, or as primitives, if they belonged to cultures that the industrializing societies sought to dominate. Indeed, in the early stages of capitalist society a great deal of attention was given to engendering in the masses a desire to compete and advance themselves. Those who did not see the importance of acquiring money and goods that could be stored up for the future were dismissed as slothful.

But a counter set of values was often articulated in the one area of human life that was not completely dominated by the ruling elites: religious communities. Much as these communities also depended on the tolerance and support of ruling elites, they often articulated a set of values that made those elites uncomfortable.

Not that religious institutions hadn't long supported patriarchy and oppressive social relations. But they had also provided an important framework in which our human desire to care for one another could be legitimated and sustained. The medieval Church, for instance, imposed "fair wage" and "fair price" demands on those who employed workers or sold goods at market. The feudal landlord was often a terrible oppressor, and yet serfs had the right to live on the land they worked and the right to bring their animals to graze and draw water from wells in land that was understood to be "the commons." In addition, extended families and country villages offered some level of support, both material and emotional, that was an expected part of communal life. Care for others was a major feature of what it meant to be a Christian, and a similar ethos has generally prevailed in religious communities around the world.

When religious institutions declined, over the past three hundred years or so, however, it became easier for the marketplace to become a haven for manipulation and domination. With the weakening of the religious framework and the demand it made for mutual support and communal responsibility, the capitalist market was freed to reshape education and to create a media that would work in tandem to teach us that our primary responsibility in the contemporary world is to maximize our own advantage. This way of being has a profound impact on our personal lives and relationships.

Joan Fletcher is a twenty-six-year-old administrative assistant in a large corporation in Atlanta. She graduated from Emory and still hopes to move up the corporate ladder once her talents are more fully recognized by her boss. Her story is similar to those we heard from hundreds of other twenty-somethings:

> In college I was too busy studying to think seriously about relationships, and in my first four years in the business world I put all my energies into learning the skills I would need. But in the last year I've been seriously looking for a partner, so I've been meeting a lot of men, and it's always the same story: the men are more interested in sex than in anything else. Sometimes they take the time to get to know you a little, but that often seems like a prelude to getting you into bed, and nothing more. I kind of feel like these guys are shopping around in a large supermarket, and I'm one of the items on the shelf.

Or consider Roberta Fox, twenty-eight, whom I interviewed in Baltimore:

Sex is all about power. I love the sex for its own sake, but I also know that everyone wants to get a piece of me, and I'm not going to let that happen unless I get a good deal back. I'm no prostitute—I don't sell sex. In fact, I'm very picky who I'm with. Men say I'm "hot," and that's cool with me. But I want a man who is going to show me a good time, spend his money, and be good in bed.

Needless to say, there are plenty of men who think in similar terms: "What's in this for me?" Frequently what they mean is: is the amount of time and money I spend likely to produce a good return on my investment?

James Allen in Seattle has a different story to tell. He tells me that he has never known how to make himself attractive to women. He works for a computer firm, although he says he's "no geek, just a bit shy." He complains bitterly about how the attractive women never look at him, never notice he exists. When I asked why he needs to have the "attractive women" and why he doesn't instead look for someone who doesn't meet conventional criteria for attractiveness but who might nevertheless be a wonderful person, he answered: "I've been dropped by some women who my friends described as 'dogs' for how they looked. So what's the point of going out with them—they are just as hard on a man as a good-looking babe, so why not fantasize about the best?" Again, I asked him whether "good-looking" is really "the best," and he responded by telling me, "Hey, I know that looks aren't what last. But nothing else lasts either. Truth is, I'd settle for a plain-looking woman if she had other qualities, but it's hard to find the right combination."

Internet dating has only intensified these dynamics. "I'm too busy to hang out in bars or wait for chance encounters," Sally Adams, a resident of a Detroit suburb, explained to me. "And every time I've tried to go to singles events, I find myself wondering whether I'm as much a loser as the people I encounter there. So I've become addicted to using the Internet. At least I get to see what I'm about to get into before I jump—and that provides me with some protection."

The Internet does provide some of that safety, avoiding the blind dates and getting "fixed up" and then rejecting a person that you could have known you wouldn't be interested in. The Internet can provide a way for several deep conversations before that first encounter, so you already know if there's enough in common to have a face-to-face meeting. I've known some wonderful relationships that have come out of Internet connections.

However, there's a downside as well because Internet dating has taken marketplace dynamics to new levels. No matter what intentions you come with, scrolling through descriptions of people who look like collections of statistics (5'4", blond, great figure, bust 36D) turns dating into shopping. And that is precisely what self-help gurus advise: the "Dating Dr." Web site tells people looking for love that "to get dates, your profile has to be better and more eye-catching than anyone else's." In short, if finding a date is about shopping, then getting asked on a date is about selling yourself. In the new dating game, people have become commodities. The special magic that can occur during a face-to-face encounter may never happen if people keep ruling out prospective partners on the basis of the superficial self-presentations that Internet exposure often encourages.

"Speed dating" has taken this to a new level. Ten men and ten women sit opposite each other in two circles and then each has two minutes to present themselves before they are required to switch to the next. This continues until everyone has met, at which point each person gets a chance to indicate who appeals to her or him. "It cuts out a lot of wasted time," one woman told me. It also cuts out any possibility of finding out who that person across the circle really is.

This dating process can continue for many years, or even for decades. No wonder that many of our respondents expressed a great deal of cynicism about relationships, experiencing them as inherently unstable and hence unlikely to last.

What people were telling us was this: there is a marketplace in relationships, and the goal is to sample as many of the potential commodities as possible before having to make a choice and settle down. After years of living in that kind of a world, it's not surprising that when people do settle down into what they intend to be a lasting relationship, they nevertheless bring a great deal of cynicism into the early years of their married life.

When people tire of the sexual marketplace and decide to choose a life partner, they frequently bring with them the bottom-line mentality they've learned from that marketplace. They have learned to see others in a utilitarian context—"How can this person be of use?"—so it seems only natural that, when it comes to seeking a mate, their first concerns will be: "Does this person satisfy more of my needs than anyone else to whom I am attracted? And will that level of needs satisfaction be enough, or should I just forget it and wait it out till someone else comes along who can satisfy more of my needs?"

For many people this process of establishing the bottom line for potential mates is not fully conscious. Instead, the computations take the form of, "Do I feel good about this person, given that he or she is x, y, and z but not a, b, and c and given that I could wait to see who else becomes available later?"

In view of the marketplace in relationships, making the decision to commit to any given person is often quite difficult. Even those who talk of falling deeply in love are aware of the long-term set of alternative options. Given that they've been taught to maximize self-interest, relatively few can enter marriage feeling certain that they have made the right choice—and even fewer among them still feel that way after the first several years. The notion that there might be someone else out there who could satisfy yet more of their needs haunts many people in relationships.

It's not only the 50 percent of marriages in American society that end in divorce that are negatively affected by this marketplace thinking. The kinds of anxieties that often precipitate divorce also exist in couples who stay together. Even in the most stable relationship, if you know that your partner has chosen you because he or she believes that you will satisfy his or her needs better than anyone else, you can never be certain that at some point your partner won't encounter someone who could satisfy even more needs. And if that person is available and interested, then, as a maximizer of self-interest, your partner would be foolish not to break with you and start a new relationship with this other person. And since that is precisely what is happening in marriages all around you, it is not unreasonable for you to feel insecure even though your own marriage seems to be working.

This nagging awareness creates tremendous anxiety throughout American society. No matter how close two people feel to each other, they know that their partners have been socialized in the very same world in which they themselves have grown up. We face the same messages at work, from the media, and from friends about the importance of "looking out for number one" and so, like everyone else, have been conditioned to see other human beings primarily in terms of how much we can satisfy our personal needs.

No wonder then that so many people report feeling lonely even in their own marriages, fearing that things could fall apart and knowing that they can never really be sure that their partners are the ones with whom they will share a lifetime. For some, that concern already manifests in prenuptial legal agreements about how to distribute the resources that one brought into the marriage should a divorce occur. Most people don't have enough resources to make such agreements necessary, but the anxiety that such contracts reflect is there just the same. It's an anxiety that creates distance, insecurity, and alienation. And it confirms in each partner a tendency toward cynicism about the possibility of a world based on love and caring, if even in this, the relationship crafted to provide lasting love, there is this deep sense of loneliness and doubt.

If the economic bottom line causes anxiety for marital partners, the psychological bottom line prevents the healing people need when a marriage does break up. Not all relationships work. As a therapist I've seen many relationships in which the best possible outcome was for the couple to separate. Yet in these cases, too often people fall into blaming themselves, thinking, "I wasn't good enough for my partner" or "I didn't do enough to keep this marriage alive." The same ethos of the market that can make it easier for a good marriage to go bad can also make it harder for people to move on when a bad marriage ends.

Our most intimate relationships are in crisis because of this cycle of me-firstism and self-blame, a questioning first of the other and then of the self.

But there is another possible orientation toward the world, the spiritual one. When we choose this approach, we value human beings not because of what they can do for us but because they are intrinsically precious and deserve to be respected and loved for who they are.

Then when we approach someone, we are not approaching a commodity, an object, an "it." We are approaching a being every bit as holy and unique as ourselves.

Once we start to believe that love is corny or sentimental, though, we shut ourselves off from this spiritual way of experiencing other human beings. When seeing the other as an embodiment of the sacred is regarded as a quaint or overly romantic idea, hopelessly out of touch with the real world, or, worse yet, when caring about someone else automatically seems to threaten our emotional integrity and need for independence, we experience a spiritual deprivation that is just as intense, painful, and destabilizing as the loss of material security.

Although some psychologists, most famously Abraham Maslow, have talked about a "hierarchy of needs," according to which our material needs must be met before we can begin to worry about our spiritual needs, our research suggested otherwise. We found that many middle-income working people whose material needs were still not secure nevertheless felt more deeply pained by the spiritual crisis that surrounded them and that shaped some of the dysfunction in their own families and loving relationships than by their economic worries. They might agree in principle with Maslow that what they needed first and foremost was economic security, but in their actual political activity they supported people who addressed the crisis in families, as those on the political Right appeared to, over people (mostly Democrats) who were more concerned with addressing their economic needs.

Once we understand how deep and real the spiritual crisis is, it no longer seems bizarre that many give precedence to the spiritual crisis in their lives and feel angry at, or at least deeply alienated from, those who don't even recognize that something fundamental to human life is missing in the contemporary world. The fact is that human beings cannot live happily without a framework of meaning that transcends the individualism, materialism, and selfishness of the marketplace and without the sense that a loving connection exists among us as well as to that larger experience the religious among us call God.

As daily life is stripped of its spiritual dimension by the seemingly unstoppable triumph of market consciousness, as work and human relationships seem to call for a continual deadening of our life energies, as our experience of the world is emptied of its magical and enchanted dimension and increasingly filled with manipulation, self-protection, and consumption, people reach out in desperation for mind-numbing devices to deaden the pain that this loss of meaning and connection to spirit inevitably generates.

The methods are obvious: we are addicted to alcohol, to drugs, even to the screens in front of our eyes—television, video games, the Internet. Each of these cultural painkillers in turn becomes the focus of a crusade ("the war on drugs" or, from the cultural Left, "turn off television and live life"), but these will never succeed until our society can answer the deep need to escape the pain of spiritual and emotional deadness that drives us to these mind deadeners. There are other, healthier distractions from the pain of living in a spiritually deadening society. But even healthy distractions, when pursued to excess, can be used to numb the mind.

Maybe you know people like that. You get them to the treadmill and they can't get off, you go with them to the swimming pool and they can't stop racing, you go to play some pickup basketball and they become ferocious competitors who forget that they are playing with friends and there is nothing at stake in winning. The very activities we choose to take us away from the market's bottom line can lead us right back into it.

Without an alternative vision of how the world could be, it is all too easy to fall back into the ethos of the marketplace.

And yet we want so much to free ourselves from that ethos. We work hard to create communities to provide us with a feeling of connection and higher purpose. Too many of these, however, are pseudo-communities that provide only the illusion of connection. The Olympics, or professional team sports, can seem to work wonders, giving to many the sense that each is part of some larger "we," a community of people connected to one another by a shared commitment to something beyond private gain. There is an aspect of our communal love of sports that seems very empowering: victory on the playing field depends on skills that, at least in theory, almost anyone might have acquired. Not surprisingly, it is often athletes from economically deprived backgrounds who become our national heroes. They live out the meritocratic fantasy that most people wish were the case in their own workplaces. Yet the celebration we feel because "we" have won the pennant or the Super Bowl or a gold medal at the Olympics is bound to be short-lived because these communities do not actually connect us to one another as individuals. They do not provide a real sense of meaning or greater purpose. Within a few days, life returns to normal, the "we" has revealed itself as a pseudocommunity, and the aloneness is back with a force.

Over and over again we heard the same story. People told us that they know what the real world is like, and they hate it. They know that they've learned how to survive, how to focus on looking out for number one, but they feel dirtied by having to be part of that kind of world. They yearn for a different reality, and yet they are so convinced that a different reality is impossible that they will scorn someone who argues otherwise.

People who feel this split in consciousness between the world they long for and the world they live in are often at a loss to know how to deal with it. So instead of tending to the spiritual crisis in their lives, they look outward, to the real world, where they are told that problems have straightforward solutions. In particular, instead of really looking at their own internal value systems, people naturally look at the values of others. This may well be one reason that crime has become such an important topic in our society. Criminals embody the crisis in values in a way that appears unambiguous: no matter how bad our choices are, theirs are worse.

For many decades now, right-wing politicians have made their crusade against crime a central element in their challenge to the liberals, and liberals have responded by trying to show that they, too, are "tough on crime." The two parties have competed with each other to see who can lengthen prison sentences more, who can find more ways to criminalize offensive behavior, or who can extend the death penalty more widely. (Bill Clinton helped to enact an anticrime bill that extended the death penalty to dozens of new crimes.)

I did a series of interviews in a federal prison in which I asked the inmates why they thought it appropriate to live by a different ethical standard than that of the mainstream. And what I heard back was this: "Hey, man, we *are* living by the same ethical standards as everyone else—just applying them in different situations." In other words, as far as they could see, everyone in American society lives by the values of the marketplace: "Get what you can for yourself, and don't worry about what that does to everyone else." That is what it means to be a maximizer of self-interest. They were merely following the same rule.

Isn't that precisely what the richest members of our society did when they supported legislation to cut their own taxes under President Bush, and before him under his father and President Reagan? The fact that the wealthy benefited disproportionately from those tax cuts is hardly a secret. The consequences have already been felt in the decline of funding for federal and state programs that benefit the poor and the powerless. And why did so many middle-income people go along with this? Because many of them imagined that they would benefit from these tax cuts in the immediate future and forgot about the longer-term consequences for others. When opponents of the legislation called attention to the effect of these tax cuts on future generations, they were often greeted by a collective shrug of indifference—as if people were saying, "What do we care about the future?" What message does cutting taxes send even when it means cutting off resources badly needed for schools and community hospitals? Doesn't virtually everyone in the society hear it as asserting the right to selfishness? This is certainly the message heard by those who are losing badly needed governmental support and who understand the depth of moral depravity shown by the rich and their representatives in government who preach moral values to the poor.

In fact, America's current economic bottom line of me-firstism leads to a massive rip-off consciousness.

This rip-off consciousness permeates every part of our lives, surrounds us, engulfs us, to the point that it almost seems normal. Who doesn't know someone who regularly hides part of their income from the IRS, or else exaggerates expenses, charitable contributions, or other deductibles—or refrains from doing so only when constrained by the fear of being caught? Many people feel that their tax money isn't serving any higher ideals anyway, so they often wonder why they shouldn't whittle down their contribution to the federal budget if they possibly can. I don't mean that most people regularly break the law. But there is certainly no shortage of people who will take advantage of any opportunity to advance their own interests and who actually feel embarrassed if they think they have missed such an opportunity.

The rip-off approach is perhaps best illustrated by the behavior of our major corporations. We all know how the key executives at Enron managed to make millions for themselves while misleading their investors and employees about the solvency of their enterprise and eventually bankrupting their corporation, thereby destroying the savings of tens of thousands of Americans, including thousands of their own employees. What is especially striking is that during the entire time this was going on, none of the executives involved appears to have thought that they were doing anything different from what every other corporate leader would do under similar circumstances.

It seems as if every few years there is a major corporate scandal of this sort, and many people think, "Well, now that such behavior has been exposed, it will stop." But it only stops for those corporations that have been exposed. In fact, most of us take for granted that corporations will lie and cheat to advance their own interests. They will take out misleading advertisements, or advertisements that use sexual imagery to sell their products, because for them it is obvious that whatever it takes to advance the bottom line is what they will do.

In this context, many people have had to struggle just to enforce even a modicum of corporate social responsibility. Corporations did not voluntarily introduce safety and health measures for their employees; they were forced to do so by laws that for years ordinary citizens had fought for. Similarly, every advance in environmental regulations was opposed by the organized representatives of corporate power for fear that the costs to their profits would far outweigh the benefits to the general public (for example, the benefits of having clean air and water). The Johns-Manville Corporation, the leading producer of asbestos, for decades hid information on the way asbestos causes cancer, and major corporations resisted the demands of health and environmental activists to clean up the many places where asbestos was a continuing hazard. It is now estimated that over 400,000 people will die from asbestos-related causes by 2027 (*Washington Post,* May 11, 1994). Instead of trying to make amends, the Manville Corporation (the successor to Johns-Manville) declared bankruptcy to escape some of its responsibility to future victims of asbestos-related cancer.

Corporations also frequently argue that if they are forced to implement environmental or health-and-safety regulations, the expense of doing so will be so great that they will have no alternative but to shut down their plants and move their operations to some part of the world where workers have not yet succeeded in organizing—where union efforts have been squelched by repressive governments. Faced with this corporate selfishness, many workers begin to resent health-and-safety and environmental advocates, fearful that the success of such advocates would mean the loss of their own jobs. It's all part of the consequences of living in a society where the bottom line is clearly to maximize money and power, and where each corporation works out for itself how exactly it can best look out for number one. This me-first mentality is not just found in renegade corporations like Enron or asbestos manufacturers. It's not just found in highly publicized cases like the cigarette companies, which continue to market cancer to teens and people of color, or the pharmaceutical companies that know their drugs may have dangerous consequences yet market them. These cases are only the extreme end of a continuum of selfishness in corporate life, where greed is the norm, not the exception. Indeed, when we find corporations acting ethically (and some do), that becomes a cause for celebration.

Barely a week goes by without some new instance of corporate crimes against the health and welfare of the American public. To take one example, on May 24, 2005, the *New York Times* reported that for three years the Guidant Corporation, which manufactures medical devices, did not reveal that a unit implanted in an estimated 24,000 people that is designed to shock a faltering heart contains a flaw that occasionally causes the unit to short-circuit. The facts came to light after one person using this device, called a defibrillator, died of cardiac arrest. According to the *Times,* if physicians had known earlier, they would have replaced this unit. The *Times* goes on to state that doctors and patients are not always told when a medical device maker has data indicating that its product has a flaw.

Sometimes liberals like to attribute this kind of criminal immorality to the excesses encouraged when Republicans are in power. Yet the evidence is that corporate greed flourishes regardless of which party is in power. Writing in salon.com on June 16, 2005, Robert F. Kennedy Jr. reported a recent discovery on the part of government scientists and health officials, who met in June 2000 at the Simpsonwood Conference Center, in Norcross, Georgia, with representatives of every major vaccine manufacturer, including GlaxoSmithKline, Merck, Wyeth, and Aventi Pasteur. Evidence had emerged that a mercury-based preservative in vaccines—thimerosal—appeared to be responsible for a dramatic increase in autism and a host of other neurological disorders among children. According to Kennedy, transcripts of the Simpsonwood conference obtained under the Freedom of Information Act show that much of the discussion was devoted to how to cover up the damaging data, given that "many at the meeting were concerned about how the damaging revelations about thimerosal would affect the vaccine industry's bottom line." Kennedy details how the companies and the Centers for Disease Control worked together to hide this data for several years. The number of vaccinations given to children had doubled between 1989 and 2003, with the result that children born during those years received heavy doses of mercury from vaccines. The drug manufacturers gradually began to "phase thimerosal out of injections given to American infants—but they continued to sell off their mercury-based supplies of vaccines until 2004." It has not been conclusively proven that the growing number of children with neurological or immune-system damage seen in the public schools, and possibly the growth of attention deficit problems that are subsequently treated by medicating problem youngsters, are related to these inoculations. But the behavior of the drug companies in the light of such a possibility speaks for itself.

Corporations are able to get away with this kind of behavior because their ownership of media combined with their powerful friends in both political parties do their best to reduce the risks to corporate irresponsibility. Kennedy reports on the role of the Republican Senate majority leader, Bill Frist, who has recently been leading the charge against "activist judges," as one of the most powerful champions of the Religious Right in the U.S. Senate. According to Kennedy, Frist, who has received $873,000 in contributions from the pharmaceutical industry,

has been working to immunize vaccine makers from liability in 4,200 lawsuits that have been filed by the parents of injured children. On five separate occasions, Frist has tried to seal all of the government's vaccine-related documents—including the Simpsonwood transcripts—and shield Eli Lilly, the developer of thimerosal, from subpoenas. In 2002, the day after Frist quietly slipped a rider known as the "Eli Lilly Protection Act" into a homeland security bill, the company contributed $10,000 to his campaign and bought 5,000 copies of his book on bioterrorism. Congress repealed the measure in 2003—but earlier this year [2005], Frist slipped another provision into an anti-terrorism bill that would deny compensation to children suffering from vaccine-related brain disorders. "The lawsuits are of such magnitude that they could put vaccine producers out of business and limit our capacity to deal with a biological attack by terrorists," says Andy Olsen, a legislative assistant to Frist.

Just because corporations often enact hurtful policies as a result of their me-first philosophy doesn't mean that the folks who work at corporations are evil. Most corporate employees and managers are, like everyone else, decent human beings who have internalized the norms of the economic sphere in which they work and then try to be as responsible as possible to their corporate investors. It is a tremendous mistake for people on the left to talk about corporate leadership as if it were composed of evil people. Demonizing these people actually underestimates the problem, which is based not in individual pathology but in a systemic disorder.

Most people in corporate leadership positions feel a powerful constraint on the choices they can make without losing their jobs. They have achieved their positions precisely because they do the best possible job to maximize a high return on investments. These corporate leaders will tell you that they have a "fiduciary responsibility" to their investors to produce high profits. They're right, too. If they don't maximize profits, the board of directors of the corporation will fire them, or their investors will remove their money and invest elsewhere in corporations where they can get a better return on the investment. So of course they are going to act according to the norms of the economic world and pursue the interests of their corporation to the greatest extent possible. They are "realistic" and accommodating to the "real world" as they know it, rarely understanding how they are simultaneously re-creating and strengthening that world.

But then how could corporate executives be expected to think otherwise when the bottom-line consciousness of the marketplace is hammered into us by the neoclassical economics taught to every college student? This theory assumes as a fundamental truth that human beings seek to maximize their own individual advantage without regard to the consequences for others and that a society in which people act this way will actually produce the greatest good for everyone. No one challenges this basic vision. Although no scientific proof exists to validate this worldview, it appears increasingly accurate as a description of how people do in fact behave.

So the logic of the marketplace permeates our thinking and shapes the way we approach many aspects of our lives both as individuals and as a community. For example, it has a direct impact on how we think about the physical world around us. In the mode of market consciousness, we learn to look at nature itself as something that can and should be turned into a commodity.

When developers take agricultural or undeveloped land and turn it into shopping malls, many Americans find it hard to resist their arguments: "If we make a great profit here, we can contribute tax monies and create jobs."

For decades now environmentalists have been calling on us to pay attention to the dire fate of the earth. But rather than heed their warnings, corporations hire scientific experts to prove that the crisis is far from imminent or that the particular damage the company in question is causing is not all that serious, at least not taken on its own. When the cumulative impact of environmentally irresponsible decisions leads to the destructiveness of a hurricane like Katrina, which devastated New Orleans and much of southern Mississippi, systemic change is briefly mentioned, then sidelined in favor of short-term assistance to the victims and token changes, while the media focuses our attention away from corporate and governmental crimes and irresponsibility to the crimes of individuals responding to the crisis. Corporate looting of the global environment is ignored while individual looting, often for survival necessities, becomes the major story.

Even though we now have overwhelming evidence of growing, and in some cases irreparable, damage to our planet, this message has not resonated deeply enough to cause American voters to rise up in anger and alarm and throw out of office those in both parties who block environmental agreements and postpone implementing measures to re-strain the worst offenders. And so the earth's ecological systems con-tinue to be undermined, its grasslands paved over, its forests torn down, and its air and waterways polluted, all in the name of progress.

The conventional wisdom claiming that people have responded to corporate-induced fears that they will lose their jobs should environ-mental constraints be implemented is true and yet misses a deeper problem that environmentalists face. How can we require corporations to behave responsibly if everyone believes that the planet is simply an-other resource available to satisfy human wants? If the earth is here for our use, why not use it?

Environmentalists are not likely to make significant headway in mo-bilizing the rest of us to lower our own levels of consumption unless environmentalism can challenge the rip-off consciousness and the self-ishness of the competitive marketplace. What the environmental move-ment has failed to emphasize is a nonutilitarian, nonreductionist, nonmaterialist view of the earth—the possibility of a consciousness that does not reduce everything to the question "What's in it for me?"

Fortunately, the past few years have seen the development of spiri-tual and religious environmental movements that teach another way of looking at the earth: drawing upon Native American traditions. The world is not to be viewed merely as a resource for humans. Rather, there is something intrinsically sacred about the planet and its life-support systems, and we must approach it with reverence, not simply with an eye to profit or usefulness.

It is this spiritual dimension of human life that is antithetical to the logic of the marketplace and to the human relationships fostered by the marketplace. The need to maximize the bottom line, along with the ethos of selfishness and materialism it promotes, has produced a world that is unsustainable, out of sorts with itself, and in deep pain. This is the core spiritual crisis of the contemporary world.

As I've noted, most people don't feel good about living in a world where the bottom line is profit and power. One might then legitimately ask, "If people really don't like this kind of world, why don't they just change it?"

Part of the answer is that they are not aware that many other people feel the same way they do. Another is our fear that we will expose ourselves to ridicule, social isolation, and loss of employment if we challenge the fundamental dynamics of our society. We've been taught to think it is naive and childish to imagine that others share our desires for a kinder, more generous world. This fearful view of the other and of what would happen to us should we act on the assumption that other people might respond to us as human beings is central to keeping people inside their established roles. In fact, most of us have had moments when we did act on our highest vision and experienced setbacks and disappointments as a result. The desire to avoid humiliation is a powerful motivator, leading us to shun situations in which our private aspirations for a more loving and generous world might be exposed. We need to look at the way this and other fears become dominant in shaping the kinds of individual and social choices we make.

THREE

The Voice of Fear and the Voice of Hope

For the past several thousand years, much of human society has been torn by a struggle between two worldviews or ways of understanding what it is to be human. The one view tells us that we are born into a world in which each person is out for themselves and life is a battle of all against all. Others will dominate you unless you dominate them first. Security for ourselves, our families, our communities, or our nation depends on our ability to get the advantage over them before they get it over us. Fear of the other is common sense, the only possible response a rational person can have in a world where competition is required for survival. I call this the view of cynical realism, and the normal psychological state accompanying it is heightened alert and fear.

The other view tells us that the world is composed of human beings who desire and need loving connection, recognition of who they are from others whom they respect, and joyous celebration of life and consciousness and freedom. According to this view, people are constantly seeking ways to cooperate, and they feel most fulfilled when they are needed by others and can generously provide care and assistance. Our fate is intrinsically bound up with the fate of others, and our own realization as human beings depends upon the fullest realization of the capacities and desires for love of everyone else on the planet. I call this the view of spiritual consciousness, or the unity of all being, and the normal psychological state accompanying it is heightened generosity and hope.

Much of what transpires in the world of politics is a reflection of the degree to which one or the other of these worldviews is on the ascendancy, though both views are almost always present and contending in the minds of most people in the Western world.

When the paradigm of fear is dominant, people look at all their experiences through that framework. At such times, politicians who speak the language of fear sound realistic, even profound, while those who talk about hope seem foolish and out of touch. These dynamics have been particularly evident in the post–9/11 world of American politics, in which the fear of terrorism has been used to manipulate the public into supporting politicians who seem to be the toughest militarists and are thus able to reassure the population that they can handle the seemingly ever-present threat. But the culture of fear extends far beyond politics. When fear prevails, those parts of our cultural heritage—religious texts, for example, or novels and poetry, or social and psychological theories—that validate our fears are deemed the most intellectually sophisticated, while those that embody elements of hope are dismissed as naive, with little to teach us. Conversely, when hope is in the ascendancy, politicians and theologians, novelists and social theorists who were previously dismissed as unsophisticated because they dared to articulate hope in a time of fear are now seen as visionary thinkers and leaders.

It's rarely the case that someone produces a decisive argument that proves one paradigm or the other. Rather, there is a flow of social energy, a movement of consciousness, both inside each person and in the society as a whole, between our most hopeful and our most fearful inclinations.

If we think of a continuum between two poles—the pole of hope and the pole of fear—then we can imagine that at any specific moment each of us is situated at some place on that continuum. In times when a large number of people feel their attention being drawn more toward the pole of fear, we can talk metaphorically about a flow of social energy moving in that direction. And we can experience in ourselves how frequently the voices of fear pop up precisely at the moment when our energies are moving toward hope.

On the most general level, the atmosphere in our society has oscillated over the years between these twin poles. After the stock market crash of 1929, when America was suddenly thrown into economic despair, many Americans felt their energy flow toward fear. The direction of the flow changed in the years of the New Deal, as President Franklin Delano Roosevelt convinced Americans that "there is nothing to fear but fear itself." Fear again became dominant during the witch hunts of the McCarthy period, and the Cold War anticommunist hysteria made the Vietnam War seem plausible to many. Yet for youth coming of age in the 1960s the pendulum swung back in the direction of hope when the civil rights movement and other social change movements began to reclaim some of the highest ideals of American democracy.

The shifting balance between fear and hope is rarely based entirely on some "obvious" meaning of any event in our personal or communal lives. We usually interpret events through the framework of the underlying theories and worldviews we already hold. Skillful political leaders or movements can call upon these preexisting frames of reference in order to characterize an event as confirming our most hopeful or fearful predilections.

Take 9/11, for example. It's certainly easy to understand why many Americans would feel frightened by such a terrible reminder of the fragility of their own lives and by the evident vulnerability of America to attack by a handful of extremists. Yet President Bush and others in both major political parties seized that moment to inculcate a much deeper level of fear in the population than the facts themselves justified. Suddenly we were told we were facing a well-organized global network of terrorists capable of launching many more 9/11s. From there came a systematic restructuring of American ideals and patterns of life. In the years since 9/11 we've been subjected to color-coded alerts to the present level of danger, rarely substantiated in any way that could be called credible. Television, radio, newspapers, and magazines have drenched us with anxiety-provoking images and unsubstantiated stories of threats against which we must be constantly vigilant. Arabs and Muslims have become instant targets of suspicion, discrimination, and arbitrary arrest. Intimidated into believing that extraordinary measures are needed to fight an ongoing war against terror that has neither well-defined enemies nor any plausible way of measuring victory, the American public has allowed its government to set up prison camps in which people are routinely tortured . And even though no link could be established between 9/11 and the dictatorship of Saddam Hussein, fear of terrorism became the primary argument for why we needed to invade and wage war against his regime, launching a struggle that has taken the lives of tens of thousands of Iraqis and has maimed or killed thousands of American soldiers. As I write, over these past four years the number of people who have died at the hands of terrorists is less than one-fortieth of the number of Americans who die in car accidents and less than one-third of the number of people around the globe who died on 9/11 from starvation and preventable diseases. All the same, since that day our social and political energies have to a large degree been devoted to preparing for a repeat of this kind of attack.

A different leadership, while acknowledging the need to take measures to protect America's borders, might have focused greater attention on the heroism of thousands of ordinary Americans who responded with generosity and courage to the attack on 9/11. Hundreds of people gave their lives and countless others risked theirs to aid the victims of the attack, while millions more gave their money and in other ways demonstrated their sympathy and concern. This was a moment that could make us all feel optimistic about the human condition and the goodness that lies at the core of so many of our neighbors. Yet these points were made only in passing, while the chief political lessons drawn by our leaders and emphasized in the media were those that confirmed our fears, not our hopes. The facts did not require this—the misuse of 9/11 was a choice. But it was a choice rooted in a deeper paradigm of fear. It is thus critical that we understand the two contending worldviews and how they operate If we are ever to move America away from its current domination by fear.

In the fear paradigm, human beings are imagined to have been thrown into a world based on the struggle of all against all, in which people seek to maximize their own advantage (or the advantage of a group to which they belong) without regard to the consequences for others.

Greed is one of the pathological consequences of fear. We believe that there won't be enough to go around, so we feel we must hoard. We suspect that others won't share with us, so we don't want to risk being exploited by sharing what we have with them. As long as we see the other as likely to take advantage of us, the idea of sharing seems self-destructive. The world is evil, and we must struggle on as best we can.

The voice of fear has its reflection in religious language. According to the paradigm of fear, God's religious path is primarily about creating boundaries and restraints and providing us with religious practices designed to prevent us from falling into the endless temptations that surround us. Individuals find meaning for their lives by being aligned with the divine energy that is protecting them and that guides them in how to deal with all the many dangers they face. Frequently, the spiritual energy of the universe is perceived as uniquely on the side of a particular group or nation (even though virtually every nation or group believes that God is on its side). Further, God is envisioned as a warrior: powerful, combative, and harsh in judgment. This is the Right Hand of God.

For some two billion people on this planet, material scarcity remains a central reality in their daily lives. To the extent that that is true, fear of destitution and abandonment may be much closer to the surface of consciousness, and trust may be harder to sustain. Voices that preach resignation, the inevitable triumph of evil, the fundamental corruptibility of the human soul, and the need to dominate before one is dominated may all seem more plausible when one's daily reality is filled with hunger, deprivation, and oppression. Even those who yearn for a different world may give up on the possibility of achieving that in any way other than through divine intervention. What an emotionally sustaining picture—to imagine the world suddenly being made right when God swoops down and decisively defeats the forces of evil in battle. God's Right Hand triumphs, and subsequently the good things of the world can flourish. I'm not surprised that many people follow the Right Hand of God.

To many on the contemporary political Left, the Right Hand of God consciousness is the only visible manifestation of religion, dominating American politics and leading people to support the war in Iraq, to attempt to pack the judiciary with right-wingers, to seek to criminalize abortion, and in numerous other ways to back policies based on domination. "Why should we listen to this talk of religion or spirituality," my friends on the Left say, "when in practice all that religious language turns out to be about is accepting domination and resigning yourself to oppression? Religion is just a way for people to accept what they believe they cannot change. Perhaps the one thing Marx actually got right was that 'religion is the opiate of the people.'" As they see it, religion is the problem, not the solution.

If the only manifestation of religion were the Right Hand of God, my friends on the Left would have a point. But the voice of fear and despair has never become the sole voice in our heads or the only melody in our souls or the only strain in religious and spiritual traditions. From the time we were born, we have heard a loving, caring voice that cannot be totally drowned out. Human infants could not survive the first several years of life without a nurturing loving other who takes care of them. Clinical studies have demonstrated that a child that is fed and clothed but not touched or given any external source of recognition will die. Without denying all the pathological behavior we may have experienced at the hands of our parents, the reality is that none of us would have survived had there not been a loving someone to nurture us, and that person could not have survived unless she or he was surrounded by a family or community that provided the primary caregiver with nurturance and support.

This initial, undivided love is the basis of the great spiritual traditions. Biblical religion does not start with evil and fear. The book of Genesis begins with a God who creates our universe and who then affirms the goodness of the world: "and God saw that it was good." Human beings are created in this divine image—we also are good. If there are distortions of that divinity in the world, they reflect mistaken choices, not the essence of what it is to be human. Cruelty is not destiny, because human beings have been created in the image of a gentle, loving God. Imperialism and class conflict, murder and rape, anger and hatred—these are not built into the fundamental structure of reality. They are not inevitable. They can be changed through human action and more compassionate choices.

None of this is to deny evil and sinfulness as part of the daily reality of human life. We in the Jewish world talk about sin as a "missing of the mark," as though we are an arrow that has gone off course, and we need periodic tuning up of our spiritual selves in order to get back on course. In Judaism, sin is overcome through repentance, a return (*teshuvah*) to the divine image in which we were created. In Christianity, sin is overcome through faith in the person of Jesus, whom they believe to be the Christ (Messiah), whose mission on earth was to enable human beings to once again find that divine good and hence repair the evils around them. In both traditions, we are told that evil can be overcome and that we need not live in fear.

The central story of the Torah is that of a people who are enslaved and then through divine intervention freed from slavery. Its message is one of hope: we *can* overcome oppression, the world can be transformed. In Judaism, the force that makes change possible is YHVH, the God-force of the universe. This God-force, a force of healing and transformation (*tikkun*), is the ultimate reality of the universe, the force that has shaped the universe from the start, the truth whose will toward goodness is manifested in the command to "pursue justice," to "love one's neighbor as oneself," and never to "oppress the stranger." This God is a loving being whose essential nature is compassionate, caring, forgiving, generous, and peace loving, even though God can at times be angry at the persistence of injustice and our indifference to the suffering we cause by participating in oppressive social or political systems. God wants us to care not only for ourselves but for everyone on the planet because we have all been created in the divine image. God needs us as partners in the healing and transformation of the world and as stewards of the well-being of the planet, and sometimes gets irritated or upset when we misuse God or Torah or Judaism as a vehicle to escape doing what we know we must do to heal the world. Although ultimately God cares for us, has compassion for our straying from our mission, God desperately needs us to get back on the path of healing the world, even with all our imperfections and weaknesses, as long as we too show compassion for others. This is how God is understood from the standpoint of the Left Hand of God.

If we want to find an answer to our current spiritual crisis and remake our society, the choice we face is not between religion and secularism. The choice we face is between the Right Hand and the Left Hand of God. Even if you are secular, you are called to choose between the paradigm of hope and the paradigm of fear, between a vision of a world in which love can be the central reality and a world in which power over others is the only realistic path. At every moment, we are unconsciously, but nevertheless quite determinedly, organizing our experience through one or the other of these paradigms. One of the goals of this book is to encourage us to become more conscious of which paradigm we are using at any given moment and to help us make it less scary to choose the paradigm of hope.

The world is not neutral. My faith tells me that the world actually tilts toward love and hope. Nor is my belief some New Age accommodation to modernity. The great interpreter of Torah, Rabbi Hillel, was challenged to recite the entire Torah while standing on one foot. Hillel responded: "Do not do anything to your neighbor that is hateful to you. This is the entire Torah. Go and learn." And the greatest expositor of Jewish law, Rabbi Akiba, taught that the central principle of Torah was, "Love your neighbor as yourself." He went on to explain that this statement was not just about inner feelings but about our relationship to property: "What is mine is yours, and what is yours is yours." Need I add that, in articulating his view of God's call to human beings, Jesus later developed this message of love to an even higher level of sophistication and centrality, while parallel developments within Judaism and later in Islam have given that message of love a deep foundation in the religions of the West, however imperfectly those who practice these religions have actually embodied it.

This call toward a world of love and hope is counterbalanced by many moments of despair and fear both in ourselves and in our holy texts and spiritual traditions. We hold elements of both paradigms in our minds, both the Right Hand and the Left Hand of God, both fear and hope, and in every encounter we hear both voices, which together shape how we experience the world and one another. Exactly where we are on that continuum at any given moment is determined by a complex interaction among several factors: the legacy of our experiences in our families and in our early socialization in schools; our current life situations; the intellectual concepts, religious beliefs, and popular ideas that we have internalized; and our assessment of the extent to which those around us are conducting their lives according to fear or to hope.

Once we understand the paradigms of hope and fear, we have a framework within which to understand the political meaning of much of the culture, intellectual life, religion, and mass psychology that surrounds us. We need only ask of any phenomenon: "Does it tend to increase our hope or our fear? Does it make us more certain that the world is basically a scary place from which we must be defended, or does it support our inner conviction that more goodness and kindness and beauty and generosity and compassion exist in the world than we have been allowing ourselves to recognize recently?"

Do your own research. Ask yourself, where would you locate what you see and hear on the hope-fear continuum? Ask this question of every movie and television show you watch, every political speech or advertisement you listen to, every commercial and magazine ad, every piece of legislation, every political demonstration, every sermon or spiritual teaching, every theory of human development or of the natural stages in spiritual evolution, every social and scientific theory, every rock concert or rave that comes your way.

What you will find is that our culture is today profoundly oriented toward the paradigm of fear. Selfishness makes sense; generosity does not. In moments of fear, the hopeful side of religious traditions recedes, and stories, theologies, and interpretations of holy texts that see the world as a dangerous place and human beings as evil or fundamentally hurtful, or that justify the use of violence, or that see God as seeking revenge and the obliteration of enemies, or that view suffering as intrinsic and inescapable, or that justify passivity and an acceptance of the distortions in the world as unchangeable, become more prevalent. Religions develop that sanctify the people in the "in" group (the nation or the community of believers) and demonize those on the outside.

These same dynamics play out in the secular world and in secular theories of social change. When fear is ascendant, it is easy for theories to catch on that blame some evil other for the ills of our society and that assume that anyone who does not share this viewpoint is deluded. Theories become popular that see the contemporary distortions in human beings as built into the structure of reality, as an inevitable feature of human nature or of complex social organizations, or even as a result of bad genes or evolution or brain structure.

In the progressive world, the paradigm of fear is manifested through a lack of trust that we can transform our society and a growing cynicism about the possibility that people can ever be mobilized to struggle for the kind of fundamental changes that the world so badly needs. Liberals and progressives develop narrowly conceived technical solutions to social problems because they imagine that people are too fearful to even think about, much less fight for, the more fundamental transformations that are really needed. As they themselves begin to lose trust in the viability of their own underlying vision of what the world needs, they unconsciously communicate their own lack of faith in the American people, which only serves to increase our collective doubt that real change is possible. But if real change is not possible, people reason, then tinkering with the system as it is may only antagonize the powerful who have the means to retaliate, for example, by moving their business to countries that offer fewer environmental restrictions and cheaper labor. If no credible vision for deep-seated transformation exists, if fear has won out over hope, then many people will try to accommodate to "reality," and this often encourages them to affiliate with the Right, which seems more equipped to deal with a world based on fear.

The Right has learned how to use the paradigm of fear to dominate politics. It can take a distinguished army hero like Senator John McCain or John Kerry and label him "soft" on military matters, as George Bush did during the Republican primaries in 2000 and again in the presidential election of 2004. It can push through the Congress spending bills totaling hundreds of billions of dollars to fight the war in Iraq on the grounds that otherwise Americans will become vulnerable to terror. It can claim that to protect us from terrorists we must reduce our funding for social services so that we have more money for homeland security.

Instead of countering with a vision that validates the Left Hand of God, the Left, particularly the Democratic Party, tries to tinker with kinder, gentler versions of the Right Hand of God. But doing so only strengthens the widespread perception that everything is moving toward fear. And the more people believe that fear is the only sensible approach to reality, the less open they are to anyone who isn't sophisticated enough or profound enough to understand how dangerous and hurtful the world truly is. To the extent that they allow their own fear to dominate, the Left becomes powerless to shift the discourse. Its supporters come to be perceived by many as a puny substitute for the right-wing "realists," who always appear to have a much more savvy understanding of the world than all these weak-kneed liberals.

There is an inherent problem for those who espouse a politics of hope and a vision of love: that achieving a world of love and kindness cannot be done using the tactics of power and domination. If the Right Hand of God seeks to "win," the Left Hand of God seeks a world in which winning is no longer the appropriate category, a world in which the humanity of all has been validated, including those who position themselves as "our enemies." The Left Hand of God looks weak in part because it does not aim to dominate and control but rather tries to elicit a spirit of generosity and hope. Such a spirit does not show up on the radar screen of those who think of power in terms of capacities to manipulate or command people and resources for the sake of self-advantage.

It is no surprise that many who espouse the Left Hand of God have used the language of women's experience to describe their vision. The Hebrew word for compassion is *ruchamim*, from the Hebrew word for womb, *rechem*. The mothering we receive during our early years leaves an indelible impression on us, a belief that love is really possible, a love that is not about manipulation and domination but about the outpouring of generosity, about the world nurturing us with mother's milk. Such images suggest a vulnerability that frightens those who believe that love and generosity are too "soft" to provide a foundation for significant victories in the tough-minded, power-oriented world of American politics. Yet the history of transformative movements from Judaism and Christianity down through psychoanalysis, feminism, civil rights, and the peace movement demonstrates the potential power that can emerge from a vision of love and kindness. Even when these movements eventually lost faith in their own transformative vision and then allied themselves with the Right Hand of God, their initial and most profound impact occurred when they actually believed in the healing potential of a world based on love, generosity, and caring for others, and on aligning oneself with the poor and the powerless and affirming peace and justice.

The logic of Pharaoh could never make sense of the logic of Moses, the logic of Rome could never make sense of the logic of Jesus, the logic of police sergeant "Bull" Connor could never make sense of the logic of Martin Luther King Jr. The spiritual politics of the Left Hand of God confronts the empires and the social practices of domination with a loving energy that by the criteria of the powerful can seem in-substantial and dismissible, like a bothersome mosquito that makes noise but ultimately can't really do much damage. That loving energy nevertheless has an immense potential to change everything, to the ex-tent that people are able to sustain the position of hope.*

Yet social reality is never static, and the moments of hope, no matter how self-validating and wonderful they feel, are often undermined by nagging doubts, the not-yet-cured legacy of past pain, and the impact of social and economic institutions that have not yet been transformed. Fear crouches at the door, ready to leap back in, and does so under the guise of an alleged realism about the best way to create and maintain a world that is safe for hope. In the name of peace, we must make war; in the name of social justice, we must accommodate to the interests of the rich; in the name of building a society that is safe for our religions of peace, we must protect ourselves from those who hate, and the only way to do that is to hate their evil ways! So slowly the energy swings back toward fear.

So how do we move the energy toward hope?

We are continually making choices that tend to reinforce one end of the spectrum or the other, both in ourselves and in those with whom

---

* And hope has its support structures, too. For centuries the voice of hope found ex-pression in the mystical traditions that became central to the kabbalah, to Sufism, and to the worship of Mary. The powerful insights of feminist theology, finding expression in the writings of Catherine Keller, Mary Grey, Sharon Welch, Judith Plaskow, Rachel Adler, Karen Baker-Fletcher, Rosemary Ruether, Sister Joan Chittister, Maria Pilar Aquino, Carter Heyward, Mary Hunt, and dozens more, have given contemporary substance to the Left Hand of God. Social theorists and theolo-gians like Thich Nhat Hanh, Jonathan Schell, Zygmunt Bauman, Cornel West, Alice Miller, Riane Eisler, bell hooks, Peter Gabel, Michael Bader, Abraham Joshua Heschel, Walter Brueggemann, Thomas Merton, John Dear, Parker J. Palmer, Matthew Fox, Zalman Schachter-Shalomi, Sylvia Boorstein, Thomas Berry, Thomas Moore, Sharon Salzberg, and countless others have provided an intellectual foundation for hope. Musicians, artists, poets, and novelists have often bucked the trendy cynicism to provide yet another frame for keeping alive the vision of the Left Hand of God.

we interact every day. Every time we take a step in a direction that reinforces hope and affirms the possibility of building a world imbued with greater love and kindness and generosity and lack of violence, we contribute to the movement of social energy toward the Left Hand of God. Every action we take has the capacity to increase the love or the anger, the hope or the fear, that are the fundamental building blocks of the world we inhabit. In the smallest acts of our everyday lives, as well as in our larger acts on the stage of politics, we are always involved in choices.

But what if we are stuck in fear or feel that others are stuck? What can we do?

I wish there were a magic bullet or one-size-fits-all solution. But each person and each moment has its unique features that can't be addressed through a general formula.

Some valuable resources and guidelines grow out of the religious and spiritual traditions of the human race and have sustained people in times of darkness, sometimes empowering them to take steps toward hope:

1. Do acts of kindness, love, and generosity every day, even when you are not in the mood.

2. Let go of a commitment to outcomes. Do acts of hopefulness even when there are no rational grounds to believe that it will all turn out okay. This is what the religious miracles are meant to say—that good outcomes can happen even when there is no rational reason to believe they will.

3. Find a friend with whom you can share your vision of the world you want. Develop that friendship so that it is one place where you can always go to share your frustrations and renew your hopes. Make it a regular commitment to see that friend and share your own inner fears and hopes and hear his or her hopes and fears too. (And when you are listening to your friend, pray for the success of that person's vision even if it isn't yours.)

4. Prayer and mediation. It's possible to focus on the source of our fears, to be fully present to them, to experience them, and see

that they are often less formidable than we may think. Meditation and prayer can sometimes help us fully accept that we are all going to die and can teach us to let go of the expectation of permanency, decreasing the fear of death and making it less scary to take risks for the sake of our beliefs in what is right and good.

5. Rituals of empowerment. The Passover Seder and the reading of the stories of liberation from Egypt helped keep up the spirits of the Jewish people for two thousand years while they endured oppression, exile, and brutality from others. The spiritual Left ought to have a comparable Seder telling the story of the liberation struggles of the world. Till we have such, why not create such a ritual for your friends and family? You'd be amazed at how empowering and hope engendering it can be.

6. Join and participate in a spiritual community that weekly celebrates a Sabbath of some sort, a day dedicated to celebrating the grandeur of creation and to remembering the moments in which hope surged forward. Don't stay in a religious community that does no such celebrating. Challenge such a group in the name of the Left Hand of God, and speak with others about the hope-based tradition within your religion, letting them know that you want to hear more of that hopeful vision being articulated. If that doesn't work, leave that group and if necessary build your own spiritual or religious community. Draw upon the rituals and practices of some existing religious or spiritual path, since it's harder to start from scratch than to modify a path that has some history and accumulated wisdom.

Some other resources, not necessarily connected with a religious or spiritual tradition, may also be helpful:

7. Individual therapy, particularly with a therapist who has a hopeful attitude toward the world and is not stuck in some fear-oriented worldview. Be sure that the therapist you pick knows that your current despair is not only a psychological issue but also a reflection of the degree to which the society as a whole

moves toward fear—and don't stick with a therapist who tries to reduce the whole thing to childhood problems. But keep in mind that all of us carry remnants of childhood and adult life that can help to undermine our capacities to sustain hope—and they should be dealt with too.

8. Participate only in political activities in which the leaders are psychologically and spiritually sophisticated enough to understand these issues and give as much attention to making sure that their activities foster hope as they do to winning a specific political goal. If you can find no such activities or leaders, you can be the leader and create the activity. If there is no alternative but to take part in an activity in which the leaders are generating fear (for example, the only peace demonstration in town), challenge the speakers and leaders publicly. Don't go along just because they created the activity. Insist on a message of hope. But do it compassionately and respectfully. And when someone comes around asking for your vote or your donation, make sure that a condition is that they start to project a hopeful vision more in accord with your own.

9. Whenever you are giving a talk, recruiting a person to some activity, writing a leaflet or op-ed, or trying to influence others in the public arena, always ask yourself: is this presentation giving enough attention to fostering hope?

10. Invite people to study this book with you as the first step in creating a group that will focus on books related to spiritual politics. It may give them some hope, and that may give you some hopeful sustenance. Then, join the Network of Spiritual Progressives, and that will give you even more: http://www.spiritualprogressives.org.

If you were the only one doing all this, it might seem scary. But guess what? You are *not* the only one! In fact, hundreds of millions of people want to build a world of greater love, kindness, generosity, awe, and wonder. Our task is to help them find one another so that they will know about you and you will know about them. That's why it's so important to join up, to become part of a movement that articulates your ideals, and to become visible.

We can change this world, and you can be an important part of that process. But we need to be smart about it, correcting mistakes of the past and being unafraid to articulate a visionary and love-filled perspective. That will be the focus of the coming chapters before we turn, in the second half of this book, to a political agenda for spiritual progressives.

FOUR

Enter the Religious Right

For over forty years now, the ongoing spiritual crisis in American society has largely been ignored by mainline churches. Liberals in the
church responded to the Left's political agenda, endorsing the central
call for "inclusion" by challenging the racism, sexism, and homophobia that existed in their local churches, often at speeds that provoked
considerable resistance among their congregations. Acquiescing to the
Left's demand to keep religion out of politics, however, they rarely
brought any spiritual consciousness to the liberal political movements
they sought to aid. While black churches were unequivocal in their integration of spiritual themes with their support for civil rights, the
largely white leadership of the mainline churches was reluctant to do
more than provide troops for peace and social justice demonstrations
and to bring prophetic sermons on these topics into their local
churches.

What they did not do was to acknowledge, analyze, and educate the
Left about the spiritual crisis in American society. Even though some
of these churches kept up a lively set of activities in support of social
change, their leaders were increasingly distanced from the inner lives of
their congregants and the struggles that they faced in daily life and in
connecting to God. Their attempts to be politically relevant had led
them to ignore the hunger for a spiritual connection to a higher meaning, to awe and wonder, and to the experience of loving community.
Secular rationality often prevailed over mystical connection to the

ultimate source of love. Although the churches spoke the language of love, they often neglected fostering the experiences and emotional intensity that are the necessary foundation for taking that language seriously.

No wonder, then, that the mainline churches began to lose their membership as an evangelical form of Christianity picked up on the energy of the 1960s and 1970s, attracting millions to a religiosity based on the personal experience of surrender to God—an inner experience of transformation, the affirmation of a higher purpose to life, and the building of religious communities in which people were challenged to move beyond the polite limits of socializing at church and involve themselves more actively and passionately in spreading the church's message. Evangelists put on massive "Jesus festivals" that drew hundreds of thousands of teenagers; they produced movies and videos; created interactive Web sites, Internet magazines, and networks of bookstores; and they turned out Christian rock music and contemporary gospel music that sometimes turned their recording artists into pop stars. Now, in the first decade of the twenty-first century, an estimated one out of every three people in the United States identifies with an evangelical church.

Not all of these evangelicals are politically right-wing. A small but still significant minority of evangelicals voted Democratic in 2004. Some sociologists estimate that as many as 35 percent of evangelicals oppose the politics of the Religious Right, and many opposed the invasion of Iraq. Under the leadership of Ron Sider, a group called Evangelicals for Social Action has played a pioneering role in struggles for social justice. The Call for Renewal, led by deeply religious progressives like Jim Wallis and Tony Campolo, has brought together thousands of evangelicals concerned about poverty and willing to challenge government policies that are detrimental to the poor. Jim Wallis's *Sojourners* magazine has become a major voice for those who are deeply committed to an evangelical approach to Christianity and yet retain a passion for peace and social justice. I had the honor of being invited by Jim Wallis to be the only rabbi to get arrested with a group of evangelical leaders engaged in nonviolent civil disobedience in the rotunda of the Capitol building—challenging budget cuts for the poor. No doubt these progressive evangelicals can, and I hope will, play a central role in building the kind of spiritual politics that I advocate in this book. I highly recommend that anyone who tends automatically to equate religion with reactionary politics have a look at some of what progressive evangelicals have written, particularly Jim Wallis's *God's Politics: Why the Right Gets It Wrong and the Left Doesn't Get It* and Tony Campolo's *Speaking My Mind: The Radical Evangelical Prophet Tackles the Tough Issues Christians Are Afraid to Face.*

Unfortunately, a far larger section of evangelicals identifies with right-wing politics. In part, that split mirrors a split about how best to interpret scripture. A large part of the evangelical movement has adopted a perspective called dispensationalism, taught in the Scofield Reference Bible and popularized in Tim LaHaye's best-selling Left Behind series and in the writings of John Nelson Darby and Hal Lindsey. Dispensationalists believe that we are living in the last stage of history prior to the Second Coming of Christ, a thousand-year period in which Satan and his demons will be imprisoned, and then a final battle will take place in which Satan and his evil followers will be destroyed by fire and a new heaven and a new earth will be established for all eternity.

Dispensationalists oppose the ecumenical movement, which it sees as suppressing true Christianity. It sees the world as on a downward spiral toward total corruption and that humans can do nothing but wait for the coming of Christ. Social action is seen as a waste of time because there will always be wars and injustice till Jesus returns to rectify it all. Feeding hungry people is legitimate not for the goodness that is involved but for the opportunity it may present to open the people being fed to accepting the gospel. Convinced that nothing much can change till Jesus returns, they often look at the evil around them as confirmation that the biblical predictions are already on their way to coming true and that Jesus will be returning soon. Jerry Falwell is reported to have responded to a TV commentator's question about the growing degradation of the environment by saying that he wasn't concerned because Jesus was coming back, and therefore we had better use it before we lose it.

Some dispensationalists believe that the government that governs best is the one that governs least. They fear the imposition of a super-government and see the United Nations as an evil force that may eventually get the power to do the work of the Antichrist and persecute

God's people. That's why many of them cheered when President Bush appointed John Bolton as the U.S. representative to the United Nations, recognizing him as a strong critic of the world body.

But while they fear the United Nations, dispensationalists are strong supporters of the Israeli right wing. They believe that the Palestinians should be expelled so as to make room for the rebuilding of the Temple, all as necessary prelude to the return of Jesus, a final struggle between Jews and Arabs, and the conversion of some Jews to Christianity, with the rest joining all those who don't accept Jesus—in eternal damnation. Right-wing Jews have embraced them, winking to each other that they will accept the political aid to Israel at this moment without worrying unduly about Jesus's imminent return.

The dispensationalists are unapologetic champions of the Right Hand of God. They would not necessarily argue with my earlier point that this approach is appropriate only when it is necessary to rectify the oppression of the powerless, because in the view of many dispensationalists that is exactly the situation of true Christians in the world today, who face overwhelming oppression in a secular culture whose pernicious ways have even poisoned the beliefs and practices of many denominations of Protestantism. Nor would they in principle reject the message of the Left Hand of God, although they would argue that its call for a world based on love, kindness, generosity, and nonviolence, so beautifully espoused in the Sermon on the Mount, has no application today but was meant instead for the thousand-year period after Jesus returns to earth and establishes God's kingdom.

Dispensationalism is contending to become the dominant view in evangelical circles. It is a view that generates fear in the present but hope for a very different kind of future that will arrive when Jesus returns. But given its conviction that human beings are incapable of altering current realities in America, it fits in well with a political Right that is quite satisfied with the status quo and is all too ready to join with the dispensationalists in doubting that any interventions on the part of government will improve things.

It's easy enough for people on the Left to dismiss the Right as pursuing a policy of selfishness and to question the integrity of the Christian Right's alliance with the political Right. The Right has been very effective in using big government to serve corporate interests, and many on the Right directly benefit when their taxes are reduced by eliminating governmental services for the poor. Rightists talk about "sacrifices" that must be made in order for America to pursue its interests abroad, but it is not they or their children who actually make those sacrifices. They talk about belt-tightening so that the society will have funds to pursue the war on terror, but the belts that get tightened are not their own or those of corporate interests but rather those of middle-income working people or the poor.

They are not ashamed of this. In fact, they frequently seem proud that they have more money than everyone else and view their prosperity as a badge of merit. Some parts of the Religious Right believe that capitalism is an economic system ordained by God, thus giving it theological legitimization. Covertly, and despite their public antagonism to the theory of evolution, they are actually social Darwinists who believe that the marketplace allows those who are most fit to benefit. Some of them rely on strands within Calvinist thought that suggest that those who are prospering are the elect of God. Some believe in a "prosperity theology," teaching that if people accept Jesus, he blesses them with the virtues that will make them economically successful in the American socioeconomic system.

Of course, some on the Right also claim that the tax benefits they receive will "trickle down" to the poor. Yet there is very little evidence that money eventually does trickle down, whereas there is a lot of evidence that those who support tax cuts benefit right away. For theorists on the Right, however, whether tax cuts will ultimately help or hurt those who are less affluent than they are is really beside the point. Their selfishness is part of their paradigm. When you live only by the Right Hand of God, when you believe you must dominate others if you don't want to be dominated yourself, then you also accept that looking out for yourself above and beyond all is nothing to be ashamed about. It's just common sense. If living that way also helps others, great, but first and foremost looking out for number one is the only rational approach to life.

Meanwhile, despite the right-wing media's efforts to dismiss certain of those on the Left as a "Hollywood elite" or as "limousine liberals," the truth of the matter is that these relatively wealthy supporters of the Left are backing policies that call for raising their own taxes in order to provide benefits for poor people. The Right disdains this cultural elite, but actually there is something quite honorable in a liberal elite that is showing some genuine willingness to sacrifice their own material interests for the sake of others—as opposed to right-wing elites, who prefer to back policies that cut much-needed services for others in order to have more money in their own pockets.

No wonder then that when the Christian Right rallies around the tax-cutting policies of the political Right, even getting many people who will suffer economically to vote for conservative politicians, liberals see psychological pathology or stupidity or venality at the core of this kind of religiosity. Liberals wonder how the Christian Right could abandon the many New Testament teachings about giving priority to the needs of the poor.

Instead of trying to understand the Religious Right, the Left too often takes the Right's advocacy of me-firstism as proof that religion itself is hypocritical. Having decided that the Right is succeeding despite its religious hypocrisy, the Left tries to point out the irrationality of the Right's positions, imagining that one more good argument will knock the socks off of the rightists and then everyone will throw away their crutches and start a stampede to the Left. Imagine their surprise when it doesn't happen.

Of course it won't happen that way. The Left ignores what is attractive about the worldview of the Right Hand of God, particularly at moments when people believe that they have very real grounds for fear. And, after 9/11, most Americans believe that they do have a lot to fear.

Moreover, the Left ignores the way the daily operations of the economy give people considerable reason to be fearful. After all, if you live in a society in which people have come to think that the only rational way to live is to maximize their own advantage, they are quite likely to be using you or trying to advance themselves at your expense. As I've shown, that perception leads many people to feel that they have no alternative but to protect themselves by dominating before they become dominated. And this in turn creates a deep spiritual crisis for our personal lives.

This spiritual crisis is sometimes dismissed by liberals as a purely personal issue. If people are in pain, they reason, let them go to a good therapist or even a good minister, rabbi, or priest. But keep all this stuff out of politics, please! Well, that might be the desire of the Left, but it has no reality in the actual behavior of people in this society. The truth is that it is the social order that is generating the spiritual crisis in people's lives, and that crisis will continue to have an important impact on the political choices people make when they vote. What the Left needs is an alternative view of who God is, not a denial of God and religion. It needs the voice of the Left Hand of God, which can acknowledge why people's experience of the deprivation of meaning is important and then can provide a progressive account of what causes that deprivation and explains how we can build a society that sustains rather than undermines loving connection and spiritual awareness.

From the interviews I conducted after the 2004 election, I learned that the Democrats are in greater trouble than they realize. True, the normal dynamic of off-year congressional elections combined with disillusionment about the war in Iraq, oil prices, and the administration's handling of the New Orleans post-hurricane flooding are likely to produce significant Democratic party gains in the elections of 2006. But when it comes to picking a president in 2008 and 2012, or having the public support to implement significantly different policies from those that flowed from the fear-oriented agenda of the Bush administration, the indifference and tone-deafness of the Democrats to the underlying spiritual crisis in America is likely to continue to undermine their political power.

Take Jane Hill, a forty-two-year-old single mother from Dayton, Ohio, who was one of dozens of middle-income Americans I talked to after the election. "I don't agree with Bush about the war or about his Social Security reforms," she told me. "But I have an eleven-year-old daughter, and I see the pressures on her to buy all kinds of things I can't afford to pay for and to dress in clothes that are sexually provocative. And I just don't like the values that she is getting in school and in the media. And Bush's people seem to care about these things, so I voted for him—because he gets that there's something wrong."

Or take Beatriz Callejo, a woman in Corpus Christi, Texas, who told me that her family has benefited greatly from the government programs sponsored by Democrats. All the same, she said, "I just can't stand the way the Democrats seem so antireligion. Sometimes it seems to me that they fear religious people more than they care about war or poverty."

Or consider James Horner, thirty-seven, a firefighter living in a sub-urb of Orlando, Florida, who told me: "I used to vote Democratic, but in the last years I've come to doubt whether they care about anything besides winning. Look at how they said they were opposed to the war and then supported Kerry, who was for the war! I don't think I can trust them to really stand for what they say they are for. I don't think that they even have core values."

The good news is this: When people talk about the spiritual cri-sis, or what the media labeled the "values" issue, for the most part they are not talking primarily about gays or even about abortion. Yes, there is a hard core of right-wing, mainly white, voters who are in fact motivated by extreme feelings of anger or fear toward those who differ ethnically from them or who have a different sexual orienta-tion, and who have a continuing anger and fear of women's role in our society now that women have finally started to break through the glass ceiling. There are some who will talk about these things when they talk of a values crisis. But for many more, the values cri-sis does not mean a fear of change or fear of the empowerment of new groups, but the fear and dislike of living in a society in which everyone seems to be looking out only for themselves. These voters really are talking about how difficult it is to live in a society gov-erned by selfishness and fear.

Why is that good news? Because it allows us to understand some-thing that many on the Left don't yet get: a significant section of the people who have turned to the Republicans are not inherently reac-tionary or stupid. Nor do they start out being people who buy into dis-pensationalism or other extreme views of the Christian Right. Instead, they are responding to something very real that is wrong in American society and using the only language that they have available to articu-late to themselves what is out of joint—a spiritual language that the culture around the Republican Party supports and that the culture around the Democratic Party rejects.

Democrats and their allies will continue to lose elections until they become open to understanding the inherent value of a spiritual vision of the world and can present a spiritual vision that validates love and kindness instead of domination and war. Once they learn to value this spiritual vision, they will find that many of the people on the periphery of the Right actually share the same values as they do on issues connected to poverty, social justice, peace, and health care.

But let me be clear. I am not arguing that the bulk of evangelical dispensationalists can be won over to a spiritually progressive worldview, though I imagine that some of them might eventually be attracted to a religious orientation that affirms the Left Hand of God if they felt safe enough to consider it. What I'm arguing instead is that there are many others in the society who are moved by the spiritual energies of the evangelical world, who recognize their own need for a spiritual dimension to their lives, and who are dismayed by the absence of that dimension in the political and economic world in which they live and particularly in the politics of the Left. These people may ultimately deal with their dismay by adopting a dispensationalist attitude of resignation about the possibility of changing the world, but they are not there yet, and they could still be persuaded to support a much more hopeful vision of what is possible now, in this world, before any messianic era. But if this is to happen, there must be a voice articulating that hope within the context of a spiritual worldview, and that voice must be compelling and attractive. They won't be won back to progressive politics by a more generous spending program or a few more entitlements thrown their way by progressives. The Democratic Party and others on the Left will need to develop a politics that has a coherent and proudly articulated spiritual foundation.

Without that alternative, the Democrats have little to offer, and the Right will persist in power, occasionally losing an election, but nevertheless growing in its ability to shape the national debate and make Democrats feel that they have no choice but to frame their own politics in terms that the Right has set. As long as the Right is the force that seems genuinely to care about the spiritual crisis, they will continue to capture the ears of many Americans who are in pain. So even if Democrats manage to take control of Congress and the presidency, as they did from 1992 until 1994, the worldview of the Right will continue to shape public discourse and Democrats will seek to prove themselves strong by the criteria of the Right Hand of God—a path that will lead to the furthering of the Right's agenda and a future erosion of support for the Democrats.

Americans give a tremendous amount of credit to anyone who can name a pain that they have been experiencing but have been unable to locate. The women's movement, for example, in creating the category of sexism, immediately relieved a tremendous amount of pain in many women's lives. Up until that point, many women blamed themselves for being inadequate because they didn't feel good about their assigned task of subordinating their needs to those of their husbands. After Betty Friedan and others named their pain, they understood that their feelings were a product of a set of social relations that could and should be changed, not a function of their own personal shortcomings.

In much the same way, the Religious Right has helped many people understand why they are experiencing family dissolution or insecurity, why they are surrounded by selfishness and materialism, and why they feel lonely and alienated. It is not because of some personal failing but because of the fundamental way our society is organized, which discounts the spiritual dimension of life.

It's important to acknowledge that the Religious Right has done something very important in identifying our spiritual crisis. Many people who belong to the Religious Right really do care deeply about creating a world in which people are not alienated or alone. We should give credit where credit is due.

Moreover, in my experience, the Religious Right often offers people a more caring community than do many religious groups on the Left.

Before I became a rabbi, I attended Shabbat (Sabbath) services at a wide variety of Jewish religious communities. And what I discovered has helped me to understand one dimension of the attractiveness of right-wing religious communities.

When I attended services at progressive or liberal Jewish congregations (generally members of the Reform, Reconstructionist, Renewal, or Conservative movements), I often found myself very much in tune with the explicit messages coming from the pulpit. But after the service, at the typical coffee and cake reception, people tended to hang out in cliques and rarely spoke to me. I occasionally went home feeling disappointed and perhaps a bit more lonely than I had been when I first arrived. By contrast, when I attended politically conservative Orthodox congregations, I hated what I heard from the rabbis or teachers. The messages were sometimes brimming with anger or even implicit hatred at the Palestinian people, Arabs, Muslims, or in a few extreme cases all non-Jews. Yet after the services people in these Orthodox congregations would come up to me to welcome me, would ask me if I had a place to go for lunch. They wanted to know who I was, what I was doing with my life, and they asked if there was anyone in my family who needed a hospital visit or some kind of assistance. They even asked me if I was single and wanted to meet someone for a potential match. Somehow I felt cared about and welcomed in a way that made me more hopeful about who human beings are than I did when I left the more liberal Jewish religious settings.

This same thing turns out to be true at many Christian churches. Ultrafundamentalist and right-wing evangelical churches often make an effort to show genuine caring for others in their community and for visitors in a way that is infectious. In a society where so few people care to find out what is really happening in someone else's life, this kind of overt display of caring can feel nurturing and delightful. The Religious Right appears to really practice what it preaches.

If only that were true.

Unfortunately, there is a radical split between the caring that gets shown on the personal level and the hostility some on the Religious Right manifest toward those in wider society who do not share their beliefs. Most readers are likely familiar with the peculiar hostility toward gays and lesbians, liberals, and secular people that has become daily fare from many of the sixteen hundred Christian radio and television broadcasters of the National Religious Broadcasters association. Their message, that Christianity is under assault by a dominant secular culture, mixes freely with calls to action against these enemies of Jesus who are determined to wipe out Christian truth. This supposedly endangered minority rarely acknowledges that their supporters occupy the White House, control the Congress, and are well on their way to shaping the decisions of the judiciary and other major parts of the government.

Listen to the broadcasts or attend the mega-churches of the Christian Right, and you will hear frequent reference to the spiritual crisis that faces most Americans. Yet instead of tracing the cause of America's spiritual crisis to the selfishness and materialism that marks corporate America's economic bottom line, the Religious Right chose to make an unholy alliance with the political Right. The political Right has traditionally argued that the best interests of all will be served if corporations and the marketplace are given freedom from all social responsibility and allowed to pursue their own path. In buying into this worldview, the Religious Right gained a foothold to bring its own religious agenda into politics. But the cost of this was to turn a blind eye to the source of the problem

This is their central contradiction: the Religious Right has become the champion of the same system that daily infuses into people a set of values that generates the very ethos of selfishness and materialism that the Religious Right rejects in principle.

For at least a century the political Right has been the voice of the corporate powerful, funding politicians who will preach and universities that will teach the importance of letting each corporation function without the constraints of any regulatory laws. The political Right resists attempts to require environmental responsibility, health and safety regulations for workers, adequate pay for workers, protections for consumers, or any other aspect of social responsibility. They argue that the well-being of society as a whole will be maximized only through a corporation's self-interested me-first pursuit of profit. Let the marketplace, which is an aggregate of the individual decisions of all people in the society, determine what is really needed in this society. In so doing, they claim, you allow each individual to be voting with each dollar they spend. They neglect to mention that the market works on the principle of "one dollar, one vote," so in a society with vast inequalities in the distribution of wealth and income those with more dollars have way more votes. Moreover, the marketplace gives no opportunity to vote for stopping production of certain environmentally destructive goods—as long as a few choose to purchase them. Nor will corporations produce goods that last longer when planned obsolescence increases their bottom line. The market won't record the vote of the vast majority who want the old-growth redwood forests preserved, because it has no mechanism to prevent a small group of people who do want to purchase those redwoods from doing so and destroying trees that will take hundreds or in some cases thousands of years to replace. This is why politics becomes such an important arena for potentially restraining the destructive choices made by the marketplace.

The me-firstism of the marketplace is not, of course, solely a creation of the political Right. Democrats often support corporate interests in order to raise the money they need to compete effectively during elections and to earn "credibility" with the media. But the Democrats have always been conflicted about this pandering to the rich, in part because, given their traditional electoral constituency, their success has typically rested on their ability to portray themselves as working on behalf of American workers.

Republicans, meanwhile, have been far less conflicted about serving the powerful. So here is the unfortunate irony and hypocrisy of the alliance between the Republican Party and the Religious Right. The Religious Right is supposedly attentive to scripture. Some even take a fundamentalist approach to the Bible. That Bible commands special sensitivity to the needs of the poor and the powerless. Yet those on the Religious Right end up giving their votes to George Bush and a group of right-wing congressional representatives whose policies starkly reject this biblical mandate.

Let us consider how the newly reelected President Bush, feeling a mandate, decided to manifest his moral agenda as he defined budget priorities in 2005 and compare this agenda to the values the Religious Right claims to embrace.

As we all know, the Bush administration has made a priority of cutting taxes for the wealthy. Although the Right argues that these tax cuts will stimulate investment, create jobs, and therefore alleviate poverty, a significant number of economists disagree. Princeton economist Paul Krugman, for example, argues that the wealthy spend their extra income on luxury items like yachts and third and fourth homes abroad or diamonds and other jewels. They don't put that extra money into manufacturing, technology, or other job-creating sectors of the economy.

What is certain is that if these tax cuts are kept in place, they will generate a budget deficit of several trillion dollars. The Bush administration has used this growing deficit to justify reducing funding for social services and other programs that benefit the underprivileged, as well as mounting a more general assault on government spending on the national and state levels. The logic is circular. As government agencies are deprived of funds, they become less competent, and that lack of competency allows the Right to justify giving them even less money. The result is fewer and less effective government services for the poor, and greater wealth for corporations and those who are already rich. We even heard this from some conservatives after the Hurricane Katrina tragedy. An underfunded government and an understaffed National Guard did not do a credible job of rescue in the first week after the flooding, so, the conservatives concluded, we should underfund governmental services even more because government once again has shown itself inefficient.

Let's look at the Bush budget submitted in 2005 as a moral document, a way of stating what the president's moral commitments are and how he intends to implement those commitments. The budget that Bush proposed literally would have taken money from the poor and given it to the rich. His spending cuts would have made it harder for working families with children to receive food stamps, terminated food aid for about 300,000 people, and denied child-care assistance to a roughly equivalent number of children in low-income working families. Meanwhile, as Krugman points out, more than half the benefits of Bush's tax cut would have gone to people with incomes of over a million dollars, and 97 percent would have gone to people with incomes exceeding $200,000 ("Bush's Class-War Budget," New York Times, February 11, 2005).

Bush's budget would also have had the Education Department eliminate forty-eight programs, including one that would provide $441 million in grants to states in 2005 to promote drug-free schools and another that would spend $33 million on reducing alcohol abuse among students. The Environmental Protection Agency would cut by $500 million its program to help poor communities build wastewater treatment plants and fund other water projects. Big budget cuts were also proposed for the Centers for Disease Control and Prevention. He even suggested cutting health insurance for children.

It's not as if Bush had no money for spending increases. Yes, you guessed it. At the same time he proposed cutting money for the poor, he recommended a substantial increase in military funding.

Is it any wonder, then, that at least some Democrats have questioned the moral integrity of the Religious Right for failing to make an outcry against the fundamental premises of such a budget?

The Right wins people to its cause by convincing them of its genuine concern about the spiritual crisis and then by providing them temporary relief with a religious community while people are in church. But the relief doesn't last long. After all, each week people return to the world of work, where they are exposed to another massive dose of "reality," and they bring that home into their daily lives in the destructive ways I've outlined above. However much the Sunday cheerleading for a more caring ethos might feel momentarily satisfying, it is not enough to offset the actual consequences of living in a world whose bottom line is money and power. So if the right-wing churches give support to the political Right, which is defending the pursuit of selfishness and materialism in the world of work and denies that the economy is connected to the moral problems in personal life, how do they account for the moral and spiritual crisis in personal life?

The answer that the political Right formulated in the late nineteenth century and that has persisted until today is this: On the one hand, they blame an intrinsic sinfulness, which will always pull people in a destructive direction no matter what form of social organization they live in. And on the other hand, they see societal distortions as a product of some group in the society that only cares for itself and promotes selfishness and materialism because it cannot embrace the "true" values of the nation or of "our" religion.

And who is that group? Typically the pundits of the Right focus on whichever group of people happens to be the major scapegoat of society at the time, the major "demeaned other," and blames that group for the problem.

In the United States, the major demeaned others have generally been Native Americans and African-Americans, although the place of dishonor has on occasion been extended to Catholics, Jews, the Irish, Italians, Poles, Mexicans, Japanese, Chinese, and, most prominently today, gays and lesbians and Muslims. Each of these groups has at various points in its history fought to be included without prejudice in American society. When that struggle starts to get a foothold, the Right often denounces these groups as "special interests" pursuing their own narrow selfish agendas and thereby introducing into what would otherwise have been a coherent community an ethos of self-centeredness that undermines community and fosters the dissolution of family ties.

These dynamics are played out somewhat more subtly in contemporary politics because the powerful impact of the civil rights movement in the 1960s and 1970s built a massive rejection of racism in the minds of the American majority. In the past several decades the Right has had to reframe and limit its use of racist categories.

Not that racism has been totally abandoned. The relatively quick transition of the "solid South" from its longstanding allegiance to the Democrats to its current surge toward Republicans was certainly fostered by the Republican willingness to oppose civil rights for blacks while the national Democratic Party supported legal equality and affirmative action. The Right's affinity toward "law and order" politics has often been associated with fear of people of color, and neatly coincides with the motivation of some to withdraw their children from integrated schools, to find homes in gated communities, and to oppose policies guaranteeing equal opportunity.

President George W. Bush has been a powerful exponent of right-wing policies while avoiding any overt demeaning of the groups his policies hurt. Bush appoints African-Americans to prominent positions while defunding social programs that had disproportionately benefited African-Americans (who, because of the lingering impact of three hundreds years of slavery, a hundred years of segregation, and a few dozen years of more subtle discrimination built into the operations of the marketplace, need such social supports more than many other groups).

But if some of the Right are reluctant to be overt in their attack on African-Americans, sections of the Religious Right helped supply them with other scapegoats. The Religious Right blamed feminists and homosexuals for the rising divorce rate, the instability in families, and the decline in private morality. It attacked activist judges who had legalized abortion and given legal rights to homosexuals. It pilloried secularists who had provided the general cultural frame within which older forms of patriarchal religion could be marginalized.

As I have argued, the key to responding to the Religious Right is to acknowledge that the spiritual crisis it is addressing is very real. Only when one has first affirmed the reality of the crisis can one then challenge their analysis of it and the solutions they propose. The Left by and large is not even in the relevant ballpark, because it doesn't recognize the spiritual crisis as real. To the extent that the Left imagines that our society's problems are all products of pathological desires on the part of the Right, and as long as they are reluctant to admit that there is a legitimate basis for the worries that attract people to the Right, they will have no plausible way to promote alternative solutions.

Yet the questions remain: How can those on the Religious Right be so blind to the obvious destructive impact on families of the capitalist culture in which we live? Why, instead, do they give blessing to a political Right that upholds the values of the marketplace, the very values that the Religious Right should be challenging if it takes its claim to be pro-family and pro-biblical values seriously?

For one thing, those on the Religious Right reflect the schizophrenia so many in this society already share—hating the dominant values of the capitalist order yet trying to live their lives by those values because they have come to believe that accommodating to the competitive marketplace is the only realistic possibility. In the churches, and likewise synagogues, of the Religious Right, one gets to have it both ways. One can affirm the vision of the Left Hand of God, talk about love and kindness and generosity, and even embody those values in the way that one treats other members of one's own religious community, while simultaneously embracing the Right Hand of God and assuming that the selfishness and mean-spiritedness of the larger world cannot be changed and that, in order to function in this world, one must simply prepare oneself and draw upon God's ability to dominate and control in order to function in it.

Once one accepts the meanness, selfishness, and materialism of the larger world as a given, the only remaining possibility is to prepare oneself to "succeed" in that context—and in that case what is needed is a tough-guy approach to politics and economics. Even though religious folk may sing praises to the baby Jesus or talk of God as compassionate and abounding in loving-kindness, they are well aware that those qualities are not what one needs to face the "real world." It is this ability to affirm both the desire for more love (which can be achieved in one's own private religious community) and the perceived need to accept the logic of the marketplace that makes the Religious Right so soothing to people who have given up on the possibility that the larger world can be changed. These rough-and-tumble fighters for self-interest can feel safe with such a Religious Right, because these kinds of religious folk fully understand the "real world," with all its competitiveness and "me-firstism."

It's a powerful deal that the Religious Right offers: affirmation of the parts of our psyche that yearn for the love, caring, and generosity that most people cling to even though they have been taught that these values are "unrealistic" for building an economy or society, coupled with acceptance of the materialism and selfishness, the need for power over others and war, as the accommodation to "the real world." So everywhere in the world you will find some version of this Religious Right, whatever the religion in question, with this same dichotomy. The right-wing churches, synagogues, mosques, ashrams, etc. can retain the voice of love, sing praises to a God or a prophet or a great teacher or a Jesus figure who embodies or preaches gentleness and caring for the poor, even while they align with a harsh, militaristic, and self-interested politics that is based on the (unstated) assumption that all that "love, kindness, and generosity" talk has no real world application outside of that church or religious institution.

As a religious Jew, I join many other theologians—not only evangelical leaders like Jim Wallis and the Reverend Tony Campolo but also Christian and Jewish theologians like Walter Brueggemann, Larry Rasmussen, Leonardo Boff, Catherine Keller, John Dear, S.J., Sister Joan Chittister, Zalman Schachter-Shalomi, Arthur Green, Abraham Joshua Heschel, Jonathan Sacks and Buddhists such as Thich Nhat Hanh, the Dalai Lama, Robert Thurman, and Sylvia Boorstein—in rejecting this approach to religious life.

Some of us analyze this theology of the Religious Right as a powerful form of idolatry. From my standpoint, YHVH, the God of the universe, is the force of transformation that makes possible the healing of the world, the shift from what is to what ought to be. The good news of Judaism, Christianity, and many other spiritual traditions is that the circumstances of the world are not fixed, that the world can be changed and healed, and that this is precisely our task. And what makes that change possible is that a God exists in the universe in Whose image we are made, and our task is to be partners with that God in the transformation of the world.

The essence of idolatry lies precisely in denying the possibility of change and then accommodating to evil—whether this be the hatred and cruelty perpetrated by others or one's own hurtfulness and indifference to the world's suffering—as though there were no alternative. To believe that no alternative exists to evil is the essence of believing there is no God. So, from the standpoint of at least some of us on the religious Left, the problem with the Religious Right is not only bad politics and bad economics but bad theology.

This bad theology has been able to flourish in part because the political Left has given little attention to its own religious Left, presenting itself instead primarily as a secular force. Unfortunately, the Left at times seems virtually tone-deaf to the spiritual crisis of capitalist society. Lacking categories within its intellectual apparatus that might allow it to comprehend and address that crisis, the Left is prone instead to dismiss the whole spiritual crisis as a right-wing fabrication.

And if this were not enough to isolate the Left from a large segment of the American public, many of whom might be responsive to the message of a spiritual Left, the secular Left often compounds its problems by adopting a harsh and judgmental attitude toward the American people and the country's history.

Although it has rightly acknowledged the bleaker moments in American history, the post-1960s Left has had a hard time celebrating all that is good about the North American embrace of democratic and human-rights values. Instead, its message to the American people can come across as something like: "You are not enough. You are descended from the white people who enslaved blacks. You are citizens of the nation that wiped out the Native Americans. You belong to the privileged class that benefits from America's global economic domination and ecological irresponsibility. You are the problem." It's not a message designed to open hearts, nor does it acknowledge the ways that the American people rallied to social change movements that sought to transform these evils, and even sometimes succeeded. Contrast that to the implicit message of right-wing religion: "You are enough simply because you are a Christian" (or a Jew or an American or a Muslim or whatever). And the message continues: "Because you are one of us, there is nothing you have to accomplish to be judged valuable. The very fact that you've become part of our group (by accepting Jesus as your personal savior, or by recognizing the right of Americans to run the world, or by recognizing the right of Israel to hold the West Bank in perpetuity, or by recognizing that we have the right path to God) is enough—you are one with us, you are saved, you are part of the elite, your life has meaning because you are one of us." This validation of the humanity and goodness of those who join with them goes a long way toward explaining why people are attracted not only to right-wing religious communities but to ultranationalist ones as well.

In contrast, at left-wing gatherings one often hears people being denounced for some aspect of their being that they can't really do much about: they are citizens of a society that has benefited from genocide, slavery, racism, and sexism, they are white, they are men, they are heterosexual, they are something that is being denounced as essentially bad, something that they can't change by virtue of their behavior. A few of the men we interviewed who had at one time attended events sponsored by the Left told us that sometimes they had wanted to jump up at one of these rallies and shout, "I can't help it if I was born white, or I was born with a penis—give me a break!"

People don't face this kind of thing in the Right, because the sinfulness that is being denounced there is said to be universal and can be overcome (for Christians) by the powerful act of embracing Jesus or (in the Jewish world) by converting to Judaism or living up to the Commandments. There is a path in these communities that allows people to feel fully validated. (There is no such path for white heterosexual males in the Left.)

Unlike people's daily experience in the competitive marketplace, on the one hand, or in the liberal and progressive social change movements, on the other hand, their experience in these religious communities is one that affirms who they are and allows them to be imperfect.

But the policies the right-wingers pursue are at striking variance with the goodness of their individual actions. Overwhelmingly, voters of the Religious Right empower Republican supporters of militarism and war. I understand why oppressed people have been attracted to the Right Hand of God with its promise of defeat for the forces of evil. But when embraced by nationalists of the most powerful military force in the history of humanity and used to justify military interventions around the world, this embrace of the Right Hand of God quickly devolves into a spirituality of cruelty that can close its ears to what is being done in its name in Guantanamo or Abu Ghraib. This may be what critical theorists Max Horkheimer and Theodor Adorno were getting at in the *Dialectic of Enlightenment* when they spoke about fascism as an inversion of religion, in which all the enlightenment elements are replaced. Pain and cruelty replace love and justice in what seems to me a perversion of the best original impulses in biblically based religious practices, a "transvaluation" (to cite Nietzsche's term) that happens in some approaches to Judaism and Islam as well as in some branches of the Christian Right.

This inversion of Christianity, Judaism, and Islam gets temporary power, but in the long run it cannot work. Its approach is not a real solution to the alienation from which it emerges. The destructive logic of the globalization of selfishness through the competitive marketplace will continue to undermine loving friendships and families. The willingness of the Religious Right to support the Bush administration's dismantling of environmental protections will accelerate the irresponsible pillaging of God's world. The destruction of the social support network by Republicans, together with a few Democratic Party allies, will produce suffering that will manifest itself in crime and other dysfunctional behavior. Military campaigns are already creating new generations of terrorists whose impact will be felt for many years to come. In the long run, the alliance of the political Right and the Religious Right will produce an ever more irrational and self-destructive world that will eventually destroy the alliance itself.

But the Left cannot and should not wait and watch as the destructive policies of the present administration and Congress play themselves out. We cannot sit by passively as the progress in human relations made when social energy flowed toward the Left Hand of God is reversed as the energy now flows to the Right Hand of God. The Left needs to intervene with all the power that a loving worldview can muster. To do that, however, it will have to think deeply about the way it has presented itself to the American people.

FIVE

Elitism on the Left

Once the Left embraces a worldview capable of articulating the spiritual crisis, it has a chance of capturing sections of the public who might supply it with electoral victory. But it faces another major obstacle: it has to overcome the perception of many people that the Left is rife with elitist contempt for ordinary Americans. That contempt is expressed partly in the disdain that the Left has for the voting behavior of Americans and partly in the ridicule and put-down it expresses toward the religious commitments that are central to the lives of so many Americans.

That perception, unfortunately, has some foundation. Because the Left has no categories to understand why Americans have not consistently rallied to its positions, it tends to belittle those who are not yet on its side. And because the political Left tends to be overwhelmingly secular, it often sees religion not merely as mistaken but as fundamentally irrational, and it gives the impression that one of the most important elements in the lives of ordinary Americans is actually deserving of ridicule.

Judging from what I heard after the 2004 election, the Left's stereotypical view of Americans who don't vote for the Democrats or the Greens is not going to change without a massive shift of consciousness.

Soon after the election, my computer mailbox was flooded with e-mails that all had pretty much the same theme: "Those who voted for Bush are either stupid or evil." Actually, the e-mailers called Bush voters everything from racist, sexist homophobes to authoritarian religious-empire builders. If you missed it on e-mail, you can catch it each week on TV when humorist Bill Maher, in the presence of liberal intellectual glitterati as his guests, accuses Red State people of being stupid and assails religious people as irrational—to the laughter and applause of an adoring audience. This humor is hilarious only until you put yourself in the place of those being ridiculed.

This kind of talk is deeply troubling—and it is a major part of the reason why many Americans can't hear any of the good things that the Left has to say. You don't have to be a genius to know when you are being treated with contempt.

The leaders of social change movements have on the whole been unwilling to consider that the problem with their message might be the messenger. Rather than look inward, they point to a set of external factors to explain why the American public has not responded more powerfully to their message. Listen to left-wing pundits or read their press releases and you will find a litany of "blame the other guy" excuses when the Left loses its political battles.

One argument the Left frequently trots out is that the Democrats can't compete with the procorporate political Right's far greater economic resources.

It's true that the Right's candidates, think tanks, magazines, and organizers are better funded. Yet it's also true that in the 2004 election the progressive wing of the Democratic Party, energized by Howard Dean and groups like Move On, were able to raise huge sums of money. The Kerry campaign had millions of unspent dollars at the end of the campaign. It had the ability to buy advertisements. It was the content of what it had to say that had not proved sufficiently appealing. Kerry was able to get out a message, but it was the wrong message.

The Left also likes to claim that the media are to blame for its predicament. According to this argument, the media, especially television, have been effectively monopolized and manipulated by the political Right—which explains, for example, why millions of Americans still believe the Bush administration's lies about Saddam Husscin's "weapons of mass destruction." As an editor and media insider myself, I've seen the way that the mainstream media favor the Right. There are dozens of talented writers on the Left capable of doing weekly columns in major newspapers, but there are barely a handful who are printed, as compared to the hundreds of mainstream and right-wing syndicated columnists. And it is rare indeed to have major media present the Left's perspective on any major domestic or foreign policy issue. Media people are often so deluded that they believe that the tepid centrists and right-wing Democrats they serve up *are* the Left—an illusion supported aggressively by the Right, which thereby defines the actual Left as extremists whose views don't have to be taken seriously.

At the same time, the Left should acknowledge that its style of communication has often been off-putting. There are individuals and groups on the Left who have serious critiques of American policies to offer but who often couch them in statements so broad that they seem to be criticizing the American people as a whole.

Right-wingers sometimes argue that the mainstream media have a pronounced "liberal bias." By defining as "liberal" the technocratic and boring discourse of the centrists who report the news, the Right brilliantly pushes the national discourse to the right. But ask any progressive activists, and they will tell you how very hard it is to get their message heard. The reason is that whereas media conservatives have no fear of aggressively putting forward their own worldview, the liberals who shape reporting and analysis on major TV and print media often pretend to have no bias and claim merely to be objectively presenting "the news" or a "balanced analysis." For that reason, they often avoid presenting the views of people with a more pronounced progressive analysis, lest they be accused of liberal bias. Right-wingers know that that is ludicrous—that there is no such thing as objective reporting. Every selection of a news item represents a perspective on what facts are "newsworthy," and this perspective is not inherent in the facts but in the values of the choosers. Each day somewhere between 10,000 and 30,000 children die from starvation and diseases that could be cured if the world distributed its resources differently. Why aren't there daily stories about that reality on every media, stories about the lives and families of those who died? It's not because of the facts but rather reflects the perspective of those who make decisions about what counts as news. Liberals in the media persist in pretending that they are delivering something that is neutral, and want kudos for doing so, but what often happens is that they make their stories boring and visionless, and that just loses them an audience. I'm certain that if major media presented news stories in ways that reflected a variety of political perspectives (say one night you were learning about the Iraq war from the standpoint of an avid supporter, another night from someone who thought it was morally abhorrent), they'd soon generate a much bigger audience for network news. Fox News Channel built its audience by being a voice for the Right. Where is a network that progressive groups would acknowledge as presenting their perspective?

When they can't blame the corporations or the media, the Left resorts to blaming the American people for failing to be more progressive. "People can be easily manipulated by the Right," pundits on the Left argue, "because they don't take the time to study issues, and so they aren't really capable of understanding the more nuanced political views of the Left." It's certainly true that most people don't have the time to read the *New York Times* or *Alternet* or the *Guardian* each morning, but that doesn't mean ordinary Americans can't grasp complex thinking. For example, a majority of the American public now believes that the war in Iraq was a mistake, despite the media's patriotic embeddedness in the military assumptions of the Pentagon. The fact that the Left blames the American people for their lack of support just shows how very far the Left is removed from the people it says it wants to reach.

To be clear, I'm not arguing that the explanations of those on the Left for the dominance of the political Right are totally incorrect. I'm saying that even when they capture part of the story they are wrong because they miss a deeper context: people are less inclined to trust the Left today than they were sixty years ago. They are tired of being put down by the Left.

Here is how Sara Waters, of Walnut Creek, California, put it to me:

> I first noticed it in college when I attended UCLA—everyone on the Left made fun of religion and made it seem as though anyone into religion was, I don't know, I guess it was like they were saying it was like being into a cult. Then I went to do a graduate degree in social work, and I can't tell you how prejudiced people were there against Americans who didn't vote for liberals. Everyone who cared about things like the Fourth of July or thought

America was basically a good place were labeled "rednecks." When the Republicans took control of the Congress in 1994, it was like the Nazis took over or something—people were in mourning, thinking the world was collapsing. And it's the same way in the neighborhood I live in—the liberals where I live all think that everyone who doesn't agree with them is a fascist. And they openly say that people are just stupid if they vote for Bush. Even though I agree with them that Bush is wrong about Social Security, I still don't want to hear from them, the way they make people feel dumb. I'm not dumb, but I'm not a Democrat either, and I just don't like that kind of person. All the liberals are like that, and all my life, that's how they've been.

Clearly, those on the Left need to change their attitude toward their fellow citizens. They need to acknowledge that while there are undeniably religious fundamentalists who use their extreme convictions to encourage militarism, authoritarianism, homophobia, sexism, and a distaste for rational thought, there are tens of millions of others who are attracted to the Right despite these extremist policies, not because of them. Instead, the Democrats seem to prefer to believe that a vast number of Americans are just plain dumb. Naturally, that contempt comes across to many people and becomes an important factor in their alienation from the Democratic Party.

It wasn't always this way. Elitism became a political problem for the Left when the new social movements of the last thirty years found it impossible to develop a common ground with the labor Left of the 1900–1968 period. Progressive politics took on a university-based, identity-politics obsessed character. This estrangement from the labor movement was partly due to the impact of McCarthyism and the silencing of progressive voices in the labor movement, coupled with the triumph of a more conservative and ultranationalistic union leadership. Added to that was the transformation of the labor force itself, as relatively well educated and culturally sophisticated workers refused to think of themselves as part of the working class and instead developed an elitist self-conception, perhaps by way of compensation for jobs that were giving them far less control over fundamental decision making than they had imagined would be theirs once they achieved semiprofessional status. The Left often reflects the consciousness of this sector of the workforce.

The Democrats showed massive contempt for the American public when they backed John Kerry for president. I don't mean that Kerry wasn't an acceptable nominee. Kerry had done some very good things in the Senate and in his career in public service. There were good reasons to like him. What I mean is that the Democrats chose John Kerry for cynical reasons, in an attempt to manipulate ordinary Americans into voting against Bush and for a Democratic candidate.

Polls indicated that over 68 percent of Democrats thought the war was fundamentally wrong. Yet in the primaries they selected a candidate who didn't hold that position. Why?

Most Democrats believed that Americans were not smart enough or virtuous enough to share their moral opposition to the war in Iraq—and wouldn't share it even if presidential debates and federal matching funds gave the Democrats a unique opportunity to present convincing antiwar arguments that had never been presented in a coherent manner to most Americans heretofore. So, they concluded, the only way to beat Bush was to choose a candidate who could be presented as a tough guy with a strong military background who had fought in Vietnam, unlike Bush, a "tough guy" who never fought anywhere. So during its national convention in the summer of 2004 the party arranged the official public launch of its chosen candidate so as to reflect the very militarism that most Democrats actually abhorred—on the grounds that this would win over to the Democrats those people who felt that the country needed a strong wartime leader.

Of course, many on the Left campaigned against Kerry in the primaries and were disheartened, even sickened, by that convention. I have no quarrel with those who voted for Kerry in the general election because they wanted to head off the damage to civil liberties, human rights, and the environment that a second Bush term would likely bring. Nonetheless, there were millions of Democrats who had the opportunity during the primaries to select a candidate with whose stand on the war they agreed but instead voted for Kerry because of his alleged electability. They decided it would be too risky to let the American public hear what they really thought, especially the pro-peace vision of the world upon which their opposition to the war in Iraq was based. They were positive that the American public was too indoctrinated with militarism to change their minds (a view that has proved false—by 2005 a majority opposed the war).

Privately, many on the Left told themselves and one another this: "Kerry is really not for this war. Once he is elected, he will, we hope, feel less pressure to be opportunistic. Then the real John Kerry, the one who testified against the war in Vietnam, will reemerge and save us from this war." And with that hope they donated millions of dollars and huge amounts of their time going door to door on behalf of the Kerry candidacy.

Let me be even clearer. The Left actually wanted Kerry to be a flip-flopper. They said to themselves: "We believe that John Kerry is an opportunist, and that's why we are for him. We sincerely hope that, once he's elected, he will flip-flop away from his stated positions. We hope he won't be a militarist, as he tries to present himself now. We hope he won't follow through on his campaign pledge and actually try to send U.S. forces to kill every living terrorist around the world. We fervently hope that he's just saying all this stuff to fool the American people into voting for him. But, once in office, he will (we pray) flip-flop and do the opposite of what he is saying he'll do now."

The response of the Republicans to the Democrats' strategy was very effective: they told the truth. They said to the American public: "This guy Kerry is a flip-flopper, and so you don't ever know where he really stands, and our proof is that his own supporters actually think there is a good chance he will flip-flop once in office. Our side has integrity because we really mean what we say; the liberals don't have that integrity. You may not like what we are saying, but we don't pretend to be pro-choice when we aren't, we don't pretend to be pacifists when we are pro-war, and we don't pretend we support programs for the poor when we're actually calling for tax benefits for the rich." Of course, we can easily identify a real lack of integrity in the way the Republicans promote some of their policies—pointing to nonexistent WMDs to justify a war in Iraq, claiming that proposed tax cuts would help the middle class, and so on. All the same, voters responded to the Republicans' argument that Kerry was unreliable because it did point out the actual inconsistencies in the Kerry campaign as well as the Democrats' mistrust of ordinary Americans, which made those inconsistencies seem necessary.

Why did the Democrats follow this path and misrepresent them-selves to the American public? Because they deeply believe that if they were to present their vision of a good world and a good society, the American people would never buy it, and then the Democratic Party would never get back into power. They decided they would have to lie to the American public. It took the Right sixteen years from its defeat in 1964 to succeed in having some of its ideas legitimated in public dis-course, but those on the Right stuck with those ideas and slowly man-aged to convince people. They did not water down the ideas in the vain hope of winning elections by pretending to believe something else. The Democrats' misguided disdain for and lack of trust in Americans has given the Right one of its most powerful weapons: the ability to de-velop a politics based on the public's resentment of the Left.

The irony of this situation is that the Right tries to manipulate pub-lic opinion every bit as much as the Left. The Right may lie about par-ticular moves it is making—and it has distorted the truth with its various stories of hidden nuclear weapons, of impending terrorist threats (at various color levels of intensity), of military service records of its friends and enemies, of the benefits of tax cuts to ordinary Amer-icans—but its overall orientation toward the world is not concealed and does not waver.

The Right believes that the best interests of the world lie in Ameri-can domination over the global economy. The Right believes in using military force as necessary to provide cover and protection for Ameri-can corporate power. It favors expansion of democracy where the democracies in question are powerful supporters of American eco-nomic power and "the free marketplace," but it resists democratic out-comes and even seeks to overthrow democratic governments (such as in Haiti or Venezuela) where democracy leads to governments that challenge American economic power (and the Right argues that real democracy must include the free market system which is the only guar-antor of liberty). It sees institutions like the United Nations and other multilateral institutions primarily as valuable only to the extent that they become adjuncts to American power. It believes that the best in-terests of all will be served by the rich having more money to spend. It believes everyone will be better off if corporations are less constrained by lawsuits or by environmental and health-and-safety regulations or by unions that might force them to pay their workers too much to guarantee adequate levels of profitability. In short, the Right doesn't pretend to be the Left.

The same cannot be said for Democrats, who often try to represent themselves as agreeing with the Republicans on many of these issues and yet portray themselves as a liberal alternative.

If I tell you that the Democrats are going to nominate two wonderful candidates for president and vice president in 2008, can you tell me whether those candidates will be ones who originally supported or opposed the war in Iraq, supported or opposed the setting of a date for withdrawal of troops from Iraq, voted for or did not vote for the tens of billions of dollars spent each year to fund the war, supported or opposed the Kyoto accords for environmental safety, supported or opposed extending NAFTA-like free-trade agreements, supported or opposed the extension of Ariel Sharon's Wall through the West Bank, supported or opposed gay marriage, supported or opposed the Bush administration's No Child Left Behind plan for education, supported or opposed single-payer universal health care, supported or opposed the Patriot Act? I can tell you what the positions of the Republican candidates will be in 2008, but I doubt if you could confidently predict where both of the Democratic candidates would stand on these issues.

If the Democrats collectively stand for anything, if there is any shared platform that unites them, other than the goal of returning to power, then most people can't figure out what it is, except that Democrats prefer a somewhat more balanced approach than do the Republicans when it comes to favoring corporate interests and the rich. Many of us hope that Howard Dean, now their national party chair, will change this—and if so, I hope that the Democrats will give serious consideration to the direction defined in this book and the Spiritual Covenant with America that I will outline below. But I'm not going to hold my breath till that happens.

Luckily, I don't have to. There's another way to think about politics.

The reason Republicans are able to trust their fellow Americans with such confidence is because they believe that Americans will remain stuck in the dominance paradigm, in which to be realistic is to get power over others and look out for number one—what I call the Right Hand of God paradigm. As long as Americans see life as a war of all against all and believe that eliminating poverty and creating world peace are fantasies and that others care only about themselves, the Republicans will fare well. Fortunately for them, the vast preponderance of the media, the educational system, and the very structure of the society teaches us this worldview. The Republicans' task is made easier still when they can share with their fellow Americans the religious passions that make America one of the most church-going societies on earth, while the Left is filled with people who radiate bold-faced contempt for religious people and ideas. And they know people will positively flock to them when the Left, as it did in 2004, opts to soft-pedal its own positions out of a depressive conviction that otherwise no one would take it seriously. And so it is that the Republicans, and the Right in general, are able to pull off the most extraordinary reversal of reality and convince a significant portion of the American working class that the Right is really on their side even though the policies the Right is pursuing in fact constitute a provocative and sustained class war.

In his brilliant book *What's the Matter with Kansas?* and in a subsequent article called "What's the Matter with Liberals?" (*New York Review,* vol. 52, no. 8), Thomas Frank painfully demonstrates how, during the 2004 presidential campaign, the Republicans systematically went about representing themselves as the articulators of class resentment against the elitism of the Democrats, while the Democrats barely fought back, unwilling to embrace a populist program or discourse. As Thomas writes:

> The hallmark of a "backlash conservative" is that he or she approaches politics not as a defender of the existing order or as a genteel aristocrat but as an average working person offended by the arrogance of the (liberal) upper class. The sensibility was perfectly caught during the campaign by onetime Republican presidential candidate Gary Bauer, who explained it to the *New York Times* like this: "Joe Six-Pack doesn't understand why the world and his culture are changing and why he doesn't have a say in it." (p. 3)

Thomas Frank goes on to show that the Democrats, advised by a host of consultants (many of whom work as corporate lobbyists), had elected to downplay the more progressive elements in their agenda such as raising the minimum wage, had made little of Wall Street corruption, had rarely challenged the impact of Wal-Mart on local communities, and had generally played down anything that might identify them with the interests of working-class people. After years during which the Republicans and their media lapdogs have repeatedly charged that Democrats are risking class war whenever liberals point out that Republican Party policies serve the interests of the rich, the Democrats seem to have lost their nerve and so have become unwilling to bring populist concerns to the center of American politics.

Frank is certainly right to point out that the Democrats' abandonment of a commitment to economic liberalism was the final nail in the coffin. Yet previous elections in which that economic liberalism had remained central, as in the 1980s, had not been sufficient to overcome the Republicans' cleverly orchestrated portrayal of the Democrats as the party of the rich and the elites. The Democrats' biggest mistake lies not only on the economic front, but in their refusal to listen to the hunger for meaning.

The Republicans' attempts to dismantle Social Security are facing rough going even after Bush's victory in 2004, but the Right's assault on the Left as anti-God has been flourishing. Portraying themselves as the victims of a cultural crusade by "leftist jihadis hunting down Jesus," the Right insisted that they were facing religious bigotry from militant secularists. "Leftist organizations are aggressively seeking to redefine America in their own God-less image," wrote Jerry Falwell, and Pat Buchanan chimed in by claiming that "they hate the idea of Christmas with a deep abiding hate." Unfortunately, the charge resonates with the experience of hostility to religion that many Americans have faced from people who identify as liberal or progressive. So although I agree with Thomas Frank that the Right is vulnerable on economic issues, I am convinced that the Left will remain politically vulnerable until it is no longer perceived as anti-God and as sneering at the religious and spiritual aspirations of the American people, a transformation that will require some deep rethinking in progressive circles along the lines I outline in the next few chapters.

SIX

The Religion of Secularism and the Fear of Spirit

The Left faces a significant obstacle to recognizing the spiritual crisis in the lives of many Americans and building a spiritual politics in response. In fact, most of those on the Left—perhaps you included—feel queasy even thinking about allying with spiritual and religious progressives, let alone building a spiritual progressive movement. Many on the Left, to be blunt, hate and fear religion.

Here's a personal example. After the 2004 election, I met with a funder from the Ford Foundation who was interested in supporting projects that could counter the growth of the Right. The meeting was going well until I showed her a poster for an upcoming conference on fostering progressive spiritual activism. Her eye fell on one workshop, which was called "God and the Economy: How Can Making a Living Become Sacred Work?" "Why do you have to bring God into this?" she asked angrily. "Don't you know all the destructive things done in the name of God?" Perhaps she forgot I was a rabbi, but what did she think a spiritual answer to the Religious Right would look like? Couldn't one of the twenty workshops mention God and speak to concerns of people who take their religious lives seriously? Had she forgotten that destructive things have also been done in the name of democracy? And yet the very mention of God was enough to alienate a potential funder. The Left's hostility to religion is one of the main reasons people who otherwise might be involved with progressive politics get turned off.

In the aftermath of November 2004, isn't the Left cured of its spiritual antipathy? After all, the most militantly secular magazine in the country, *The Nation,* ran a cover on religion. Hasn't the Left opened itself to progressive religious voices?

Unfortunately, no.

On one level, of course, left-wing hostility toward religion is not hard to understand. The Left has good reason to be suspicious of the ways that conservatives have historically used religion to justify oppressive social systems and political regimes and to be appalled when right-wingers today talk of religious and spiritual values in order to justify war, social injustice, and ecological blindness.

But then it's not as if the Left has never seen anyone misuse its own ideas to serve hateful and repressive purposes. From the Terror during the French Revolution (when the Left was named for those who sat on the left side of the national assembly) to the Stalinist gulag in the Soviet Union, the ideals of equality, fraternity, and liberty have often been contorted into serving violence and oppression. Saying that the Crusades evolved naturally from Jesus's teaching, however, is like saying that Kim Jong Il's "communist" North Korea arose inevitably from Marx's teachings. Those of us who work on the Left know that Fidel Castro's persecution of gays and lesbians and repression of dissent are not the essence of socialism, that the anti-Semitism encouraged by communists in Eastern Europe in an effort to win popular appeal with the masses after the Second World War is not endemic to socialist ideals, that the killing fields of Cambodia are not what third-world liberation struggles are about even if, at the time, certain radical left-wing groups on American college campuses argued that such horrors were justified. The Left knows how to distinguish between the core values of a tradition and its misappropriation—and the Right does too.

Unless the contemporary Left wants to take the rap for the deaths of tens of millions of people killed by Russian and Chinese communists, it ought to have the integrity to stop blaming all religion for the way religion has been appropriated to justify cruelty and oppression and instead to acknowledge that, just as aspects of the language and the standard analytical categories of the Left need to be reevaluated and revised because of the ease with which they have been misused, so it may be that religious traditions need similar reassessment and transformation rather than wholesale dismissal. But we who seek that kind of renewal and transformation within our own religious communities often find it much harder to build support for a progressive reading of our traditions when our more conservative coreligionists can point to the experience so many religious people have had of hostility toward God and religion on the part of mainstream liberal and progressive culture.

Many of the most rigidly antireligious folk on the Left are themselves refugees from repressive religious communities. People who experienced the homophobia, the sexism, the patriarchal authoritarianism, the racism, and the moral obtuseness that fundamentalist religious communities sometimes manifest are understandably angry at those communities and so find it difficult to hear that religion need not be oppressive in its essence. I know how difficult it is to work through trauma, and I don't want to condemn anyone who has suffered at the hands of an oppressive religious community or family. But acknowledging the right of such people to be angry doesn't mean we must accept their anger as our own. Why is it that the Left, which so often prides itself on its own rationality, fails to make these distinctions?

Is it perhaps because the Left has never seen a religious community that embodies progressive values?

But that is clearly false. Every time secular leftists sing "We shall overcome," they are drawing on the power of a religious community. The Left enjoyed some of its greatest success in the 1960s when it was led by a black religious community and by a religious leader, Martin Luther King Jr. The civil rights movement succeeded because the black churches mobilized their members. The churches became the locus not only for demonstrations but for voter registration drives, and perhaps most important, organizing for local political power. Churches became the centers for self-education, often creating after-school and career-day programs to advance the process of integration.

A religion of the spirit, powerfully linking its vision of God with its vision of political liberation, developed, supported by black theology and by a renewal of spiritual energy. Many black churches adopted Pentecostal-style worship with its strongly participatory focus, transcending denominational lines and creating a black ecumenicism. It was precisely the black churches' long tradition of biblical literacy, and particularly the Torah's central story of the liberation of Jewish slaves from Egypt, that gave these churches a language for liberation struggles upon which the civil rights movement could draw for hope.

And yet, overwhelmingly, the white activists who shaped the Left of the 1960s have remained mired in a culture of hostility toward religion and spirituality. If this were merely a historical curiosity, I'd leave this issue to the cultural historians. But since the Left's hostility to religion and spirituality has become such a major stumbling block to the chances that progressive forces will ever win enough power to actually change the socially and environmentally destructive policies of the West, it becomes important to explore the roots of this hostility to discover how it can be eradicated, or at least reduced.

Scientism

In part, what underlies the secular Left's deep skepticism about religion is their strong faith in a different kind of belief system. Even though many people on the Left think of themselves as merely trying to hold on to a rational consciousness and resist the emotionalism that can contribute to fascistic movements, it's not true that the Left is without belief. The Left believes in the power of empirical observation to determine truth and guide decisions. They are captivated by a belief that has been called scientism.

Science is not the same as scientism. One of the great advances in human history was the emergence of science. Science relies on empirical observation to describe the world. The information it has produced has allowed us to cure diseases, improve the material conditions of our life, and to gain insight into the complexity of the universe. Science offers us a degree of control over the natural world and hence a heightened sense of security in the face of some of its very real dangers. One of the scariest aspects of the Religious Right is the hostility it sometimes expresses toward science itself. I want to be clear that I am a strong advocate for science and believe it to be a form of human knowledge that should be preserved and extended, and an activity that should be funded by our collective social resources and government tax monies.

However, it is important to distinguish between science as a field of knowledge and scientism, which is a worldview that accompanied the rise of science and has played a major role in shaping thinking in the modern world. One can be a passionate advocate of science, as I am, and yet be a strong opponent of scientism.

Scientism is the belief that nothing is real in the world except that which can be observed and measured. As a religious person, I rely on science to tell me about many aspects of the world I live in—about how my body functions, about the relationship between my body and mind, and perhaps even about the relationship between my life and the life of the planet. However, I don't rely on science to tell me what is right and wrong or what love means or why my life is important. I understand that such questions fundamentally cannot be answered through empirical observations. I don't expect to find the meaning of life as an explorer might find a long-lost valley that had never been charted by cartographers. I don't expect science to discover a gene that will explain beauty or tell me why I respond with awe and radical amazement at the grandeur of the universe (although part of what I am responding to is an understanding of the universe and how it operates that I have gained from science). A person who adopts a scientistic worldview, however, believes that science can answer every question that can be answered. Science, for them, is the means to absolute truth (even if the absolute truth is that all things are relative or that there is no meaning in life).

The scientistic worldview holds that everything that can be known is known through empirical observation, through sensory perceptions, and any claim we make about the world that cannot be validated or falsified on the basis of such data is meaningless. Not false, because for a claim to be false it must in principle be verifiable. If we say, for example, that the moon is made of green cheese, and then, when we arrive on the moon, we find that it is not made of cheese at all, we know that our claim was false. For the thousands of years before we got to the moon, that claim was still false, but meaningful, because it could in principle be verified or falsified. In contrast, a claim like, "Caring for other people is morally right" cannot be verified or falsified through any set of observations. In fact, it really isn't a claim about the world at all but merely a statement of our personal tastes or choices or proclivities. Similarly, claims about God, ethics, beauty, and any other facet of human experience that is not subject to empirical verification—all these spiritual dimensions of life—are dismissed by the scientistic worldview as inherently unknowable and hence meaningless.

Scientism thus extends far beyond an understanding and appreciation of the role of science in society. It has become the religion of the secular consciousness. Why do I say it's a religion? Because it is a belief system that has no more scientific foundation than any other belief system. Consider its central belief: "That which is real is that which can be verified or falsified by empirical observation." The claim sounds tough minded and rational, but what scientific experiment could you perform to prove that it is either true or false? The fact is that there is no such test.

Scientism is really a belief system that presents itself as science but isn't.

Secular people often think that scientism is simply saying what it means to be rational in the contemporary world. But why should we adopt that standard of rationality? Is there some scientific test that can prove that this is indeed the rational way to think? Absolutely not.

If the viewpoint of scientism appears to many to be obvious, it is merely because that viewpoint is so prevalent: we live in a world dominated by the religion of scientism. But that doesn't make scientism justified by science. Spiritual progressives therefore insist on the importance of distinguishing between our strong support for science, as the best method for learning about the natural world, and our opposition to scientism, a religion that teaches us to value only those things that can be discovered and verified by means of the scientific method.

So why has the Left become so attached to scientism? The Left emerged as part of the broad movement against the feudal order. Feudalism was sanctified by the Church, which taught that God had appointed people to their place in the hierarchical economic and political order for the good of the greater whole. Within the feudal order, the Church assigned rights and responsibilities for everyone, prevented social mobility, and legitimated the use of force by the powerful lords of the manor to extract payment from the powerless serfs.

Our current economic system, capitalism, was created by challenging the Church's role in organizing social life. It was founded on the principle of scientism, the belief that empirical observation and a scientistic version of rational thought will lead to truth more surely than reliance on revealed texts, spiritual experience, or religious faith. The tools of science—empirical observation and rational thought—became the battering ram the merchant class used to weaken the Church's authority, hoping to create the space for greater freedom in the marketplace. By insisting that the scientific method, based on information that came through our senses, was the only reliable path to knowledge, and that all else was literally non- "sense," they were able to undermine the intellectual credibility of the religious order.

I'm glad that the capitalists were able to overthrow feudalism, and I'm glad that many religious traditions have evolved beyond their feudalistic formulations and developed new ways of thinking about God, humanity, and our obligations to one another. Scientism, though a flawed worldview, played a positive role in that development, but it then went on to play a less positive role in the next few hundred years.

This isn't to suggest that there was a meeting in which a group of people conspired to overthrow the feudal order by adopting a scientistic worldview. In the 1500s, the merchants who championed science probably did not believe they were undermining religion. They didn't like the Church as an institution, which is one reason many members of the merchant class eventually became Protestants (Martin Luther, the founder of Protestantism, lived from 1483 to 1546). They didn't abandon religion itself, only one particular form of religion, the Catholic Church. These early capitalists were almost all religious people who believed they could apply the principles of science to society without denying God's existence. They tried to avoid a conflict between what were really two different ideologies by assigning them to separate spheres: religion became the ruler of private life, while scientism became the ruler of public life.

When this new class, which came to be called the bourgeoisie, actually won power for itself in the aftermath of the American and French revolutions, it carefully placed restrictions on religion, curtailing its influence in the public sphere. Public life, the bourgeoisie imagined, should be governed by the "rational." The rest—that is, ideas and convictions that could not be empirically verified—could be allowed to continue but relegated to the private sphere of personal belief.

These "revolutionaries" immediately faced a serious problem, how-ever: the need to legitimate their own authority. After all, there could be no scientific justification for the notion that the best society is run by men who own property (including slaves, as many people in the new United States did in 1776). And yet the laws of the fledgling American republic restricted voting to white, male property owners. What exactly was the scientific evidence that a society based on a democratic vote would be the best sort of society?

The radicals who had fought against feudalism now faced a difficult dilemma. How could they remain true to their scientism and yet justify the new social order, one that had from the start vast inequalities of wealth and power? Two main positions on the issue emerged in the subsequent conversations: liberalism and Marxism. Bear in mind that in this historical context *liberalism* didn't mean you were on the Left. In fact, the people who were called liberals hundreds of years ago would today qualify as politically conservative. Liberals' main goal was not to defeat the Church but to create capitalism. They didn't really care what the social order looked like, as long as it permitted the oper-ation of a free market.

Edmund Burke, who had watched the radicalism of the French Rev-olution play out from the safety of England's shores, was a key figure in resolving the liberals' problem with religion. Burke urged the new rul-ing elites of the postfeudal world to revive some form of religious be-lief, one that would exert a comforting and pacifying influence on society by suggesting that the new order had also been sanctified by God. Burke's belief that God was the ultimate mover behind the social order was quickly adopted by the rulers of the newly emerging capital-ist states.

The advantage of Burke's idea was that it did not require any further involvement on the part of God in the operations of the society. Once God had provided a justification for democracy and the Constitution, for example, human beings would take over from there. This was the position adopted by the American revolutionaries, many of whom were inspired by John Locke's theory of natural rights and believed in the existence of a natural law that God made immediately available to any rational thinker. Many of the founders of the United States suggested in their various declarations that God had inspired a core of universal principles that were available to any rational being who listened carefully to his (or her) own intuitions and that their society would be founded on such principles: "We hold these truths to be self-evident, that all men are created equal and endowed by their creator with certain inalienable rights, among these being life, liberty and the pursuit of happiness." Once the principles had been spelled out, God could disappear, and society could be ordered along rational lines.

Once capitalism was firmly established, this form of liberalism also made it possible to set aside scientism as a principle and return to faith, albeit a faith different and much less powerful than that espoused by a theocratic church. Today, many Americans adhere to some version of Burkean faith, the belief that truth ultimately comes from God and then manifests itself through science, rather than to the more radical scientistic belief that science itself is the basis of all truth.

Burke brought God back into the equation. From the standpoint of scientism, no truths can be "self-evident." At the time of the American Revolution, for example, men generally believed it was self-evident that they had the right to rule over women. Similarly, most property owners believed it was self-evident that they had the right to enslave Africans. Self-evidence has been a slippery slope throughout human history, often shaped by the existing norms of a given social order.*

Science, with its emphasis on empirical observation and rational thought, seemed to be making the world a better place, bringing it electric light, refrigerated food, modern medicine, improved means for communication and transportation, and more leisure time for workers. In short, science seemed to be enhancing people's lives. As a result, people increasingly became interested in building a society based on a completely secular scientistic worldview. Among them were champions of the capitalist marketplace, who saw how their own corporations

---

* Though I personally believe that a deeper truth is self-evident—namely, that all human beings deserve to be respected and their opportunities to develop their capacities for love, generosity, creativity, beauty, freedom, knowledge, expanding consciousness, solidarity with others, and connection to spirit given as much support as possible—I don't think there is anything self-evident about how to apply such a principle in any given historical situation. And so I remain very cautious about those who think there is one and only one right way to apply this or any other ethical or spiritual intuition.

could appropriate the latest innovations of science to create new technologies that would allow for innovations in production and endless new consumer items. Science could also help them develop techniques whereby they could manipulate consumer desires and thus increase potential sales. "Progress" allowed for endless innovation in the creation of new consumer items, and anyone who sought to limit these possibilities for some moral or ethical reason could simply be dismissed as "reactionary." Yet there were other champions of science, particularly the Marxists, who rejected the class structure of capitalist society and argued that science should be appropriated in the service of creating a more egalitarian system, whether socialist, communist, or even anarchic. They believed that the religious props for capitalist society would be discarded once people rejected religion and the "self-evident truths" that had been used to justify capitalist society. Science, for these radicals, would be the basis for a new society, and scientism could be used to dismiss religion and ethical systems that had been created to justify capitalist oppression.

Central to the thought of Marx and his successors was the portrayal of their theories as a "scientific" socialism that did not rely on subjective or unproven assumptions. Although Marx himself had a more sophisticated view, Marxists in subsequent generations argued that the only reality was people's material needs—needs that could be empirically observed—and that the only rational way to answer to people's material needs was communism: "from each according to his ability, to each according to his needs." The march of history toward socialism was a fact, just like other facts established by science. In their view, scientific socialism was a socioeconomic system based in hard reality, not some God-sponsored system such as capitalism that actually benefited the rich or some utopian fantasy. In contrast, religion, spiritual insight, ethical longings were all "soft" and subjective—something that reflected a misguided emotional response to the real world.

Marx famously stated that "religion was the opiate of the masses." He understood that it provided emotional compensation for real-world suffering, but he saw this compensation as illusory, in that it did nothing to change the real source of that suffering. What was needed instead was to wean people from this delusion so that they could be mobilized to fight against the social conditions that were at the root of their pain.

Marx was a little less clear in his thinking about whether there is any foundation for human desire other than material needs. In his early works, Marx suggested that there was something about human beings, other than their material needs, that motivated them to struggle. In his *Economic and Philosophic Manuscripts* (1844), for example, he noted that, as a species, human beings are in essence quite different from other species: "An animal only produces what it immediately needs for itself or its young. It . . . produces only under the dominion of immediate physical need, whilst man produces even when he is free from physical need and only truly produces in freedom therefrom. . . . An animal forms things in accordance with the standard and the need of the species to which it belongs, whilst man knows how to produce in accordance with the standards of every species, and knows how to apply everywhere the inherent standard to the object. Man therefore also forms things in accordance with the laws of beauty" (*Marx-Engels Reader*, ed. Robert C. Tucker, Norton, 1972, p. 62).

In my own PhD thesis on ethics and democracy I detail how Marx's thinking actually presupposes an ethical or spiritual foundation. Some of his early writings reflect a deep spiritual wisdom that was, regrettably, lost because of his attempts in many of his post-1844 writings to play down what was essentially a moral critique of capitalism. He presented his theory as a scientific description of inevitable social developments that happen not because of ethical choices but because of larger forces. All the same, there are places in his later works, such as *Contribution to a Critique of Political Economy* (1857) and *Capital* (1867), where Marx hints again at the moral and spiritual underpinnings of his ideas, in what otherwise read like technical discussions of economic theory.

While Marx understood that people turn to religion in response to deep suffering, and while he perhaps alluded to meaning needs, most of his followers identified that suffering in strictly material terms.

Unlike the early Marx, most of his followers saw material well-being and ownership of the means of production by the working class as the answer to everything. Many believed socialism was inevitable, the only possible resolution of the crises in capitalism. Most ridiculed anyone who sought a spiritual or religious foundation for social change, insisting that the transformations that were needed must occur first by satisfying material needs. Although Marx's early writings were rediscovered in the twentieth century, and writers like Gramsci, Lukacs, and Sartre and a significant grouping of New Left theorists in mid-twentieth-century academic and intellectual circles sought to renew a Marxist focus on alienation from what Marx called "species being" and I might call the spiritual foundations of human existence, the majority of those involved in Marxist movements could not unequivocally embrace human needs that could not be verified through scientistic criteria.

In fact, many of Marx's followers thought they were merely drawing out the full implications of their new worldview when they adopted a scientistic approach to the world that not only dismissed God and Spirit as without empirical foundation but also reduced all ethical and aesthetic judgments to little more than reflections of class interests. According to the most mechanistic of these Marxists, people were motivated not by ethical or spiritual beliefs but by their material needs: the sole motivation for any action, they argued, was self-interest. Moreover, a great many, although not all, of the people writing in this tradition held a very narrow conception of self, ignoring the ways in which it might be in people's self-interest to be in loving relationships characterized by mutual recognition and respect, or to fulfill their need to be creative and to contribute to some higher purpose, or to be free to develop a deeper understanding of their place in the universe. Even when some Marxists in Western academic circles eventually began to insist on this broader conception of human needs, they were often ignored or dismissed by the Social-Democratic and Communist Parties, which were the major expression of Marxist politics in the public domain.

The mechanistic Marxists deduced that if everyone is acting only out of narrowly construed material self-interest, the interests of the most powerful are bound to win. When idealistic young Americans read Marx in 1890 or again in 1920 or again in 1950 and looked around them, what they observed was that, indeed, the self-interest of the most powerful governed society. But they also noticed that the powerful sought to hide the extent to which they controlled society by presenting their own selfish interests as in fact being in the best interests of all. Some Marxists believed that all they needed to do was to unmask this kind of deception and rouse the working class to its own self-interest, and then the powerful would be overthrown. The larger working class would build a new society based on their best interests, which would exclude those of the rich but would at least represent those of the majority. No higher values need be invoked for this revolution—the material self-interest of those oppressed by the capitalist order would mobilize people for struggle.

This radical application of scientism to social life, this idea that people are only motivated by material self-interest, became the basis for a significant part of what we now call the political Left, or labor movement, and the Democratic Party. Over the course of the twentieth century, though, the way this scientism was expressed changed. In the earlier part of the century, those on the Left focused on helping the "working man." They fought for labor unions and for women's suffrage. By the 1960s, however, when the United States was awash in prosperity, the average American worker looked pretty well off, at least considering the economic opportunities available to his or her grandparents, and certainly in comparison to the level of material well-being elsewhere in the world. Those on the Left then argued that the real battle was between advanced industrial countries like the United States and impoverished and colonized third-world countries. The United States and its peers were the capitalists, and the third world, the new proletariat. Many on the Left spoke up in dismay when the first thing third-world governments often did after winning their liberation struggles was go to the World Bank and ask how they could become capitalist countries. But if the goal really is to raise the material well-being of a society, third-world leaders responded to their critics, why shouldn't we seek support from whoever has the most money to help spur development?

Does Self-Interest Drive the Left?

There was from the start a deep contradiction built into the secular Left's thinking that surfaced in its attempt to mobilize people to fight third-world oppression. If one was truly a scientific materialist, then what could be the basis for one's identification with these others? What could be motivating these largely middle-class, largely white, almost entirely first-world activists, and was that motivation legitimate? After all, these people could make a reasonably good living for themselves independent of social change. So why, given the secular materialist account, should they care about the fate of these others in the third world? They should, in theory, have been concerned only about their own material self-interest. In fact, there were some on the Left who took this reasoning seriously and insisted that anyone not sharing their particular circumstances should be distrusted, since altruistic motives were, on their supposition, normally just a cover for self-interest.

It's important to understand that these white, middle-class, first-world activists genuinely did care about others—even when their own brand of moral reductionism, which reduced their compassion to self-interest, could not provide a compelling explanation of why they had taken personal risks for the sake of others not in their ethnic, national, or class groups.

One of the greatest failings of the Left has been its refusal to acknowledge that the greater number of its members are motivated by love, caring, generosity, and other spiritual values.

At first the intellectuals of the Left sought to develop the scientific study of society and participated in the shaping of disciplines like political science, sociology, anthropology, and social welfare. Those in the university who continued to pursue more humanistic studies, however, soon found themselves on the defensive. They realized that if in the humanities there is no authoritative scientific way to determine what is right or wrong, then there is also no way to justify continuing to pursue the kind of ethical and aesthetic studies that they themselves were doing. They could find only two possible solutions to this problem. One was to fall into a position of extreme relativism: my moral choices reflect my desires or tastes and have no more objective foundation than my taste in flavors of ice cream, although I can supply internal reasons for why I favor these particular desires. The other was to focus on negative critique, pointing out flaws in the positions of others without trying to put forward any new ideas of one's own. These leftist academics could deconstruct the position of others, showing the class biases, racist preoccupations, or patriarchal assumptions that might underlie the thinking of anyone who proposed theories that claimed universal validity. They could ridicule the ideas of "dead white men" and show that the classics of the West were covers for sexism, racism, homophobia, anti-Semitism, and other insidious prejudices, and many times their criticisms were brilliant and insightful. Yet lacking any positive vision, this approach led to nihilism and so failed to foster a new generation of social change activists to replace those who were now building their university careers.

The Left consistently attacked religion and spirituality as ways of thinking that would mystify people and draw them away from the rational observation that human beings act out of self-interest. In part to do something more positive, early in the 1960s some activists and intellectuals on the Left began to rethink the concept of self-interest. Perhaps material deprivation was too narrow a framework for understanding self-interest, they realized, and so they began to look toward other forms of deprivation, especially those that might furnish a basis for larger social change. The continuing oppression of African-Americans and other peoples of color, of women, of gays, lesbians, bisexuals, and transsexuals were all highlighted as areas where the Left could persist in challenging contemporary social attitudes and arrangements. These movements burst into the consciousness of the Western world in the 1960s and 1970s with talk of a new kind of world in which the old divisions between human beings would be overcome, the shared humanity of people everywhere would be celebrated, and racist, patriarchal, and homophobic conceptions of human reality would be transcended.

Obviously, these were terms that moved beyond the old Marxist frameworks, and there were some on the traditional Left who resisted this New Left, with its emphasis on issues that could not be reduced to material needs. For a brief transformative moment the Left was energized by a spiritual vision of human beings that emphasized love, an expansion of consciousness, and the recognition of the interdependence of human beings with one another and with the planet. The voice of hope sprang to the fore, and people allowed themselves to imagine a very different kind of world, though no one dared call this revolution spiritual. Yet that is exactly what it was.

A spiritual vision emphasizes our common humanity. This was what made Martin Luther King Jr.'s appeal so powerful—what gave him the ability to encourage people to move beyond conceptualizing their interests as opposed to those of others so that they could see that their interests would be best fulfilled in a world in which everyone else's were also fulfilled. Yet that religious and spiritual vision emerging from the biblically rooted consciousness of a black Baptist preacher faced harsh resistance from the voice of fear and the cynical realism that had taken hold in all of us, including the most courageous movement activists.

Without that spiritual vision, many movement activists were unable to acknowledge that the power of the civil rights movement was precisely that it touched and liberated a generosity of spirit that had enabled "black and white together" to "overcome" the system of racial injustice. If people are motivated only by self-interest, the voices of cynical realism insisted, then whites who joined with blacks were really just looking out for their own interests, and no real transcendence was happening. And if other groups were recognizing their own oppression, their concerns might take away from the support your own group needed. So a cynical consciousness fostered mutual suspicion rather than solidarity among oppressed groups. Each group felt a scarcity of recognition that made it insist that its own oppression was more fundamental and that it was more oppressed than anyone else.

The civil rights movement fell apart for many reasons, but the movement certainly was not strengthened when blacks decided they could not accept the presence of white activists. Whites were hounded out of the civil rights movement by militant Black activists who told them, as Stokely Carmichael once said at a meeting I attended in 1966, "We don't want you white folk anymore, because politics isn't about 'black and white together' and all that Martin Luther King shit gratifying white egos, but about everyone getting their own, and we want to get our own." Many of these whites, who had been moved by the message of King and the civil rights movement toward hopefulness and idealism and who were for the first time in their lives willing to imagine that they could act on their own more hopeful inner voices, heard this kind of rejection as confirmation of their most fearful and cynical voices: "See, everyone is just out for themselves." They not only turned away from the civil rights movement, they turned away from the Left.

This dynamic replayed itself in the women's movement as well. A movement that started out with a profound critique of the way that patriarchal assumptions and worldviews had permeated the consciousness of humanity and shaped institutions to perpetuate sexist outcomes was very quickly taken over by more "realistic" women. Many shared the materialist assumptions of the Left and were oriented toward "concrete" achievements. This often meant little more than slight improvements in their wages or getting more women into positions of power in male-dominated institutions so that women could adopt the logic and styles of leadership that men had shaped for hundreds of years. We could eventually have Secretary of State Condoleezza Rice, an African-American woman, articulate the logic of American global domination for the Bush administration. While the material advancement of women was an important achievement, the triumph of a narrow materialist vision of women's liberation limited its revolutionary potential.

I have deep respect for the achievements of these courageous women. The early consciousness raising of the women's movement had an amazing and profound impact on global history. I believe that the huge increase in power and self-esteem with which women in the twenty-first century are able to negotiate personal relationships and the respect that they command throughout the society constitute some of the most significant changes in human life in the last thousand years.

Nevertheless, the early theorists of the crusade against patriarchy went much further. They imagined that what society had previously devalued—women's work in the home, their caring capacities—would become recognized as one of the most important elements in human life. While the materialists tried to reduce this vision to a demand for "wages for housework," the most visionary feminists rightly imagined a much more profound transformation in which every part of our society would be reconstructed in ways that gave prominence to the caring that human beings needed, to love, and to generosity of spirit. In short, though avoiding religious language, they were actually envisioning a return and renewal of the Left Hand of God. But given the dominant materialist assumptions that prevailed in the Left, and in capitalist society as well, these visionaries were quickly relegated to the sidelines while more "realistic" concerns could be foregrounded. Caring itself was eventually dismissed as a covert way to push women back into traditional roles, since women, said the materialists, had always provided love and caring services for free.

While the enormous impact of the women's movement in transforming the status of women around the globe was largely due to the breakthroughs in consciousness stimulated by feminist visionaries, it was the more practical and materialist women, whose more limited concerns focused on economic mobility and individual freedom, who came to be seen as the public representatives of the women's movement. But since many of their materialist demands were well on their way to being achieved for upper-middle-class women, many women in the next generation dismissed feminism as passé, taking professional opportunities for granted and largely unaware of the more visionary aspects of feminism, which had been sidelined by the realists who ran the major women's organizations and those who became political leaders in the political parties. So by the early twenty-first century many of the younger women looking for a place to express their idealism no longer placed their primary energies in the women's movement.

The logic of the Left's scientism produced a fragmentation of efforts and a resurgence of narrow self-interest. If we think that everyone else is motivated only by a narrow material self-interest, we are more prone to narrow the political struggles we engage in to those that will produce concrete material gains and can therefore be imagined to be "winnable." So activism shies away from visionary change, and it becomes popular in the Left to denounce ideologies, to urge people to stop being so intellectual and instead be more practical. In place of a unifying vision and shared moral ideals we get coalitions with a laundry list of campaigns to support, with no attempt made to educate each other about the underlying spiritual or moral values that could unite these different agendas. Pressed by the reality of inadequate funding, activist groups approach foundations and other potential donors who in turn ask them to prove that their projects will have a measurable impact in a relatively short time. The funders rarely have any vision of how their various projects will add up to social change, and so they press these activists to be realistic, funding only those projects that can have realistic outcomes. The more visionary, the less fundable.

Ironically, those with the greatest power in society feel least threatened by a Left whose highest calling is material self-interest. After all, if the loftiest goal that the Democrats can articulate is based on the assumption that everyone is looking out for number one and struggling to get more of what the ruling elites already have, how powerfully can their critique of ruling-class selfishness resonate? If the Left tells us that everyone is just out for themselves, why should we be surprised, much less upset, that Dick Cheney's former company, Halliburton, is making billions on contracts connected to the war effort in Iraq or that Bush has allowed his environmental agenda to be shaped by donors connected to environmentally polluting corporations? Many people begin to reason that in a society based on material self-interest they would be best off finding ways to join the group of the successful, whether through winning the lottery, insider trading, or clever maneuvering in the world of work. More and more people begin to fantasize about experiencing an instant "makeover" that will allow them to live the lives of the rich and the famous, be endowed with ever-young bodies, and find their every whim gratified. No wonder that people who think this way can support tax cuts for the rich even when that means a decrease in their own social services—because they imagine that they, too, will someday be rich. Even if they only have a one-in-a-million shot at riches or stardom, that appears more possible than being able to successfully challenge the powerful. After all, to mount such a challenge would require a movement composed of people who were willing to at least partially transcend their narrow self-interest. Instead, they think, "I'll let others engage in this struggle, and when they've won, I'll share in the benefits."

One of the deeply self-deceptive aspects of thinking that human needs can be satisfied in narrow material terms is that it ignores the real spiritual pain that rich people also suffer. The deprivation of love and meaning can never be adequately compensated for by money.

Try to say that to people who have been fully indoctrinated in the materialist thinking of this society, however, and you'll be met with derision. Granted, most people on the Left would probably agree, in the abstract, that money can't buy love (or meaning). But when it comes down to the choices they make in trying to formulate goals for a union or a political party or a social change organization, they often revert to their deeply internalized materialistic assumptions, which leads them to deny the potential efficacy of addressing the meaning needs.

Of course, a healthy movement would never totally separate meaning needs from material needs. As Jacob S. Hacker correctly argues in the *New Republic* (June 27, 2005), the globalization of capital has created economic uncertainty and instability in the advanced industrial societies of today not only for the traditional working class but across class boundaries. Collectively, Americans are, for example, richer than in previous generations, but they face the possibility of more dramatic shifts in their income. Over the past decade, Hacker notes, "insecurity has moved up the economic ladder. Increasingly, educated middle-class Americans are riding the economic roller coaster once reserved for the working poor." Guaranteed pensions are virtually a matter of the past, and "employment-based benefits have been in steep decline for more than two decades, particularly for low-wage workers. Meanwhile, public social programs have growing gaps" (viewed July 2005 at http://www.newrepublic.com). But to achieve a transformation in this reality, the Left will need a vision powerful enough to counter the escape fantasies that allow so many economically insecure people to identify with the interests of the rich. To begin to see themselves as part of a "we" with common interests that transcend those of one's own narrow group requires moving past the "looking out for number one" mentality of the capitalist market. Ironically, the Left's capacity to foster that alternative consciousness is weakened when it clings to a materialist vision of self-interest that can be validated only on scientistic grounds.

The Bush administration understands this point very well, and that is precisely why it advocates changes in Social Security that it euphemistically calls "progressive indexation." Under this scheme, the benefits of poor workers would remain where they are while the benefits of middle-income workers would be significantly reduced, thus undermining the cross-class solidarity that has traditionally existed for Social Security. Then, once middle-income workers have lost interest in the program, at some future time benefits for the poor could also be reduced.

In emphasizing that caring for people's economic well-being is only part of what's necessary, I am not, of course, proposing that we discard that caring as irrelevant. To deny that human beings are *solely* motivated by economic needs is not to deny the importance of those needs. On the contrary, in judging how far people are living up to God's command to love their neighbor and not oppress the stranger, virtually every biblical prophet used as a criterion the way people treat the widow, the orphan, and the powerless. The response to the growing economic dislocations that globalization will bring to American society, of which we have tasted only the beginning, could be a fearful and frenetic intensification of conflict, as each person seeks his or her own well-being at the expense of everyone else, or it could be a resurgence of solidarity and mutual support. To the extent that the Left can move social energy toward hope and articulate a spiritual vision that reinforces our ability to see our mutual interconnectedness, it can begin to popularize an expanded conception of self-interest so that more of us can allow ourselves to imagine and to fight for a world that leaves no one behind. We can refuse to accept as "collateral damage" the material suffering of large sections of the human race in the name of progress as it is being defined by the globalization of capital.

As I have said, to prepare for this mother of all economic battles, we are going to need a sustaining moral vision. The truth is that most people on the Left already have a set of moral principles that guide their lives and have led them to be Democrats or Greens or social change activists. But their scientistic worldview makes them feel slightly embarrassed to acknowledge and articulate those values. And the intense skepticism about religion and spirituality in the Left makes them reluctant to talk in a language that could be seen as inherently religious or spiritual. Mistakenly thinking that the best way to counter the Religious Right's attempts to impose its values in the public sphere is to insist on the value-neutrality of public life, some on the Left have embraced as their only explicit moral value a commitment to tolerance: "People can do what they want and say what they want as long as nobody tramples on the interests of somebody else."

But that principle is inadequate. Social change requires trampling on the self-perceived interests of the wealthy, most of whom want to keep as much of their money as they can and do with it as they like. Raising their taxes, regulating their corporations, preventing them from outsourcing their factories—these are acts that we would not normally undertake unless we were convinced we had a moral obligation to do so. But if morality itself is nothing more than an expression of subjective desire, then the Left has no right, any more than the Right does, to impose its morality on others—and that renders it incapable of forcefully challenging the current distribution of wealth and power.

In short, liberals become liberal about their liberalism, which makes it hard for others to feel that they can count on them to stand up for anything. One reason why those who are concerned about national security often feel uncomfortable with the idea of putting the Democratic Party in power is that they suspect that liberals don't have the moral backbone to fight for their own beliefs—so how can they be expected to fight to defend the interests of the rest of the country? I don't agree with this logic, but it is one of the consequences of not being willing to stand behind one's deepest convictions and declare: "This is right and that is wrong, and I'm saying this not just because I happen to have personal feelings about it." Of course, deep down most liberals and progressives really do believe, for example, that genocide or the denial of human rights or the economic oppression of the poor is objectively wrong, not merely "wrong for me but possibly right for you if you happen to feel differently about it." But what they currently lack is any adequate foundation in their own worldview for this belief.

A last attempt at saving the self-interested materialist viewpoint has been made on ecological grounds. We are all in the same sinking ship, the argument runs, and so we need to work together, not because we share some sort of spiritual interconnectedness but rather out of simple self-interest—because we are all going to go down together into global destruction unless we do so.

But this argument, too, is filled with holes.

The reality is that in the short run, the worst impact of our environmental destructiveness will be felt by third-world peoples and by those least able to afford to protect themselves. Even when the effects of global warming reach our shores, they are unlikely to affect everyone equally, as we saw in the aftermath of the Katrina hurricane and subsequent flooding in New Orleans in 2005. Most of the American population over the age of forty will be dead before the worst impact of the environmental crisis really starts to hurt the upper middle classes of the Western world. So if the ecological argument is being made on narrow self-interest grounds, because anything more idealistic smacks of religious or spiritual unscientific sentimentality, then on those same grounds someone could well argue, "I don't care about what happens after I'm dead. Let my currently ungrateful children and grandchildren inherit that unfortunate consequence of our contemporary selfishness." Or, as a popular bumper sticker on SUVs in retirement cities proclaims, "I'm spending my children's inheritance."

Of course, the Left is going to support environmental protection anyway, whether it benefits them, their children, or even someone else's children. When it comes down to it, the Left does have values. The Left values the environment. It values labor. It values equal rights and, in fact, human rights generally. The Left values the possibility that each of us can live in peace with our neighbors and ourselves. The Left has very deep values commitments. In fact, the reason I've been a social change activist with liberal and progressive social change movements for the past four decades of my life is precisely because I deeply respect the real underlying values that have often energized the Left.

The problem with the Left, the source of its elitism and of its inability to attract voters, is that it has robbed itself of a discourse that would allow it to proclaim the spiritual principles and transcendent values that underlie its humanistic commitments. It can't talk about love or kindness or generosity without feeling that it has violated its commitment to a scientistic form of rationalism. When people on the Left say they feel "uncomfortable" with this kind of language, they are reflecting a long history of indoctrination into the scientistic assumptions of the dominant secular society, assumptions that have shaped our educational system, permeated our economic marketplace, and been internalized as "sophisticated thinking" by the self-appointed (and capital-sustained) arbitrators of culture.

Immanuel Kant tried to provide a rational ground for ethics by insisting that rationality itself required us to act only in a way that we could wish to see universalized. So if we think x is good for me, it will need to be good for everyone similarly situated. As a method for decision making, Kant's call for universalizability is sometimes helpful, assuming we can figure out which aspects of a given situation need to be universalized. As a rational foundation for ethical judgment, however, it is as much lacking in scientific verifiability as any other.

But if the Left's values aren't based on science, logic, or empirical observation, what are they based upon? The Left believes these values to be good in and of themselves—to be "self-evident." In short, the Left is right back, intellectually, where it started, without any scientific or rational foundation for its belief system. That's appropriate. But then why act as though it is on a higher ground than those who base their moral values in a religious or spiritual foundation?

On the whole, I appreciate the belief system of the so-called secular Left. I also believe in values like justice, peace, love, caring, and generosity. My beliefs are grounded in my Jewish faith that there is a Force in this world that heals and transforms and is moving all of creation toward greater consciousness, freedom, and loving connection—and that this Force is the primary creative Force of the universe. This turn to God does not appeal to many on the Left, but it's time for them to acknowledge that they have their own position of faith. They are not secular in the scientistic sense that they affirm only that which can be validated by empirical observation. They have their values, and those values are not on a higher level of rational foundation than those who root their values in religion or spiritual awareness.

Religious believers cannot provide a set of empirical data to prove the validity of their religious or spiritual commitments. They can show you what is fulfilling about their commitments, what makes sense to them and speaks to their hearts. They can show you the strength and beauty of families rooted in that belief system. But they cannot point to any scientific foundation for their beliefs. And neither can the Left.

Nor should those on the Left seek such a foundation. The view that moral beliefs are not "rational" reflects a particular usage of the word *rationality* that got established when the antispiritual and antireligious forces of the bourgeoisie came to power. It is a usage based on a scientism that claims that anything that can't be validated through science is meaningless, quite literally "non-sense." But this view itself is just another faith position, one that cannot be validated through science, and hence, by its own criterion, is meaningless. It just happens to be the dominant worldview governing the marketplace, the university, and the centers of power. But, as a worldview, it has no greater foundation than the worldview that says it is rational to value that which contributes to love, kindness, and generosity.

Science as an enterprise is something I highly value. But scientism as a worldview is a belief system that has no greater rational status than any other belief system, including those often dismissed by leftists or secularist rationalists as irrational religion. I share the faith of these left-

ists in peace and social justice, but I don't pretend that this faith is
something other than a faith position.

Once you understand that the Left really operates on faith—faith in
their values—you unlock the secret as to why so many people are
angry at what they see as an arrogant elitism coming from people on
the secular Left. The secular Left often presents itself as if it is operating on a higher moral plane than everyone else, precisely because it
imagines that its worldview has been sanctioned by science and rationality. Not only is the Left's scientism a false theoretical support, however, but it leads the Left to convey this kind of wrongheaded attitude
of superiority.

I've taken this long excursion into the history of thought to coax
people on the Left off their high horses. I am not trying to convert anyone on the Left to a particular religious belief. I am happy to find allies
who agree with my values, no matter what foundation they have for
those values. I often ally myself with Christians, Buddhists, Muslims,
Hindus, Native American shamans, and many others, and I have been
actively allying myself with secular Leftists for many decades. However,
the spiritual Left often finds it emotionally challenging to ally with secular Leftists who claim that they are embodiments of rationality,
whereas we religious folk are deluded by irrational fantasies. What's
true is that the secularist position is a belief system neither higher nor
lower, neither smarter nor dumber, than other religious and spiritual
belief systems.

Nor does it help for secularists to say, "My views are ethical, not
spiritual," as though somehow their ethical beliefs are epistemologi-
cally better grounded. The truth is, they have no better foundation for
their ethical views than I for my spiritual views if *foundation* means
"rooted in science, objective empirical observation, or universally accepted truth."

In saying that the secular Left has a belief system like any others, I
am not saying that all belief systems are equal or that we are obliged to
"tolerate" anyone who has a belief system. The Nazis had a belief system, and it was not tolerable. Tolerance is one of our values, but it is
not always our highest value.

A friend of mine who is a Christian evangelist once got on my case
for talking in terms of tolerance. "You leftists call 'tolerance' your

operating principle," he said. "Well, I want to tell you that you are full of it. You don't operate according to a principle of tolerance when you face what you perceive to be 'objectively evil,' as you did when you made wars against slavery and fascism in the past, or when you try to uproot what you perceive to be racism or suppression of human rights in the present. You don't approach these with tolerance but with righteous indignation. But you get all huffy when we on the Right are intolerant of other things like abortion that evoke our righteous indignation because you don't agree with our judgment. And then you invoke your principle of tolerance, as though somehow that was above the moral fray, whereas actually tolerance is just another one of your beliefs that you'd like to position above the struggle. But it isn't: it's just another one of your religious beliefs. If you would just recognize that your belief system is a religious system like mine, equally based on beliefs that cannot be validated by science or empirical observation, you'd stop thinking you were on such a higher plane than we believing Christians are on."

I hated to admit it, but I've been forced to conclude that there is something powerfully correct in his critique—not that this stops me from criticizing his position on abortion or demanding that the state protect abortion clinics that are under siege by threatening mobs.

Yet I do recognize that if leftists could heed his complaint, this might soften the hostility and sense of superiority that many Americans find so offensive about the secular Left.

I don't mean that the secular Left ought to give up its secularism! I am not suggesting that a secularist should convert to some particular religion in order to garner popularity and win votes. What I do mean is that a leftist secularist ought to approach other belief systems with a greater spirit of humility, recognizing that secularism is one possible answer among many to the question of how to understand the universe and how to live one's life. Secularism is not "the rational approach" but "a rational approach" among other rational approaches. I know that may be a lot to ask at a moment when secularism itself is under attack from the Religious Right. But then again the claim that it is "under attack" is precisely what the Religious Right uses to justify its intolerance of secularism. It's time to let go of that kind of thinking. To the extent that we ourselves can remain respectful both of militant secularists and of those on the Religious Right, we who seek to create a spiritual Left could serve as models for a new ethos of respecting those with whom we disagree.

In building a social change movement, we would not tolerate religious people who refuse to ally with us unless we adopt their belief system. In exactly the same way, secularists should not be saying, "Keep your religious perspective out of this conversation, because if you want a genuine coalition, it can't be based on your imposing your religion on me." To be effective, a social change movement will need to make a place for everyone who shares the same political values even though they may belong to different religious traditions or hold different philosophical positions. As I have argued, rather than acknowledge the spectrum of beliefs that members of a coalition bring to the table, the Left too often ends up with a boiled-down mush of "neutral" language. But there is no such thing as neutral language: every position, including taking no position on ultimate questions of faith or spirituality, is a particular position. A movement that truly seeks to transform society must be open to a wide range of articulations. Speaking from a religious perspective should be normal in political meetings or public events sponsored by the Left—and the Left should work as hard to create an inclusive feel for them as it does to include any other constituency.

Why Men on the Left Fear the Left Hand of God

Once it becomes clear to the Left that their antireligious scientism has actually retarded the progress of peace and social justice movements, the Left could be well positioned to address the spiritual crisis in American society. A Left that was ready to overcome its history of hostility to religious and spiritual concerns would show that it recognizes the difference between repressive and liberatory tendencies within religions, would be free to honor and support religious communities that are committed to women's equality and gay liberation and a vision of God based on love rather than repression, and could make substantial efforts to ally itself with a progressive spiritual politics.

So you'd expect that to happen, right? No. Not so fast.

Clearly, there are good reasons why the Left should change its perspective. But there are also deep-seated sociohistorical and psychological reasons why the Left, and particularly male leftists, are fearful of and resistant to a progressive spirituality. In some important ways, "muscular" forms of religion may be much easier to sell to men because of the way we view gender roles in our society than is a progressive spiritual politics that affirms the Left Hand of God.

Despite all the advances of the past century, our culture continues to inculcate patriarchal values as it educates and socializes its children. It continues to value strength over compassion, power over vulnerability, "hardness" over "softness," and to view the first of each of these pairs as appropriate for men and the second as appropriate for women.

As psychologists have pointed out, parents work hard, consciously as well as unconsciously, to ensure that boys develop the masculine traits they will need to succeed. Mothers, who are usually our first caretakers and thus embody the nurturing traits of femininity for us, tend to push sons away from them earlier than they do daughters so that boys will learn independence, a quality we assign to men.

Boys learn early, from their own parents, from TV, and from the surrounding society, that to be considered a man they must strongly disidentify with their mothers and suppress the "feminine" inside of them. Becoming the school-yard bully, greeting a friend by giving him a punch in the arm, focusing on guns and superheroes and video games that feature war and conquest and killing, emphasizing victory in competitive sports, making fun of girls—all these are ways that preadolescent and adolescent boys learn to repress that part of them that actually wants very much to run back to mother, to be accepted by her, embraced by her, and even to be like her.

Girls, meanwhile, are given the mixed message that they should identify with their mothers and yet that they should not value that identity. This mixed message causes serious self-esteem problems in preadolescent girls, manifested in falling grades, eating disorders, and other self-destructive behaviors.

Given this culture, it's understandable why so many of the politicians and pundits of the Left—women as well as men—gravitate toward worldviews that will make them look hard, tough, and powerful. No wonder, then, that so many on the Left find spirituality, religion, and even words like *love, caring, kindness,* and *generosity* so very threatening. These Leftists have already put themselves in the position of championing causes like peace ("sissies who are scared to fight"), the environment ("tree huggers"), and social justice ("liberal do-gooders") that the Right puts down as soft and girlish. From a marketing standpoint, many Leftist believe, the central challenge in a patriarchal society is to create an approach to politics that will appeal to men, and that means showing them that they are not going to be too vulnerable to the charges of softness. They feel the sting when California's governor, Arnold Schwarzenegger, decries the "girlie men" on the Left.

For many on the Left, the solution seems obvious: Cling with tenacious ferocity to the world of science, with its "hard facts," and to a scientism that dismisses spirituality and religion as lacking the hard foundation that facts provide. Distance yourself from anything that suggests emotionality and vulnerability. Build your strategies around the accumulation of power, not around the maximizing of loving experiences. Stay away from the talk of awe and wonder about nature or about unnecessary suffering, and instead quantify, quantify, quantify. Show that you've got measurements that can back your case, that you are not relying on any of that silly girlish stuff like feelings and intuitions—forms of knowing that cannot be verified through empirical observation and confirmed through redoing the experiment under controlled circumstances. Show them you are tough.

The gendering of political life manifests itself in larger geopolitical movements as well and explains why so many people get attracted to visions of strength and power even when objective conditions seem to warrant the possibility of greater softness. In the years immediately following the collapse of communism in the Soviet Union and in surrounding Eastern European states, we might have expected to see a surge of energy in the United States toward disarmament and the redirection of government spending toward social needs. Instead, most politicians sought to reassure the population that we would keep vigilant and work to build a modernized army, while finding other potential enemies (as in the first Gulf War, fought to save the feudal monarchy in Kuwait from the expansionism of Saddam Hussein). This is not to deny the economic importance of the military-industrial complex and its powerful impact on the U.S. media and political discourse. Still, other possibilities might have emerged politically but for the fear of appearing soft. The danger of appearing too vulnerable is even greater when we

are actually attacked, as the United States was on 9/11. Our psychoso-
cial conditioning led us to respond to our own vulnerability by seeking
safety and security in a powerful, "tough" male leader.

Seen in this light, the attraction of many Americans to the Right and
to the Republicans Party is not hard to understand. Throughout the
world the right wing is the political voice for toughness, for using
power to dominate others, for striking at others before they can strike
at you.

This analysis also explains why some of those men who are part of
the spiritual and religious world would be attracted to a muscular
Christianity. That muscular quality prevents men from being seen as
weak or powerless and attracts women who feel they lack strength and
want it in some other form.

Men in the Left face a particularly difficult challenge because the
basic prerequisite for peace and justice in the world is some degree of
mutual trust between human beings. Concern about the well-being of
others around the world, concern about animals suffering and trees
being destroyed by clear-cutting, and concern about the oppression
faced by minorities or foreigners are all connected to a generalized sensitivity to the suffering of others—and that kind of sensitivity our culture paints as feminine.

In fact, it is precisely those so-called feminine qualities of love, softness, vulnerability, caring for others, generosity—the Left Hand of
God—that are desperately needed in a society that has gotten so out of
balance, so male dominated, so out of touch with its own soul, that it
reeks of spiritual crisis and disturbance.

Moreover, without being able to affirm those feminine qualities, liberal and progressive social change movements quickly find themselves
in debates on the terrain of the Right, trying to argue who has better
statistics and more "hard facts" on their side. So leftists rush to get the
statistics and the facts and to reshape their own policies so that they are
reduced to aspects that can be bolstered by some set of "hard data."
Meanwhile, the Right can always pull out its innuendoes, reminding
the audience that no matter how many statistics or "hard facts" the
Left can muster, the underlying message of the Left really is soft, emotional, generous, love-oriented, and thus unacceptable to anyone who
is really hard rather than soft. And the Left, having done all that it can

to distance itself from the loving, emotional, spiritual, and soft aspects of its message, finds itself tongue-tied. It doesn't want to acknowledge what is obvious to everyone, because its own strategy is to find a way to avoid being perceived as soft. So it counters with more technical information, more hard facts, more convoluted arguments that avoid emotions. And the listeners? They change the channel. For most, it's way too boring.

It's too boring because so many of the policy debates that liberals get dragged into are framed in a way that is divorced from anything that might enhance the larger meaning to the lives of those who are listening, divorced from their desire for a world that nurtures more human connection, divorced from people's desire to be saved from the deadness of work and media, divorced from the energies that might inspire people.

The Right doesn't have this difficulty because the policies that the Right is advocating flow from the Right Hand of God—they already embody the militarism and domination and selfishness that trump all cynicism and proclaim their hardness. They can be emotional, they can connect to spirit, because ultimately they are protected from being called "sissies" by being prowar and prodomination.

It's not just the outsiders to politics who turn away from the resulting policy-wonkishness and emotional deadness that too often characterize the candidates of the Democrats and the meetings of the Left. Without a larger framework of meaning guiding the specific strategies and tactics of progressive movements, the activists themselves begin to feel alienated or "burned out." Since the leadership of these projects does not have within its conceptual framework the notion that people hunger for meaning and purpose as a central and legitimate part of their need structure, they create nonprofit organizations and social change movements that give only passing attention to what they sometimes dismissively call "cultural issues."

Already under the intense burden of trying to challenge the huge concentrations of power that the corporate cheerleaders of the Right can mobilize through their ownership of the media and the huge financial resources they can amass to back candidates who accept the Right's vision of what is realistic, social change activists and workers in the nonprofit sector find that they are doubly disadvantaged because the

Left pays inadequate attention to their emotional and spiritual needs. Whereas the Right affirms a strong connection to a religious world that directly addresses those needs, people working in progressive social change movements discover that they must fend for their own spiritual needs and rarely find that their comrades at work or in movement activity feel comfortable joining them in so doing. Of course, most activists don't even have a language to express these needs and would feel that they were betraying the cause if they used religious language. So they tend to blame themselves for not having more fortitude, feel bad about what they imagine to be their own selfishness, and then depart from their years of activism with very conflicted feelings. Many still believe that their cause was right. They talk of feeling burned out, but often what they are talking about is that their experience in the Left did not adequately nurture their souls.

The secular Left consistently disarms itself of what could be its most powerful weapon: a spiritual vision of a world based on love, kindness, and generosity, a vision that most hold privately but that is rarely articulated publicly. This vision is precisely what a spiritual Left could contribute to the political Left, not only strengthening the Left's ability to reach out to people who have moved to the Right but also deepening the commitment of those whose intellect is on the Left but whose hearts and souls do not feel nourished by that affiliation. It could re-ensoul politics.

I've used the word *spiritual* as a label to identify a meaning-oriented approach to politics. Its focus is on the yearning of human beings for a world of love and caring, for genuine connection and mutual recognition, for kindness and generosity, for connection to the common good, to the sacred, and to a transcendent purpose for our lives. Understand human history and contemporary society and individual psychology from the standpoint of these needs and the ways in which they have been frustrated, and then develop a strategy that seeks to address those needs, and you will be able to build a movement and a political party that will be in a position to bring about all the good things liberals and progressives have fought for with such limited success over the past one hundred years.

I've taken this long journey through the origin of the Left's hostility toward religion in the fight against feudalism, its adherence to an antireligious scientism that became its calling card in the nineteenth and twentieth centuries, and the negative impact that such scientism had in restricting the way the secular Left conceived of its options in framing political struggles in order to show you that this marriage of the forces for social change with an antireligious and antispiritual worldview is not good for the cause of peace and justice.

SEVEN

How the Left Lost Hope

The Left was not always afraid of talking about love and generosity, kindness and compassion. To understand the current dominance of the Right, we need to look back at political history a bit. We need to discover how liberals and progressives forgot the Left Hand of God.

For religious progressives in the United States, the first decades of the twentieth century were imbued with a vision of hope, often tied politically to a belief that the United States would bring democratic values to the rest of the world. The *Christian Century*, a magazine that articulated a vision of social justice rooted in liberal Protestant values, took what seemed to its white middle-class constituency to be remarkably courageous stands, supporting suffrage for women, championing organized labor and the right to strike, and preaching a vision of Christian social responsibility that became known as the Social Gospel. Walter Rauschenbusch, a Baptist minister whose work in New York City's Hell's Kitchen, an area inhabited by the poor and down-and-out, symbolized the religious political activism of this period, might be taken as a representative figure of the aspirations of the Social Gospel and its vision that God's kingdom might be achieved through the democratization of the American economic system.

However, when the smoke cleared after the First World War, it became clear that the hopes for an international working-class solidarity had been subsumed by the steaming energies of nationalism. American fantasies of a "war to end all wars" or "to spread democracy" were revealed to be founded on hollow rhetoric that obscured the colonial needs and expansionist desires of the industrializing capitalist world. At that moment, a new level of cynicism and despair blossomed throughout much of the Western world, intensified in the late twenties and thirties by the breakdown of the country's economic engine in the stock market crash of 1929.

The harsh terms imposed on Germany and the other defeated countries by the victorious allies after World War I created economic turmoil and suffering, coupled with a sense of despair among the youth of those nations, who had sacrificed for a war that seemed pointless in retrospect. The turn from hope to fear was especially harsh, and many sought relief in fascism. Fascism had a powerful appeal. Not only did the fascists promise to jump-start the economies through military spending and government rationalizing of production, but they also spoke to a very real human need to be part of something beyond self and beyond money, in striking contrast to the liberal democracy of the Weimar government, which had opened an era of materialism, selfishness, and sexual licentiousness.

The economic collapse intensified the already-existing feelings that people had given up too much by abandoning the supportive institutions of the feudal world, the Church, and the village communities of the past for a new world of competitive individualism in which rootless self-interested groups could advance themselves without regard to the well-being of the community. Romanticizing the past, minimizing the oppressive nature of feudal social relations and patriarchal family structures, many people responded to fascism because it promised some relief from the ultra-individualism of a marketplace that seemed to reward selfishness and to discard all forms of community.

The newly emerging capitalist marketplace in central and eastern Europe communicated to people the message that they were valuable only to the extent that they could maximize profit for themselves or for the owners of the businesses for which they worked. Countering that harsh message, the radical right-wing nationalism of the fascists told people that they were valuable not because of what they accomplished in the marketplace but solely and simply because they were members of the Aryan master race. Membership in the nation or race was a gift of birth, not something one could lose by failing an objective test (which those Jews were so very good at passing) or by failing to make lots of money. The nation became for the fascists the locus of meaning, a framework that could transcend the selfishness of the marketplace and provide an image of enduring worth—but only if the nation could be purified of its polluting elements (Jews, communists, homosexuals, and other such subversives).

Under fascism, the goodness of all humanity is replaced by the goodness of Us in opposition to Them. The alienation people feel is not a communal problem that they can solve among themselves but the result of the presence of an evil Other that is undermining the spiritual coherence of the national community and hence must be destroyed. For the fascists in Germany, the demeaned Other was most infamously the Jews. The Nazis also rounded up gays and Roma (gypsies). For the fascists in Japan the Other was the Chinese and Koreans. For the fascists in the United States, it was people of color and Jews. But it's important to remember that the fascists' goal in identifying an Other was to resolve their spiritual crisis. And the way to solve the problem was to exercise domination over others and to extol military power and brute strength while demeaning weakness of any sort.

When fascism came to power, the world experienced a moment in which extremes of fear trumped hope. Its victory did not reveal a lasting truth about the human condition, however, but rather a reflection of the inadequacy of secular liberalism to provide a satisfactory strategy to combat the appeal of fascism or to alleviate the conditions, described above, that had given rise to it. Communists and socialists, when they were not wasting their energies on fighting each other, offered a vision of a new economy. But they were completely tone-deaf to the hunger for some framework of meaning and purpose to life that was attracting people to the Church or to visions of a *Volk* (the national community of the people) that conjured up hopes of genuine recognition and community. We will never be certain that fascism could have been wiped out in Europe without war and before the Holocaust occurred. But the meaning-oriented strategies that could have been used in the 1920s before fascists had won state power were never seriously tried. An antifascist movement that offered hope instead of fear, that acknowledged the legitimacy of the complaints about the breakdown of community, and that made the desire for transcendent meaning central to its agenda would have been far more likely to have stopped the fascists, especially in the 1920s and early 1930s, before they came to power, than what was actually tried.

After the defeat of German fascism in World War II, the communist and socialist movements that sought support of the working masses understood the economic dimensions of postwar suffering, but did not understand the crisis in meaning and purpose to life that had only intensified as a result of the violence of that war. Deeply rooted in a Marxist worldview that saw human beings as primarily motivated by economic need, the Left could offer little to the displaced and lonely masses of Europe besides a promise to achieve economic security. It should not surprise us that the country that set out on the most antispiritual path, Soviet Russia, ended up with another version of fascism under Stalin.

With the rise of fascism, the American religious Left abandoned the Social Gospel of its pre–World War II past, with its cheery hope of steady progress toward the Kingdom of God. Instead, the chief theologian of the period, Reinhold Niebuhr, began to write of the need for a new realism about the world of power. Nazi violence and oppression had to be stopped, and to do that Niebuhr switched his previous focus from the need for a democratic socialism that would challenge capitalism and instead sought to mobilize his own capitalist democracy, the United States, to stand up against the threat of Nazi totalitarianism.

Niebuhr rooted his antifascism in a Christian theology that stressed the limits of human perfectibility and the centrality of human sinfulness. Christians needed a new sense of realism, and that meant not only the use of force against Hitler but also the abandonment of any hopes of building a social order that could dramatically improve the human condition. For Niebuhr and the Christian realists who rallied around his writings, sinfulness required recognizing the limitations of any politics aimed at fundamental social change, accommodating to the inequities of their own capitalist societies and championing the Cold War. The Christian "realists" helped reenforce individualism when they focused religious energy away from social movements and toward building a "moral man," while excepting as inevitable an "immoral society."

•   •   •

There is a powerful tendency inside all of us toward fear. When our consciousness moves in that direction, we believe that the Other is a serious threat that needs to be dominated and controlled before it does likewise to us. The Bible describes Pharaoh's fear of the Israelites in these terms—they had to be enslaved lest they potentially ally with the enemy. His next step was to attempt to kill every firstborn Jewish male. So the genocidal tendency was there at the very beginning of Jewish history—and yet the thrust of biblical religions is a countermessage: that we don't have to act out of fear. There is a different and more powerful possibility: to respond to the voice of a God who commands us to "love your neighbor as yourself" and to not "oppress the stranger" but to "remember that you were strangers in the land of Egypt."

Understandably overwhelmed by the level of carnage during the twentieth century, religious leaders all too often abandoned the hope that love and kindness and generosity and nonviolence could ultimately triumph.

Of course, there are times when fear is necessary. But even in moments when the Right Hand of God is needed to inspire struggle against fascist oppression, it must be balanced by the Left Hand of God. Instead of reminding their followers that we need not despair, that even when we meet evil we can remember hope, too many American religious leaders allowed the Hitlers of human history to define for them what was "reality" and, in so doing, awarded those Hitlers a posthumous victory.

In the second half of the twentieth century a deep post-Holocaust cynicism about humanity led many American intellectuals and even religious leaders to conclude that power over others was the only path to security. Frequently they abandoned hope for a world based on love and kindness, ideas that in the period from 1945 to 1965 were dismissed as utopian, adolescent, and unsophisticated. In other words, they abandoned the Left Hand of God.

As cynical realism parading as religious truth covered over the realities of global and domestic inequalities, the tendency in human life toward love and caring and generosity that had once been the "good news" of the religious world was not actually extinguished but rather found other forms of expression. By the mid-1960s a secular movement was developing in the United States and in many of the other advanced industrial societies that took up the banner of hope that had been laid down by much of the religious world.

The social change movements of the 1960s were in large part a response to the spiritual deadening that happens to a society when it loses its voice of hope. The anticommunist crusade of the cold war that shaped American life in the 1950s silenced those who believed that politics could be a realm in which a community could actualize its highest ideals.

The aftermath of the Second World War could have seen the countries of the world uniting in common purpose, using the incredible scientific and technological advances spurred by the war to solve global problems. Instead, it became a period of narrow self-interest in which the victorious countries sought to advance their own power and in which the peoples of the West were encouraged to imagine that the highest goal of life was the endless accumulation of material goods. With television providing new ways to create consumer demands and inculcate a vision of "the good life" as one in which isolated family units maximized their own advantage and their own wealth, many people in the Western world withdrew their attention from the public sphere and sought to find fulfillment in private life.

Private life devoid of a higher purpose than the accumulation of goods could not and did not provide spiritual satisfaction, however. What social theorist Peter Gabel describes as the emotional and spiritual deadness people experienced all day in the world of work could not be healed by an increasingly passive and complacent consumer life or even by the pseudosubstitutes available through frantic accumulation of material goods, binge eating, drugs, alcohol, television, sports, psychoanalysis, or whatever else could be introduced to give momentary highs. Yet to the extent that the religious world had become cheerleaders for the Western capitalist status quo, it had stripped itself of the intellectual and spiritual categories that could provide an alternative spiritual path.

It was in this context that spontaneous movements, largely composed of students and other young people, emerged to critique the social and political realities of the Western world and to challenge the alienation, spiritual deadness, and emotional flatness of a society whose highest goal was consumption. Neither the religious world nor the old Left had any language in which to express these concerns, so students aligned themselves with single-issue causes like the civil rights and antiwar movements. But they brought to these causes a set of concerns that were sometimes dismissed as merely "countercultural" because they spoke to yearnings for human connection that seemed to transcend the political categories that the Democrats and Left movements mostly employed. Using the categories of democracy and human rights as their framework, these social movements called upon the countries of the Western world to live up to their own promises of equality and justice. What made this Left "new" was that alongside these demands for rights and for the expansion of democracy was a willingness to champion the ideal of non-alienated social relations rooted in the biblical notion that human beings are created in the image of God. This New Left was largely unaware of the religious foundation of its own ideals, however. Because it often encountered resistance from the mainstream religious communities of the 1950s and 1960s, and because it attracted as part of its base young people who rebelled against the authoritarian, racist, and sexist aspects of the religious traditions in which they had grown up, it quickly inherited and intensified the Old Left's hostility toward religion, even though its critique affirmed the values of the spiritual heritage of the human race.

The civil rights movement, the antiwar movement, the feminist movement, the environmental movement, the movement for gay and lesbian rights all emerged in reaction to the deprivation of rights. Each movement sought at first to have America live up to its own ideals. But as they faced unexpected resistance from the government, the media, and the mainstream religious world, each began to develop a more radical critique of the society that questioned the very foundations of American society and the legitimacy of the religious communities in which many of these new social change activists had been raised. They incorporated a critique of the cultural and spiritual deadness they experienced in American society, one that opened the way to a much deeper understanding of the ways that racism, sexism, militarism, and homophobia actually paralyzed the soul.

I am proud to have been part of many of these movements. I believe that their appearance in the 1960s and 1970s represented a great surge forward in the positive and hopeful energy of the universe. Within a very short period of time, racist, sexist, and homophobic attitudes that had been part of the unconscious structure of Western societies for millenia were exposed and challenged in unprecedented ways. Even though the deep legacy of these attitudes in culture and politics has not yet been fully dislodged, the progress made on all three fronts over the past forty years has completely surpassed the expectations and predictions of even the most hopeful early exponents of liberation and has been no less miraculous than any other miracle in human history.

It would be a terrible distortion to deny that these movements received significant support from some sectors of the liberal religious community. Quite apart from the energy it drew from African-American forms of Christianity, the civil rights movement received considerable support from liberal churches and synagogues, as did the antiwar movement. The heroic role played by progressive Catholics in fighting the war in Vietnam, as well as the well-known role of the Catholic liberation theology movement in challenging U.S. policies in Central and South America, was matched by the powerful commitment to peace and justice movements on the part of the mainstream institutions of the Episcopalians, Methodists, Lutherans, Presbyterians, Unitarians, the United Churches of Christ, and Reform Judaism, side by side with the inspirational work of smaller denominations like the Quakers, the Mennonites, and the Church of the Brethren.

While these religious movements ended up playing decisive roles in bringing social change movements into the mainstream, they rarely supported activists at the most difficult moment, generally at the beginning of the struggle. Usually, religious leaders followed on the heels of secular activists in supporting an issue or a new way of thinking rather than vice versa. (One notable exception was the issue of providing sanctuary for Central American refugees, in which the Catholic Church played a leading role.) At the same time, although secular activists—whose attention was focused most on what was happening in large urban centers on the East and West Coasts and on university campuses—frequently knew that their ideas were "catching on" throughout the country, they rarely understood the powerful contribution made by mainstream Protestant churches in bringing progressive ideas to large sections of the American population that the secular Left could never have reached on its own.

The civil rights movement, led by the Reverend Martin Luther King Jr. was an important exception to the Left's resistance to the religious world. But even in that movement the acceleration of activists' demands (from ending segregation to achieving racial equality to seeking black liberation) was met by criticism from religious institutions rather than by generous acceptance. Churches and synagogues were ready to challenge the treatment of blacks in the South by a few overt racists, but they were much more reluctant to champion a more fundamental rethinking of racism as a pivotal element in the daily life of American society.

Those who participated in the movements for social change experienced a sense of liberation and joy that accompanied their tilt toward the vision of hope. As they sought to transform their society, they felt that the scales were falling from their eyes—the feeling of hope seemed to beget more hope. What they had been taught growing up was just "common sense"—that people were out for themselves and cared for no one else—was suddenly being proven false in front of their very eyes. This feeling ran particularly deep among white Americans. As thousands of young people from the North streamed into the South to challenge segregation, often facing jailings and beatings and in some cases even death, their transparent idealism began to sweep college campuses and inspire a new vision of human possibility. Caring about the fate of black people in their own country soon escalated into caring about the fate of other people of color around the world, first and foremost in Vietnam.

Though the holders of established power tried in the later decades of the twentieth century to portray the antiwar movement as merely a reflection of narrow self-interest on the part of young people seeking to escape the draft, the reality was quite different for many who actually participated. Self-interest led some to oppose the war, to be sure. But self-interest would have also led students to quietly hold on to their student deferments rather than risk expulsion from school by participating in disruptive campus demonstrations challenging the recruitment efforts of the ROTC and the CIA. Nor could self-interest account for the fact that the largest and most militant antiwar demonstrations occurred in 1970 and 1971, after the draft was essentially suspended for middle- and upper-middle-class youth.

What many of the participants in these movements reported was a dramatic decrease of fear in their lives, even at the very moment when they were engaged in fear-inducing experiences. Moral strength and courage were valued in this movement, while money and social power lost their allure for the activists, many of whom believed they were putting their professional futures in danger. Their experience of moral solidarity would have been called religious or spiritual had those terms not been in such disrepute among the activists. What was undeniable was that people were experiencing the kind of mutual recognition and sense of community that had been absent through much of their lives. It was an experience that was at once self-validating and empowering, creating a hunger for deeper connection and a society that could support rather than undermine the flourishing of what some dared call the human essence (and what others used to call the soul).

When such experiences are available, they are infectious. Identification with "the movement," which started with just a few tens of thousands of people in 1965, mushroomed to over twelve million, according to a *Fortune* magazine estimate in January of 1969, and grew even more dramatically in the next few years. The experience of recognition, the feeling that one's life was connected to a higher ethical purpose gave meaning to each day's activities and provided for an ecstatic life that seemed to match the intensity and purposefulness that passionate religious communities and ultranationalist movements had offered in the past.

No wonder, then, that the existing liberal religious communities seemed pale and artificial in comparison. The post–World War II theology of realism in mainstream Christianity and Judaism seemed to many to be little more than a clap and a half for a society that was increasingly being revealed as sexist, racist, homophobic, and committed to spreading its power through overt wars of aggression (Vietnam, Santo Domingo) or covert overthrows of governments that did not abide by the American will (Salvador Allende in Chile).

Even though the counterculture defined itself as a secular movement, I can say with the hindsight of history that it was indeed a spiritual movement. Those who partook in the movement insisted that it was central to their being, and they celebrated the vision of hope they had found with their own rituals and communal rites. Indeed, the spiritual aspect of the movement came forth most clearly in the activists' drug-assisted gatherings of music and poetry, where they came to know themselves as reaching for a transcendent vision that affirmed the most hopeful, the most love-oriented, the most generosity-oriented, the most peace-oriented aspects of the human experience. Although few people from this time talked about having created a secular spirituality, many recognized that their aspirations were in fundamental conflict with the one-dimensional power orientation of the capitalist marketplace, the military-industrial complex, and its media cheerleaders.

What we witnessed in the 1960s and early 1970s was an explosion of desire. For a brief historical moment, millions of people allowed themselves to imagine what the world could be if love prevailed and a more authentic existence could be forged. Though the institutions and requirements of daily life kept chugging along and making their demands, the joyous experience of allowing authenticity, a generosity of spirit, and a freeing of creativity spread hope in ways that seemed to open new pathways in the mind. Participants in the movements of the 1960s and early 1970s often spoke in retrospect of being alive in a way unlike anything they had experienced previously or since—the kind of words used by those who have experienced being resurrected from the dead or "born again in Christ" or those who talk of the joy of serving God experienced in Jewish Hasidic and mystical communities. Free to "Imagine," as John Lennon put it, they found that it "isn't hard to do," because, as Lennon went on, "I'm not the only one—I hope someday you'll join us and the world will live as one." This was a community that had tilted as far toward the Left Hand of God as any in living memory—a community that was strongly committed to affirming hope and living as though love and caring and mutual recognition were really possible.

And yet, as is always the case, even at the height of this religious ecstatic experience there were countervoices in the consciousness of the actors in these movements. At the center of the movements were, after all, ordinary people who had grown up and been socialized in a world that deeply internalized cynicism and doubt about the possibility of a world based on anything but domination. The major spokespeople for the Democratic Party were, in that regard, no different from those of the Republicans in their certainty that the world was a fundamentally dangerous place, and their hostility toward this new energy was not even thinly concealed. And the Nixon administration was filled with people who imagined that the entire social order was on the verge of dissolution or overthrow and had to be defended by an extraordinary set of repressive measures.

No ecstatic consciousness can last long when agents of the government are sent into your movement with the goal of creating as much dissension as possible. The FBI's COINTELPRO program, which began in the late 1960s, placed paid police agents and patriotic right-wing volunteers in local chapters of antiwar movement organizations, where they proceeded to sow dissension. These infiltrators, presenting themselves as ultramilitants, put down the movement's own grassroots leaders for not being militant enough, while themselves suggesting and sometimes implementing violent activities. They sent forged letters to members of these groups that sought to "prove" that some of the most effective leaders were actually racist, sexist, money hungry, power hungry, or only looking out for themselves. In countless ways these agents helped undermine group cohesion. Many of the most idealistic activists quit their own organizations when they saw these kinds of dynamics emerging, never imagining that some of the most destructive and violent behavior surging up around them was actually being generated by undercover police, the FBI, and their volunteer associates.

I've talked about the spiritual or religious nature of some of the experiences that people were having as part of the social change movements. Yet what was missing from these movements was any sense of their own human limitations, or sinfulness. They understood the Left Hand of God but ignored the Right Hand of God. They understood hope but ignored fear. Lacking the conceptual or spiritual tools needed to deal with sinfulness, the social change activists were unable to respond to "sinners" (themselves and their comrades) with compassion. They had no capacity to provide routes for repentance, atonement, and forgiveness. These brilliant spiritual techniques derived from the religious traditions of the human race, which had given lasting strength to previous movements of hope around the globe, were absent in the secular movements of the 1960s and 1970s.

As a result, movement people who had rejoiced in discovering the possibilities of transcendence and profound transformation were totally unprepared to accept their own limitations with any sense of self-compassion or gentleness. They expected to instantaneously become pure embodiments of their own highest ideals, and when they discovered the many ways in which they failed to do so, they became ruthlessly self-critical. Activists were overwhelmed with self-doubt and self-loathing as a result, without ever developing a compassionate process by which they could accept their flaws while simultaneously working to overcome them.

Self-blaming is carefully woven into the fabric of Western societies. Yet it reached new heights with a generation of young people reared on television-induced fantasies of the immediate gratification of all one's desires. Expecting to instantaneously achieve a social order based on love, challenged to see how they actually had self-defeating flaws like everyone else, many of the white activists in these movements were able to sustain their hopefulness about everything except themselves.

The process began when the civil rights movement took a turn toward black nationalism and Black Power. As I mentioned earlier, in the years from 1965 to 1969 a significant number of black activists in the civil rights movement broke with their former white allies, accusing them of using the cause of black people to overcome their own feelings of guilt, and claiming that they could no longer work with white progressives whose racism was just as deeply ingrained as that of Southern segregationists. While the charge felt deeply unfair to most whites, many of whom had been risking their own lives in support of civil rights, it reflected a continuing experience of subordination and lack of respect that is the reality of life for most African-Americans in a racist society. Moreover, in the politics of American society, the civil rights movement truly was being appropriated by the Democratic Party, which was dominated by white liberals who used the fight against racism in the South as a rallying cry while refusing to confront the deep and systemic nature of racism in the North and elsewhere. The anger appropriately directed by African-Americans against these powerful forces was misdirected against the white radicals who were their allies.

Many white activists internalized the charges and began to doubt their own capacity to remain politically active. They adopted a "victim consciousness" and gave up on antiracist politics rather than acknowledge the experiences that had led some blacks to distrust whites. Others sought to twist the politics of their own organizations so as to meet black demands and show that they were less racist by following black leadership. This sometimes led to a rather convoluted path because, like whites, blacks in America held a variety of different and sometimes mutually contradictory political stances, and so organizations that sought to overcome their own racism became mired in fighting over the question of which black leadership to follow. Still other activists decided that the best way to continue to help blacks was to end the war in Vietnam, since the draft was ensuring that a disproportionate number of blacks were getting wounded or killed.

The assault on white racism and privilege in the movement in 1965–67 was followed in 1968–73 by a similar assault on the part of certain feminists who charged that the male activists working in the antiwar movement were as sexist as any in the society and that the movement was in fact so distorted by sexism that women would have to leave it. Again, many of these charges were true—many women in the movement were relegated to secretarial work while men took the leadership roles. Yet it was hard for the men under attack to consider these charges while they were simultaneously risking their lives and abandoning their path to comfortable careers to fight on behalf of the well-being of the Vietnamese peasants being murdered by the thousands by U.S. troops. The more these male activists resisted the charges of chauvinism, the more powerful became the critique of entrenched male power, a critique that was so transparently true that most men in the movement eventually began to agree with it. Yet the pain of that recognition—that they who had been fighting for the good were simultaneously acting in oppressive ways toward the women in their lives—was at times overwhelming and debilitating, particularly since the accusation was being made with such force by the very women with whom they were involved in work and/or love relationships.

And men were not the only target of feminist rage. Many middle-class heterosexual feminists distanced themselves from their more outspoken lesbian "sisters" in an effort to make feminism more palatable to the average American woman, often ignoring the analysis of heterosexual privilege that gays and lesbians were articulating. This in turn

led to a powerful backlash from other feminists. Some women were denounced by their radical feminist sisters for being male-identified, that
is, for giving precedence in time and loyalty to their male partners over
their women friends. It was not unusual for heterosexual women on
college campuses in the late 1960s and early 1970s to find themselves
on the defensive for being in relationships with men, thereby rejecting
the advances of their lesbian sisters. And these dynamics continued for
several decades in the experience of feminists in colleges where
women's-studies programs had been established to challenge the male-
dominated knowledge that shaped the Western canon ("dead white
men" became a term of ridicule). Women who chose to give priority to
building a family over building a career reported that they frequently
felt put down or were made to feel they were being disloyal to the
women's movement. For all the talk about respect for choice, it was
clear that from a feminist perspective some choices were better than
others and some women more legitimate or more representative of
women's consciousness than others.

For the most part, however, the women's movement was characterized by a flood of generosity toward other women and a spirit of sister-
hood that stood in powerful contrast to the individualist ethos of the
society. There were some militant and angry feminists, but there were
also a whole lot of women with or without families who went to consciousness-raising groups and began to see the world and their own relationships in new ways. These women were greatly empowered by the
insights and experiences they had in the movement. But the media typically played up the angry elements of the women's movement far more
than it communicated the positive energies that were at its heart, the
affirmation of the dignity and worth of women who began to shake
themselves free from the indoctrination they had received into demeaning patriarchal assumptions and life patterns, or the joyous experiences so many women had when they connected with each other in a
deep and not necessarily sexual way.

I don't want to suggest that all of the questioning of attachment to
men or questioning of heterosexuality was illegitimate. The pervasive
and deeply ingrained sexist and heterosexist assumptions harbored by
virtually everyone raised in patriarchal society needed, and still need,
to be challenged and critiqued. But the occasional lack of compassion

shown by some radical feminists and lesbians to their feminist sisters was amplified by a hostile male media and so helped to undermine the power those critiques might have had if they had been accompanied by a more generous attitude. The mainstream media also publicized these attacks as a way of discrediting the liberatory thrust of feminism and gay liberation. Similarly, by focusing on the demands of a small minority of movement activists who claimed that the family itself was inherently patriarchal or heterosexist, the media accelerated the feeling that some heterosexual activists were experiencing—that their own sexual proclivities were not okay, that their desire for family was a betrayal of the movement, and that their desire to raise children was a sign that they really had not aligned themselves with the forces of liberation.

Finally, a powerful group of movement activists became convinced that the reason they had so far been unsuccessful in winning the majority of the American people over to the side of the people of the third world struggling against global imperialism was that white Americans of the working and middle classes had bought into "white-skin privilege" and taken advantage of their special situation as beneficiaries of the spoils of American imperialism. It became popular in some movement circles to denounce America's working class as self-satisfied racist pigs.

If that weren't enough to undermine the political credibility and potential impact of antiwar activists, some people in the movement began to criticize each other for having failed to transcend their own egos. To their own horror and shock, movement activists discovered that underneath their own idealism they had egos (can you believe it?) and that their perception of themselves as selflessly sacrificing for others sometimes masked powerful needs for recognition and admiration that sometimes actually influenced their behavior!

By the beginning of the 1970s, as activists became increasingly despondent about their failure to have ended the war in Vietnam, many in the movement began to turn on each other with great emotional ferocity, accusing each other (and often themselves) of "not having dealt with" their alleged racism, sexism, homophobia, white-skin privilege, egos, and other serious defects.

I don't mean to minimize the truth in any of these charges. I don't blame people who exploded with anger as they became aware of the depth of racism, sexism, and homophobia in the society, in themselves, and in their comrades. Righteous indignation at oppression is an important contributor to the energy that builds awareness and social change. But there is an important distinction between attacking a set of practices and behaviors that need to be changed, on the one hand, and acting in ways that demean the humanity of those who need to change, on the other. And the sad truth is that the way many of these legitimate criticisms were made led those who were the targets of these criticisms to feel that their very humanity was being called into question.

The yearning for connection to one's highest self becomes more intense the closer one comes to experiencing that possibility—and the frustration at not being able to actualize that desire becomes ever more intense and can lead to self-hatred and to extremely self-destructive behavior.

That's why some movement activists directed the greatest ruthlessness of their critique at themselves. Too often the participants in the movement had expectations of unlimited and immediate transformation and transcendence. Many had actually experienced amazing transformations and growth in the course of their participation in the movement, so when they discovered that they still were limited human beings who had, after all, been socialized in a sexist, racist, homophobic society that privileged self-interest, they were filled with self-loathing. Some concluded that they had no right to be challenging the larger society when they had so much of their own internal psychological work yet to do. I still hear people who dropped out of activism say something like, "I joined the movement because I wanted to build a different kind of world but then got disillusioned when I found that people in those movements had so many of the defects of the rest of the society." A famous Pogo comic strip of the time had a slogan that embodied this (in my view deeply mistaken) consciousness: "We have met the enemy," Pogo proclaims, "and it is us."

To which I say, "Duh. What in the world did you imagine you would find in a movement composed of people who had joined just a short while ago? Did you really expect that people would become saints overnight just because they had realized a few months earlier that the war in Vietnam was a moral evil or that racism was more pervasive than they had previously acknowledged?"

Actually, the fact that movement activists expected instant transformation reflected the way in which they had themselves been shaped by the instant gratification ethos of the consumer culture.

What activists lacked were the tools that a psychologically informed and spiritually deep consciousness could provide. From the world of psychology, activists could have learned how deep and sometimes intractable the ways of seeing ourselves and the world that we have internalized throughout our childhood and adult life can be. From the world of the spirit, activists could have learned that people simultaneously have a yearning for loving community, a tremendous fear and cynicism about whether such a community could ever come about, and a tendency to run from it just when deep transformation might happen. Spiritual traditions teach that such fear takes time and effort to overcome, something that is best accomplished through a repeated process of repentance, atonement, acceptance, and forgiveness, each step refracted through a general attitude of compassion for ourselves and other people. But when we fail to show compassion or to experience it from others, our most fearful responses get "confirmed," and we become all the more convinced that our momentary experience of loving connection and mutual recognition was nothing but drug-induced fantasies or adolescent idealism that must be left behind.

One tragic dimension of this lack of compassion is that the people who took huge risks for their ideals, who experienced incredible levels of ecstasy as they fought for social justice and peace and women's liberation, who brought powerful new ideas into public discourse and managed to smash down oppressive racist and sexist practices, were never able to fully appreciate how much they had achieved.

Segregation was dismantled and paths to genuine mobility were opened to African-Americans. Patriarchy, a set of social and economic practices that seemed so deeply embedded in our culture that people thought it utopian to suggest that it could be challenged, was shown to be capable of being significantly weakened within a very short period of time. The unconscious processes by which women subordinated their lives to the will of men were exposed and often dislodged, opening up possibilities for a higher level of human fulfillment for half of the human race.

To be alive at this historical moment was like being alive when Prometheus stole fire from the gods to make it available for human use, or when the slaves broke out of Egypt and proved that slavery could be overcome, or when Jesus and Buddha taught, or when Athenians developed democracy, or when the Enlightenment affirmed human reason and helped people undercut the assumptions of feudalism.

How incredibly sad that the people who participated in this moment couldn't appreciate it more, couldn't feel their own accomplishments as proof of how dramatically the world could be changed, but instead were focused on their own and one another's deficiencies.

The turning inward that occurred in the 1970s, as people sought to explore their private psychological dynamics and even to reopen themselves to a spiritual dimension that had been unarticulated and needed discovery, could have afforded a wonderful opportunity for building a healthier Left. Framed as a supplement and balance to political activism, this self-scrutiny could have been a powerful tool for creating an ever more successful Left. Instead, most people took this route as an alternative to political action and—with the help of a cynical media and a Nixon presidency that consciously sought to convince activists that their demonstrations were pointless and were either counterproductive or ignored by the powerful—sweepingly invalidated much of what they had just contributed to American political life.

Unfortunately, many activists turned the lack of compassion they had for themselves outward against those who still did not agree with them. Activists who had themselves converted to a radical perspective only months before would project a deep contempt for anyone who did not share their intense anger at the war in Vietnam and at the manifestations of racism that surrounded them.

Prophetic jeremiads and righteous indignation are at the heart of a spiritual critique of society. But such a critique must distinguish between policies and institutions that perpetuate evil and individual human beings who may be caught up in those practices but whose humanity needs to be affirmed even as their practices need to be challenged.

Unfortunately, though, the New Left was unable to leaven its critique with compassion and spiritual awareness and as a result produced a backlash that continues to shape politics in the early decades of the twenty-first century in the form of a powerful Religious Right.

Some people who had previously voted Democratic moved to the Right in the period between 1968 and 1980 because they were not ready for the critique the liberal and progressive social change movements made of racism, sexism, and homophobia. Some Americans felt most comfortable with patriarchal and authoritarian family dynamics and discriminatory social and economic policies that were particularly well entrenched in the South, though they were pervasive throughout much of American history. Some traditional Democratic voters felt angry and threatened when their institutions and social practices came under attack from the movements of the sixties. Still, there were many others who might have been more responsive to the critique of the Left had it been offered in ways that were openly caring and compassionate rather than put-downish and elitist.

Given the crude way that members of the New Left assaulted the dominant cultural assumptions of the societies in which they lived (both in the United States and Europe) and the way that this New Left found little to praise and much to denounce in the history and present reality of America, it is not hard to understand why many Americans felt personally assaulted and demeaned, as well as outraged at the absence of respect for the country in which they believed. So even when they could agree with parts of the Left's analysis, they felt angry and assaulted and in need of protection from these critics.

Some of the harshness in the New Left's critique can be attributed to the fact that "the Left" of the 1960s and early 1970s was primarily a youth movement. As such, it had an important generational component, in the form of young adults rebelling against what they perceived to be the failures of their parents' generation ("Don't trust anyone over thirty")—and this came with its own brand of "I know better than you because I'm younger and hipper and more in tune with what's really in the future than you are." But for many in the society, the assault was remembered not as that of brash twenty-year-olds but as their only encounter with liberals and "the Left." It was an encounter that left deep psychic scars on many who had felt pushed "up against the wall" by the abrasiveness of this critique of virtually every aspect of American society.

That upset was shared by many people under thirty who resented having their whole generation spoken for by radicals and social change activists whose values and political orientation they did not share. Millions of them in their teens and twenties saw that their whole way of being was being "dissed" by these liberals and progressives, who frequently made them feel that their worldview was reactionary and essentially racist, sexist, and xenophobic. And they resented the characterizations and the invisibility imposed upon them by the media and by the liberals. Many of these would play a leadership role in the development of the Religious Right and the return to power of the political Right in the following decades.

In almost every sphere, from environmentalism to economic justice, activists persuaded many to join them in the earliest days of the movement, when they were full of utopian energy. As they grew more angry and less compassionate, however, activists found that they ceased being able to persuade. Because they blamed and ridiculed those with whom they disagreed, their pointed, rational, and well-evidenced analysis was taken by many Americans as nothing more than a cloak for left-wing condescension and elitism.

It is probably true that many people would have been resistant to progressive arguments no matter how compassionate the spirit of those who tried to inform them about American imperialism, racism, and sexism. We will never know for sure. What we do know is that the attitude of disdain and condescension conveyed by the Left at the time when the Left was at its highest visibility (the late sixties and early seventies) left a lasting impression. Millions of Americans who eventually came to agree with the Left's message on issues like racism, sexism, and the war in Vietnam nevertheless felt put down and dismissed by the proponents of social change.

The crusading flavor of the Left's approach to its issues manifested in a lack of tolerance for difference and frequent insistence by vocal social change groups that people who were not 100 percent in agreement with the Left's positions on sexism or racism or homophobia were actually "the enemy." This made it easy for right-wingers in the 1980s and 1990s to characterize the whole progressive movement as attempting to impose a totalitarian agenda that those on the Right labeled "political correctness." "PC" became a term of popular derision, a way of reminding the Left that no matter how smart its ideas were, its way of approaching people had bombed. Conversely, putting down the Left for its elitism and abusive style protected many Americans from the anxiety that people experience when they momentarily glimpse the possibility of a world based on kindness and love. That anxiety at the thought that they might open themselves up to hope and once again be disappointed and humiliated, as they had been so many times in their lives, gave people an unconscious motive to intensify their anger at leftists who seemed to have no respect or compassion for the emotional complexities in the lives of ordinary Americans.

Recognizing that something was deeply wrong in the way they had been doing politics, yet lacking the tools to correct it, many of those inspired by social change movements withdrew into personal life, some imagining that they could make their best contribution to social healing by working on their own psyches, some believing that their own professional lives as doctors, lawyers, teachers, social workers, scientists, union organizers, or government employees might provide a more effective conduit for their idealism than the Left had proved to be, still others simply burnt out and despairing of politics and believing that the only kind of loving society they would ever see would be that which they might create in their own families. Lacking a spiritual vision that could combine compassion for one's own limitations with an ongoing commitment to transcendent ideals, it was hard for many of the progressive activists of this period to sustain a social movement that had revealed itself to be, alas, human and partially flawed.

EIGHT

From Power to Purposelessness: The Fate of the Democrats

The surge of hopeful energies of the 1960s and 1970s that took the form of the civil rights movement, the antiwar movement, the women's movement, and the counterculture rippled through the society, at once generating excitement about new possibilities (and liberating creative energies in music, poetry, fiction, film, and almost every other sphere of human creativity) and fear (that all that people had relied upon for stability in their lives might suddenly come crashing down around them). The attraction of social movements with a utopian vision led some in the mainstream churches to ally themselves politically with the Left, and it also challenged right-wing Christians to find their own way to attract the baby-boomer generation to commit to something beyond personal fulfillment and success in the capitalist marketplace. Evangelical energies that seemed on the wane in the middle of the twentieth century were revitalized and gained new ground as those who could not identify with the Left sought some other way to reconnect with their own higher callings. A revitalized Religious Right would play an important role in reversing what appeared in the 1960s to be a kind of unstoppable surge of energy toward social transformation, moving that energy toward the political Right.

The Campus Crusade for Christ provides an excellent example of how the spiritual energy of the sixties became channeled into religion, moved rightward, and eventually was taken over by the political Right. The Campus Crusade for Christ sprang up just as the Left was dissolving into recriminations and self-blaming. It fed off the antiauthoritarian consciousness and desire for self-exploration that had been fostered by the social change movements. The Campus Crusade for Christ simply took those ideas one step further, helping people see that, if they looked deeply enough, they would find a spiritual need that could not be satisfied by the secular political movements or even by the newly emerging 1970s New Age consciousness or by self-exploration grounded purely in psychological theory. What the Campus Crusade recognized was that people were not only interested in exploration but were also looking for direction. So it put forward deep questions that pushed young people to ask, "Who am I, really? What is the purpose of my life?" Fully aware of the antiauthoritarianism that had become central to the cultural critique promoted by the Left, which found fertile ground in the individualism of American culture, the CCC aligned itself with the notion that "You don't have to take any official religious answers for these questions for granted—these are your personal issues and you need to explore them and see what fits for you" while simultaneously suggesting that "If you really think these through, you'll find that there are some timeless truths that you can access by studying a text that others have used when they faced these questions—the Bible."

Like the small consciousness-raising groups in the women's movement and the small groups that had been used in the Student Nonviolent Coordinating Committee (SNCC) and by the early organizers of Students for a Democratic Society (SDS), the Campus Crusade organized itself around small group discussions in which people were encouraged to share about their own lives and experiences. But these groups were often led by well-trained group leaders who affirmed strong religious principles, were committed to the authority of the Bible, and had great impact in leading the discussions toward fuller commitment to orthodox Christian religious perspectives.

In its early days, the Campus Crusade for Christ was primarily a spiritual movement. But the positive energy it released also sought to find a more political expression, and the genius of the Right was to tie that desire to a very narrow right-wing interpretation of Christianity. That version of the Christian tradition championed sexual restraint and traditional gender roles as the vehicle for achieving the sanctity of family life, as well as support for the sacredness of all life, which soon slipped into the doctrine of the sanctity of the fetus. Playing on a deep sense that the sexual freedom of the sixties, the undermining of patriotism, and the exclusive focus on personal freedom and autonomy had gone too far and had produced chaos rather than loving relationships, the Campus Crusade for Christ became a powerful recruiting ground for a Religious Right that would increasingly dominate the politics of the 1980s, as it continues to do today.

Nothing gave more powerful impetus to this development than the identification with the fetus and the resistance to *Roe v. Wade.* The Pill had freed women to have sexual relationships of their own choosing inside or outside the bonds of marriage without fearing disastrous personal consequences like having to raise an unwanted child. For some men reared with patriarchal expectations, this new freedom for women was very threatening, particularly for those men whose powerlessness in the rest of their lives made their relationships with women the only sphere in which they could experience power at all.

For many women, of course, the liberation from sexual restraints was experienced as one of the greatest freedoms they could imagine. Many women in our research groups at the Institute for Labor and Mental Health repeated one version or another of the following mantra: "No one is going to tell me what I am going to do with my body—it's mine."

Yet, for others, sexual "freedom" had often been defined by the men in their lives in ugly ways. As a thirty-two-year-old administrative assistant in a government office described the message that men were giving to many women she knew: "Now that they have the Pill and the last-resort-abortion as a possibility, women should make themselves endlessly available to us sexually and should stop being 'up tight' about sleeping with any man who wants to. It's just about fun and pleasure, so get into it."

The Christian right insisted that sex was not just about fun but about loving commitment, which should be sanctified by holy intention and sacrament. For the Campus Crusade types, sexuality was not to be demeaned as "cursed" or as nothing more than a reminder of Eve's sin—they would affirm sexuality as pleasure within marriage, but they insisted on the commitment part. In that consciousness, abortion was seen as a way for men and women to free themselves from the responsibility of caring for each other, and that was one reason for this group's intense feelings of opposition to abortion.

Yet there was also another level to the energy that the Christian Right gave to abortion, which *Tikkun* magazine's associate editor, Peter Gabel, pointed out. Peter has been my primary collaborator in developing the politics of meaning and many of the ideas in this book. I've been greatly influenced by his insistence that people's longing for mutual recognition and connection to each other is frequently coupled with melancholy resignation to the idea that such longing is utopian and cannot be fulfilled in this world. Yet the desire for this connection remains a driving force in the unconscious lives of most Americans.

Part of the energy of the antiabortion movement, Gabel argued, comes from its ability to symbolically address this desire. The fetus is a symbol of an idealized, innocent being, actually the little child within us, who is not being adequately loved and accepted in our daily experience. The desire to be loved and accepted as human beings—a completely rational desire—is split off by these antiabortionists, in part because they themselves (like so many of the rest of us in this society) have been taught to view that part of themselves as scary, unobtainable, and narcissistic. Acknowledging it would require getting in touch with our anger at all of the things that prevent us and have always prevented us from getting that love and recognition. So instead we project this desire onto the fetus, which is then conceptualized as the idealized and pure version of ourselves—an innocent and perfect unborn creature, and, because unborn, not yet sullied by the world. Those who felt conflicted about standing up for themselves when, as children, they did not receive the love and recognition they badly needed, and deeply wounded because no one stood up for them when they were vulnerable as children, can now symbolically stand up for the beautiful part of themselves, which was underappreciated, by standing up for this fetus.

It may have been a similar dynamic that made possible in the spring of 2005 a sudden explosion of concern to save the life of Terri Schiavo, a woman who had been in a vegetative state for fifteen years and hence could be experienced as both pure and helpless, by people who had shown no similar interest in saving the lives of tens of thousands of Iraqi civilians killed over the six previous months as "collateral damage" during the American invasion and occupation.

But because this projection and process of idealization involves an evasion and denial of the actual pain in our own lives, it is accompanied by another split from consciousness—a denial of the rage and hatred that people carry within themselves all their lives to the extent that they live lives in which their fundamental humanity is not fully confirmed or was not adequately confirmed when they were children. So what to do with that rage? In the case of some right-wing antiabortion activists, Gabel argues, that rage is directed against a demonized Other whose humanity is ignored or denied, transformed by imagination into the "murderers" killing little babies—or, in other instances, against the evil criminals who must be executed, the drug addicts upon whom we must wage war, the Muslims or terrorists who are imagined to be posed to take over the world unless we forcibly stop them, the liberal judges who are willing to allow Schiavo to die, or whoever else pops up as a possible target for their anger and who appears in their minds as the slaughterers of the innocent.

This may help explain how it is possible for so many "pro-lifers" to fanatically oppose abortion and yet support the death penalty and American militarism. At the rational level these views may seem inconsistent, but at the deeper psychological level they are expressive of the same distorted dynamic. As Gabel told me, "Both the unborn fetus and the evil 'other' are imaginary constructs that carry an unconscious meaning, reflecting repression of people's most fundamental social need."

In short, the anger at not being adequately recognized by parents and others when we were children and our inability to articulate, at that time or subsequently, either to others or to ourselves, our rage at not being affirmed for who we really are but only for how we might fulfill the needs and expectations of others, along with the anger at living in a society that systematically frustrates our desire to connect to a higher purpose in our lives, led to a free-floating rage that the antiabortion movement harnessed into defense of the fetus.

I do not mean to suggest that there are not other, quite rational, reasons to be concerned about the escalating level of abortions or to want to find ways to provide good alternatives. I myself, a strong opponent of any attempts to place legal constraints on abortion, share with many other Americans a deep dismay at the high number of abortions each year and believe that progressives should be working to make abortions rare (in ways that I'll discuss in the next section of this book). But the specific form that the antiabortion movement has taken—its bizarre combination of "pro-life" activism on abortion with what seems to be a complete lack of interest in promoting policies that could be called pro-life when it came to militarism, the death penalty, or adequate support for children once born—cannot be understood solely in terms of the rational desire to reduce the number of abortions. While I honor those in the Catholic Church who not only talk about the "seamless garment of life" but who have actually fought against the Iraq war, the death penalty, and the Bush administration's budget cuts to programs that would support the life of the baby once born, the fact is that the overwhelming majority of those Catholics and Protestants who claim to care for the life of the fetus have demonstrated deep hypocrisy in electing politicians who implement government policies, like war and the death penalty, that destroy life and who slash funding for programs that could serve the needs of the fetus once it is born as a child.

Nor can it be rationally explained how this issue would become the defining issue for a religious renewal, given its rather minor role in the teachings of Jesus or in the history of Christianity. It's only when we understand this symbolic function of the fetus as a way that many have found to indirectly stand up for the purity and innocence inside themselves that was never adequately defended when they were young and unprotected that we get a more sympathetic account of the pain that underlies some of the murderous violence and hatred that some "pro-life" demonstrators have exhibited at times.

But once it became a central focus for a religious renewal, it was not hard to understand why those involved would be seeking a way to have their antiabortion perspective turned into actual legislation. And that would require political power.

Enter the developing New Right that was seeking new direction after the marginalization of conservative thought following the landslide defeat of right-wing Republican Barry Goldwater in the 1964 presidential election. Unhappy with the kind of Republicanism represented by Richard Nixon (who, in part to protect his ability to wage war in Vietnam, had signed into law environmental and worker safety regulations that were anathema to corporate interests), the conservative movement had entered into a period of serious self-criticism and reconstruction. That movement had lacked a source of energy and vision to cover its rather narrow self-interested procorporate agenda. An alliance with the Christian Right would provide it with a new life. In the Christian Right's rage against abortion, the political Right saw an energy that could be leveraged.

It would have been a difficult alliance if the Christian Right retained Jesus's priority commitment to social justice for the poor. It was precisely this commitment that had led many Catholic priests in Central and South America in the 1970s and 1980s to develop a liberation theology that set them against the interests of the large landowners with whom the Church had traditionally been in alliance. But in North America concern for the poor and powerless among the Christian Right most frequently took the form of individual acts of charity; a given church might support a mission to the poor in which assistance was laced with evangelizing for the sake of recruitment to Jesus, rather than support for governmental programs like universal health care or a higher minimum wage or support for the right of workers to organize and collectively bargain or support for governmental health-and-safety legislation. Instead, the interest of those on the Christian Right was largely restricted to issues of personal life, challenging feminists and eventually gays and lesbians, as they argued in favor of what they called a "pro-family" vision.

The Christian Right, it turned out, would not challenge the fat cats of the political Right and in fact would be happy for their support. Similarly, the champions of corporations and the ruling elite did not feel threatened by the Christian Right's focus on the family. After all, the rich can fly to other countries for their abortions and prefer not to talk about their intimate relationships anyway.

When the energy of these idealistic Christians joined with the economic politics of the political Right, they created an unholy merger of corporate power and Christian fervor. The Left generated much of the energy of the sixties, but it was the Right that took that energy and brought it to electoral politics. It was the Right, not the Left, that understood the power of Spirit and the extent to which people need to have meaning in their lives. As the Christian Right created a wide network of study groups that included prayer and affirmation of their shared spiritual truth and linked up with conservative think tanks funded by people who recognized the importance of integrating a political focus with a religious and spiritual focus, the power of the political Right grew, while the power of the political Left waned.

The Right could never have come to power again, particularly after the twin debacles of the war in Vietnam and Watergate, without the tremendous failure of the Democratic Party to harness the legacy of hopeful energy that had been released in the 1960s.

The story you hear told in history books and TV documentaries gets it all wrong. That conventional story goes like this: the Democrats were captured by the New Left in the primaries of the 1972 election, and their politics, articulated by George McGovern, were resoundingly rejected by the American public, which embraced the reelection of Richard Nixon. In this telling, the trauma of that defeat has shaped Democrats ever since, forcing them to be realistic and choose their most conservative candidates for future national elections.

But that's not what happened. From the standpoint of social change activists, the 1972 election barely mobilized a fraction of their attention. The McGovernites who took power in the 1972 Democratic Party may have been the left-wing of the party, but they were the right-wing of the social change movements, most of which gave little credence in 1972 to electoral politics of any sort. Their concern about liberal politics was confirmed immediately after the Democratic Convention, when, as if to formally concretize the notion that liberals were unreliable and never fought for principles when under attack, McGovern abandoned his own vice-presidential nominee, Thomas Eagleton, after it was revealed that Eagleton had years before been hospitalized for depression. Instead of using this as a moment to identify with all those who had ever suffered from depression and to challenge the stigma connected with seeking mental health services, McGovern opportunistically pressured Eagleton to resign from the ticket. This was a man who would supposedly symbolize the vision of a new way of doing politics?

Moreover, while it was true that the liberals in the party had been able to change party rules and select George McGovern as the nominee, the party hacks quickly took control of the candidate and his message, totally undermining the intent of the liberals to give antiwar energies an electoral focus. The hacks convinced McGovern that he must run his campaign on economic issues and in particular focus on reassuring Wall Street that, should he be elected, he would not make any radical assault on corporate power. The antiwar forces that had secured the nomination for McGovern were totally sidelined within a month of the convention.

I was at the time a member of the national leadership group of the National Coalition for Peace and Justice, an umbrella group that brought together a wide variety of peace organizations. So in early September 1972 I met with McGovern aide Gary Hart (later to become a U.S. senator and subsequently a presidential candidate himself) to urge a return to the antiwar focus. I found him totally dispirited at having lost any influence on the shape of the campaign and despairing at the stupidity and crass opportunism that had led McGovern to listen to "the professionals" who advised that the campaign totally avoid the issue of the war—which it mostly did throughout September and October!

For the millions of social change activists who had been energized by the movements of hope, the McGovern campaign seemed to be an embodiment of the wimpy and unprincipled politics that had led so many to become disillusioned with liberals in the past. The television ads bought by the McGovern campaign in the months preceding the election mostly avoided mention of the war in Vietnam, or racism, or sexism, or inequalities of power and wealth. Yet once the campaign was over, the media and the establishment Democrats rushed in to draw the false conclusion that the left's politics had been given a chance and had proven to be a losing path for a party seeking national power.

Armed with this story, the media convinced many voters in 1976 that they must be responsible and choose the least radical, the most timid and conventional, among the major contenders for the Democratic Party nomination, a born-again Christian farmer from Georgia, Jimmy Carter.

In the years following his presidency Carter has distinguished himself as a fighter for human rights and peace, and that is how he deserves to be remembered. But that was not what he was about in the years when he actually had power as president of the United States and was shaping the country's vision of what Democrats in power would fight for. Carter was a representative of the "New South," a governor of Georgia who opposed segregation and supported the liberal pro-inclusion agenda for those who had been left out of America's economic success. He ran on a platform calling for nuclear disarmament, which seemed politically feasible at that moment following the American defeat in Vietnam, the exposure of the lies told by the military and intelligence communities, the dishonorable departure of Richard Nixon, and the election of powerful Democratic majorities to Congress.

For those tens of millions of Americans who had been imbued with an antiwar consciousness, the promise of nuclear disarmament was a significant reason to take electoral politics seriously and to reengage with the idea that a transformed Democratic Party might become a vehicle for their hopes. But within months of his election, Carter unilaterally abandoned this promise and began to cater to the professionals and Washington insiders who taught him to rethink any antiwar inclinations he had within the context of the alleged need to show strength in the face of the "Soviet threat."

The alleged "present danger" that conservatives sought to revive in public consciousness as they fought against what they labeled the "Vietnam syndrome" (namely, the desire to end militarism and seek global peace and disarmament) was, as subsequent studies have shown, a fantasy generated by right-wing think tanks: at no point in the 1970s was the Soviet Union militarily prepared to engage in war with the United States. The Soviet Union did support liberation struggles that the United States opposed and did insist, like the imperial power it was, on controlling the countries within its geographic sphere. But the Soviet Union was not a real geopolitical threat to the United States itself.

In fact, the 1970s offered a unique historical moment for a liberal president to build a whole new way of thinking about the role of America in the world. Such a transformation in thinking could have started by acknowledging that the war in Vietnam had been a tragic error, that many of the real patriots were those who had the courage to reveal the lies, to protest the interventions, to resist participation in an immoral venture, to offer amnesty for war and draft resisters, and in the name of the political party that had opposed the war in the 1970s to welcome home and provide emotional support for Vietnam vets.

Carter could have then gone on to insist that the United States take a new path in the world, one that would have accelerated the aspirations for democracy and freedom in the communist world by showing that America was ready for a world of peace. A principled liberal would have reversed American support for dictatorial regimes like that of the Shah of Iran, supported the Frei social democratic party forces emerging in Chile, developed an economic boycott of the Argentine generals, fought for universal health care and child care, and proposed a comprehensive plan to convert military production to domestic projects without causing huge unemployment. Such an agenda would have revived the hopeful energies of the previous years.

Sadly, Carter capitulated to the program of the militarists in the Pentagon and the Committee on the Present Danger. Instead of developing a comprehensive plan for disarmament and implementing it through his role as commander in chief, Carter sought only the most minimal reorientation of the defense budget. He allowed the CIA to support insurgencies against regimes friendly to the Soviet Union, particularly in Afghanistan, thereby signaling to the Soviets that the cold-war mentality still reigned in this country and thereby giving support to the most militarist wing of the Soviet leadership, which decided, insanely and self-destructively, to prop up a Soviet regime on its borders by sending in its own troops to quell a Muslim rebellion, an act that further confirmed to the Cold Warriors that there was indeed a Soviet danger and placed greater pressure on Carter to accede to their view of the world.

Nothing gives greater credibility to the claim that Democrats are unable to defend the U.S. from potential threats than the wishy-washy way Democrats fail to fight for their own beliefs. Having won election, Carter could not fight for what he had said he would stand for, and that made many people wonder how he could possibly stand up to a serious challenge from the Soviet Union if such should occur.

Those baby boomers who looked to Democratic party politics for inspiration and a way to preserve their idealism quickly despaired. This lack of political leadership on the part of Democrats accelerated their own fear that nothing could be done to change things and hence spurred their individual decisions to start looking for professional careers or ways to fit back into a society that had proved less malleable than they had originally believed. The society suffered a deep emotional depression as the hopeful energies of earlier years receded into "business as usual."

Carter himself picked up this feeling and articulated it when he talked of what the media later described as national "malaise" facing the American people. Instead of recognizing that people were in fact suffering the impact of a society-wide depression generated by the loss of hope in the possibility of a world based on peace and justice, Carter blamed the malaise on the American people itself. This misguided articulation hooked into the self-blaming and despair that were already crippling so many Americans after Vietnam.

No wonder, then, that Ronald Reagan's irrepressible humor and promise for a new dawn in American life, a reclaiming of older visions of an America with a purpose and a goal, a nostalgic attempt to revive the memories of a time when America and the world were less complex, seemed so refreshing to many.

Liberals inside the Democratic Party tried to resurrect the progressive vision by running Senator Ted Kennedy of Massachusetts in the primaries, but in some ways this attempt was already too late. The hope of the sixties had largely dissolved, and few could be mobilized to take the Democratic Party seriously as a vehicle for change. Instead, the remnants of the social change movements withdrew into a variety of "localist" politics ("We can't change the big picture, but we will work to promote change in our local community") or identity politics ("We focus on our liberation as African-Americans, Latinos, women, or gays and lesbians because this is the real arena for social change").

Others took some of the inspiration that they had maintained from their years of activism and channeled it into alternative spiritualities, into Transcendental Meditation and the creation of an American style of Buddhism, into Esalen-type explorations of self, into new forms of psychology and theories of personal growth, into a burgeoning interest in alternative medicine, into developing organic foods, and into renewal efforts inside traditional religious communities.

Yet split apart into these many directions, many of them hidden well below the media's radar screen, these energies were barely noticed any longer by the majority of Americans in the 1980s. Instead, cheered on by a media that was increasingly seeking to reposition itself as a "responsible" voice of the political center (a position it fancied itself as having lost because of its self-proclaimed courage at exposing the lies of the American government in relationship to the war in Vietnam), the Christian Right was able to present itself as the new source of vision and energy by the late 1970s and into the 1980s, and has managed to retain that position in public discourse ever since.

The Right in America included many conflicting strands that were woven together by the Reaganites into a powerful political force. There were, to be sure, hard-line economic conservatives whose primary goal was to ensure the wealth of the rich and the power of American corporations. They were joined by a growing constituency of those who resented the advances made by blacks and women, an odd assortment that included Southern whites (some of whom still yearned for the days when blacks "knew their place"), Northern whites who resented the imposition of school busing and the court-ordered integration of ethnic neighborhoods, and many men, particularly in the working class, who felt their economic security and place in the world threatened by affirmative action programs for minorities and women.

Many of these groups would not have felt able to express such retrograde and selfish desires without such desires being linked to a larger framework of meaning and purpose that gave the Right a vision of a better world. For example, rather than openly champion racism and repression, the Right found a way to oppose the advances of women, blacks, and other minorities by claiming that the expansive powers of the capitalist market would right all wrongs—if only, the conservatives argued, it could be freed from the constraints that liberals had placed upon it by trying through social engineering to shackle its creativity.

These economic arguments interested a small part of the population but never were sufficiently convincing to give the Right the energy it needed to become the leading political force. What gave the Right its momentum was its alliance with the Christian Right and the Christian Right's ability to call upon the Right Hand of God. The Christian Right was able to enunciate the existence of a spiritual crisis that most Americans by then felt and to cast it as a crisis in family life. It didn't hurt their cause that they then claimed the crisis was the fault of the liberals and of special interests (read women, blacks, Latinos, homosexuals, Jews, labor unions and liberals).

The Right was able to portray itself as the champion of the family because the Left had little if any clue that there was in fact a real problem. Coming out of the sixties, the Left thought the problem the country faced was an excess of militarism and patriotism. The country needed more rationality and greater cynicism about its actor-turned-president Reagan. A few creative thinkers on the Left talked about shaping a patriotism that could celebrate the way people's struggles were at the heart of what should make Americans genuinely proud of our history. Howard Zinn's *A People's History of the United States* highlighted this approach on an intellectual level, and Jeremy Rifkin's attempts to create a progressive alternative to the bicentennial celebration of July 4, 1976, on a more activist level. But most liberals and progressives had little interest in addressing the ever-more-pressing meaning needs that were shaping American politics. They countered those needs with cynical arguments about the sexism of pro-life politics and the racism of trickle-down economics. The Left got the facts right, but they missed the message.

It's hard now to believe how cynical the Left was in the 1970s and 1980s. For example, we at the Institute for Labor and Mental Health decided to respond to the Right's new emphasis on the family by putting together our own progressive organization called Friends of Families, insisting that to be a friend of the family also required support for single-parent families and gay and lesbian families as well as support for flexible work schedules, health care, child care, and more. Co-chaired by Betty Friedan and Benjamin Spock, Friends of Families sponsored a series of "Family Day" celebrations to promote our alternative analysis. Yet we were assaulted by many on the Left who explicitly called Friends of Families a sell-out to the Right and insisted that any support for family was necessarily reactionary! Even those on the Left who didn't openly attack us thought that we didn't "get it." "Why bother mucking around with 'quality of life' issues," they argued, "when Reagan will be defeated once the American people see how his economic programs undercut their own economic well-being?"

Perhaps the Left's newly cynical belief that people would act primarily on their economic interests explains why the Democratic

Congress decided to capitulate to the Reagan tax cuts and to cooperate with much of the Reagan program—maybe they thought that the suffering that came out of that misguided economic program would lead to Reagan's defeat. I was told by the national president of the AFL-CIO that the labor movement had no interest in hearing about the spiritual needs of its members. After all, the Democrats were bound to defeat Reagan in 1984 because his economics had failed so badly and hurt so many working people.

They were wrong.

Many Americans cared less than liberals expected that no money trickled down to them. They reelected Ronald Reagan because his message made them feel good about themselves and connected to a vision of America they could be proud of.

By not standing up to Reagan or offering an equally spiritual message in answer to his powerful vision of America, the Democrats became irrelevant. Worse, Americans perceived the party of the Left as spineless, gutless, and visionless. Ever since Goldwater's defeat in 1964 the New Right had been developing think tanks and intellectual journals to promote a coherent worldview based on the notion that human freedom would be enhanced by dismantling "big government." Briefly, their argument is that significant tax cuts will stimulate the economy by prompting the rich benefactors of these tax cuts to use their extra money to increase consumer spending directly or to increase investment in corporations that in turn will increase production (either way, thereby increasing employment).

Meanwhile, they argue, government should be pared down to the barest of necessities, with its main role being the defense of our nation. With the economy freed from the constraints of government—including environmental constraints and health-and-safety regulations, a higher minimum wage, or taxes to fund health care, Social Security, and retirement programs—capitalism will be unshackled and then be able to work its magic. And government will play the minimal role of making sure that regimes abroad open themselves to American corporate penetration, which, the Right argues, not only will benefit the United States directly, because corporations will acquire new markets, but also will benefit the peoples of these countries, who will gain employment at wages higher than they would otherwise be able to achieve.

From 1980, when Ronald Reagan was elected, to 1994, when they lost their majority in the House, and still to this day, the Democrats have failed to present a coherent alternative vision to this Republican economic program. As the remnants of the New Left of the 1960s and 1970s became increasingly focused on identity politics or on single-issue campaigns, from ending the nuclear arms race to increasing the minimum wage, creating a unified vision seemed less pressing.

In fact, many of the intellectuals of the Left bought into a new philosophical movement, deconstruction, that denied the possibility that there could be any coherent universalist theory of the good. At best, they said, all the Left could hope for were alliances on particular issues.

Lacking a unifying vision or a coherent ideology with which to counter the increasingly well-oiled idea machine of right-wing think tanks, backed by the Republicans' friends in the media and their ability to support right-wing students on campus, the Democrats did what they could to try to paste together a coalition of disparate (and sometimes antagonistic) groups. Jesse Jackson, a former lieutenant of Martin Luther King Jr., tried to revive the left wing of the Democrats with his image of a rainbow, creating what he called a "Rainbow Coalition" to unite the Left's disparate pieces into one whole. At the Democratic Convention in 1988, where Jackson gave a speech outlining his perspective, he suggested that the Rainbow Coalition could go so far as to include both "hawks and doves," as though clarity meant nothing— What, after all, could a voter expect a political party to do once in office if it represented both Martin Luther King Jr.'s commitment to nonviolence and neocon visions of using violence to spread American power?—and getting everyone inside the Democratic Party electoral tent meant everything.

This lack of clarity, however, does not go over well with anyone. Instead of widening the tent and making people feel welcome, it makes people feel that politicians are only interested in power and will say anything to get it. For example, later that year, when Democratic Party candidate Michael Dukakis, who was a supporter of the ACLU and a self-proclaimed liberal, was asked by the press if he was in fact a liberal and a supporter of the ACLU, he hemmed and hawed. Dukakis was unwilling to speak proudly about his beliefs, which only solidified further the certainty so many Americans had that the Democrats stood for nothing but getting power for what the Republicans called "special interests" (even though it was the Republicans who were in fact championing the most powerful special interest: corporate power and the rich).

It was only when Bill and Hillary Clinton managed to articulate a different kind of theme in the 1992 election that there was momentarily a possibility that energy might shift from the side of fear to a renewed commitment to the common good. After the Dukakis defeat in 1988, I had written an extensive analysis of the failure of the Democrats to address the hunger for meaning or to provide a coherent worldview as an alternative to the ethos of selfishness and materialism that the Republicans embraced in their slavish championing of the interests of the rich. I explained why the Democrats needed a politics of meaning that would counter the Right. I didn't have the language at the time, but I really was calling on the Left to embrace the Left Hand of God to counter the way the Right had embraced the Right Hand of God. I wanted the Left to reclaim a vision of hope and to use that hope to drive a spiritual progressive politics.

I didn't pay much attention when a young governor from Arkansas named Bill Clinton wrote me, quite out of the blue. I had no idea he was reading *Tikkun,* the magazine I helped create as a voice for spiritual politics that could disseminate the information we were gathering at the Institute for Labor and Mental Health about the psychodynamics of American society. Clinton told me that he had been quite influenced by my perspective. I was at that point so cynical about the lack of vision of the Democrats that I couldn't imagine that they were about to change. I filed the letter away and ignored the weekly reports his office sent me about what a great job Clinton was doing in Arkansas.

Imagine my surprise in 1992 when I was invited to a meeting of national Jewish leaders with Clinton and there heard him give a speech about the politics of meaning that was quoting virtually word for word from my own editorials of the past years.

When I went up to introduce myself, Clinton not only acknowledged that he was still using this material but also quoted word for word from other articles he had been reading in *Tikkun.* He also told me that he would like me to become more deeply involved with his campaign. As I traveled to hear other speeches, I heard him articulate a consistent theme of spiritual politics: that it was time to move from fear to hope, and from selfishness and materialism to a genuine ethos of generosity and caring for each other. As a major part of how that would be done, Clinton promised a health care plan to cover the tens of millions of poorer Americans who had no coverage and who often relied on hospitals' emergency care facilities, usually at high cost to the taxpayers because the care they sought came only after illnesses had gotten to the point beyond which preventive, relatively simple treatments might have worked.

Many of those who cheered excitedly were not themselves lacking in health care plans—what excited them was the notion of being part of a movement focused on caring for one another.

What was even more astounding was that while these talks produced huge swells of enthusiasm and wakened dormant hopefulness in millions, the media barely covered a word of it. Instead, they listened to the slogan of Clinton adviser James Carville, who explained Clinton's surging popularity by claiming, "It's the economy, stupid." The media and the Democratic establishment got the message that what people "really" cared about was that the policies of President George H. W. Bush—actually, the cumulative impact of right-wing policies under Reagan—were not working. They never got the message that Americans wanted a spiritual politics of hope to replace the Religious Right's politics of fear.

For the media and its hard-boiled political insiders, politics is a game like football, and reportage is about cynically tearing down ideas to show them to be mere pretexts for self-interested candidates to advance toward the goal of winning an election. They dismiss idealistic talk as a way of manipulating the ignorant public for the sake of power. Yet the public is not ignorant. They wanted to hear someone speak to their meaning needs. The Clinton message was the first time they had heard a Democratic Party politician proclaim a vision of plausible idealism since John F. Kennedy in the early 1960s, some thirty years before.

Clinton told me he was translating my politics of meaning into a discourse that could work in the election, and indeed it did. On election night, when Bill and Hillary Clinton and Al and "Tipper" Gore danced on the stage in celebration of their victory, the newly elected president promised again a serious move forward to a new society of caring and generosity.

But to the mainstream political analysts and their followers in the Democratic Party, the Congress, and the mass media, the Clinton victory was little more than a reflection of the basic truth that people care about their own economic self-interest and had voted out the Republicans because Republicans were not delivering employment and material well-being. They didn't question this assumption or ask why it had been that sections of the country who had suffered economically under Reagan continued to vote for Reagan and then Bush. Nor would they ask at the end of the Clinton administration, why the tens of millions who had benefited materially from the economic expansion under Clinton didn't vote on economic concerns again in 2000.

For most of these "common sense" ideologues, the idea that people might have as strong a desire to care for others as to advance their own economic interests would simply "not compute." Such an idea fell too far outside the realm of what they most deeply believed about the world. So it was inexplicable and disturbing to these media cynics and policy hard hats that, immediately after the 1992 election, polls indicated skyrocketing support for Clinton's call for universal health care. In particular, what challenged the cynics' religion—namely, their belief that all that is real is money and material self-interest—was the repeated and growing willingness of Americans to say that they would be willing to see their taxes or their health care premiums rise in order to provide funds to pay for universal health care coverage.

What was happening, of course, was that energy was suddenly moving, actually exploding, toward hope and possibility, and as societal energy moves in that direction, more and more people begin to abandon the safety of narrow self-interest and allow themselves to imagine being part of a different kind of world.

When energy flows toward hope in a sudden rush of enthusiasm, however, a corresponding negative energy is elicited inside everyone. The voices of fear jump into the fray, reminding people of all the times they have been abandoned and betrayed in the past when they trusted in others, and particularly of the humiliations that they have gone through for hoping in the possibility of a different kind of world. The disappointments of the sixties, especially, were in the back of many voters' minds. This fear was mobilized by the Right, which opposed universal health care because it would diminish the profits of health care corporations and threaten to offer free and legal abortions, and by the media, which had a stake in believing any idealistic program was really a cover for power.

Eventually, fear triumphed in reversing the early enthusiasm for the Clintons and for their health care plan. People on the Left often point to the unbelievably hostile coverage given to the Clintons in their first months in office, totally unlike the coverage given to Reagan or either of the Bushes. In fact, it was even more vitriolic than the media attention George W. received in 2000 when he got into office despite not winning a majority of the popular vote. It's incredible, looking back, to believe that the nation's business was halted while the media criticized Bill Clinton for delaying an airplane flight for an hour, having an expensive haircut, or firing some support staff in the travel office. Personal tragedies like the suicide of a staffer were turned into scandals without merit, including the largest of these, an allegation that the Clintons scammed money in Arkansas—an allegation that proved to be entirely false. Historians will shake their heads when they compare these fictions to the real scandals of the current Republican administration. Republican scandals—Bush's avoidance of military service, the links of members of his cabinet to firms profiting from the war in Iraq, Bush's personal connections to Enron, and so forth—have gone almost unnoticed. Seeing all this, the Left has claimed that right-wing ownership of the media guaranteed that Clinton would have a rough ride while Republicans would be given endless honeymoons.

Despite the media bias, the Clintons were still in a position to lead the country to significant change. Unfortunately, they themselves fell victim to internal doubts about what support they could generate from the American people. The Clintons, like everyone else in the society, struggled with their own internal alternation between the voice of fear and the voice of hope. Bill Clinton was receptive to the voice of hope, but he also felt an almost obsessive need to read poll results, evidently imagining that if he stayed close enough to what people were saying they wanted in these polls he would retain the confidence of the American people.

The meaning of poll results, however, is not always so clear, and how we read them is almost always shaped by our own inner voices. The media assault on Clinton during his first few months in office had a powerful impact, strengthening the new president's voice of fear. As a result, Clinton would start an idealistic project and then back down.

For example, he took a courageous step forward by announcing his intention to allow gays into the military, but then quickly backed down when his pollsters told him the public wasn't ready to support it. The policy he backed into, "Don't ask, don't tell," has had the effect of keeping gays out of the military and has in some ways made life more difficult for gay soldiers. This is the way fear undoes hope.

It was in the midst of these kinds of struggles that Hillary Rodham Clinton had a moment of conscience in which she asked herself why she was being so narrowly pragmatic instead of speaking her deepest truth. The day before her first major speech as First Lady, she had visited her father, who was on the verge of death. Instead of giving the speech she had planned on health care, she threw away the written speech and spoke from her heart, and as a result made the most powerful anticapitalist speech ever heard from an occupant of the White House. "The market," she told her thousands of listeners, "knows the price of everything, but the value of nothing." She went on to say that what the country needs is the Politics of Meaning.

Her words were astounding because she was articulating a spiritual politics at a time when the vast majority of official spokespeople for the Democrats did not even have an inkling of the need to address the spiritual dimension of human needs. In fact, the only place on the Left where anyone could read about a spiritual politics was *Tikkun,* a fact quickly noted by the *New Republic.*

The *New Republic* had started out as a magazine of progressives but had changed dramatically under the leadership of Martin Peretz, a former liberal who was quite reasonably angered by anti-Semitic rhetoric he encountered from a handful of black radicals in 1967. And so he had gone on from there to reject much of the liberals' peace and affirmative action agendas, becoming a foreign policy hawk and a blind supporter of the Israeli occupation of the West Bank and Gaza. Peretz and his sidekick Leon Wieseltier had shaped the *New Republic* into the mother of all cynical media. Peretz had been a close ally of Al Gore. He was disappointed when Bill Clinton, someone he considered a country bumpkin, had become president while his Harvard student and protégé was merely vice president. Peretz had, however, hoped that Gore would for all practical purposes run domestic policy under Clinton and was shocked and angered when Hillary stepped forward to take command of Bill Clinton's major domestic initiative, health care, along with much else.

Hillary Clinton's speech seemed to present a golden opportunity for Peretz to strike out against the First Lady, perhaps enabling critics to dislodge her from her domestic policy role. But not only that. Criticizing her speech gave Peretz the opportunity to reassert the religion of much of the media: a deep commitment to cynical realism and the Right Hand of God, whose ideological roots they hide from themselves by deluding themselves into the belief that they are merely practicing media objectivity. And strike out is just what the *New Republic* did, with a series of attack pieces that, purporting not to understand what a desire for meaning in one's life could be about or how it could possibly be connected to the social and economic institutions of a society, went after Hillary Clinton herself and the very idea of a politics of meaning.

Other parts of the media followed suit. Unable to critique the substance of the claim that there was a deep spiritual hunger for something more than money or power or fame, the media simply ignored the claim and focused on me as the editor of *Tikkun* and my alleged power over Hillary Clinton! The *Washington Post* ran a series by former *New Republic* writer Charles Krauthammer called "Home Alone," the thesis of which was that poor Hillary's attraction to a spiritual politics was an adolescent identity crisis. In a feature that appeared in the Styles section, the *Post* outdid its normal cynicism by running a full-page article about me titled "The Guru of the White House," in which I was compared to Svengali, to Rasputin, and to the séance leader who had advised Nancy Reagan. The theme of my alleged power over the First Lady was picked up by the *Wall Street Journal,* the *New York Times, Newsweek, People,* and by hundreds of other media sources (not to mention the daily denunciations of Hillary Clinton and me by radio host Rush Limbaugh, whose book *See, I Told You So* devoted an entire chapter to the topic of "Lernerism" and "Rodhamism."

Anyone who knows Hillary Clinton knows how ludicrous this charge was. It was true that she had invited me to the White House, that she had quoted my ideas and identified with them, and that she had told me that she was going to work with me to ensure that the Clinton White House would become a bully pulpit for the politics of meaning. It was true that she had asked a staff member to ask me to vet all my public talks and writings on the politics of meaning with the White House staff. But it was also true that my ideas then, like the ideas in this book, came directly out of the great spiritual and religious wisdom of the past. Hillary Clinton did not need me to come to these ideas. Rather, one of the first things she told me was that she became engaged in these questions of spirit and meaning during her own teenage years as a Methodist youth activist and that she quoted my articles in *Tikkun* about a politics of meaning only because she found there a clear articulation and application to politics of spiritual views she had responded to and held all her life.

This whole episode concerning my role in Hillary Clinton's political life was a tiny moment that might have had no lasting impact but for the fact that it coincided with a deep struggle going on in the White House between a set of "realists," who were trying to convince Clinton that he should wise up and play insider politics, and a set of advisors who advocated a more "populist" strategy, telling Clinton to "go over the heads of the insiders" in order to build support for his programs directly with the American people.

I was, of course, in the populist camp, and the attack on my association with Hillary was used by those in the "realist" camp to show the president that going for ideals and sticking up for a visionary approach to the world would be far too costly and likely subject him to ridicule.

So the Clintons withdrew from this path and distanced themselves from me. Not that I had ever been a major part of the Clinton presidency. But I had been given a momentary opportunity to see the dynamics up close.*

---

* Senator Clinton's subsequent transformation from the dove on Israel/Palestine questions, which led her to tell me that she fully identified with my "middle path" position of being both pro-Israel and pro-Palestine and agreed with *Tikkun*'s call for an end to the Israeli occupation of the West Bank, to a hard-line pro-Sharon antagonist to Palestinian rights paralleled her born-again militarism that manifested itself in her support for the war in Iraq. In essence, Clinton has turned her back on the politics of meaning and the Left Hand of God. But that hasn't prevented right-wingers from continuing to try to identify her with such a politics. Consider Jonah Goldberg's attack on November 8, 2004, in the *National Review Online,* in which he analyzed the liberal antagonism toward religion: "What has offended the Left since Marx, and American liberalism since Dewey, is the notion that moral authority should be

There was another possible response, however. Hillary Clinton could have stood up to the critics, dismissed the notion that there was anything wrong with her commitment to a spiritual politics, and, as I had suggested to her, instead make the issue the cynicism of the media. But she told me that she doubted that she would have enough support to do that, while her husband doubted he would have enough support to go directly to the people in support of the health care plan she was developing.

She was already listening to the voice of fear.

And it's true—once you believe that society is all about me-first and who has the most power, you can't use the spiritual power you have. Once you start playing those power games under the Right Hand of God, you lose the ability to speak the language of generosity and compassion in a way that people can hear.

Rather than trying to speak the truth of the Left Hand of God, the Clintons decided that the safer path would be to attempt to work within the constraints of power as it currently existed. They would stop being perceived as visionaries fighting for a fundamentally new way of doing politics. Instead, they would carefully follow the advice of their pollsters and design a health care plan that would play to the interests of everyone and not offend anyone.

And that is just what they did.

The plan that they developed was in fact a monstrosity of accommodationism. Instead of following the single-payer plan that had

---

derived from any place other than the state or 'the people' (conveniently defined as citizens who vote liberal). Voting on values not sanctified by secular priests is how they define 'ignorance.' This was the real goal of Hillary Clinton's 'politics of meaning'—to replace traditional religion with a secular one that derived its authority not from ancient texts and 'superstitions' but from good intentions of an activist state and its anointed priests." But nothing could have been further from Clinton's intent in the brief moment in 1993 when she espoused a politics of meaning. The politics of meaning is an attempt to reintroduce into American politics the spiritual truths that some of us, Clinton and me included, derive from our attachment to God and the inspiration we receive from the ancient texts whose authority we accept (even as we recognize that the meaning of those texts has been a subject of evolving interpretation over the past several thousand years) and to state that truth in a way that allows those who have arrived at those same spiritual truths in ways that do not depend on God to also be part of the community that supports them. My commitment to building a world of worked well in Canada, they devised a plan that would have found a way to enlarge the profits of the insurance industry, the health care middlemen, the hospitals, the medical professionals, and everyone else, at huge expense and with bureaucracy piled on top of bureaucracy.

It was so complicated that almost no one could explain it to their friends or neighbors. But it did seem more aimed at protecting the interests of the profiteers than the interests of the public.

As ordinary citizens watched the Clintons move away from their campaign idealism and begin to allow their positions to be determined by their pollsters, the voice of doubt, of fear, of cynicism, was recharged. Many Americans had reasoned that if this was really going to be a moment in which a new moral community would emerge, a "we" that could reshape American politics, then they wanted to be in that number when the visionaries came marching in. But if that was not what was going to happen—if instead the very person who had promised a time in which selfishness and me-firstism was to be replaced by idealism and caring for others was now letting his own decisions be governed not by idealism but by what the pollsters told him would be in his interests—then why should they, ordinary Americans, be left holding the bag of idealism and face higher taxes or higher health care costs? So the energy that had been flowing toward hope began to flow toward fear, and it was this that led many people to respond to the clever anti–health care advertising of the Right.

---

love, generosity, social justice, and peace derives from my attachment to God. Others derive the same commitment from secular sources or personal experiences. To claim that these are only secular values parading as religious values is as misleading as to claim that they are only religious values masquerading as secular. They are obviously both religious and secular.

The politics of meaning is an attempt to bring the Left Hand of God into politics, not to eliminate but to reclaim a significant role for God's values in the public sphere, yet to do so in a way that does not assert or imply that one must be religious or believe in God in order to be moral or to have a foundation for one's belief in a world of kindness and love.

I only wish that Clinton and other Democrats had the courage to remain committed to the values for which Goldberg and other right-wingers seek to criticize her. The irony is that she, like many of her colleagues in the Democratic Party, are doing everything they can to show that their real commitments are to the Right Hand of

This same dynamic led to the victory of Newt Gingrich and the Right in the 1994 congressional elections. Gingrich was the aggressive minority leader of the House Republicans, and his brilliance lay in catching onto the switch in Clinton's self-presentation from idealist to inside-the-beltway realist. Gingrich picked up where Clinton left off by proposing his own visionary plan—a Contract with America that tied together the Right's worldview and made it the foundation for the 1994 elections. Because Clinton had been unable to get House Democratic leaders to move beyond their own egos far enough to actually pass a health care bill, and because he appeared to have abandoned the language of vision, Clinton was a perfect target for the right-wing politics that Gingrich presented.

I am not writing this history in order to pass judgment on the Clintons. They acted the way most other Democratic Party politicians have acted for the past forty-five years, letting their own perceived self-interest trump their vision of the good. Democrats attempt to be "realists," assessing the political forces and acting as though politics is "the art of the possible."

What the Democrats have consistently failed to recognize is that "the possible" is shaped by our choices. You don't actually know what is possible until you struggle for it.

When we choose to believe that everyone else is stuck in narrow self-interest, this perception leads us to believe that there is no alterna-

---

God, rejecting completely the politics of meaning that she had the courage to espouse for a few months in 1993. A reporter recently asked me whether I thought that Clinton's statements reasserting her religious commitments were merely post-2004 election opportunism. I responded that the religiosity was, in my view, the core of her real self that she had revealed to me and to many others in the early 1990s: I was not the only spiritual person she had run away from when she judged us political liabilities. The real opportunism lay in her abandoning the Left Hand of God. If she returns to those values as she and other Democrats slowly recognize that these values are in fact more likely to be helpful in reconnecting them to an important part of the American electorate, that move, for her, will not be solely an act of opportunism. Rather it will be a return to the core of her being that she opportunistically abandoned out of the same fear that makes so many of us shut our ears to the voice of the Left Hand of God, a fear reinforced by the kind of right-wing distortions of the position that Goldberg so strikingly illustrates.

tive and hence that we ourselves must be careful about our own self-interest.

When this paradigm of fear becomes dominant, politics moves to the Right, toward those who are most articulate about the need for narrow self-interest, and the voices of idealism begin to recede. Vision becomes authoritarian and is all about recreating an imaginary past that was safe and free of the interference of some Other.

If you are on the Left—whether Democrat or Green, liberal or progressive—the strategy of realism is a huge mistake. When you stop asking, "What do I really believe in?" and substitute instead a focus on asking, "What is realistic?" you are on a slippery slope toward the values of materialism and selfishness that receive much clearer statement by the Republicans and the Right. When the question is, "What's realistic?" it is only the Republicans who look like they have the answer. When you believe you must always put "me first" and play the power game, the Republicans will always appear less hypocritical, because they've been fighting for selfishness without apology.

So, watch the Democrats out of power. What is their shared vision? The Right could answer that question even when they were out of power. In fact, they were willing to stay in the position of a minority in order to continue championing their vision of the good—a vision I find uncompelling and even quite distasteful, but a vision nevertheless. But it is impossible to know what the Democrats' vision was in 2000 when Al Gore spoke, or four years later when John Kerry campaigned, just as it is impossible to detect any clear vision coming from the lackluster statements of Democrats today.

Some Democrats jockeying to position themselves for presidential primaries in 2008 or 2012 think they are being savvy by criticizing Bush, often rather mildly, yet also portraying themselves as wanting to "support the troops" in Iraq by voting for huge expenditures and by not calling for an immediate or phased withdrawal with a clear-cut time schedule. This way they imagine they can keep the loyalty of the antiwar forces while simultaneously showing how aligned they are with a Right Hand of God consciousness. But this is the game they've tried for the past several decades, and it has only succeeded in moving the Democrats from the majority to the minority in both houses of

Congress and in reelecting a president widely perceived as presiding over a failing economy and a failing war.

Democrats, to this day, remain confused: they don't understand why their realism hasn't succeeded. However, to those of us who understand the paradigm of hope and fear, the Democrats' defeat makes a lot of sense. If people want to go with the voice of hope, they need to have a framework of support that is strong and unflinching. If we are going to support withdrawal from Iraq or universal health care or any other policy that collides with the interests of economic elites, we are going to face the powerful voices of cynical realism, not only from the media but from our own inner doubts. We want to feel that the political party with which we affiliate has enough backbone to stand up for peace, social justice, and ecological sanity in a way that will support our best selves. No wonder that so many people lose enthusiasm for politics and withdraw into focusing their energies purely on personal issues when they find that the Democrats are ducking for cover and trying to play both sides of the street, and are unwilling to stand up for a principled critique of morally bankrupt policies.

Faced with two parties that are advocates of self-interest, people on the Religious Right will follow the same logic as the midwestern Catholic priest I talked with, who told me why he no longer voted Democratic:

"Neither of these parties really share a high moral vision, but at least the Republicans share our perception of what will strengthen family life and avoid what we consider to be the moral evil of abortion, so we can more wholeheartedly align with them."

If the Democrats are going to win again, they will have to stop being "realistic." They will have to turn instead back to the visionary hopefulness they had in the New Deal and in the early sixties, the kind of hopefulness that makes you willing to fight for your highest ideals and take risks to make them happen.

What I learned from my brief encounters with the Clinton administration confirmed something I had known before. If your goal is to win narrow material rewards or ego gratification or fame, then getting close to the powerful, whispering in their ears, having "access," can make a huge difference. But if your goal is to heal and repair the society, and you want to enlist the politicians to pursue policies that require courage, if you want them to feel safe to examine the part of their own selves that is responsive to the Left Hand of God, then there is only one thing that can work: building a social and political movement in the larger society that is so visible, noisy, and persistent that the powerful cannot ignore it and instead feel that it provides them with the political cover to take stands that might otherwise be perceived as risky.

If I look back at the major positive transformations in this society over the past fifty years—the transformation in the status of women, the ending of segregation, the emergence of an environmental consciousness—they were all accomplished because of powerful movements of ordinary people who were mobilized behind a set of ideas that were originally considered utopian and unrealistic. Once those movements had achieved momentum and visibility and had attracted growing numbers of people who felt they had made that cause their number one priority, then it became possible for individuals who were part of that movement to whisper in the ears of the powerful and have them listen. At the moment when those with access to power could point to large movements of people who were organized, committed, willing to take risks, and could sustain their commitment to the movement for years or even decades, then the politicians no longer felt that it was "unrealistic" for them to listen to the message of that movement.

So when people say to me today, "Do you see a candidate or a political leader that you think will be a champion for the Left Hand of God?" I respond: there are many decent and principled people in public life today, and there are many more who would like to be. But as the Good Book tell us, "Do not put your trust in the princes" (Psalms 146:3). Those people will respond when there is a social movement that makes it safe for them to do what their best instincts tell them to do. In fact, only at that point will they begin to hear the voice of hope and the voice of a politics that believes in the possibility of a world of love. And that's not because politicians are unprincipled, but rather because they are just like the rest of us—and just as likely as the rest of us to ignore the pull toward a world of love, caring, and generosity as long as it seems that paying attention to that pull is likely to be self-destructive and put them at risk of humiliation and isolation.

When President Franklin Delano Roosevelt met with a group of labor leaders in 1934 who were trying to convince him to support the

Lehman Act, which would extend rights for union organizing, he listened intently for three hours. At the end he said, "You've convinced me and I fully support this legislation. Now go out there and force me to do this." He was saying what I'm saying: social change can be helped along by people in power, but only when they themselves feel that some significant section of their constituents is pushing them very hard, and in a direction that has already received national support and attention from a movement that is not going to go away.

So we need to stop fantasizing that we are going to find a magical candidate who embodies all that we believe in and instead create a movement that makes it necessary for any candidate to respond to our message. To give the values of the Left Hand of God a chance to transform politics, we need to be actively championing a vision of love and generosity for our society and refusing to settle for less. This was what my teacher Abraham Joshua Heschel was trying to communicate in his book *God in Search of Man:* the sacred energy of the universe, in whose image we are created, is calling upon us to bring that energy into the public sphere and to remake our world in ways that are consistent with our highest values.

A first step is to build an alliance between secular, religious, and "spiritual but not religious" progressives. That is the goal of the Network of Spiritual Progressives.

Still, you might reasonably ask, what might be the shared political agenda? To that we will now turn, in the second part of this book.

PART TWO

The Spiritual Agenda for American Politics: A New Bottom Line

Introduction

I could not be leading a religious life unless I identified with the whole of humanity, and that I could not do unless I took part in politics. The whole gamut of human activities today constitutes an indivisible whole. You cannot divide social, economic, political and purely religious work into watertight compartments.
  —Mahatma Gandhi

Learn to do good, seek justice, aid the oppressed, Uphold the rights of the orphan, defend the cause of the widow.
  —Isaiah 1:17

The essence of the spiritual crisis of the Western world is this: our economic and political order rewards us for selfishness and punishes us for openheartedness and caring for others. We value the Right Hand of God, with its emphasis on fear and dominion, rather than the sense of hope and generosity that accompanies the Left Hand of God. We no longer listen to our highest aspirations but content ourselves with what is "realistic."

The solution to our society's ethos of selfishness and materialism cannot be a set of mild reforms that seek to make daily life slightly more humane. Of course, we must do everything we can to eliminate hunger and homelessness and to protect Social Security and other programs designed to provide a safety net against the worst consequences of the competitive marketplace. Such reforms on their own, however, have not proven to be enough to create a sense of safety or security or solidarity.

Greed, selfishness, and materialism are all products of fear. Fear that we cannot count on others. Fear that everyone is looking out for themselves. Fear that there won't be enough and that we will be the losers unless we get more than we need right now to protect us against the possibly dangerous future.

These fears rarely get dispelled by the kinds of demonstrations and protests that are launched by the Left against the bad policies of whoever happens to be in government at the time. I've gone to my fair share of marches and supported the antiwar and antiglobalization demonstrations of the past decade. But protests that are focused primarily on what is wrong, that are devoid of a positive alternative, have been largely ineffective because they have been unable to create in their participants, much less in those who only hear about them, a sense that there exists a community of people who are willing to care for one another and build a different kind of society together. Instead, too often what predominates and gets communicated to others is the voice of anger and fear. Yet what is really needed is the voice of hope. We need to offer Americans something to be for. We need to present Americans with a vision of a progressive spiritual politics that will bring home the Left Hand of God.

There are some on the Left who insist that they can regenerate hope by putting forward a more radical program of social and economic reforms. They believe that had the Democrats nominated candidates who affirmed a consistent populist agenda, they would have been more successful politically.

But they are only partly right. The part that is right is this: if Democrats were perceived as having the backbone to stand up for their own ideals and fight for them, rather than always compromising them in order to show how "reasonable" they are, they would go part of the way toward reassuring Americans that they could be trusted with power. Consistency and the courage to fight for what you believe in make a big difference in reassuring others that it's safe to take the risk of joining you.

The first half of this book demonstrates why that's not going to be enough. A populist politics is unlikely to succeed without simultaneously presenting a spiritual agenda that speaks to the needs and deepest aspirations of a community that cares about something beyond money and self-interest. A populist agenda, to the extent that it is presented without that larger spiritual framework, often appears to be little more than a power or money grab by one section of the population in opposition to another, what the media ridicules as "class war."

Too often liberal programs seem to conceptualize human beings as a set of isolated individuals, each of whom possesses material needs and political rights, and the liberal goal is to make sure that everyone gets as many of their material needs met as possible without violating the rights of anyone. What is continually missed is the universal desire for connection, mutual recognition, and higher meaning. It's only when we can root a populist agenda in a much deeper (and universal, cross-class lines) vision of the good that we stand any chance of countering the appeal of the Religious Right. So, yes, we are for using the common wealth for the common good to better all of our lives. But we are also for a world that promotes love, kindness, generosity, gentleness, awe, and wonder.

I know that this makes some people on the Left very uneasy. Their fear is that if we introduce our own vision of the good into public discourse, we are actually going to weaken the separation between church and state. Instead of introducing our own values, they imagine we should be putting more energy into keeping all values out of the public discourse.

But this strategy has already been tried, and it failed. The radical "keep values out of the public sphere" people have failed to keep values out of the public sphere. They have managed only to keep their own values out of the public sphere, while the Right, faced with no coherent alternative worldview, has been able to promote its views without any serious challenge.

As you'll notice, the Spiritual Covenat with America includes the array of issues from health care, employment, sustainable energy, and education that the Democrats will be promoting in 2006 and 2008. In asking them to embrace a "spiritual agenda," I am asking them to go to a deeper level of human need, and to explicitly affirm a commitment to building a society that promotes love, caring, generosity, awe and wonder at the grandeur of creation, and a host of other values that will almost certainly make them vulnerable to put-downs by the cynical media as either New Age flakiness, utopian hopefulness, or even communistic oppressiveness.

Spiritual progressives can respond by noting that most of the world's religious traditions talk about love, caring, generosity, kindness, nonviolence, and awe and wonder at creation and see these as an intrincsic part of what it means to be human and to respond to what God and the universe seek from us.

The Torah tells us not only "Love your neighbor as yourself" but also "Do not oppress the stranger." The Talmudic rabbis tell us that the sin of Sodom was not sexual licentiousness but the failure to welcome strangers and provide the homeless with safety and security. They reference the strange passage in Deuteronomy 21:1–10, in which the Israelites are told that if some stranger is found slain in the fields outside city boundaries, the elders of the nearest city must make a sin offering. The rabbis pointed out that the elders of the city could not reasonably be thought to have killed the stranger, but they are nevertheless thought to be responsible. The rabbis speculate that perhaps that person came by and was not given food or clothing or shelter and thus was made vulnerable to attack, so the responsibility falls on the community, as though they had themselves participated in killing this stranger. From the standpoint of Jewish tradition, caring for the stranger, the Other, is not a sentimentality or utopian fantasy but a legally enforceable requirement on the community.

Jesus takes a similar stance in Matthew 25:34–46, when talking about the punishment of the righteous and wicked. Jesus tells people that God will say to the condemned: "For I was hungry, and you gave me no food, I was thirsty and you gave me no drink, I was a stranger and you did not take me in, naked and you clothed me not, sick and in prison and you visited me not." And the condemned are astounded and want to know when they ignored the suffering of the Lord, and Jesus responds, "Indeed, I say to you, what you did not do on behalf of the small people around you, you did not do for me." The way we treat the powerless, the homeless, the hungry—that is how we are treating God.

So why do these values suddenly seem flaky when articulated by someone on the Left? Here we face the fundamental asymmetry between the situation of the Religious Right and a spiritual or religious Left. The Religious Right can say all this and get away with it because when it comes down to actual policies the Religious Right sides with the Right Hand of God and champions militarism and the self-interest of corporations and the rich. As a result, it doesn't have to worry about being labeled soft or utopian or too "New Age." Those on the Religious Right don't try to take seriously Jesus's call to "turn the other cheek" in the face of violence. They may be fundamentalists about homosexuality, but they are remarkable moral relativists and flexible modernist interpreters when it comes to the Bible's command to forgive all debts once every seven years and to redistribute land during the Jubilee every fifty years. The corporate-dominated media don't call them on these inconsistencies, because as they see it, the Religious Right is being "realistic." But anyone who would actually take Torah or Jesus seriously when it comes to peace and social justice agenda is a target for ridicule.

It's no solution to this dilemma to have the Democrats try to present themselves as though they, too, are "realistic" and committed to the Right Hand of God. Doing that may make it possible to gather up enough credibility to win a given election, but at that point the logic of the Right Hand God places these opportunists in a very difficult position. They may be momentarily in power, but they haven't convinced their own base to support them in making significant changes, and without that support they face not only the well-orchestrated campaigns of the wealthy and entrenched power interests but also their own inner doubts about whether they have the right to push for their own ideals. The only way you can change anything politically is to build public support for a different way of thinking. And that means that you have to be arguing for the Left Hand of God, defending the spiritual vision that has been the common wisdom of the human race for most of our existence, and facing up to those who will ridicule policies that seek to support our capacities for love, generosity, kindness, nonviolence, caring, openheartedness, and so on.

Publicly advocating for a world based on these values is what it will take to revive an effective social change movement.

Such a movement need not be, and should not be, an explicitly religious movement, but it should be inclusive of religious progressives, "spiritual but not religious" progressives, and secular people as well. The values of the Left Hand of God are supported by many people who do not believe in any supreme being (just as, conversely, there are many religious people who don't actually believe in those values).

To the extent that a social or political movement or a party like the Democrats is willing to stand up for these values—to champion them in the face of all the cynicism, all the attempts to humiliate those who hold these beliefs, all the attempts to find inconsistencies, all the attempts to expose the ways that people holding these beliefs actually don't embody them in their own lives (something that is certain to be true of most of us to some extent), all the attempts to portray these views as childish or utopian or self-destructive or whatever else is thrown at us—to that extent it will begin to make it safe for the tens of millions of people who share these values to actually take them more seriously, back them publicly, and then become more involved in backing the movement or party that is promoting this vision. This is what it will take: a Democratic Party that has the courage to stand up for a whole new way of doing politics, a way that affirms the highest values of the human race, and does so with a willingness to challenge the critics and the voices of cynical realism, whether these come from the outside and from within oneself.

Fear is the root of greed and selfishness and materialism. The key, then, is to engender a political movement that knows that one of its major tasks is to take the energy that has been flowing toward fear and turn it toward hope.

Our task is to make people feel safe to champion the values that they actually hold in part of their being but which they feel too afraid to trust, given the way that cynical realism rules in the public sphere. Creating that atmosphere of safety is the path to the revival of a Left capable of transforming the fundamental distortions in American economic and political life. And the first and indispensable step in fostering a sense of safety is for us, every one of us, to say publicly that we really want a different kind of world, a world in which love and generosity are the foundation of our public life together.

The emphasis on creating a politics that meets our meaning needs as well as our material needs will have a tremendous appeal across political parties and across class lines. The Right, very brilliantly, was able to appeal across class lines by taking the spiritual needs of working people seriously while putting the economic interests of the wealthy first. A progressive spiritual politics will cross class lines by a different route. We will put the economic interests of middle income and poor people first, while taking the spiritual needs of all classes seriously.

There are many people who are already engaged in this kind of progressive spiritual politics: greening the planet, developing sustainable forms of agriculture and production of goods, creating co-ops and neighborhood associations, transforming unions and civic associations, developing socially responsible investment and encouraging corporations to embrace a greater degree of accountability, transparency, and ecological sensitivity. The goodness and hopefulness of the American people is already moving on many of the issues that I will describe in the second half of this book. Up until now, however, much of that caring and socially responsible energy has not been unified by a clearly articulated worldview or had a presence in public consciousness. By articulating a spiritual politics, we may be able to both reinforce these positive tendencies that are already happening and make all of them more visible, not only to other people but among ourselves. The more people recognize that they are not alone, the more they will be willing to take the principle of generosity and caring for others and for the planet that motivates them in one sphere (for example, ecology) and apply to other spheres (for example, foreign policy).

Please keep this in mind when reading the Spiritual Covenant with America, particularly at those moments when you say to yourself, "The Democrats will never buy this—it's too idealistic for them." It is precisely when people act from their idealism that they generate the change in society from fear to hope, which makes it possible for others to overcome their own depressive certainty that everyone is just out for themselves, so they have to be that way also. That's why the Democrats are always more powerful when they are fighting for a clear principle. When Democrats in the past put forward a vision asserting that we are all in this together, that we need to take care of each other, and that we are going to leave nobody behind, people responded, and they will respond again. But when Democrats try to show how "realistic" they are, most of their constituents lose interest because if the message is, "Take care of some people but not all people," then each person says, "Fine, let me take care of myself first—so don't raise my taxes."

Take as an example the struggle over Social Security, one of the great inventions of the New Deal that affirmed a principle of intergenerational solidarity. The Bush administration, seeking to undermine this sense of solidarity and caring, proposed measures that would result in each person worrying about his or her own retirement. The Democrats' response, to the extent that it would reaffirm the principle of intergenerational solidarity, could potentially build powerful political support in every congressional district and defeat the Republicans on this point in the 2006 and 2008 congressional elections. But to the extent that Democrats propose some compromise measure that does not preserve the intent to help one another across generational lines—the intent at the heart of Social Security—they will undermine this solidarity, and people will retreat into fear, asking, "Well, how much will this pay me personally?" And at that point people will turn to the Republicans, who do self-interest best.

The same thinking should guide Democrats in how they approach the rebuilding of New Orleans. Shortly after *Tikkun* magazine proposed a Domestic Marshall Plan, the Democrats picked up on that language but without the substance of what we are saying. Their vision is tepid and unlikely to produce mass support precisely because it offers too little (lots of money but concentrated in only one area). The Domestic Marshall Plan that is needed must address not only the problems of New Orleans, but also the problems facing the whole country that have been revealed through the Katrina disaster. This must have three foci:

1. The permanent elimination of poverty in the United States. This can be accomplished by:

    a. A massive housing program to provide adequate housing for every person living in this country, citizen or not. End homelessness, and replace shabby ghetto housing with well-constructed, ecologically sound apartments built in central cities or in areas close to potential employment.

    b. Guaranteed full employment through massive construction work and other socially necessary programs funded through federal taxes.

    c. A national single-payer health plan providing universal coverage for everyone residing in the United States.

2. A total transformation in our society to make it sustainable and to begin to repair the damage being done to the environment. This can be accomplished by:

a. Ending our reliance on fossil fuels. This means immediately requiring all cars produced in this country to be hybrid and specifying that within a certain number of years they be entirely independent of oil, coal, or other destructive fuels. The production of energy for our factories and our sources of electricity must be converted quickly to environmentally safe forms, and this conversion must be completed without constraints put on it by those worrying about how to save their investments in oil, gas, and coal. Meanwhile, we must enforce emission standards tougher than those in the Kyoto accords.

b. Retooling factories to produce environmentally sustainable ways of manufacturing goods.

c. Developing a global labeling system for goods that have been produced in ways that are ethically appropriate (in terms of the conditions under which workers produced and delivered them to market) and ecologically sensitive—and then committing the U.S. government to buying only goods with such a label; encouraging American consumers to do likewise with an ad campaign similar to those used to discourage tobacco consumption.

3. A massive retooling of the infrastructure of our cities, including the bridges, the levees, the ports, and all other parts that might fail in a natural disaster.

What does this have to do with New Orleans?

Everything.

It is precisely because we didn't take these steps that we faced the New Orleans tragedy, and it is only if we take these steps that a similar disaster can be averted in the future. And the tragedy will be not just for us but for the entire earth.

Talking in these terms, and proposing something massive that will help not only the people of New Orleans but all Americans is far more likely to generate enthusiasm in the coming years, whereas sticking to the narrow focus of New Orleans will sooner or later come into conflict with other societal needs, particularly since President Bush stated that funds for this massive rebuilding will come not from new taxes but from further cuts in existing social programs. If the Democrats call for new taxes to make sure that existing social services are not cut, they end up in a bind because many Americans have noticed that existing programs don't really solve anything but only perpetuate poverty. So instead of being placed in that position, the Democrats need to be more idealistic, more visionary, more able to get at the roots of the problem by embracing the vision I've just articulated. And far from being politically unwise, such a move would in fact be far likelier to inspire people than anything that the scaled down, unimaginative, realistic programs of the Democrats.

So it turns out that thinking in the more idealistic terms proposed in the covenant below is smart politics, not utopian fantasy.

You'll see in the Spiritual Covenant, some elements of overlap with the Democratic Congressional agenda developed for the 2006 election, including energy independence, free college education, saving Social Security, adequately funding education, and post-Katrina rebuilding. But in the larger spiritual framework, most of the details, the New Bottom Line and how it applies, the generosity approach to foreign policy and much else is strikingly different in philosophy and worldview. This is *not* a call for more of the liberal programs. It is a fundamentally different vision that incorporates liberal programs but moves in a spiritual direction with categories that are painfully lacking in the worldview reflected by the 2006 Democratic agenda.

It's amazing what can happen when we practice the politics of the Left Hand of God. In our lifetime, a vision of hope overthrew apartheid in South Africa and helped tear down the walls of totalitarianism in Eastern Europe. All around the world, events are happening like the July 2004 meeting of the Parliament of the World's Religions, when some eight thousand members of diverse religious communities gathered in Barcelona, all of them committed to combating religious violence, ensuring access to safe water, and eliminating the debts of developing countries. Whenever people allow their yearning for a world of love and generosity to overcome their fears and cynicism, real change can happen.

I remember the day my eight-year-old son returned from his first day at Hebrew School, where Jewish religious instruction took place in the late afternoons twice a week after public school. He excitedly told me the following story from the Talmud he had been taught on his first day there:

Once upon a time there were two brothers who loved each other very much. They worked together in their field all year, and when harvesttime came, they shared the produce equally. That night the older brother could not fall asleep. He kept thinking: "My brother is married and has two children, while I am single. He needs more food than I do." Turning his thoughts into action, he arose from his bed, gathered up a great gift of produce, and secretly started walking toward his brother's house.

That same night, the younger brother also could not sleep. He reflected, "My older brother is all alone in the world. He has no one to work for him and sustain him in his old age, whereas I have my two children. He needs extra profit from our labors so that he can save up for those difficult days." And with that thought, he arose, gathered up a great gift of produce, and he, too, secretly started walking toward his brother's house.

Next day each arose to find that although they had left a large quantity of their produce at the other's house, their own produce had not been diminished. They could not understand what was happening, and each resolved to try again. This happened for many nights, until one night, on the hillside separating their two homes, under the moonlight, the two brothers met as each was halfway to the other's house. For a moment they were both shocked, but they suddenly realized what the other was doing, and they embraced and kissed and cried for the love they felt in their hearts and the way that love was being shown through acts of generosity and caring.

Years later, during the time of King David and his son Solomon, that very spot where the brothers met and embraced was selected to be the site for the building of the Holy Temple, the Temple of Peace at the center of the world.

That's the story my son told me, and I cried with joy that day some twenty-five years ago when he shared it with me. The message my son learned was that giving and caring for others is the center of our Jewish culture, and it is the foundation upon which any future religious or spiritual practice must be built. I only wish that the Temple Mount, now at the center of controversy between Israelis and Palestinians, could once again become the spot for a new spirit of generosity among all peoples.

My point in recalling the story is this: a culture can be built that fosters generosity and caring. It doesn't have to be connected to a particular religion. It doesn't violate human nature but fulfills a deep aspiration that we all have. A progressive social change movement can draw upon the cultural resources of existing religious and spiritual traditions. But it should also seek to build its own cultural resources and traditions—because a spiritual politics must also be one that speaks to the intuitions and emotional needs of secular people. We need music, stories, rituals, and much more to build that culture. One part of that process is to articulate a vision of what the political dimensions and program of this spiritual movement might look like, and that is what I will do in the coming chapters.

NINE

The Spiritual Covenant
with America

In the 1994 elections, Newt Gingrich and the Republican minority of Congress unveiled a Contract with America that presented a coherent vision of what the Republicans would offer if elected. Gingrich won, and parts of his contract were subsequently implemented by the Republican Congress and now by the second Bush administration.

It's the Democrats' turn. But the platform they put forward in 2006 reflects a limited vision. I support all that they are for and parts of it are included in the Spiritual Covenant with America. I urge you to compare their approach with the details of the Spiritual Covenant to get a fuller picture of how a progressive spiritual politics is quite different from secular liberalism even as it incorporates liberal programs.

I do not mean to suggest that the Spiritual Covenant with America that I will present in this chapter is all it will take for the Democrats to win. They must also really believe what they say and manifest their belief in the way that they express themselves. Many Americans experience themselves as disconnected from others and barely able to relate to what the media talks about as "politics" and the social world. They end up not voting, or voting halfheartedly, with zero real enthusiasm for their candidate or party, or simply voting for whichever candidate seems to have the most energy and be the most genuine, regardless of the candidate's specific policies. These voters will only respond to Democrats who passionately embrace their own ideals, who are willing to stand up and be "for something" despite the cynicism they are likely to face, and who embody in the way they are in the world the values that they urge others to follow.

The Spiritual Covenant with America could actually be heard by a significant part of the American people, those who have not been moved deeply enough by what Democrats have been saying for the past thirty years. So spiritual progressives should do what we can to convince the Democrats and their constituent groups, such as the labor movement, the women's movement, environmentalists, civil libertarians, peace activists, and other fighters for social justice, that this framework, visionary though it is, can in fact be an important contribution to practical political advances in the coming years.

The Spiritual Covenant with America

We, the people of the United States, are proud of our accomplishments over the twenty-three decades that have passed since we declared our independence and began to build a society based on shared values and democratic processes. Over the course of those many decades, we've been able to extend our democratic system, eliminate slavery and segregation, welcome and integrate into our society refugees from around the world, reduce sexist practices in our economy and in our personal lives, challenge discrimination against people whose lifestyles differ from those of the majority, and increase our commitment to human rights around the world.

We recognize that another major challenge faces us: to transform economic and political arrangements that have allowed selfishness and materialism to shape too many aspects of our lives. The fundamental goodness of the American people is now awakening to the need for a new bottom line based not only on economic success but also on our deepest spiritual values, values that are shared by religious as well as secular people, values that were and are central to the building of American society.

We hereby proclaim our commitment to these traditional spiritual values: love, generosity, kindness, responsibility, respect, gratitude, humility, honesty, awe, and wonder at the grandeur of the universe.

We reject the assumptions that productivity, efficiency, and rationality are defined solely in terms of maximizing money and power. Instead, economic and political institutions, social practices, legislation, and corporations will be judged by a new standard. They should be considered efficient, rational, and productive not only to the extent that they maximize money or power, but also to the extent that they maximize love and caring, kindness and generosity, peace and social justice, ethically and ecologically responsible behavior, and to the extent that they enhance our capacities to transcend a manipulative, technocratic, and utilitarian way of treating others so that we can respond to other people as embodiments of the sacred and enhance our capacities to respond to the universe with awe and wonder.

We invite our fellow Americans to join us in building a society based on this new bottom line. In the covenants listed below we begin to articulate what can be accomplished if we work together to transform our society.

We offer this in a spirit of humility, knowing that this is only the beginning of articulating all the consequences of having a new bottom line based on these spiritual values, and knowing also that our own best interests as Americans can only be met if we are equally committed to the fulfillment of the best interests of all people on our planet.

1. Covenant with American Families

All families deserve a living wage, full employment, affordable high-quality child care, affordable health care, access to excellent education, starting with preschool, and flexible work schedules. But strong families need more than that. We need a culture that nurtures the spiritual and emotional underpinnings of family life—a culture that honors nurturing, love, gentleness, and kindness, that rejects the physical and emotional abuse of children, and that provides equal respect to both women and men.

We may not all live in small-town USA anymore, but we can still embody the spirit of caring for others, neighborliness, and generosity that helped make America great. If we build a society that rewards "looking out for number one" and tells us all day long that what really counts is the economic bottom line, then we weaken our capacities to love and care for others.

But if we instead reward love and caring, building a new bottom line of generosity and kindness, we will be far better equipped to sustain loving family commitments. Similarly, if we respect the real contributions to the common good made each day in our communities by tens of millions of people who rarely get the recognition they deserve, we all benefit. If we create workplaces that offer us more opportunities to use our intelligence, our creativity, and our desire to contribute, more recognition and respect, and more reward for caring for others, we will make it more likely that people will come home from work with higher levels of self-respect and a greater capacity to be nurturing and to care for their family members, neighbors, and the larger communities in which they live.

We support economic and political institutions that foster kindness and generosity, mutual respect, and commitment to the common good—recognizing that strong families need a social context that promotes solidarity and rewards generosity, and a societal environment that reinforces what we teach our children.

We encourage family support networks and a culture that promotes families in all their various forms, including single-parent families and gay and lesbian families, understanding that the more love flourishes in a society, the stronger all families will be. And we will support men in developing the capacity to be nurturing, gentle, and intimate, qualities once thought to be primarily female strengths, and the capacity of women to share leadership roles in family life, so that we can assist in the evolution of families from a model based on domination to one based on a spiritual partnership.

2. Covenant of Personal Responsibility

Each of us individually has personal responsibility for the choices we make in our own lives. We promise to live with integrity, joy, honesty, kindness, openheartedness, compassion, forgiveness, and generosity. We resist the easy excuses of blaming our problems on society or on people who let us down. And we do not rely exclusively on government to rectify aspects of our lives that could be changed through individual or community effort.

We honor each other as created in the image of God—as embodiments of the sacred. We recognize and support each other's aspirations to contribute to the common good and to each other's well-being. We resist the message of our society that encourages us to view people as an amalgam of material needs and instead recognize each other's yearnings for lives of higher meaning and purpose. We join with others to challenge left- or right-wing politics that implicitly see human beings as little more than maximizers of self-interest.

We build purpose-driven lives and take the time to discover how we can best serve God, humanity, our country, our community, our families, and our friends, and we find and build meaning in our own lives and in the lives of those around us. We bring humor, joy, and celebration into our lives and the lives of others.

We respect the privacy of others, avoid gossip or spreading negative stories, and practice righteous speech—using our words to enhance love and not dissension or hurtfulness. We consume responsibly and respect the earth. We affirm sexual pleasure within the context of mutually respectful, responsible, and loving relationships.

We take time to nourish our souls and deepen our inner lives and celebrate the wonders of the world that surrounds us. We expand beyond our constricted limitations and evolve our consciousness beyond a smallness of vision in accord with our highest capacities, connecting to the ultimate unity of all, developing a compassionate holistic view of ourselves and each other, of human history and of human destiny. We accept that not all spiritual experience can adequately be expressed in words, so we take responsibility for creating the music and dance, art and poetry that can give voice to our ecstasy in the joy of living and also to our sadness at the persistence of human suffering. We channel God's blessings and seek, through acts of spontaneous loving and unprovoked generosity and openheartedness, to become a blessing in the lives of all we encounter. We accept people at whatever stage they are in their own intellectual, emotional, and spiritual development and help them to become the healthiest and most fulfilled beings they could possibly be.

We join with others to fund and support spiritual communities that embody our values. We take the responsibility to inform ourselves of what is happening in the world around us—and what we can do to create positive change. We challenge illegitimate authority. We honor and learn from our elders, provide them with opportunities to share their life experiences with us and our children, and see aging as an opportunity for spiritual growth and not a disease that should be cured or an affliction that needs to be hidden from others. We are endlessly curious, develop our minds, and care for our bodies.

We respect diversity, honor those with whom we disagree, and forgive those who offend us. We engage in genuine dialogue, not just waiting for our chance to shout our truth but truly learning from others. Wherever possible, we alleviate suffering. We are compassionate toward one another, recognizing that each of us has limitations that make it unlikely that we will ever perfectly embody all our values, and yet we will support each other in moving closer to actually living what we believe.

3. Covenant of Social Responsibility

We will break through the social disconnection that traps so many people in loneliness and alienation. We will resist the cynical realism that reduces all public discourse to the manipulation of that which can be measured, ignoring precisely what is most deeply human: the spiritual dimension of our experience.

We seek to eliminate poverty, ensure full employment, provide for public safety, and require that those who regulate our economy, our health systems, our communications, our utilities, and environmental and consumer safety do so in ways that protect the common good. We will halt the revolving door from the boardroom to government and back that leads to so many ethical scandals, increases cynicism, and robs citizens of the protections we deserve.

We will protect the rights of seniors, people in poverty, the young, and all those at risk of being left behind.

We will not allow discrimination in any form or create false distinctions between those who deserve our care and those who do not. We will reduce the gap between rich and poor, both in our own country and around the world.

We celebrate and honor the contributions of ordinary citizens to the good of our communities. Tens of millions of people pour their life energies into work that is essential to our well-being but do not receive adequate pay or public recognition for their efforts. We will reinstill the value of working for the common good and find ways to honor those who do so. Employers must provide time for volunteer activities, and government must be reimagined as the public service it was meant to be. We will revive a sense of civic-mindedness and make government an attractive place for our best, brightest, and most compassionate.

We reward institutions, including corporations, that promote the value of caring for others. We salute the many corporations that are already socially responsible. We applaud voluntary corporate codes of conduct and the aspirations of many businesses to improve their labor and environmental standards.

We will aid the best instincts and intentions of America's many ethically oriented business people by supporting a Social Responsibility Amendment to the Constitution that requires corporations to apply for a new corporate charter every ten years. Such a charter would be granted only to corporations that can demonstrate to a jury of ordinary citizens a satisfactory record of social responsibility. The jury will consider testimony not only from corporate leaders but from employees of the company as well as from environmental, labor, and community groups.

The Social Responsibility Amendment will give teeth to the new bottom line and extend our democratic principles into our economic lives. It will help responsible corporate leaders to put a brake on those economic pressures that have pushed corporations into policies that are destroying the environment and undermining the moral fabric and spiritual integrity of life on this planet. Love of money needs to be replaced by love of life, love of the earth, love of God, and love of each other at the center of our economic lives.

4. Covenant for a Values-Based Education

We support education that fosters children's capacities to be loving and caring human beings and helps students grow into responsible, ethically and ecologically attuned adults. Unfortunately, our current system often teaches students that they can advance themselves only at the expense of others and that the highest good is to impart skills that will enable them to find high-paying jobs and achieve positions of power and prestige. We will replace that old bottom line with a new bottom line that values learning as an activity that is a pleasure in itself. We value knowledge and the joy of exploration even when the sole reward is to enhance our openness to the wonders of the universe and the goodness of human beings. We will make teaching a more highly valued (and better paid) vocation, building schools that inspire learning rather than simply warehousing children, and create programs that encourage students to cooperate as well as compete.

We will teach our highest values: generosity and compassion, kindness and responsibility, respect and caring for others, joyous celebration, awe and wonder in response to the grandeur and beauty of the universe, gratitude and humility, intellectual curiosity and love of learning, emotional and spiritual intelligence and a powerful commitment to freedom, justice, nonviolence, and peace. And we will provide free college education for everyone who demonstrates a capacity to do college-level study.

5. Covenant for Health Care

Everyone deserves affordable health care.

Health care is not just an individual concern; we all bear the financial burden when those who are ill do not receive adequate care. Equally important, the bonds of trust and caring are shattered in a society when we feel that no one cares whether we live or die unless we have enough money for expensive treatments or costly insurance. In a world where the air we breathe, the foods we eat, and the water we drink have become health hazards, we owe it to each other to solve these new health problems and eliminate their causes.

We will give ourselves the same health care that the president and the Congress receive: a single-payer system that allows us to choose our doctors, hospitals, and treatments and that gives our doctors the freedom to worry about us, unconstrained by bureaucrats who limit our care in order to enhance the profitability of insurance companies or health care providers.

We propose a new model of care that looks after our health in all dimensions: physical, mental, emotional, and spiritual.

Mother Earth

6. Covenant of Environmental Stewardship

We will joyously preserve and protect the earth and will seek to reverse the damage done through ignorance and irresponsibility. We will halt the reckless wasting of the world's resources. We will build new technologies, new systems of transportation, new forms of planning for our cities that release us from dependence on fossil fuels and help us live in a more sustainable manner. We will reward individual, corporate, and governmental responsibility, encourage family planning and education to reduce population growth, support ways to reduce overconsumption, and dramatically reduce pollutants and poisons in our air, water, and land. And we will create an international system of ethical consumption so that consumers will be informed of how and where to purchase food and consumer goods that have been produced in ways that are just to those who produce them and environmentally

sound and healthy for the planet, and we will encourage governments to provide economic assistance to firms that are environmentally responsible and socially just.

7. Covenant for Building a Safer World

We value safety and security. We also recognize that no wall can
block every threat. Reliance on military and unilateral strength interventions does not make the world more secure. As much as we
must protect our families and communities, we understand that
our well-being as Americans is intrinsically tied to the well-being
of everyone else on this planet. So we will support the Strategy of
Generosity to ensure homeland security, not only because it is
morally right but also because it is in our best interests. We will
harness American generosity to heal the pain caused by hatred,
poverty, hunger, inadequate health care, inadequate education,
and the manipulation of the global economy so as to serve the interests of advanced industrial societies and their allies among the
elites of third-world countries.

We will replace the globalization of selfishness with the globalization of spirit. Rather than export a glorification of the "me-
first" mentality and old-bottom-line consciousness, we will
embody a spirit of caring and responsibility not only for America
but for the entire planet.

The United States will join with other advanced industrial societies in creating a Global Marshall Plan to dedicate part of our
GDP each year to eliminating homelessness, hunger, poverty, inadequate education, and inadequate health care. Within twenty
years we will help raise the standard of living in the developing
world so dramatically that terrorists will find it almost impossible
to recruit people who are angry enough to want to give their lives
to fight the values and power of the United States and its allies.
Our Global Marshall Plan will not seek to impose our own culture
but will instead be implemented in ways that respect the cultural
and religious traditions of the peoples of the world.

We are rightly proud of America's democratic achievements

and of the long history of struggles to extend the original democratic promise of America. We will reduce dramatically the role of money in elections, eliminate the electoral college, guarantee access to the media for all candidates and perspectives, and allow candidates to receive votes for public office on multiple-party slates and instant runoff voting. Aware of the dangers of a tyranny of the majority, whether at home or abroad, we will resist political correctness that is not respectful of alternative perspectives, will fight vigorously to maintain and extend civil liberties, will champion privacy and penalize governmental or corporate forces that collect, sell, or manipulate information about private citizens without prior authorization. The more America lives up to its democratic and civil liberties ideals, the more it can provide morally coherent global leadership.

We will make the world safer by building strong international institutions and a standing international nonviolent force that can intervene where necessary to protect populations from genocide or oppression. We will strengthen the International Court of Justice to punish violators of human rights. And we will end all use of torture in United States and U.S.-affiliated detention centers and ratify and implement international agreements against torture. We will dramatically reduce nuclear armaments and seek global disarmament of conventional weapons as well. Even though we recognize the need for transitional periods in which protections are in place, our intention is to work toward global nonviolence and the abolition of war, both as an outcome and as the means to achieving that outcome. Seizing on this moment in world history, when the United States exercises virtually undisputed global hegemony, we will model for all future times how a superpower can communicate genuine respect and concern for others. As a first step, we will replace all U.S. forces in Iraq with an international force that will conduct a plebiscite among all three ethnic communities to determine whether and how they stay together as one country or become independent states.

8. Covenant to Separate Church and State and Science

Trouble

We seek to keep religion out of government and government out of religion, and both out of science.

We will not allow anyone to use government to impose a particular religious worldview on the rest of us. Religious liberty, or what our Constitution calls the free exercise of religion, requires protection of all our religious communities as well as those secular or "spiritual but not religious" people who follow a different path.

The values we seek to introduce to shape our public life—kindness and generosity, caring about the impact of our actions on the well-being of others, love of knowledge and an appreciation of the accumulated wisdom of humanity, gratitude for all the goodness that surrounds us, awe and wonder and humility in recognition of the grandeur of creation, respect for teachers and elders, justice and peace—are shared by many secular as well as many religious people. Holding these values does not commit one to a belief in a supreme being or to any particular religious or spiritual path. It is precisely by fighting for these values that we provide an effective counterweight to those who use the absence of values in the public sphere as their springboard to try to impose their particular religious tradition on our public life. We will uncover the ways that supposedly value-neutral concepts like productivity, efficiency, and rationality actually mask a commitment to the materialist values that undermine beliefs Americans hold dear.

We will protect religion from government interference, and we will protect the sanctity of religion from those who try to turn God into their private property. We will foster respect and tolerance for all religious communities and paths, as well as for nonreligious orientations.

We will curb government-funded efforts that directly or indirectly support recruitment to any particular religious community. But we encourage spiritually sensitive programs that operate in an interfaith spirit of generosity and openness to diverse beliefs. We know that programs that address the spiritual dimension of human life are often more effective in healing and supporting people than cold, technocratic interventions alone.

We will generously fund and promote scientific research and rational thought and will not allow the priorities of science to be set by the corporate marketplace or scientific research to be restricted by religious dogma. We will also foster a deep respect for the wisdom that comes from literature, poetry, music, art, and the spiritual heritage of the human race. We will dramatically increase funding research aimed at curing disease and increasing human well-being in ways that are ecologically sustainable and life sustaining.

By maintaining a strict separation of religion from government, we will create a safe public arena for a serious discussion of fundamental questions of meaning and value and how they should apply to the directions we move in as a society. We encourage that discussion in our public institutions, our workplaces, and our governmental bodies and seek to ensure respectful and open-hearted conversation.

A spiritual politics based on these eight covenants will provide a new vision and a powerful message, the message of the Left Hand of God. We recognize that many Americans are suffering from the loss of spiritual meaning in life. This is not their fault but is rather the consequence of living in a society in which everyone is rewarded for looking out for themselves. Despite the personal decency and generosity of most Americans, despite the efforts of ordinary Americans through two centuries to share the common wealth of our society and to generously assist those who are in need, we know we have not yet succeeded in creating a society in which everyone has enough.

In the past, social movements have focused narrowly on repairing the worst damage caused by institutions and social practices rooted in materialism and selfishness, but the amount of good we have been able to do in that way, problem by problem, has not kept up with the rate of new problems. It is time now to address the source of our social suffering. We need to replace a culture of fear with a culture a hope. Agree to these eight covenants, and you will create a powerful cross-class progressive alliance that will bring a new bottom line to America. Your willingness to publicly identify with the kind of vision articulated in this Spiritual Covenant will itself be a factor in making others feel more hopeful, thus contributing to the shift in cultural and social energy from fear to hope.

The following chapters will provide more detail about the eight covenants and what it would mean to use them as the center of a progressive spiritual politics. Please understand that the covenants and their elaboration are my attempt to give flesh to a new bottom line. I do this with a sense of humility, recognizing that you might agree with the new bottom line yet have very different ideas about how that would translate into specific policies. The covenants are only one possible way, and the emerging movement of spiritual progressives will include plenty of room for other ideas on how to bring the new bottom line into public discourse.

TEN

The Family, Sexuality, and Personal Responsibility

Most people in the United States, when asked to say which social institution means the most to them, overwhelmingly choose family—and for one important reason. No matter what our own childhood experiences may have been, no matter how much we had to struggle later in life to repair some of the damage done by less-than-perfect parents, almost all of us recognize that the family is the only institution in our society whose explicit goal is to provide love and caring.

What Families Teach Us

Ideally, families provide our first and most enduring experiences with love, caring, and well-being. In the family, we are loved for who we are, not what we have achieved or how much money we make. Families offer us refuge from the world of work and competition, and they allow us our first taste of the deep joy that comes from sustained intimacy.

No wonder, then, that people feel so attached to family. They use words like *brother* and *sister* to address people they really care about. They talk of their closest affiliations with others "as though they were family." There is an implied loyalty and solidarity in family life that is rarely experienced elsewhere in the society.

Of course, not all families live up to the ideal of being a place where genuine caring and nurturance are given. Nor have families always represented our highest values. One great achievement of the twentieth century was our realization that the patriarchal family oppressed women and children and supported class divisions in the larger society, by legitimating the notion that inequalities of power are "natural."

Feminists have worked hard to tear down patriarchy and have succeeded in many ways. For example, women now find it much easier to leave oppressive family situations than they did fifty years ago. Gay and lesbian activists, feminists, and others on the Left have helped us reimagine the family as a nonhierarchical unit that can be created by single parents, same-sex parents, two parents, and intergenerational groupings. Control over their own reproductive choices plus the opening of the employment market has given some women options for shaping their own lives that never before existed.

These important changes have not been without their sometimes painful or morally challenging sides, causing some women to worry that their own family life may be less secure when so many women choose to go to work rather than remain as housewives, and increasing the ability of both men and women to have sexual relationships without fear of unwanted pregnancies. It's certainly different to live in a world where real choices are available for most of our society, when less than a hundred years ago such choices about personal life seemed restricted to the upper classes. Yet vive la différence. Now more than ever, families are created purposefully to cultivate love and to cement caring relationships.

Spiritual progressives seek to encourage the evolution of families from a structure based on domination to one founded on a spiritual partnership. We want to encourage individual freedom and choice, and we also want to encourage a greater flourishing of loving commitment to one another, a rejection of family violence, and the fostering of "equalitarian" leadership so that both women and men share in making the fundamental decisions of family life. A spiritual partnership seeks to promote the fullest flourishing of the talents and capacities of each member of the family, supports each to grow in her or his own chosen direction, fosters solidarity and mutual caring, and provides privacy and safety for each to develop his or her own spirituality. A spiritual partnership seeks to build a shared sense of meaning and purpose in the service of God and humanity, to help develop a balance between individuality and service to community, and yet to protect family members from subtle or overt coercion in the development of their relationship to ultimate issues. This means, in part, respecting the right of any family member not to adopt the family's or community's spiritual approach, not to believe, and not to feel that the amount of love that they receive is tied to sharing the perceptions and belief systems of others.

Supporting families as they try to incorporate greater amounts of love and freedom, enhancing women's power while honoring men, must become fundamental political commitments for the Left. A spiritual Left should make the Covenant with American Families its first program, and its focus should be on building a society that is safe for love and intimacy, that supports caring rather than competition, generosity rather than selfishness.

The Right has been all too happy to present itself as the "pro-family" force in American life. But has the Right actually strengthened the family? Not if divorce figures are relevant, because it turns out that many of the Red states have the highest levels of divorce. As I showed in the first part of this book, a major factor undermining families is the way our economic life generates a "looking out for number one" consciousness in the world of work that shapes how we think about people in the rest of our lives. Brought home, this way of thinking plays a major role in making loving relationships difficult to sustain. Yet the Right is the primary political force encouraging this mentality in the world of work, always fighting against attempts to bring into the economy concepts of social responsibility and caring about the consequences of corporate selfishness. So even though the Right says it supports "the family," we should not assume that the Right truly is willing to support a true "pro-family" agenda. To be fair, many on the Right sincerely believe that the policies they pursue will in the long run make everyone more successful, and that will contribute to family stability. But since the Right's policies actually encourage the competitive consciousness that undermines solidarity with others, they inadvertently jeopardize the very family stability that they genuinely want to advance. In effect, the Right acts as though it is more invested in making sure the wealthy keep their money and the corporations keep their power than it is in creating a new way of doing business that would give priority to the love and caring necessary to promote healthy families. The policies and worldview of the Right are actually a menace to family life.

All the more reason why we need to teach people about what it is that undermines love. We live in a society that rewards those who are best at looking out for themselves. Once we recognize that everyone is acculturated in this society to be a rational maximizer of self-interest, we feel alone and doubt we can trust even people who are close to us. This way of thinking undermines loving relationships.

The covenant we make with American families is that we will build a society that rewards the qualities of soul and self that provide the powerful underpinning of family life. We will take the values of love and caring present in the family as guideposts for all our relationships—at home, with friends, and even in the world of work. And we will make sure that our society gives each of us the time and resources to celebrate and enjoy family life. You want strong families? Build a society that encourages and rewards caring for others, nurturing, kindness, generosity, openheartedness, and love.

Building such a society is a major goal of a progressive spiritual politics, and the underlying aim of the Spiritual Covenant with America. In terms of values, the other parts of the covenant must be understood as stemming from the Covenant with American Families. For example, when we talk about the Social Responsibility Amendment (SRA) to the Constitution, we are talking about a program that, if implemented, would encourage a whole new set of values in the world of work, values like caring for others and generosity and kindness that would, over time, have a massive impact on people's psyches. The more these values are reinforced in the daily life experience of people at work, the more people come home with the psychological attitude that makes them capable of sustaining loving relationships. This is what I mean by saying that our demand is to build a society that is safe for love and intimacy, rather than a society that undermines loving relationships.

Once we understand this dynamic, we see how transparently ludicrous it is to have the Right claim to be pro-family when in fact it is the political force that guarantees that the values of the marketplace and the world of work will continue to be the values that, when brought home, are sure to make family life less stable and more problematic.

Moreover, as Riane Eisler points out, the Right uses slogans like "traditional values" to promote a family in which fathers make the rules and harshly punish disobedience, preparing children to accept the notion of "strong leaders" who allow no dissent and use force to impose their will. People raised in such families will tend, particularly when frightened (for example, by the possibility of renewed terrorism), to seek the protection that a strong father figure as national leader can provide. If, by contrast, we want to build a world in which people have the psychological capacity for cooperation, generosity, reconciliation of antagonisms, environmental sensitivity, and global peace, we need to raise children in families that operate with a partnership model in which people treat each other with real caring and in which love is more than sexual attraction because it translates into equality of worth and respect. In a partnership love means giving to the other without expectation of return on the investment, a giving that is guided by generosity and openheartedness rather than a "giving to get." Because we want to build a world based on love, we need to foster that in the way we build strong families.

Personal Responsibility

What is the meaning of the Biblical verse, "Ye shall walk after the Lord your God"? (Deuteronomy 13:5). Hama Ben Hanina [third century C.E.] teaches: Walk after the attributes of God. Just as He clothes the naked, so must you clothe the naked, as He visits the sick, so should you visit the sick, as He comforts mourners, so should you comfort mourners.
—Talmud, Sotah 14a

Many of the changes that must be made if our society is to follow the Left Hand of God go beyond the individual. Our goal in challenging the bottom line in this society is to develop social and economic arrangements so that our individual capacities will be strengthened rather than undermined all day in the world of work.

Yet even though an important dimension of support for families is to change the world of work, there is much that we as individuals can do in the meantime while we are seeking those larger societal changes.

It's particularly important to stress personal responsibility to counter the charge by some on the Right that liberals and progressives want the government to do everything for us, rather than hold people accountable for their own choices.

The Right argues that liberal social programs create a culture of dependency that actually weakens the motivation of poor people to get off welfare and encourages people to see themselves solely as victims. Although the Republicans have contributed to the creation of a culture of dependency by blocking attempts to promote full employment, so that there would actually be jobs for people who are willing to take them, and while this assault on welfare programs has often been mean-spirited and insensitive to the needs of children born into poverty, I nevertheless believe that there is something correct in this critique that the Right has put forward. I've seen too many people use oppression and past discrimination as an excuse for current behavior that is morally unacceptable. I have witnessed people relying on their grievances to justify passivity or a generalized anger at the world that disempowers them or leads them to the mistaken belief that they are no longer subject to the moral constraints of others. I've witnessed people who perceived themselves as powerless use that as a rationale for developing a rip-off mentality, in which they think that they have every right to take whatever they can get without regard to the consequences for others.

One reason why people on the Left have been reluctant to include a focus on personal responsibility in their politics lies in the tendency by America's elites of wealth and power to blame the victims for their poverty and powerlessness. A major prop to the class structure of American society has been the ability of the powerful to convince the powerless that they live in a meritocracy, a society in which you can make it if you really try, and therefore that if your life isn't really fulfilled you have no one to blame but yourself. Over and over again we are taught that "you create your own reality," and so you should take personal responsibility for the world you live in.

The Left has been correct to challenge that worldview and to help people understand the way that class realities, sexism, racism, and other factors have limited our possibilities. But it is also true that all these limitations are socially constructed. When women began to understand this, they began to internalize the message of personal responsibility in a different way: not as "I" create my own reality but as "we" create our own reality. And whereas no individual woman could have successfully challenged sexism, when women got together to create a social change movement, they were taking responsibility and acting to change their reality. Often, then, what "I" can do is to find others to work with so that "we" can change things together.

Each of us needs to take personal responsibility for building that "we." I've met so many people who tell me that they really support what I'm saying and really hope that a network of spiritual progressives can work but that they can't get involved personally right now in giving time or more than a token amount of money. Somehow they expect that others will create a movement for them. Or they tell me that they are waiting for the "right" candidate to show up to run for public office or a new Martin Luther King Jr., to appear in public space. But none of this will happen as long as people are waiting for someone else. Taking personal responsibility means that it isn't someone else that will make it happen.

This was a point God made to Moses in the book of Exodus. Moses had had his early rebellious period, but after escaping from the wrath of Pharaoh, he had built a comfortable life for himself. Living with his wife, children, and sheep in Midian, Moses was in his yuppie phase, divorced from the consciousness of pain that he knew continued to exist in the central cities of Egypt. But, comfortable though he was, there was a fire within him that burned but could not be quenched, and out of what appeared to be a burning bush came the voice of God telling Moses to return to the land of oppression and challenge the power of Pharaoh. Moses' response was that he was not the right person to do it, that he stuttered, that he really couldn't provide the leadership that was needed. And God's response was that even though Moses couldn't do it by himself, once he made the commitment, others would be able to make their own contributions, and together they could overthrow the tyrant. The point of the biblical story is that you don't have to be perfectly equipped or to be the one person who will do everything, but what you do have to do is take what talents you have, commit them to your highest vision, and enter the struggle for social change.

And when you do, you'll encounter many obstacles. I know many people who go to a political meeting out of a momentary enthusiasm for social change, then quickly get disillusioned because they've watched others at the meeting talk too much, get too involved in their egos, or say things that seemed unintelligent. So these people despair and don't show up at the next meeting, leaving the whole thing to the ego-trippers and flakes. What doesn't occur to them is that they could start their own group or that they could change the dynamics in this one.

Changing those dynamics requires a recognition that many people who come to political gatherings do so with a complex mixture of feelings. On the one hand, they want the same thing that you want: a world of kindness, generosity, social justice, ecological sanity, nonviolence, and love. On the other hand, they have their doubts that such a world is possible, and that makes them panicked and afraid. So they try to get control of their panic by talking a lot or by trying to reassure themselves that others really will see them and love them or to get confirmation that everyone genuinely knows and understands and shares with them every bit of their own ideology.

If we could realize that most of these people are really good people who are, like everyone else on the planet, needy in various ways, we might take personal responsibility and try to inspire more functional meetings. And if we can't do that in a given organization, we might start our own and create a different dynamic.

It's self-delusion to say, "I'll wait till someone else gets it together to create a political movement that feels good to me." There is no such other person. You are Moses, or at least you can create the circumstances under which Moses will emerge in you and others. Martin Luther King Jr. was not the heroic figure he became until others had begun to create a movement that made it safe for him to develop his own capacities. And at first there were many black pastors who stood in his way, who told him that he was doing the wrong thing. It is easy to romanticize the later King and ignore all the inner struggles he had to go through and all the craziness he had to deal with around him. Luckily, there were people like you and me who took the responsibility of stepping forward and building a movement from which a Martin

Luther King Jr. or a Nelson Mandela could eventually emerge. It won't happen without you.

To have that kind of inner strength, though, requires that we also take time away from politics to work on our own lives. Many of us can benefit from the regular practice of meditation, prayer, yoga, observance of the Sabbath, or some other spiritual observance. We can take the time to reflect on our lives and choose for ourselves a framework of higher meaning and purpose that will give us inner direction—for example, locating our lives within the framework of a community or social movement or religious tradition dedicated to healing the pain of the human race before it irrevocably destroys the life-support systems of this planet.

Similarly, we need to take responsibility in our personal lives to attend to our own inner needs and to the needs of our partners, spouses, children, and friends. Often the dysfunctions we face can be rectified by loving attention offered in a consistent way.

The Covenant of Personal Responsibility articulates some of the areas in which we can assume personal responsibility. We can take responsibility in our own families and relationships for bringing into them a sense of humor and playfulness, a willingness to share our own vulnerabilities and to be gentle toward our own limitations and the limitations of others around us. We can take responsibility to carry out spontaneous small acts of compassion, generosity, and love, to be careful in our speech not to say things that might be hurtful, to not bear a grudge or take revenge, and to forgive others who have offended us. We don't have to wait for a messianic era or a political revolution to be more present to others in our lives, to show them that we see them as precious, and to devote time and energy to caring for them.

The quality of our own moral lives has a tremendous impact on the movements we seek to build. The Talmud (Yoma 86a) tells us that when the Torah says, "You shall love the Lord your God," this means that God should become beloved through you. When people witness the lives of those who serve God, they should see them as so decent and pleasing that they are drawn to love God through this encounter. A spiritually aligned social movement should be filled with people whose loving qualities are so beautiful that people will be attracted to their politics because they want to know what kind of a worldview helps sustain such wonderful, loving, kind, and generous people.

Of course, as I've warned before, part of the danger here is that we will be too critical of the ways that people fail to fully embody their own highest ideals. We need to take responsibility for showing compassion toward our own and each other's limitations and weaknesses.

In the Talmud, this principle of compassion toward others takes the form of an injunction against embarrassing others. The formula given in the ancient Jewish text called the Mishnah, "Do not judge your fellow until you stand in his place," is extended in the Talmud to say that adultery is less of a crime than shaming someone in public. The Talmud cites the biblical story of Jacob sleeping with his daughter-in-law Tamar, who for this act is accused of adultery and about to be executed but declines to publicly identify Jacob as the perpetrator of the pregnancy that is the proof of her alleged crime. She sends a private message to Jacob, but she protects him from public scorn. For this, Tamar becomes an ancestor of the Davidic line that will produce the Messiah. As the Talmud concludes: "Better for one to haul himself to a fiery furnace than shame his fellow in public."

It should be noted that privileging sexual sins above the sins of taking life (war) and taking from people the means of life (dismantling social programs for the poor) has become the hallmark of the contemporary Christian Right. The secular media sensationalizes sexual offenses while giving little attention to the far more devastating crimes of war and violence. So while President Clinton might well have been criticized for his failure to act decisively to intervene against genocide in Bosnia and Rwanda, the crime for which he lost public support is the crime that at least one element in Jewish tradition claims should never have become a matter of public discourse.

I have tried to maintain this line in editing *Tikkun* magazine. I have rejected articles that contained sly put-downs of individuals with whom the author disagreed politically. For example, I always thought it unacceptable to make jokes or references to the alleged lack of intelligence of President George W. Bush or to his trouble with articulating his thoughts. I don't agree with President Bush on many matters, but I don't think that makes him or any other Republican leader "fair game" for personal criticism. I don't even care whether or not he fulfilled his military obligation or whether his not doing so did or did not indicate personal cowardice. Similarly, I thought that the sexual proclivities or sins of people in both the Democratic and Republican parties were not a proper focus for discussion in our magazine. We allow critiques of the public positions taken by political, religious, and cultural leaders, but we have refused to give space to innuendo or to charges about personal defects or personal lives.

Taking personal responsibility in regard to one's own discourse, according to Jewish tradition, requires not only not participating in this kind of "evil language" but even not listening to it when it is being presented to you by others. Jewish tradition says that one must interrupt the person engaged in such discourse and not be a passive recipient of negative stories about other people, including people in positions of authority or power. One can, however, critique their ideologies and policies, just as one can and should critique sexism, racism, or homophobia. But one can do so without having to embarrass specific people.

There are many other areas, articulated above in the covenant, in which we can pursue personal responsibility without waiting for larger social change to occur. And the more compassion we bring to our own lives and our encounters with others, the more we empower each other to believe in the possibility of a world based on love and kindness.

A Culture of Respect

The rabbis understood the command to love our fellow humans as including both love and honor. Be careful to honor all people, with the thought that you are thereby giving honor to God, because they are the work of God's hands, God's creatures.
—Avot d'Rabbi Natan

After working for twenty years as a therapist and spiritual advisor for middle-income working people, I've come to the conclusion that most people feel underrecognized, underappreciated, and underrespected. Most people spend most of their waking hours in the world of work, yet many complain that their work feels meaningless. They can't see how what they do contributes to the larger society—their work seems only to be about money, the profits they earn for the company and the (usually much smaller) amount they make for themselves. Some people are actually ashamed of their work, realizing that they are contributing to global pollution or increasing disparity in wealth but feeling there is little they can do about that. Even when people do feel good about their work, they often don't feel that others respect them for it.

When people come home from work feeling underrecognized or lacking in respect, they often make unfair demands on their spouses or children. They want to get from them some of the respect that they didn't get at work. But their spouses or children may have similar needs and not be in the perfect psychological position to deliver the needed support. Too often, when that happens, people withdraw from each other in mutual agitation, anger, or loneliness.

Whenever we recognize these dynamics, we can take steps to show one another some of the respect that every one of us needs. But we also need to make larger societal changes. We have to find a way to create workplaces in which people are recognized and appreciated for the important work they do.

In the Occupational Stress and Respect for Workers groups we ran at the Institute for Labor and Mental Health I asked postal workers what might they suggest could be done at their workplace to make them feel more respected. They said that the postal service could hand each person who comes into the post office a laminated notice explaining that the long lines are a function of trying to keep expenses down in order to be able to make mail affordable for poorer people and that, as a result, many of the postal workers were somewhat overworked and underpaid and deserved the appreciation of the public. Each person would then turn in the laminated sheet when they reached the front of the line. They also mentioned that the workplace would be more efficient if they could elect their own supervisors and recall from that position anyone who acted abusively. And, most important, they wanted to have more say about how the whole postal operation worked. They said that they would have a lot more respect for their own jobs if the management of the postal service showed more respect for them, consulted them about the major directions the service is considering, and took seriously their feedback. Working people want and deserve this kind of respect.

I once had a family member who told his wife that he "worked for the City of Newark." Eventually, we discovered he was a bathroom cleaner for the city latrines. There were people in my family who were outraged that a good Jewish boy had failed to achieve a more honorable job for himself. As a preteen, I joined in the general family mockery. But when I was twenty-two, I had the privilege of spending many months working on a kibbutz in Israel. I learned to think very differently about the nature of work. On the kibbutz, all work was valuable because we realized the whole venture could not function without all of us. We were a collective, and every single person, from dishwasher to kibbutz leader, was invited to participate in making economic decisions and to use their highest capacities to share in decision making. As a result, almost every person I met at the kibbutz felt proud of what they were creating each day in the world of work. They came home tired but often invigorated, certain that their work was contributing to higher purpose.

Imagine a workplace in which management was required to share important economic information with their workers and in which the workers themselves had an important voice in management policies, elected members to the boards of directors, and were empowered to elect their own supervisors. Their voices and concerns would be taken much more seriously. When employees feel that level of respect, they sometimes respond by working harder and really caring about the enterprise.

I say "sometimes" because it is going to take some time for people who have been manipulated and demeaned in the world of work all their lives to trust that any such consultation is about respect and not merely a new management trick to induce higher levels of productivity. I've known of some socially conscious enterprises that have failed because even though the originators of the venture were highly committed to respect and the involvement of workers in decision making, the workers who got hired never really believed that this commitment was real and could not abandon the (many times quite reasonable) suspicion that these consultations were merely new and more clever forms of manipulation. One reason why we need thoroughgoing societal change, as opposed to reforming businesses one capitalist enterprise at a time, is that people are not going to easily believe that they no longer live in a "looking out for number one" social reality unless they see all businesses acting on a different ethical foundation than that of greed and self-aggrandizement.

254 THE LEFT HAND OF GOD

To the extent that people see themselves as part of that more caring society, they will give more of themselves to each other and to the companies for which they work. But to the extent that people believe themselves part of a society in which most people are trying to maximize their own advantage, they are going to be very distrusting of any given corporation or political party that calls upon them to "sacrifice" or work for the "common good." They've heard the wealthy and their representatives in government talk about shared sacrifices for the common good, only to discover that it was middle-income and poor people who were actually making real sacrifices, while the wealthy were only further consolidating their own relative advantage over everyone else. Just ask yourself how many congressional leaders and Bush administration officials have their own children or grandchildren serving in the army in Iraq and risking their lives for the administration's war policies, and you'll see what I mean.

And yet it is this same healthy skepticism about the intentions of the powerful that can sometimes slide into an unhealthy cynical realism and doubts that anything much can be changed. When that happens, working people become their own worst enemies, insisting that they "know" that nothing can be different, resisting opportunities for unionizing, and discounting any vision of an alternative way to organize their own society. They even end up voting for candidates who oppose workers' rights. They imagine that they are just being smart by not falling for the promises made by politicians (often liberal Democrats) who told them in the past that things really could be different but then failed to deliver once they had won public office.

One way to counter this cynicism was developed in the Respect for Workers groups that we ran at the Institute for Labor and Mental Health. People met once a month, often over the course of several years, to discuss their working conditions and how these might be improved so as to create higher levels of respect for working people. The groups had as their task to envision what kinds of changes would take place at their workplace, in their union, and/or within their profession if there were a new bottom line that replaced money and power with love, caring, generosity, kindness, openheartedness, solidarity, and genuine respect.

I don't want to pretend that getting people to join or remain in such groups was easy. The internalized voices of the reality police—voices that said there was some "they" out there who would never let any real changes take place, and so what was the point of even thinking about it?—were often dominant. Yet, over time, some of these groups evolved in ways that empowered many of the people in them and made them potential vehicles for social transformation. People began to envision a workplace that was emotionally and spiritually nurturing, and some of them began to bring those ideas into their unions and professional gatherings, or even directly into their own workplaces. The more concrete the thinking, the more powerful became the suggestions about how to reorganize work and the more people who had originally been deeply skeptical became energized to fight for these changes. And that is the point, ultimately. The Respect for Workers groups were not meant to provide a place where people could let off steam so that they could better adjust to the existing reality. Rather, they offered a context in which people could work through the various ways that they had internalized self-blame so that they could overcome it and then begin to imagine and develop strategies to transform their world of work so that it would be more fulfilling and democratic and would provide them with an opportunity to serve the common good.

I think similar groups need to be created in our neighborhoods, our PTAs, our religious institutions, and our community centers, groups that would imagine a new bottom line. The task of each group would be to envision the changes that they would want to make in specific institutions—schools, courts and the legal system, businesses, government offices, hospitals and health care organizations, sports teams, and so on—and then to work together to push for those changes.

It may seem unrealistic to imagine that a simple set of neighborly discussions could change the way we work or organize institutions in America. But to the reality police, let me just say that the most successful movement of the twentieth century followed this path. When groups of women said they were going to go to their "consciousness-raising" group, many laughed at them. "Let those women hang out with their friends," they said. "Nothing will ever come of it." What came of it was the women's movement, along with vast changes in our economic and political life. Title IX—the law that provides federal money for girls' sports equal to that for boys—came out of it, as well as legal access to birth control, equal rights in the workplace, to say nothing of women like Carly Fiorina, Meg Whitman, Hillary Clinton, Barbara Boxer, and many others who now lead America's biggest businesses and play a significant role in our government. All that resulted from small groups of women meeting with each other and envisioning what the world might be like without its patriarchal underpinnings. That's what can happen today with Respect for Workers and New Bottom Line groups aimed at envisioning how the Left Hand of God could manifest itself at work and in areas like our schools, our legal system, our health care organizations, the media, and the world of scientific research.

The more people feel respected, the more empowered they feel to ask the central questions: How can we make our working world more connected to our highest values? How can we make sure that the hours we spend at work are actually contributing to some higher good in which we can believe? And how can we change the bottom line from money and power to a higher spiritual vision of "what really counts"?

What I've found in my work as a therapist and as a rabbi is that the more people feel they are part of a community that is able to ask these kinds of questions and to engage in concrete struggles to change their work, to connect it more deeply to the values they believe in, and the more hopeful they become that such struggles might actually succeed in giving their work real meaning and respect, the more they are able to separate themselves from the "common sense" of looking out for number one. Hence the more they are able to bring greater levels of loving and openness into their family lives and friendships. As hope increases about the possibility of a world filled with love, generosity, and higher purpose, people who are moved by that hope are able to be more open to the energy of the Left Hand of God within themselves and thus more open to letting that hopefulness make it safe for them to experience the vulnerability that acting from a place of love, kindness, and generosity tends to elicit. And so they become more receptive to the ideas in the other parts of this spiritual covenant, like the Social Responsibility Amendment to the Constitution.

One of the Ten Commandments reads: "Six days shalt thou labor and do all thy work, and on the seventh day is a Shabbat to God." We need to give attention to the fact that work is a divine command and thus has the potential to be sacred. In secular spiritual language, work has the potential to be a vocation, an opportunity to be of service to humanity and to the evolution of consciousness of the human race. The more we can turn our work in that direction, the more we will feel fulfilled in our humanity.

Here's a simple test that you can use to know when we've succeeded. If you can say the following blessing at the end of each workday with full conviction, you know we have built the kind of world that is congruent with a spiritual vision: "Thank you, the Creative and Transformative Power of the Universe, for giving me this opportunity to serve humanity with my talents, intelligence, and creativity and for providing me with work that is personally fulfilling and that affords a real contribution to the well-being of humanity and of our planet. Thank you for making this kind of work available not only for me but for everyone I know."

It will take many generations to get to this place, I believe, but a movement that has a clear commitment to seeking a world in which this kind of work is available to everyone will win the support and loyalty of many who now suffer through work with a depressed feeling of resignation at a life that seems meaningless and empty.

One important caveat, however. No matter how fulfilling the work, it is also important to have time away from work and its demands. The cell phone and computer have made it harder for us to find that time and space away—it seems increasingly as if the demands of the marketplace follow us home. One part of Sabbath energy consists in having twenty-five hours when we turn off all the electronic devices, forget about work, and create a space for ourselves that is just about nourishing our own souls.

It is also important to remember that being part of a community must not mean forgoing privacy. Each of us needs some time free from the demands of work and of the political and social world—a place in our lives where we get to define ourselves without worrying about our impact on others, be as eccentric as we please, as irreverent and playful as we wish, and simply focus on what brings us pleasure and joy.

Sexuality Is Sacred

The word *love* is easy to say but often hard to understand. We all can imagine a Hallmark™ world of smiling parents and happy children. However, when we talk about the love between adults, the picture grows less clear. Those on the Right often fear the power of unconditional love and wrongly attempt to create rules to enforce a rigid view of the family as a two-parent, heterosexual household. Our Covenant with American Families emphasizes the sacred power of love in all its forms.

The Jewish tradition reminds us that sexuality is a potentially holy element of love. Maimonides tells us, "Our sages said: when a man and woman unite sexually in holiness, God's divine presence (the Shechinah) rests between them" (Reshit Hochmah, Sh'ar ha-Kedusha, chap. 16, no. 54). All the religious traditions acknowledge that there can be forms of love between people that do not involve sex, a love that is sometimes said to be the love of the soul (*agape*) as opposed to love of the body (*eros*). But when it does involve eros, it is meant to be celebrated as something beautiful and joyous. And pleasurable—not ascetic! As Rabbi Tzvi Hirsch taught: "Before sexual intercourse, a couple should give thanks to God for the pleasure that God created" (Yifrach biYamav Tzaddkik, para. 48b).

One of the most startling accomplishments of the Religious Right has been its ability to make its desire to control sexuality a central political issue. In a world filled with the pain of war, starvation, and homelessness, the Religious Right manages to refocus attention on who is sleeping with whom and how and what they do and what happens afterward.

At first I, like many on the Left, believed that those on the Religious Right were simply repressing their own sexual desires. To those who come from a place of fear and who value order and control, sexuality is frightening. Sexual desire is a largely unconscious process; we may believe that our sexual desires are inappropriate, but that does not stop the desire (although we can decide whether we will act upon it). Nor is sexual pleasure entirely ours to control. Often, fulfilling the needs of our sexual partner means we must loosen our own internal restraints and reject the voices that have told us that it is selfish to focus on our own pleasure or that doing so will hurt our partner or that too much pleasure is evil. Such fear often results in sexual repression. And to some this seemed to be precisely what the Right wanted—a repression of desire and a rejection of sexual pleasure. Especially when I was a young man in the 1960s and 1970s, it was easy for me and many of my friends in social change movements and the counterculture to dismiss those on the Religious Right as uptight, sexually repressed neurotics because their message seemed to be so rejecting of pleasure.

I started to feel something was missing in the Left's analysis in the 1980s, when I lived in Jerusalem. There I encountered women who had been feminist activists in the 1960s but had then become involved with various right-wing fundamentalist Jewish sects in Israel. These were not people who had grown up with a fear of sex; they had grown up in the sexually liberating countercultures in the United States or Tel Aviv.

These women—women like Shoshana Lichtman—told me that they had felt pressured into sex in the liberal culture. "There was little in the way of real caring," Shoshana recalled. "It was an endless set of sexual demands, posed as liberation, but actually it felt quite exploitative and unliberating. I began to look for some other path, and by chance someone introduced me to Chabad Hassidus [a Jewish fundamentalist sect famous for its proselytizing of nonpracticing Jews]. They gave a very persuasive argument against free sex and lack of commitment that nailed the way people on the Left behaved. So I started to get involved with this community. Though I still have some differences with them, I also feel very supportive of the good things they do, and I feel recognized. Now I dress modestly and reveal what my body looks like only to my husband. But I feel a lot more liberated now than I felt then. I feel safe here, not the prey of sexual conquistadors, and I think that most of the women I know here feel more powerful in this context, with all the boundaries around sexuality, than we ever felt in the liberal culture that was supposedly liberating us."

As I heard Shoshana's story repeated by others who had joined right-wing Christian, Buddhist, and Muslim communities, I found that I wasn't willing to dismiss their problem with "liberated sexuality" as entirely a manifestation of uptight personalities. I began to realize that at least some of these fundamentalists had a point: there is something very screwed up in the way that sex is handled, both in some parts of the liberal world and in many parts of the capitalist marketplace. I realized I had experienced something similar myself. When I was in my twenties, I was attracted to the writings of Wilhelm Reich and others who claimed that the growth of fascist movements could be traced to the psychological and physical legacy of the repression of our sexual desire. But after a period in which I and millions of others pursued our sexual desires without very much trace of what could be called repression, it became clear to me that this was what Ecclesiastes calls "a chasing after the wind." What we were desperately seeking was not sex but love and an experience of being recognized at our soul's deepest level, and that required a deeper commitment to the other than the sexual freedom of that period had encouraged.

We who sought to liberate sex from repression had been right to value pleasure, but we had been wrong to forget that the pleasure of sex can be greatly enhanced when it comes in the context of a loving and deeply intimate and "honoring" relationship. I'm not suggesting that we impose rigid rules that would forbid sexual exploration among singles not seeking long-term commitments. Yet it's time for spiritual progressives to advocate for the advantages of sacred sex, sex in a context that is not only respectful and loving (which could happen in short-term encounters) but is also consecrated by the commitment to integrate sex into a deeper and lasting loving relationship supported by a community that is spiritually grounded and oriented toward *tikkun,* the healing and transformation of the world. Unlike Christian rightists who want to define good and bad sex, we need to talk about our aspiration to build a world in which this integration is more plausible, less of a long reach beyond the available possibilities. To do so, we need to reaffirm this central truth: every human being is a manifestation of the most holy and precious sacred energy of the universe, or in biblical language, is created in the image of God. And, for that reason, every person deserves to be treated as such. So when spiritual progressives say that they don't want sex separated from love and the sacred, it is because we don't want anything human to be separated from love and the sacred. It's not that sex is scary to us and must be tamed by making it sacred; it is that human beings are embodiments of the sacred, and so all aspects of our lives should reflect that. Sacred sexuality is an integral element of a spiritual politics.

To allow for the flourishing of sacred sexuality, we must challenge the commercialization and misuse of sex.

In our society, sex is for sale, or it is used to evoke repressed sexual desires and to associate them with goods that the manipulators of mass consciousness (politely called advertisers) are trying to sell us. There is a marketplace free-for-all of "sexual liberation," with people charging for "workshops" on various sexual techniques that are then practiced by the participants, so that sex becomes all about technique or "lifestyle," or even becomes a form of theater, rather than being about loving connection. The sacred dimension is ignored. Here, at the most intimate level of our experience, the marketplace consciousness is once again asserting itself, reducing human relationships to techniques of manipulation. And then there is the advertising industry, continually attempting to arouse sexual desire, which is then linked to some particular product or behavior that the mass manipulators are trying to sell.

When I understood this, I began to see that some of the people who were moving toward fundamentalism were not "uptight" or "repressed." Rather, they were criticizing, on a personal level, the ethos of selfishness and materialism that permeates this society. They were upset about the way that sex had become a product in the market.

I'm also upset about the way that sexuality is manipulated by the media. I was distressed when I attended a conference on the media and social responsibility to hear so many media executives claim that they were actually being socially responsible by standing up to right-wing groups that criticized the amount of promiscuity on the air. They dismissed as ridiculous the idea that the way sex and violence are used on TV to manipulate viewers into watching shows and purchasing goods might have a negative impact on the way people think about sexuality and violence in the rest of their lives. There is no evidence, these executives claimed, that television influences the behavior or thought patterns of anyone. They were startled when the CEO of one major network challenged that line of argument, reminding his colleagues that their success in selling advertisements was based on their own marketing studies, which told them that viewers were influenced by what they saw on TV.

The Right wants to end this objectifying use of sexuality by censoring the media and banning any forms of sexuality it finds objectionable. That is the path of the Right Hand of God, the path of fear. I am completely opposed to any form of governmental power being used to constrain speech or sexual expression. Individuals and social movements, however, could decide to use market pressures against those who demean the image of God in humanity (starting, in my view, with those who use violence to attract an audience), but government should stay out of the picture.

Sexuality should not be censored. Media censorship in particular is a slippery slope that leads to the repression of ideas rather than to their expression. We want to erase the climate of fear that has prompted the government to intrude so deeply into our personal lives and to replace that kind of fear with a society based on openness. In any case, censorship would not solve the larger problem of sexual exploitation. The exploitation of sexuality does not arise from people's unregulated sexual desire but from the existence of a marketplace that turns all desire into a commodity. If we had a society that was based on generosity, a society in which love was widely available, a society in which caring for others was so abundant that people felt surrounded by nurturing energies rather than by selfishness and materialism, I believe the most objectionable uses of sexual imagery would soon disappear.

When social energy flows from hope to fear, when sexuality is split off from love and becomes a thing unto itself, it becomes distorted. God becomes identified with power rather than with love, and people seek refuge in alienated forms of life, repressing sexual pleasure entirely or immersing themselves in a pornographic sexuality that lacks any human connection. To redeem sexuality, we need to redeem our society, which today denies and undermines the sanctity of loving connections. And that will happen when we have a political movement that is not afraid to champion either love or pleasure.

Get the Government Out of Marriage

Marriage has traditionally been a holy union sanctified by some spiritual community. And that is what it ought to remain. The government should have nothing to do with it.

Instead, the government should create for its own secular and civil purposes a civil union. All legal rights that the state now gives to married couples should be given to civil unions, including tax benefits, property-sharing rights, child visitation rights, power over the other's health care in the event of incapacity, shared pensions, and inheritance rights. All contracts and civil agreements that have previously specified the rights or obligations of married couples shall henceforth be given only to civil unions, although all existing marriages previously sanctioned by the state will be "grandfathered in" so that they become civil unions. Civil unions should be available to any two consenting adults. There should be no criteria with regard to gender of partners or their sexual orientation, ethnicity, race, religion or political orientation. Thus the state will confer civil union licenses on people whose unions it has sanctioned, while marriages will henceforth be the province of any religious or spiritual community and only of those communities.

With this plan, the state will stay totally clear of marriage issues. It will not enforce civil agreements made in connection with a spiritual or religious marriage but only those based on civil unions for which it has issued a license. Similarly, the state will have no power over the dissolution of marriages, nor will it seek to regulate or control any aspect of marriage or its dissolution. The communities that sanctioned these marriages will have sole jurisdiction over the terms of marriage and divorce and cannot use the state to enforce any of these agreements or arrangements. Once existing marriages have been "grandfathered in" as civil unions, no further relationship will exist between marriage and the state, so people who are married in religious communities will not have received a civil-union license. That will take place totally independently of marriage. The state will be prohibited from conferring any benefits or any other form of recognition on marriages. The state will make its own regulations for dissolution of civil unions and will place legal obligations and responsibilities on anyone who chooses to raise children.

Gays and lesbians will be able to enter into a civil union the same way as everyone else. And those who wish to affiliate with a religious or spiritual community that confers marriage on homosexual couples can do so. These are two separate acts.

Keeping the state out of marriage will not end all controversies. There will be some who will claim that religious communities that sanctify gay marriages aren't real religious communities. But that will also be true for some who will complain that religious communities that support military interventions or tax benefits for the rich are not real religious communities either. To make sure that this works appropriately, in determining which groups or organizations deserve to be granted nonprofit status, the state will be prohibited from considering that group's stance on any issue of political or religious significance. The only consideration will be whether it in fact performs an educational, religious, cultural, or social service or serves the goal of social, medical, or psychological healing, and without accruing a profit to anyone.

What About the Bible's Condemnation of Homosexual Sex?

Actually, the condemnation in the Hebrew Bible is somewhat ambiguous. What the Torah says is that it is forbidden for a man to lie with a man as he lies with a woman. Those are the words, and they allow for the interpretation that men should develop sexual behaviors appropriate for gay relationships that do not seek to imitate the behaviors appropriate for heterosexual relationships. In the New Testament there are condemnations of something the term for which would today be translated as homosexuality, but there is little reason to think that what was being condemned was the sexuality itself but rather a specific occurrence of that behavior in imperial Rome, where young male slaves were forced into homosexual prostitution. In other words, it may well have been a particular application that was being condemned, just as when witchcraft was condemned in the Torah, it was a very particular instance of witchcraft that had been associated with rituals relating to child sacrifice.

I find it odd, sometimes even a bit humorous, when I hear people telling me that they are fundamentalists (that is, biblical literalists), and then I find out that they don't know Hebrew, the language in which the Hebrew Bible was written, or Aramaic, the language that Jesus spoke, or *koine,* the form of Greek in which the New Testament was written.

I don't imagine that a close reading of the original texts is going to influence those who are deeply opposed to homosexual relationships.

But I have sometimes imagined that the tenderness and loving behavior I've seen many times in the homosexual relationships of some of my friends and members of my synagogue might help cure those who have been taught that homosexuality is a moral sickness. If those who demean homosexuality are not themselves so deeply perverted by hate that they cannot see, I imagine that they would be deeply moved by the loving connections that exist within many stable homosexual relationships, a loving that could be honored and sanctified by those religious communities that make love a central criterion in judging which relationships deserve to be honored and preserved. Unfortunately, I doubt if many of those currently crusading against gay marriage will ever allow themselves to be exposed to homosexual relationships over any extended period of time so that they could actually witness this reality. So I doubt this will be a successful strategy for defusing this issue. Nor will appeals to civil rights. Those who advocate against gay marriage have a right to fight for their own concept of sanctity—although they have no right to drag the state into validating their particular vision of sanctification. That's why the separation of the sanctity of marriage from the power of the state may eventually have the greatest public appeal.

I've often wondered why people get so very upset about homosexuality. Both Catholic and evangelical leaders with whom I've raised this question have pointed to the evidence that children raised in gay families don't do as well as those raised in heterosexual families. But when they are asked to produce the evidence, they find it very difficult to do so, particularly when the effects of discrimination against gay families are factored out (as is possible in the case of some communities where gay families are accepted and respected). The claim that homosexuality will undermine the traditional family also withers under scrutiny: it is very rare for a marriage to dissolve because there are other families in the neighborhood who are homosexual. It is not that there are too many people loving each other in unconventional ways but that there are not enough people loving each other at all that is far more likely to undermine families.

The best way to defend gays and lesbians from the Religious Right and the homophobia it generates is to build a world of love and generosity. When people feel secure in receiving enough recognition, kindness, and generosity from others, they will be far less inclined to need scapegoats.

One aspect of homophobia may be the unconscious but powerful messages given to boys that tell them to stop identifying with their mothers and take on the tough exteriors that they will need to succeed in a world in which everyone is looking out for number one. Popular culture often identifies the man who isn't tough with homosexuality and suggests that these men are not going to be "real men" who can protect themselves and their families from the dangers of the "real world." Our countermessage is that this kind of "real man" is actually a gross distortion of our humanity, a product of fear and an approach to life that we do not want to sustain. I don't blame men who have been made to feel so insecure about their manhood that they feel the need to prove it by dominating others or by distancing themselves from men who don't act out these traditional male roles. But I certainly don't want to let their pathologies become the standard of normal behavior. Whenever a politician baits others about being "girlie men," as California Governor Arnold Schwarzenegger did in 2004, it is important for the rest of us, and particularly heterosexual men, to affirm that being a "girlie" man is a good thing, not something to fear. I believe our movement will be much stronger when heterosexual progressive men take as part of our responsibility the task of teaching other men that the traits usually associated with girls—nurturing, compassion, caring for others, putting a loving relationship ahead of domination or conquest—are all wonderful qualities that we men need more of, and that's one important reason why we embrace the Left Hand of God. We have to embrace these qualities vigorously and publicly, in a powerful and not wimpy or apologetic way. Stand up to the ridicule of the bullies who seek to humiliate boys or men who affirm love, gentleness, and compassion. Recognize that their need to make fun of these qualities comes from their inner panic that they might be perceived as too soft. Stand strong on behalf of sensitivity, generosity, and vulnerability! If we do, and if we do not collapse under the first waves of media cynicism and attempts to humiliate us, we can eventually make it safe for these other men to reconnect to the part of their own psyches that yearns for a gentler world.

Abortion

Make it safe, legal, and rare. And make childrearing safe, economically supported, and surrounded by a loving community that celebrates the mystery and miracle of life and that honors and rewards the parent or parents who have undertaken the difficult and beautiful task of raising children.

Many liberals point to the fact that there were fewer abortions during the Clinton administration, when sex education and contraception were more abundant and financial support for the needy was better funded. Their correct conclusion: If you want to reduce the number of abortions, provide adequate contraception and sex education that does not stigmatize sex or tell people that they've been bad unless they've lived up to a supposed ideal of abstinence. Make it easier for young and poor women to support their children with dignity rather than cutting funds for needed social services.

Economic reductionism is never a full account, however, so I would point to another factor influencing the abortion rate: the level of social trust. When people feel that they can count on each other more, there is a greater willingness to bring babies to term. So if you are in the section of the population that is financially unstable or outright poor and are surrounded by messages that tell you that this is your own fault and that you should fend for yourself, it is harder to convince young pregnant women that they are living in a world that is safe. If they live in a world in which they can count on others to help them out, it will seem much less dangerous to take the risk of having a child as opposed to aborting it. It's not absolute levels of money that will be determinative, but the flow of social energy between fear and hope.

Spiritual progressives should be unequivocal in opposing any attempts to make abortion illegal. But we should be equally unequivocal in recognizing abortion as a tragic loss not only for the individual woman who has chosen to undergo it but also for the entire community. The miracle of life flowing through us deserves to be treated with sanctity and care, and when life is snuffed out, this is an occasion for communal sadness and mourning.

Most women who have gone through abortions will tell you how very emotionally painful it has been to experience this loss of life. A spiritual community should be there to provide emotional and spiritual support, to make it possible for the woman to really grieve the loss, and to affirm a shared vision of the sanctity of life.

The overwhelming majority of Americans today are opposed to returning to the days when abortion was illegal and women often risked or lost their lives seeking illegal abortions. I hope it stays that way. But I'm not sure it will, partly because the discourse that has developed that reduces abortion to a matter of an individual choice on the part of the woman seems so out of touch with the spiritual dimension of what is going on in the situations in which women are making these decisions.

A growing number of younger spiritual feminists are making this kind of point. We don't quite know when a fetus becomes a person, but it does happen at some point. And though we may not be able to define exactly when that is, we certainly want to recognize that the medical procedure in question is not like any other, in that it involves a loss of life not just the loss of a body part. And this loss of life affects not only the woman, but the man who was a part of the conception, and the community in which this woman lives, and the entire global community. So these spiritual feminists reject the extreme individualism implicit in the language that frames this whole process as merely a matter of a woman's right to control her own body. Instead of viewing people as fundamentally separate beings, each with a private right to control his or her own space and life, and then imagining the planet as filled with six billion such separate individuals (in which case, it's a bit difficult to understand where moral obligations to care for the well-being of others derive), they see each individual woman and man as part of the unity of all being, as fundamentally interconnected, and each decision we make as one that emanates from our link to all others, having consequences that will affect all others.

When one talks in a language of mutual interconnection, one affirms everyone's obligation to take into account the well-being of others and the impact on others of one's own choices. That does not relieve one of the burden and moral responsibility of making those choices, nor does it empower a community to intervene and make our choices for us. But it situates us as fundamentally linked to one another and as having some responsibility to check in with others about the impact of our actions on them. This is not a checking-in that can or should be legally mandated. I talked above about building a movement that created an ethos in the liberal and progressive culture that was disapproving of the demeaning of sexuality. So, too, we should seek to create an ethos in which women feel invited to consult and receive support from others affected by their decision to abort, and conversely for those involved to offer support and comfort should such a decision be taken by the pregnant woman. At every stage of this process, the relevant community needs to be involved in a caring and supportive way.

But is this possible in an America riven by conflict about abortion, and in a society where the "relevant community" may include a man who has imposed his will on a woman (through either brute force or subtle forms of domination or manipulation)? I want to see efforts to develop training programs for people that would teach them how to be compassionate and supportive, so that they could be genuinely helpful in this kind of community context. And I want to caution against anyone trying to pressure a woman to be part of this community process.

It is the absence of that community of support and the absence of mourning rituals and processes, coupled with the attempt by some to describe this whole process as nothing more than an individual right to choose a medical procedure, that might someday lead people to join sections of the Religious Right who have their own reasons for opposing abortion. Heading off this possibility is yet another reason for a spiritual Left to seek to place abortion within a more spiritual frame and to evolve a more developed process for consultation with others and for mourning.

One reason that many feminists have not gone in this direction is that they sense that many of those in the Religious Right who have been most radical in their opposition to legalizing abortion have not been motivated by concerns about the tragedy of lost life. Rather, they are disturbed about the way that abortions have empowered women to take control of their own lives. The underlying agenda for many of these men and women on the Right was to restore themselves to a world that felt safer, a world in which women stayed in relationships all their lives, and hence a world in which their own families would be more secure—less threatened by the changing emotional terrain of the modern world. I sympathize with these right-wingers' desire for greater stability, but I oppose their solution: reinforcing patriarchal family forms and opposing changes that have given women more freedom, including the freedom to leave families that feel oppressive and loveless. If right-wingers want stability in family life, they should join with spiritual progressives in challenging the ethos of selfishness and materialism that has undermined loving relationships and lasting friendships and turned sacred territory into market relationships.

Some religious right-wingers respond that that's just what they are doing when they challenge the selfishness of women who want to leave a marriage and go elsewhere, as though they had no obligation to the well-being of their children. It is their selfishness that is undermining family life, they argue, and this is why they (Catholics and some fundamentalist Protestants) oppose divorce and oppose the way that abortion rights have contributed to freeing women to engage in selfishness. But while their desire for stability in families is understandable, it is an illusion to believe that we as a society will ever recapture a time in which stability could be imposed by force or social coercion. People who have tasted the joys and empowerment of being free from societal coercion in their personal lives will not tolerate attempts at physical, emotional, or spiritual coercion in areas of their lives that they consider personal. Stability in family life can only be achieved by making that family life so fulfilling that people will voluntarily choose to stay in it. To make that happen, we must build on love, not on coercion. If we value stable families, we must promote love, choice, and independence. These are the conditions for the flourishing of families that stay together.

Until people on the Right really understand this, I will join in the suspicions of many feminists that the right-wing antiabortion agenda is not so much about life as about patriarchy. And I'll join those women in resisting any restoration of patriarchal practices and in exposing the hypocrisies of those who claim to be pro-life but who are unwilling to provide economic and political and social supports for children once they are born, who support American military interventions in which tens of thousands of innocent men, women, and children are killed, who support the death penalty, and who are remarkably unconcerned about the between 20,000 and 30,000 children around the world (according to different estimates) who die each day from malnutrition or preventable diseases. While I acknowledge that there are a small group of Christians who are more consistent in opposing the denial of life in all these forms, the majority of pro-lifers seem not to care about all these other ways in which life is being undermined. This inconsistency suggests that we look a little deeper and uncover the not-very-well-hidden patriarchal restoration that many of the right-wingers yearn for.

Nor can I support the various attempts to legally restrict abortions by defining specific situations and then making abortions under those circumstances illegal—outlawing abortions during the final trimester of pregnancy, for example, or making it illegal to help a teenage girl cross state lines to receive an abortion, or prohibiting teenagers from getting an abortion without parental consent. On the face of each of these, the restrictions make some sense. But the proposals are usually written without nuance and sensitivity to the many complexities in life that require important exceptions. Is this because the proponents are stupid and can't think in complex ways? No. It is because these proposals are actually being put forward by people who believe that abortion is always morally wrong because the Bible told them so.

Of course, the Bible did no such thing. Jesus, who opposed divorce, never mentioned abortion, nor did anyone else in either the Hebrew Bible or the New Testament. Most Jews do not believe that their Jewish faith mandates any blanket prohibition of abortion, so if American law were to make abortion illegal, it would only be because a section of the Religious Right had been able to impose its religious practices on the entire civic community.

Some feminists today have grown distrustful of the discourse of "choice" because they see that language of choice as morally empty, reinforcing the individualistic worldview that has been shown to be a central prop of the spiritual crisis of the contemporary age and contributing to the de-meaning of life and the triumph of a one-dimensional technocratic rationality that they abhor.

But I would be cautious about taking that stance without giving it a lot more nuance. In view of the long history of women being socialized to serve the interests of men, encouraging a bit more in the way of individualism and taking on more traditionally masculine postures may be part of a necessary rebalancing of sexual roles, just as men need to be encouraged to move toward greater connectivity and vulnerability. In this sense, women's ability to choose how to create their own lives is not "morally empty" but much more affirming of an important process of consolidating what women have won for themselves over the past few decades.

The language of "choice" in matters of reproduction has a very distressing and fundamentally misleading implication: that somehow ending a pregnancy is a choice that is analogous to and in the same league as, say, deciding to have one's moles surgically removed or even the choice of which stockings to wear. We need to affirm the sanctity of life and develop spiritual processes to mark the decision to terminate a pregnancy, and rituals of mourning and purification to acknowledge what is, in the absence of these rituals, usually experienced only as a personal tragedy. It is not enough to keep antiabortion protesters away from Planned Parenthood or other clinics offering the medical procedures to terminate a pregnancy. We also need to put in place a ritual that provides support and comfort to women who face this difficult and often emotionally and spiritually draining experience, while recognizing that some women need the abortion process to be a purely personal experience (a desire we should respect).

Here, as in all matters facing spiritual progressives, the goal is to achieve a rebalancing on both the personal and societal levels.

Family Support Projects

In an earlier section of this book I discussed the way many of us have internalized the meritocratic fantasy that this is a society in which the kind of work we do reflects our actual worth—as though we could have been anything had we only been smart enough and together enough to go for it, and as though where we've actually ended up shows who we "really are." Not only is that false—a total misreading of the realities of living in a class-dominated society—but it also creates a dynamic of self-blaming that is emotionally crippling for many people.

As if that isn't bad enough, there's another element of the meritocratic ideology that operates in our personal lives. We are told that quite apart from the fact that the work we do may not be so fulfilling, we shouldn't invest too much energy there because, after all, we can find a perfect relationship that will deliver to us all the loving and all the meaning for our life that we couldn't find in the public world of work. That expectation—that we will find the perfect "other" who will provide emotional and spiritual compensation for the alienation we experience in every other corner of our lives—is almost always unrealistic. Further, it places a burden of expectation on any relationship that it can rarely fulfill. And when our relationships don't quite seem to compensate for the lives we have lost in a world of work that feels so unfulfilling, we either get angry at our spouses or children or at ourselves.

We often blame ourselves for not having been more terrific, imagining that if only we had been more attractive, or intelligent, or something, we would have found the spouse or partner who would have truly been the fulfillment of our fantasy. That disappointment often shows up in depression, emotional withdrawal, and deep unhappiness. Yet, because we feel that this is all our own fault, many of us try to cover this all up, burying our feelings in drugs, alcohol, television abuse, or in frenetic activity: sports, exercise, computer games, or endless hours at work. And the impact of all this is that our families experience us as not present, and soon our spouse and children are themselves acting in angry or hurtful ways toward us.

Not everyone goes through this in the exactly same way, of course. For some, there already exists enough awareness of the negative impact of work that they are able simply to feel angry at the workplace and not lay that anger on their partner, spouse, or children. Yet most of us need a safe place to talk about the frustrations of our day and about the relationship between our family and work lives, without feeling like we are supposed to be fixing anything. The Covenant with American Families thus includes the creation of family support networks.

The task of the family support network is first of all to help people understand a central truth about families: everyone has problems in their family life. Demystifying this reality is central, because even sophisticated people who know that everyone has problems in family life tend nevertheless to believe that their own particular personal family is worse than that of most others and that they themselves are worse than most other people.

A second function of family support networks is to provide opportunities for parents to learn parenting skills and for families to learn family communication skills.

While the acquisition of these skills can be aided by the contributions of professional family therapists, the key to the success of family support networks is to model themselves on Twelve Step programs, at least with regard to this: that they cost nothing, that they are led by their members and not by professionals, and that they have an explicit goal of affirming the human spiritual essence.

There are already family support networks that have been created by various religious communities. A progressive spiritual politics, however, would separate this process from any particular religious community and seek to promote family support groups that do not require a belief in a particular God and would be equally welcoming to secular and religious people. Yet these groups would share a commitment to the values of the Left Hand of God.

Almost all families face problems with communication and mutual support. They are as prevalent among the rich as the poor. Family support is a cross-class issue that has the potential to unite people from very diverse backgrounds.

But there are also problems that are more tied to not having adequate resources, and they, too, must be addressed as part of a pro-families agenda for a movement of spiritual progressives. For some families, the needs are most immediately material. For these people, society doesn't provide the basics, so a pro-families movement must fight for legislation and programs that can solve the following:

1. *A living wage.* If people have to take two or even three jobs in order to be able to support their families, they may be too exhausted to have time to actually be with their families and build the loving ties that are necessary to sustain loving commitments.

2. *Ending poverty.* According to the Children's Defense Fund, "In 2003, 12.9 million American children younger than 18 lived below the poverty line and more than one out of every six American children (17.6 percent) was poor. There are more children living in poverty today than 30 or 35 years ago. A child in America is more likely to live in poverty than a child in any of the 18 other wealthy industrialized nations for which data exist." We cannot have healthy families while children still go hungry.

3. *Full employment.* Unemployment is one of those things that always seems far away, a problem happening to someone else, until it hits your family or your community. But it has hit many Americans. According to the AFL-CIO, "By February 2005, 8 million were officially jobless—but experts estimate the total number of unemployed and underemployed is nearly 14 million." Every person who wants to work should be able to work.

4. *Quality child care.* Each of us alive today has been the beneficiary of the kindness and generosity of past generations. We have an obligation to pass on the same benefits to coming generations. Quality child care is so hard to find because many parents cannot afford good child care on their own and the state does nothing to help. In fact, child-care workers are among the lowest paid workers in the United States—their average wage is $15,430 a year, usually with no benefits or paid leave. As the AFL-CIO points out, on average, child-care workers earn less than parking-lot attendants. A spiritual politics insists that publicly financed high-quality child care be available as a right for every family and that child-care workers be paid at the same rate as other critically important civil servants like police and firefighters.

5. *Quality health care.* I will say more about health care in the next chapter. Let me just say here that the United States spends more on health care than any other country in the world, yet nearly 47 million Americans lack medical coverage. We must offer all Americans affordable, single-payer health insurance.

6. *Quality time.* Our society does not value our time. The poor work multiple jobs to make a living. Professionals and managers are told that they can advance only by working extra hours and by being available to work "24/7." Such hours do not give us a chance to connect to each other or to nourish our own souls. My Jewish faith calls on me to take a Sabbath day at least once a week as an opportunity to reflect on the world in which I live. We all need time for sacred rest. A spiritual politics advocates making time in the week for ourselves and the others in our

lives, and that might involve a 32-hour (that is, four-day) work week or flex-time schedules.

These policies are critical to creating a new bottom line for our families. They will be more powerful when we frame them as part of our covenant with families, because most Americans actually want strong families. Yet they rarely hear people on the Left talking about a pro-families program that coherently addresses the fears they have about instability in family life.

Imagine how deeply people would appreciate the Democratic Party that was pro-families in all the ways described in this chapter—supporting a living wage and adequate health care, ending poverty, ensuring full employment, providing quality child care, shortening the work week to allow more time for families, restoring the sacred dimension to sexuality, encouraging personal responsibility, helping to create a world of work in which people felt respected, participated in shaping decisions, and were encouraged to and rewarded for showing caring for others and for the well-being of the world. A Democratic Party that insisted that the most effective way to be pro-families was to fight for a world in which love and generosity was the bottom line could have a powerful and transformative impact on American politics, winning to its side many who today imagine that the best way to support families is to vote for the Right.

In the next chapter we will turn to the question of how to build an economy and a society that actually would be able to encourage the development of the character traits and behaviors that strengthen the family by building a world in which pro-family values like love and generosity are the norm rather than the exception.

The Limits of Love

Families and loving relationships will be far more stable and fulfilling when they are part of a society that values love and caring, generosity and kindness. But spiritual traditions teach that part of what makes people unhappy is a level of desire that can never be fulfilled. Some Buddhists teach us not to be attached to the fulfillment of our desires. No matter how much pleasure we get, there will always be a nagging

feeling that something is lacking in our lives. Suffering comes from desire. It is by learning a path of nonattachment that we free ourselves
from desire.

In *Open to Desire: Embracing a Lust for Life Using Insights from
Buddhism and Psychotherapy* (Gotham Books, 2005), Mark Epstein
speaks of the distinction in Buddhism between "the right-handed path
of renunciation and monasticism in which sensory desires are avoided
and the left-handed path of passion and relationship in which sensory
desires are not avoided but are made into objects of meditation"
(p. 40). As he explains: "What the Buddha actually suggested is that it
is the avoidance of the elusiveness of the object of desire that is the origin of suffering. The problem is not desire: it is clinging to, or craving,
a particular outcome, one in which there is no remainder, in which the
object is completely under our power" (p. 41). Epstein contrasts this
craving with "being fully present in the moment, aware without judgment and able to live fully in the Now," but he goes on to acknowledge
that "as many a meditator has belatedly had to admit, even this goal is
impossible to achieve" (p. 65). Desire can never be entirely eliminated,
nor can it ever be entirely satisfied.

And this applies directly to love. The love we seek, Epstein argues,
is too often a desire for "total surrender, complete immersion, or indis-
putable closeness. . . . Desire moves us toward climax, but its resolution
is anticlimactic." Love raises for us the possibility of transcending ego
boundaries, but often we come away feeling a certain otherness and
loneliness.

So, the skeptic might argue, all this stuff about social change is just a
way of denying the inevitable limitations of human connections.

I think there is an important point here, but it does not invalidate
the enterprise of the Left Hand of God. I have never argued that
achieving a society based on love and generosity, on kindness and caring for others, will be the end of history, a utopian finish to all suffering
and loneliness. What we need to do is distinguish between the loneliness and suffering that are built into the human condition—it will be
there no matter how we organize our society—and the huge amount of
what I'd call "surplus suffering," that is, suffering that is not a function
of the nature of human life but rather is caused by the way we have
chosen to organize our social order today.

The Left Hand of God calls upon us to create a world in which the bottom line is love and caring and suggests that, when such a world is built, we will have taken monumental steps to reduce the level of suffering in our society. It will be far easier to sustain loving relationships and families, far easier to convince people to live by their own highest ethical standards, far easier to eliminate war, poverty, and ecological irresponsibility. But that does not mean that all suffering will disappear.

It is recognizing that suffering can be dramatically reduced that leads us to engage in building a network of spiritual progressives aimed at mobilizing action to transform the way we organize economic and political life, the media, government, and many other institutions. In acknowledging that suffering will not be totally eliminated, we also affirm the importance of developing an inner life as well as spiritual practices that can help us accept the impermanence of life and the limitations on the fulfillment of desire, help us relinquish the fantasy that some great achievement or the acquisition of wealth or fame will allow us to overcome death, help us to become aware of our interconnectedness with all other beings, and help us stay present to those realities in the world that cannot be transformed and that will always partially frustrate desire.

Limitations need not generate emotional depression or despair. They can also generate compassion and the capacity to rejoice in what is ours. "Happy are we, how wonderful is our portion, how beautiful all that we have inherited from the universe and from the past of the human race, including the opportunity to affirm the unity of all with all through our participation in the divine energy of the universe." Most Jews don't even arrive at services early enough to hear this prayer, which falls in the first few pages of the morning service, but rejoicing in our portion really is part of worship, and a part that acknowledges limits.

It is in establishing a spiritual balance between the social, the economic, and the political, on the one hand, and the demands of a healthy inner life, on the other, that is the great challenge that each of us faces. And it is this challenge that a spiritually sensitive social change movement must acknowledge and make space for in the way that it constructs its program and organizes itself. I'll have more to say about this in the appendix.

ELEVEN

The Caring Economy and Nurturing Society: From Social Responsibility to Human Connectedness

Reb David'l of Lelov told Rabbi Yitzhak of Vorki, "Everyone in their innermost heart, even when they don't know it, actually wants to do good to other human beings. So everyone who works, as a shoemaker or tailor or baker or whatever who serves others, on the inside he doesn't do this work in order to make money, but in order to do good to his fellow human being—even though he does receive money for his trouble, but this is just secondary and unimportant, but the inner meaning of his work is that he wants to do good and show kindness to his fellow human being."
—Gedulat Mordechai ve Gedulat haTzadikkim

The new bottom line emphasizes the importance of social responsibility and the common good. The premise of the Left Hand of God is that we have a common interest in caring for everyone in our society— that each of us flourishes when we all thrive emotionally, spiritually, economically, intellectually, culturally, and physically. One natural consequence of such mutuality is a deep and immediate responsibility to build a world based on justice, equality, fairness, and peace, a world that cares for the well-being of everyone on the planet.

Yet it would be a mistake to characterize our social role in terms of what we "must" do or "should" do for others. "Responsibility" too often conjures up an image of a stern teacher or relative or preacher shaking their hands at us, scolding us for not being "responsible" enough. We are seeking a world governed by love and generosity, not by emotional or moral coercion, and certainly not by rules of political correctness or by bureaucratic attempts to reduce love to a series of bank checks for anonymous citizen-beneficiaries. It's time to reaffirm how very good it feels to live in a society in which people care for each other, how much that by itself raises the quality of life and the standard of living for everyone. Social responsibility is a joyous activity that deeply connects us to others.

When caring is separated from this joyous opportunity to enhance human connectedness and becomes instead just an external act of giving money to someone else, it feels less satisfying to everyone involved. When the part of us that really wants to care about others is activated, people act with incredible generosity and are willing to take personal risks, pay higher taxes, and make fundamental changes in their lives. But when they feel that a governmental program is really just about satisfying selfish needs of special interests, they get cynical, resentful of government and its taxes, and angry at those who seem to benefit from these programs.

Not understanding this was one of the great failures of the New Deal and the Great Society. Many of the New Deal and Great Society programs were motivated by a desire to be loving and caring toward others. But because the Left did not have a spiritual politics, they did not understand that delivering money was a necessary but not sufficient part of a program of caring for others. And they particularly didn't understand that their programs needed to be delivered in a loving way.

So what they ended up delivering was objective caring. People received various kinds of economic assistance from the state. Meanwhile, conservatives seeking to curtail the effectiveness of social programs and cut government spending often sought to curtail this objective caring delivered to the needy. As liberals compromised to prove that they were being fiscally responsible, the programs that were actually funded were frequently insufficient to provide more than subsistence survival for economically struggling families.

What was most frequently missing was subjective caring, the experience of feeling cared for by others. Bureaucratic regulations and impersonal ways of delivering governmental social programs undermined the ability of people to experience themselves as deserving recipients of the generosity of their caring neighbors.

In the interviews we conducted at the Institute for Labor and Mental Health, we raised this issue with government workers. They explained that they often wished they could be more caring in their treatment of the public, but that there was no place for this in the way their work was evaluated. No one ever gave them support for being nice to the public. On the contrary, they felt a constant pressure to do more and do it more quickly. They endured endless bureaucratic checks on their activity designed to prove to the Republicans that no one was stealing or otherwise ripping off the government. If only the Republicans exercised the same vigilance when it came to the programs that provided welfare for the rich and for corporations and government giveaways to the military-industrial complex!

Instead of programs that would have created full employment and permanently ended poverty, the programs that actually were funded only sought to relieve the worst impact of the competitive marketplace, leaving in place a considerable army of the unemployed whose very existence guaranteed a strong hand for corporations when it came to bargaining with workers over working conditions and wages: a corporation could always threaten to hire the unemployed if its current workers were not more compliant. Ordinary citizens, originally wanting to help the poor, found that the liberal programs did not actually serve to eliminate poverty but seemed only to be pouring working families' hard-earned cash into what many perceived to be a bottomless pit of benefits to an increasingly chronic class of poor people.

No wonder, then, that the political Right could build a successful movement aimed at reducing government programs. On the one hand, they could count on an educational system and media that failed to teach people how their current material well-being depended in larger part on the intervention of government programs, including in many cases government-sponsored housing and education programs that had enabled their own parents or grandparents to get out of poverty and begin a rise into middle-class security. On the other hand, they could count on people having the experience of paying taxes for programs that claimed to be about caring for someone else without it being obvious to anyone that government was actually solving anything by handing out money. To make matters worse, the beneficiaries rarely felt respected by the government workers who administered these programs. They felt condescended to, and this vitiated the gratitude that they might have felt for social programs, particularly when the programs themselves were often underfunded. Yet absent an experience of gratitude from those benefiting from the programs, many who were paying taxes began to feel unappreciated and then resentful at having to give over this part of their income to no apparent benefit.

A spiritual politics must create a psychospiritual context for the communal sharing of resources. That means we must bring compassion down to the level of the individual and create what I call the subjective experience of caring. Such an approach must reward government workers to the extent that they are successful in showing a caring attitude toward the public, and it must find ways to convey to the population as a whole the appreciation and gratitude of those who benefit from public support. It must reward corporate workers for contributing to the common good. It must find ways to generate in those who pay taxes a deep sense of satisfaction that they are thereby making a real contribution to the common good, enabling them to feel proud that, by paying taxes, they are affirming the deep part of themselves that really does want to care for others.

Satisfaction about caring for others won't be hard to generate, because it already exists—it's just hidden. Economists talk a lot about human nature, emphasizing the "reality" of human selfishness and greed. What is missing from that supposedly commonsense analysis is any account of the joy that comes from being able to give to others. We can receive tangible pleasure in knowing that our lives and our work truly do benefit others and are genuinely appreciated.

In our society, status often comes from having and controlling the most things. Anthropologist Lewis Hyde, however, has described some societies that have a "gift economy," in which status comes to people in proportion to how much they are able to give away. Despite all the societal conditioning we've received insisting that people have a "natural desire" to hold on to things, societies have existed in which the greatest good was to be able to give away material possessions. And, of course, since everyone was giving, there was a constant rotation of gifts, so that people were receiving as well as giving. Some spiritual traditions have linked into that consciousness, seeing our whole lives as a gift to God or to the spiritual well-being of the universe. Our society has concealed a secret that the Left Hand of God reveals: a life of giving is a life of joy. It opens us to new levels of human connectedness. It helps us fulfill the deepest spiritual aspirations of our souls, namely, the need to be needed and to feel that you have contributed your energy to something of value.

We have a long way to go before we would be able to base our social order on the gift economy. We could take powerful steps toward that goal by adopting the Covenant of Social Responsibility. To get there we need to break through the social disconnection that leaves so many people trapped in loneliness (even when they are with other people) or unsuccessfully seeking to find meaning in the shallowness of mass culture. Whether we are walking down the street, standing in an elevator in a store or office building, sitting in a bus or a subway, we are all too familiar with the experience of being surrounded by people with glazed looks on their faces, each sending out to others a clear signal: "Don't you dare try to connect with me." Even though most of us have an innate curiosity about who these others are, we get a strong signal that "no one is really at home" behind the blank stares and emotionally empty faces. That same emotional and spiritual emptiness characterizes the people on our television screens, from the characters in TV sit-coms, to the amiable but fundamentally staged personalities of news anchors, to the politicians whom we rarely meet in person but who are carefully presented to us as our leaders. Our task is to break through that facade and build a society in which mutual recognition and subjective caring are supported rather than undermined by our jobs and our economy, our educational system, our health care system, and our relationship to the environment.

The Social Responsibility Amendment to the Constitution

However powerful individual efforts at social responsibility may be, we are up against a massive problem: corporations are subordinate to the demands of the competitive market system that encourages the bottom line of materialism and selfishness. I've made this case fully in the first part of the book, so here I will only remind you that corporate leaders can be held legally responsible if they do not exercise due diligence toward their fiduciary responsibility to maximize the financial return of profits to their investors.

Corporate leaders know that they can and will be replaced if they can't show that they have come up with a strategy that works to increase the profits of their investors. If its level is not improving, investors will tend to sell their stock in a company in order to get a better return on their investments. In turn, as investors seek to sell, that will reduce the value of the stock to those who continue to hold it. Thus corporate leaders, no matter how personally socially conscious they may be, have to repeatedly make decisions that favor high profit margins. For example, the auto industry knows that the emissions from SUVs are more destructive to the environment and that these vehicles consume more gasoline and oil than other cars, but even though they may truly care about the environment, they go right ahead and produce SUVs because they can see the clear potential for profit. Similarly, when companies face the decision about where to locate their factories, the appeal of the lower wages that can be paid to workers in foreign countries or the prospect of fewer environmental restrictions far outweigh the demand to provide support to the communities in which they functioned in the past or the workers who previously built their products.

It's key to understand that this has nothing to do with evil people. The people who work in these institutions are, under most circumstances, just as moral as anyone else in the society. But they are working under constraints that often appear overwhelming, unchangeable, and "natural."

That's precisely why we need the Social Responsibility Amendment to the Constitution. The SRA says the following: "Every corporation with income above $50 million a year must apply for a new corporate charter once every ten years, and that new charter will be granted only to corporations that can prove a satisfactory history of social responsibility to a jury of ordinary citizens. No branch of government shall make any treaties or enter into international agreements that limit the right of the United States to insist on the corporate social responsibility of any firm that operates or sells goods within the boundaries of the United States and any territory under the functional control of the United States or its military. Any such treaties already concluded, or any part of the Constitution that cannot be reconciled with this amendment, or any national or state legislation that has the effect of protecting companies or corporations from ethical and ecological responsibility is hereby declared null and void."

The SRA will speak to the many morally grounded business people who would actually love to live in a world in which their corporations could be more socially responsible, only they fear that promoting such a world would be irresponsible to investors and risky to their own futures. The SRA provides them with a powerful incentive to make their corporations more socially responsible: the concern that if they fail to do so, they will risk their investors' entire investment. It thus aids them in debates with shareholders who are looking for a fast return on their money by giving them an important counterargument: "Your investment may be worthless unless we can periodically prove that our corporation has in fact been operating at a satisfactory history of social responsibility."

The SRA has the advantage that it does not require setting up a new government bureaucracy, whether at the federal or the state level. Community organizations both in the United States and around the world will be invited to submit testimony to juries made up of ordinary citizens, as will corporate representatives and representatives of the employees. The juries will have the right to subpoena documents and impose jail sentences on any corporate leaders who do not supply the requested information or who in other ways thwart the process. The juries may solicit legal help or advice, but they will not be supervised by a judge telling them what they can or cannot do. Instead they will function like an investigative grand jury. The juries will be empowered to hire their own investigators from private companies that they will select in a process of open bidding.

Each jury will be given a list of criteria to consider, in the form of an Ethical Impact Report, but will also be legally mandated to make their own decisions about what other factors might need to be added to the list.

An Ethical Impact Report will offer guidelines for corporations to pass the test of social responsibility. Such a report would require corporations to state how they have fulfilled obligations such as the following:

Gives global and local environmental concerns a high priority in making investment and production decisions

Produces socially valuable products, not merely products for which a desire must be generated through mass advertising

Promotes the value of truth-telling and personal integrity in its day-to-day operations and respect in the presentation of itself and its products to the public

Makes information about its operations freely available to the public

Requires accountability for corporate executives and members of the board of directors—accountability both to their own employees and to the public whose lives are affected by that corporation's decisions

Provides workers with a decent living within physically and psychologically healthy and safe working conditions

Allows workers adequate time to attend to their family needs

Provides workers with adequate opportunities to organize themselves and participate in corporate decision making

Encourages workers to use their intelligence and creativity at work and fosters cooperation among its employees and an attitude of service toward the public, and rewards workers who find ways to use corporate resources to serve the common good

Creates time for workers to have short periods each day for emotional and spiritual renewal on their own, without dictating a specific format or imposing any particular spiritual or religious practices, as well as time for workers to periodically assess the operations and products of their corporation from the standpoint of its contribution to the common good and service toward humanity

Shows loyalty to its workers and to the community

Avoids discrimination in hiring and promotions

Encourages an environment of openheartedness and generosity and rewards workers who find ways that the corporation can be more socially responsible on both a local and a global level

These are just some of the aspects of corporate functioning that an Ethical Impact Report could aim to assess.

Giving this level of power over the future of corporations to ordinary citizens is in accord with the fundamental democratic instincts of American tradition, instincts that tell us to trust the people. If we allow a jury of ordinary citizens to hear capital offenses and to deliberate about whether to impose the death sentence on someone, surely they can handle the responsibility of judging corporate behavior just as well. Because work on a community jury may take many weeks, jurors should be compensated for their services out of a fund paid into by all the firms with earnings above $50 million a year. For a period not to exceed four months, jury members will be paid at the level of the median average pay for corporate executives in the totality of firms being investigated, after which their pay will return to the level they were being paid in their own jobs, so as to limit any financial incentive to keep these investigations going on for an overly long time.

There are some who believe that the intent of the SRA can be achieved without an amendment to the Constitution, through state licensing requirements. That should certainly be tried, though the threat of corporations ready to move their operations to other parts of the world might prevent some state legislatures from being willing to take on this challenge. There are others who will argue that something like the SRA could never be passed, given the difficulties of amending the

Constitution and the dangers of opening up that process. That may be. History, however, suggests a possible advantage of trying to pass a constitutional amendment. The Equal Rights Amendment was never passed. But the struggle for the ERA had a powerful impact in advancing the consciousness of women's equality, and the struggle for the SRA is likely to have a powerful effect on making workplaces and our economy more family friendly, more environmentally conscious, and more sensitive to the needs of the employees and communities who are affected by the work of the corporations in question.

If passed, the SRA would actually institute a new bottom line in most workplaces, even in workplaces that had not yet grown to be the size of those subject to evaluation by the SRA. Employers would have a massive incentive to cooperate with their own workers in creating working conditions that remained profitable yet also felt fulfilling to the workers. And they would have a massive incentive to change what and how they produced so as to bring their operations more into harmony with the needs of our global physical environment. Many of the changes we've said are needed in the workplace to strengthen family life would no longer seem utopian once the SRA had been passed. Most importantly, employers would have a massive incentive to encourage rather than discourage the promotion of a new set of values, so that people began to learn that the work world was not only about profit but also about human connectedness, about acknowledging the sacred in each other and acting accordingly.

If other countries didn't go along with it, wouldn't a new bottom line make the United States less competitive in the globalizing marketplace of the future? Of course, it's possible to imagine that such a thoroughgoing transformation in the way Americans do business would have a tremendously powerful impact on other countries and would generate a new global dynamic so that other countries would soon follow the path of the most powerful and richest nation on earth. However, let's imagine worst-case scenarios, in which that does not happen. How then could we sustain our economy?

There are two possible responses. The first is that the new bottom line might actually turn out to be more productive in terms of the old bottom line. A growing number of corporate managers have argued that giving greater priority to cooperation, mutual support, caring for others, and concern for the environmental and safety consequences of what is being produced may actually enhance, rather than decrease, a firm's profitability and success in international competition. In fact, there may be a growing world market precisely for corporations that can prove that they are run by the criteria of the new bottom line. This kind of direction has been a central theme in the work of organizations like the Social Ventures Network and Business for Social Responsibility as well as a growingly popular movement for socially responsible investments. It is very important for spiritual progressives to link up with the many morally and spiritually sensitive people in the corporate world who are already aware of the need for a new bottom line.

But what if the cynical realist is right and there were a conflict between economic growth and environmental sustainability, so that choosing the new bottom line really did require a loss of position in the international marketplace? If so, we in the United States would have to restructure our economic life in major ways, and the SRA is a useful first step.

What if adopting the SRA meant that the United States could no longer dominate international trade and set the terms for globalization? Would that be a disaster?

Not at all. We could survive just fine. What it would require is a new mind-set. Imagine that the United States could provide its citizens with only present-day technology and that it had to seek zero population growth. Imagine the "tragedy" of a United States in which we couldn't get huge new supplies of oil from the world but had to make do with creating our own energy-efficient cars. Imagine if we couldn't buy the newest models of computers and computer games, but we had to stick with what we could do at the current level of broadband technology. Imagine if we had to restructure our economy so that we fed ourselves (we already have an agricultural base sufficient to do that and have plenty left for trading with the rest of the world), had to build new homes and apartment buildings in ways that were far more environmentally sustainable, had to restructure transportation to create vastly more mass transportation and reduce the amount of travel by individual automobiles, had to restructure work so that people had more time with their families, had to restructure schools so that they were more oriented to developing loving and caring children, and had to restructure our expectations so that we didn't produce as many consumer goods.

Far from being a disaster, the path "forced" upon us by a choice of a new bottom line would open up a life in which we had enough basic goods (food, clothing, housing, transportation) and a far greater amount of human satisfaction.

Jerome Segal, in his book *Graceful Simplicity,* argues that our current economy forces people to spend too much of their time pursuing basic needs and that leaves too little time for "gracefulness" or the aesthetic dimension of life. There have always been two competing conceptions of the American dream, the first centered on the accumulation of wealth and an ever-growing power of consumption, and the second on a life of leisure and grace, where money and materials, while instrumental to creating such a life, are not ends in and of themselves. From this perspective, we need only acquire the goods that meet our "core needs," enabling us to pursue lives of dignity and beauty. But we could do that right now, using our own societal wealth and agricultural productivity as the foundation.

Segal sets up a model that is both simple and convincing and relies on no more than textbook economics. Because of industrialization and technology, we are phenomenally more productive than we used to be: we have achieved far greater output per unit of labor input. The question to be put to society is whether we should therefore keep our amount of leisure time fixed and maintain our increased levels of output (which give us a higher income) or keep the output fixed and allow ourselves more time for leisure (which would mean a reduced income). Segal argues for the latter, while recognizing that such a choice demands economic policies that would reduce the costs of "core needs."

"More generally," he writes, "we need societies in which the level of NRI [needs-required income] is low, or, to put it differently, a society in which the efficiency of need satisfaction per unit of income is high" (p. 71). He calls this ratio the measure of "social efficiency." The argument is that costs like housing, transportation, education, insurance, and so on must be dramatically reduced, so as to free up time that would have been spent earning the necessary income to be put toward the appreciation of beauty. I'd simply add, time to be put toward developing our loving and caring capacities, our connection to nature, and our spiritual well-being.

What the cynical realist relies upon is a long history of indoctrination in which we've come to measure the value of things in terms of price and to see as valueless those things that cost nothing. We have been taught to think that diamonds are more valuable than water, whereas actually we can live without the former but not without the latter! To the extent that we allow ourselves to be misled in this way, we can then be intimidated by the cynical realist who will point out that the standard of living in a society with a new bottom line will fall (at least by the standard criteria).

My argument, however, is that a spiritual consciousness will recognize that our standard of living, even if we are cut off from "success" in international competition, will actually rise—because of the accruing benefits to friendships, relationships, family life, our relationship to our children, our satisfactions in work, our sense of personal safety as crime and violence decrease, and our pleasure in nature and fulfillment in having a meaning to our lives that is not based on how well we do in the competitive marketplace.

If we understand the value in this kind of transformation, we have an obligation to move quickly toward this kind of economic organization while it is still a possible choice to be made by a wealthy and flourishing society. The alternative is to keep jumping into the worldwide struggle to make money, and then face a reality in which some of us will live well materially in gated communities with heavy police forces to protect us, while the vast majority will live in an America of declining material standards, with nothing but anger and frustration and self-blame to fill their consciousness, or alternatively, fall prey to fascistic ideas and movements.

The best economic future for America lies with the best spiritual future. Americans will be happier and more fulfilled in their daily lives when a spiritual politics shapes the institutions and workplaces of our society. As social energy moves from fear to hope, as we develop a life more consonant with the Left Hand of God, we will find a huge surge of generosity and kindness enveloping our lives.

This is an amazing moment to be alive. The women's movement already showed us that one of the core assumptions about "human nature," the alleged intractability of sex roles, could be dramatically transformed. Now we are about to enter into an equally profound revolution in consciousness and social roles as people begin to reclaim their capacities for generosity, caring, and kindness and to extend them from the private sphere, where they've been nurtured in personal life, into the public sphere, where they can play a decisive role in shaping the destiny of the globe. Our spiritual lives will be rebalanced as the Left Hand of God takes its appropriate place. And the result will be a flourishing of love, compassion, awe and wonder, ecological sensitivity, and joy beyond anything in living memory. This is both our unique opportunity and our challenge.

The good news is that it is possible, though not inevitable.

Let's make it happen. To build the infrastructure for that change, let's talk about changes needed in education.

A Values-Based Education

Humanity will not perish from want of information but only for want of appreciation.... Life without wonder is not worth living.
—Abraham Joshua Heschel

A change to a socially responsible corporate structure would go far to increase the commitment to the common good in our society. Yet we know that the changes we need also must be manifested in our governmental and social institutions as well as in corporate America. We face a crisis today in the very fabric of our society, particularly in the areas of education, health care, and our relationship to the environment. Enlisting corporate America to help fund child-care centers, support a viable and just health care system, and implement policies to end pollution and support sustainable practices will help, but we must do even more.

Education is one realm that crosses over the personal and the social. Our society and each individual family share major responsibilities in transmitting our highest values to children. The clear bottom line for educating children must be recognizing that children seek and need to be recognized and loved for who they are. Their spiritual and ethical consciousness must be enhanced, and their capacity to think independently and to care for the well-being of others and the planet must also be fostered. Love and recognition are fundamental to human beings. Therefore, our schools should develop rather than retard these ways of thinking and being in the world.

Most parents feel love for their children and do their best to communicate it. Yet that communication is often tainted by a competing feeling: an anxiety that their child may not succeed unless he or she develops a certain set of skills that are rewarded in the larger society and are tested (at least in some urban areas) as soon as parents seek to enter children into preschool, at age three or four. A growing number of parents, recognizing that their children will be more successful if they are good at manipulating objects, test taking, and presenting themselves as having "pleasing" personalities, look at their children through this evaluative framework. Because they love their children, many parents become fixated on helping their children develop the skills that will all too soon be measured in order to determine whether this child will get into the "right" preschool, which in turn will lead to the right grammar and high schools, which in turn will lead to the right college and the right graduate or professional school, which then in turn will lead to the right job.

Given this anxiety about how their children will do in the world, it's hard for parents not to see their children through the eyes of societal expectations and to put energy into getting their children to "improve" in one area or another of the knowledge and skills that will be assessed by others later on. This act of caring, however, unconsciously but powerfully conveys to many children that they are not enough. Add to that parents' own childhood experiences of being perceived as not enough, and you get the recipe for misrecognition and an experience of love that seems not fully satisfying, in some ways making children feel invisible to their parents, who are evaluating them in the same way the parents fear others will evaluate them in "the real world."

The irony here is that most parents are moved by genuine caring about the well-being of their children. Yet many children get a somewhat complicated message in which the love that they receive is mixed with a feeling that they are not quite right, that something needs to be fixed in them, and that their parents do not quite understand who they are. And the resulting disappointment at not being fully seen weighs heavily on children, causing some to refuse to try to learn because they fear they won't succeed on any level. Others focus instead on accomplishments in the hope that, if they jump successfully through enough hoops, their parents might be more fully present to them. More likely, however, their efforts will be largely in vain, because they cannot fully overcome the fears that their parents have about who they are and what they will become.

It has often been remarked that children have a natural spiritual awareness. (See, for example, Robert Coles's study *The Spiritual Life of Children,* Joseph Chilton Pearce's *Magical Child,* and Tobin Hart's *The Secret Spiritual World of Children.*) Children have a wonder and fascination with nature and a simple sense of generosity that comes straight from the Left Hand of God. Too often, however, the implicit demand on children to develop the skills and habits of mind necessary to succeed in school blunts this spiritual consciousness. Parents and schools quickly seek to interfere with what they perceive to be a child's "daydreaming"—that is, the natural wandering of children's minds to all that fascinates them in their world—so that they can teach their children to "pay attention" to the aspects of their environment that will be useful for them in terms of future success. Can they teach their children to manipulate objects to fit into the right size and shape of container? Can they teach them to develop the proper kind of hand-eye coordination? Can they teach them to read early enough, so that they will do well in school? These preoccupations, of course, are not destructive in and of themselves, but when they are accompanied by high levels of anxiety about their children's need to excel scholastically and high levels of disapproval at children's attention going elsewhere, in "nonproductive" directions, they can leave a permanent scar, repressing the child's spiritual hunger.

It's true that children need to learn how to survive in our society, but they also need the kind of loving attention that is not connected to success. As parents, we must learn how to spend quiet, unstructured time with our children and to discover their world, rather than simply to educate them to ours. As they get older, we have to learn how to listen to them with a kind of generous patience. And we need to make sure we provide our children with an education that will nurture their native compassion and encourage in them an optimistic faith in that the healing and transformation of our world is possible.

Nurturing children's spiritual consciousness is one of the great challenges for parents caught between their love and their sense of obligation to prepare children to live in the "real world." All the more reason why we need to change that world so that it will be friendlier to our childrens' spiritual needs. But that requires social transformations that go beyond what can be accomplished with our covenant of personal responsibility and our covenant with the family. One place to start is by creating a new bottom line for our educational system.

Society has a responsibility to every child to provide that child with the tools to succeed in contemporary life. Every student should know enough of our language to be able to read and write effectively, enough mathematics to function in daily life, enough history to tell the story of our own and other cultures and enough science to understand the material world around us. Any curricular reform must retain these critical elements.

Given the legitimate concern parents have to ensure their children gain these skills, it is understandable that some parents will fear any curriculum that does not focus exclusively on the three *R*s. Parents worry for good reason. In the 1960s and 1970s educational reformers on the Left equated democratic policies with empowering students to decide for themselves what learning they thought was valuable or relevant. That tactic backfired badly. Left to themselves to make choices in a society dominated by the capitalist marketplace, students will often be more influenced by the media and other social messages than by what their souls most deeply yearn to know. We ought to fight for a commercial-free childhood and for TV and video games that teach loving values, but till that happens we have to take responsibility for combating the dominant culture by teaching children what they need to become morally responsible and spiritually sensitive citizens.

The idea of teaching values in schools sends shudders through some of my progressive friends. They are afraid *values* is a code word for particular religious ideas. And it's true that the Religious Right often uses "values" to talk about the particular brand of Christian fundamentalism they want everyone to adopt. Just because the Right has tried to co-opt the word *values,* however, does not mean that values don't exist, or that they don't exist in schools. The fact is that our schools are not morally neutral institutions conveying a set of morally neutral facts and skills that can be used in any way the individual decides. Rather, schools impart these skills and facts within a context that teaches selfishness and materialism as part of the underlying assumptions of every subject area and all the discourse.

Most schools teach the ethos of the competitive marketplace. Walk into any school, and if you stay long enough, you will discover that the school day is all about testing—preparing for tests, taking tests, evaluating test results. As early as preschool, children are evaluated against the backdrop of a marketplace that doesn't care who they are, only what they will be able to produce. For most children and for most teachers, the content of the tests becomes secondary to the testing process itself. Children get the message that it really doesn't pay to be curious or creative or innovative—what pays is the ability to jump through someone else's hoops. And the goal? Material success.

These materialist goals led the Clinton administration to require testing of every child in public school and the Bush administration to embrace its "No Child Left Behind" policy. The result was that these administrations, one Democratic and the other Republican, have together managed to squeeze out of education the last vestiges of humane values. Children who are bored in school or who have problems sitting for a long time have increasingly been pathologized and then overmedicated so that they will fit into a one-size-fits-all form of education. While some genuinely hyperactive children benefit from these medications, the easy path of sedation allows school systems to avoid questions about whether this kind of skills-based education for the marketplace is the right bottom line for our children.

A spiritually sensitive education seeks a different goal: to foster in students their capacities to live the path of the Left Hand of God. The Covenant for a Values-Based Education is a promise to nurture generosity and compassion for others, a sense of wonder about nature, environmental sensitivity, a love of learning, and a spirit of openness and hopefulness. In such a school environment, students would be asked to manifest the qualities the school was trying to foster, in their studies and in their behavior, in the schoolroom and out of it. Teachers would be trained to teach these skills and would be given time off to develop their own intellectual and spiritual capacities. Schools would become a place to be inspired and to inspire.

In addition to structured teaching around curriculum basics, students would from an early age be given the opportunity to perform community service. Even young children can pick up litter, care for community lands, and spend time with seniors. Older students can work with food banks, protect wildlife, and develop their own projects to care for the physical and social environment. These projects can easily be integrated into a science and social studies curriculum. After graduation from high school, each student would be required to spend two years in a Public Service Corps, at least one year of which would be devoted to service in a non-English-speaking country. The Public Service Corps will provide language training, plus skills training, so that each student can contribute to the upgrading of the economic, educational, health, or environmental infrastructure of a country that does not have the adequate economic means to provide these services on its own to all of its population. Students electing to spend one of the two years inside the United States will work with sectors of the population that face inequalities in health, education, or environmental safety or on projects related to providing adequate housing and environmentally healthy forms of transportation and energy.

Along with learning to work with the larger community, students should also learn to interact with one another in positive ways. One teacher I know has a "care box," in which students put notes when they see their peers engage in helpful or generous activity. At the end of the week, the notes are read out loud so that students are rewarded for caring and they see how important such generosity is to others. If every workplace had a care box, it might feel better to come to work!

But respect and generosity can be encouraged outside the classroom as well. There is little more satisfying for an older student than becoming a mentor to a younger one. The older student gains respect and takes on responsibility, while the younger student receives extra care and attention. If every student is adequately supervised in their mentoring of younger students, and each student does this from sixth through twelfth grade, the capacity to take care of another person will become a major aspect of what children learn in school. On the playground, the older student becomes aware of how bullying hurts younger students and tries to become a better role model. When the school community becomes a more caring place, teachers can worry less about discipline and the learning environment will improve.

Part of building a caring educational environment must include the recognition that there are multiple ways of knowing the world. Feminists have pointed out that our culture tends to value knowledge that is distanced, abstract, and "objective" rather than relational, concrete, and "subjective." The ancient Greeks imagined that rational thought could reveal the world to self-sufficient thinkers, while ancient Israelites (and their offspring in rabbinic Judaism, Christianity, and Islam) suggested that knowledge flows from our relationship with God, so that the deepest knowledge comes through our mutual dependence and openness to the nonrational and mystical. Too many students get turned off from school because their own ways of knowing are not valued. A school system must be prepared to provide a variety of forms of learning and reward a variety of forms of knowledge.

Schools should try to discourage the notion that some students are smarter or more together than others and instead work on the assumption that differences in competence tend to be based primarily on differences in privilege. Privilege in this sense is not only about money or class background, but it is about emotional and spiritual support. The most privileged students are those who got the most encouragement and support in their earlier years to explore freely, to develop their mental capacities, and to love deeply. So we need a redistribution program—not a redistribution of money but a redistribution of loving recognition. The magical thing about redistributing loving recognition is that to give away love never depletes those who give it. The more recognition is given, the more there is to go around.

In such an institution, where students are constantly recognized for who they are and reminded of the way their actions can have a positive impact on others in their school and social community, students can be trusted with more responsibility. Older children can be offered electives to explore and express their own interests. Younger children should also be given as much free time as possible, including unstructured free play during some of the school day, plus freedom after school from onerous homework. Child psychologists agree that play is one of the most important tools younger children use to discover their world. Young children must be given the time to benefit from such unstructured play.

Teachers cannot be left out if we hope to create a better educational environment. Like other workers, teachers should be treated with respect and encouraged to join worker support networks. In recognition of the importance of teachers to our society, we would strive to create enough funding to enable all teachers to take a sabbatical year designed around spiritual or intellectual development. During this time off, teachers could engage with new ideas for the curriculum that could promote learning based on curiosity rather than on test scores.

The curriculum of a progressive, spiritually based education will convey to students why these subjects matter. For example, the goal of science courses should be to open the student to seeing the marvelous within the ordinary. Instead of having students memorize a set of facts, the focus should be on learning how to experiment with nature, how to observe regularities, how to use scientific principles for the purpose of prediction and control, and how to recognize the ways that material reality as presented to our senses is only one level of the realities that exist all around us. Science in this kind of curriculum is not a set of cold, dry facts but is instead integrated into other parts of learning. Children learn science by going out into the natural world on field trips. Urban kids could go on overnight trips to the country to experience the stars at night and the noises of animals in the day.

Let students know that they can value the experience of awe and wonder at the complexities and marvels of creation. Art, poetry, music, dance—all are creative ways children can express their reactions to the natural world. Let children also know that one of the best things about awe and wonder is that it is useless, that is, it can't be used to give them a better shot at dominating or controlling other people. Too often, we adults focus on those aspects of our environment that can be of use. Imagine how many fewer environmental problems we would have if we would linger in the moment of wonder at the beauty of the world. So students should be encouraged to develop poetry, music, dance, art. stories, and community rituals that celebrate the grandeur of creation.

To empower them to be equipped to make the world a better place, we should teach students the history of human cooperation throughout the past millennia. One of the greatest such contributions of the past was the development of language itself, and then the beautiful use of language in speech, poetry, song, prayer, philosophy, and literature. Each generation has built on what was transmitted to it and passed on to the next generation what it has received and what it has added. In each such act of development and sharing, the human race manifests its inclination toward giving to others. True, there are also counter-tendencies, so students should be taught about the way societal energies and individual energies flow between fear and hope. They should learn about the development of class societies, inequalities, slavery, feudalism, class struggle in capitalist society, colonialism, imperialism, patriarchy, racism, homophobia, and nationalism—but all in the context of the fundamental desire of human beings to actualize their highest human essence. Part of understanding the goodness of the human experience requires an openness to difference and conflicting worldviews, so we shall also teach appreciation for cultural diversity and experiential knowledge.

Martin Marty, the cultural historian of religion who was for decades a guiding light of the Protestant magazine the *Christian Century,* pointed out in an interview in *Tikkun* that teaching religion in schools is perfectly legal in the United States as long as we teach a wide variety of religious approaches without advocating for any one of them. Indeed, it's hard to know how one could possibly understand Western civilization or the development of American history or even the current moment in U.S. history without having some understanding of the religious beliefs that shaped politicians and social movements. Similarly, there is no reason why various religious explanations for the creation of the universe should not be taught to students, as long as they are not taught as science but as cultural history in a humanities or social science course—as long as, Marty says, the Genesis story is taught alongside the Navajo creation myth about the Grand Canyon and the Babylonian and other accounts. I don't mean to imply that I'm satisfied with the account of evolution that appears in most science courses, because it shares the same one-dimensionality that cannot fully address the whole range of human experience that all of science shares. But that is what science is, and as I've argued earlier in this book, even with all its limitations science is an important human activity that should be preserved and supported, and religious and spiritual worldviews (for example, about evolution) should not be presented in science classrooms as though they were alternative scientific explanations.

Because I'm worried about the slippery slope toward advocacy for specific forms of Christianity that may be prevalent in a given community that elects to teach about religion, I've imagined a way to offset that: Let each major global religious tradition, including that of secular humanists, Native American religions, and feminist versions of established religions, prepare videotapes in which they present and advocate for their worldview—two such for each grade level starting in sixth grade—and let publicly funded schools that opt to teach about religions be required to show these tapes as the only way they present religion, thus ensuring that each religion gets equal opportunity to advocate for its worldview in a way that it thinks would make greatest sense to the children of America. While some communities will decide that presenting these alternative views might be too confusing for their children, and hence will choose to expose children to religion only outside of school, other school systems will feel confident that their children can make their own decisions with the support of parents and existing religious communities and thus will feel perfectly fine about having their local public schools add this dimension to their children's education.

Just as exposing children to the range of religious options helps prepare them for the real world, so too does introducing them to the economic system in which their parents live their lives. Students should be exposed to the banking system, the stock market, the housing market, the commodities market—in short, to all the ways that contemporary economics works as well as to some of the alternatives to our current system.

Students will be encouraged to develop the skills they need to actively participate in a democracy, rather than passively accept the messages fed into them by leaders and media. These skills do not have a particular political bias: the Right and Left both have had much to say about the way that the media shapes the news and the way our consumer culture shapes the media. Our educational system must challenge the unthinking and unquestioning disposition toward politics and culture that diminish democratic participation. We need to foster individuals who have the capacity, courage, and conscience to question or challenge what is inequitable, wasteful, and manipulative in our culture. When our children learn to be active learners rather than passive recipients, they will become better citizens. They will become adults who can challenge the "taken-for-granted" world of materialism, conformity, and alienation and create a better world in its place.

Public schools that incorporate the approach outlined here have a far greater chance of political and economic survival than the morally and spiritually deadened institutions in which our children are currently trained. On the one hand, they will meet the challenge from the Religious Right that can argue, in my view persuasively, that the current school system either teaches no values or bad values. Progressives should not meet that challenge by talking about how our schools are going to do a better job of preparing our students to compete in the international marketplace, because that would only encourage schools to continue teaching the wrong values. If we want to prevent the Religious Right from convincing the Christian majority in America to teach Christianity in public schools, we need to have a way of incorporating those Christian values that are universal—and that is what the approach I've presented allows us to do. At the same time, it also answers the concern of "spiritual but not religious" parents who are increasingly withdrawing their children from public schools in favor of private education where values are taught. Here instead we have an approach that teaches values that are spiritually and ethically based yet are presented in ways that can make sense to people who normally do not think of themselves as spiritual and certainly not as religious.

Some on the Religious Right are already mobilized to get their version of the world taught in schools. Those of us who are spiritual progressives similarly need to be mobilized—not around the banner of civil liberties and "keep the values out of school" but around a different and more universal vision of what the values should be. So although I've outlined above a vision of what schools could be, I of course invite you to take this as a jumping-off place for further discussion, just as I do for every other part of our covenant. A spiritual Left will fight for the centrality of the New Bottom Line in defining how to bring values into the curriculum and how to resist patriarchal and oppressive values and religious indoctrination.

Spiritually Progressive Health Care

A caring economy is likely to want to put "care" back into health care, saving it from the distortions that have occurred in the past centuries and that have reached their apex in the last decade of medical selfishness and cynicism in the United States.

Medicine began to miss the boat a long time ago when it took, as the model for the human body, the anatomy of a corpse. The scientific study of dead bodies yielded important information, but deep philosophical mistakes accompanied the attainment of this knowledge. A human being is not a corpse; we are made of a mind, body, and spirit deeply influenced by our environment. To talk about a spiritually progressive health care, we need to rethink the philosophical frame in which the field of medicine arose. For example, it's sometimes helpful in medicine to compare a human heart to a mechanical pump. But a heart is fundamentally different from a pump—and, indeed, unlike anything we know of in the rest of the universe. It's not just a metaphor to say that a heart can experience compassion. There are numerous studies showing that compassion and tolerance improve cardiac functioning, whereas the experience of anger, intolerance, and hostility worsens it. Stress-reduction groups that really work are those that generate the experiences of compassion, caring for each other, and interconnectedness.

The World Health Organization defines health as "a state of complete physical, mental and social well-being, and not merely the absence of disease or infirmity." That well-being can only be achieved by a health care system that pays attention to all the dimensions of human life. The Covenant for Health Care recognizes that we can have healthy bodies only if we are living in a healthy environment. What we take in, through our stomachs, our lungs, and our pores, has a powerful impact on our health. It's no news today that environmental conditions are central to our health. The air we breathe, the water we drink, the clothes we wear, the products we use to clean our bodies, and the food we eat have all become so filled with carcinogens and other poisons that we are constantly at risk. We must have a strategy to reclaim our natural world, and I will detail one later in this chapter.

Even if our air and water were pure, however, that would not be enough to guarantee our health. A healthy environment also will be one in which people have meaningful work. A healthy environment will make careful use of the planet's energy and resources. This environment will give people many opportunities each day to exercise their bodies, to meditate, to sing and dance, to engage in aesthetic creativity, to do physical labor as well as mental labor, to be with others in community and to be alone in moments of quiet—to celebrate the universe in community and to connect with God in privacy.

Most important, to fix our health care system, we have to fix a society in which everyone is just out for themselves. When we only look out for number one, we don't think about the ways in which our choices might hurt someone else. What's worse, we don't think about how our choices hurt us. We get so caught up in the desire to have more, buy more, and be more that we forget to take the time to be ourselves and to take care of ourselves. That's why we need a spiritual politics if we are going to solve our health care crisis. The need for meaning is as significant as the need for food or economic well-being, and it has significant physiological consequences for our health.

Eating is an example of this relationship writ large. When you walk into a large grocery store, many of the foods you see are products of the exploitation of the earth, produced by labor that is demeaned and underpaid, nurtured with pesticides and chemical fertilizers, and harvested with gas-guzzling machines. These foods have already contributed to the poor health of migrant farmworkers and to the destruction of our physical world. They start out unhealthy. It's better not to buy such foods if you have the option. But we can't blame people who don't have that option or who can't afford organic locally grown heirloom tomatoes that cost three times as much as the chainstore brand.

What's more, whether we buy organic, healthier products or not, many of us are buying food in quantities far beyond what our bodies actually need. Too many Americans are overweight. We eat to offset the emotional, ethical, and spiritual distress in our lives. We find momentary consolation, but it never lasts long. You can never eat enough to feed a hungry soul. Instead of relying on dangerous diet pills or quick fixes to lose weight, we need to provide the emotional, ethical, and spiritual nurturing people need so that they don't take their pain out on their bodies.

In spiritually oriented medicine, we would understand that the health of our body is linked to health of the economic, political, and ecological systems outside the body. Doctors would ask us not only about our physical bodies but about our environment. "How is your family?" a doctor might ask. "What have you been eating lately?" "Do you have time for yourself?" And we would visit the doctor as just one item in our personal health care, which would also include taking the time for exercise, reflection, and working with others to build a better world.

Ultimately, there is no health for the individual without health for all individuals and health for the entire planet. The caring world that we seek in this covenant is thus integrally linked with, and the precondition for, the promotion of global health.

In its powerful series of articles collectively titled "Class Matters," published in the spring of 2005, the *New York Times* demonstrated that the kind of health care we get and our ability to take steps to keep healthy are shaped by our class position. Following in detail the lives of three people who had recently had heart attacks, the *Times* concluded that class is an important factor in health care: "Class informed everything from the circumstances of their heart attacks to the emergency care each received, the households they returned to and the jobs they hoped to resume. It shaped their understanding of their illness, the support they got from their families, their relationships with their doctors. It helped define their ability to change their lives and shaped their odds of getting better" ("Class in America: Shadowy Lines That Still Divide," May 15, 2005).

All this describes a moral evil that needs to be changed. And it can be.

Let's start with support for a worldwide system of universal health care.

Only a society whose sense of morals is deeply distorted would allocate health care on the basis of how much money the ill person has. There is no moral reason why someone born into poverty should have less opportunity to have their basic health needs met than someone born into wealth. Yet over 41 million people in the United States have no insurance, and each year thousands of people who do have insurance are nevertheless bankrupted when they have a serious accident or illness. The underlying principle of our health care system should be:

everyone equally deserves first-class health care because everyone is equally valuable and deserving of respect. All human beings participate in God's holiness, and those who work in delivering health care and creating medicines and medical technologies are engaged in sacred work. Just as we do not ask individuals to pay when they need police or fire assistance, so society should provide health care for all, which would include paying for the training and salaries of doctors, nurses, and public health experts as well as for the construction and provision of hospitals and community health care centers. Schools from grade one through twelve should provide health education, including a focus on diet, exercise, and alternative approaches to illness prevention and health maintenance.

Previous efforts at health care reform have failed not because they went too far, but because they did not go far enough. Large health care insurers and profiteers fight every attempt at minimal health care distribution reforms by buying television ads purporting to show ordinary citizens talking to each other about how misguided these reforms are— as though the companies are really trying to champion the interests of ordinary citizens. Even when the Clinton administration proposed reforms that seemed designed more to ensure the well-being of the health care profiteers and drug companies than to make significant improvements in people's health, it faced crushing opposition from the insurance and drug companies. Since it takes enormous amounts of energy to fight even for the most minimal reforms, we might as well fight for the greater cause—a national health insurance plan that places the sanctity of human beings at the center of the way we think about health care.

A national health insurance plan would work the way Medicare does today. The plan would be paid for by our taxes and through the government, but the services would be provided through the private, but mostly not-for-profit, sector. Doctors would remain in private practice and would be paid on a fee-for-service basis. The government would not own or manage hospitals or private medical practices. In short, a national health insurance plan would not be "socialized medicine" but would instead be the socialized financing of health insurance. Such a plan has been proposed by the Physicians for a National Health Program, whose reasoning and arguments I am largely quoting in the discussion below. (For a more detailed discussion from

which I draw the language and concepts below, visit their Web site at
www.pnhp.org.)

We need a universal public system of health care because our current system is regressive. The poor pay a much higher percentage of their income for health care than higher-income individuals do. In essence, we ration health care: if you can afford care, you get it; if you can't, you don't. A recent study by the prestigious Institute of Medicine found that 18,000 Americans *die* every year because they don't have health insurance. That's rationing. No other industrialized nation rations health care to the degree that the United States does.

A universal public system would retain Medicare and Medicaid financing as is and would add on a payroll tax on employers plus an income tax on individuals. The payroll tax would replace all other employer expenses for employees' health care. The income tax would take the place of all current insurance premiums, co-pays, deductibles, and other out-of-pocket costs. For the vast majority of people, the estimated 2 percent income tax needed to cover these expenses would be less than what they now pay for health care. Everyone would have the same comprehensive health coverage, including all medical and hospital care (including eye care and dental care), long-term care, and mental health services.

In a publicly financed, universal health care system, medical decisions are left to the patient and doctor. This is true even in countries like Britain and Spain that practice socialized medicine, and this is how our current Medicare program works. But there has to be a cost-containment measure, which can be managed at the state level by an elected and appointed body that represents the people of that state. This body decides on the benefit package and negotiates doctor fees and hospital budgets. It also is responsible for health planning and the distribution of expensive technology. According to calculations by the Physicians for a National Health Program, a national health insurance plan would save at least $150 billion annually by eliminating the high overhead and profits of the private, investor-owned insurance industry and by reducing spending for marketing and other satellite services. Doctors and hospitals would be freed from the concomitant burdens and expenses of paperwork created by having to deal with multiple insurers with different rules—often rules designed to avoid having to make payments.

Because covered costs would be under public rather than private control, we could more easily add care based on a holistic view of human needs. We could fund much more effective mental health care, as well as chiropractic care, acupuncture, and even exercise and meditation programs. We could use funds to develop research in these areas as well as in traditional areas of Western medicine.

Medical research does not disappear under systems of universal health care, as some critics claim. Much current medical research already is publicly financed through the National Institutes of Health. For example, all the clinical trials for the AIDS drug AZT were funded by the government, not by drug companies. Many famous discoveries have been made in countries that have national health care systems. Laparoscopic removal of the gallbladder was pioneered in Canada. The CT scan was invented in England. The new method of curing juvenile diabetics by transplanting pancreatic cells was developed in Canada. Currently, drug companies spend most of their money marketing drugs. When there is no longer a need to spend money to create artificial demand for drugs like Viagra, we will be able to put more money into research that will cure human illness and promote human health.

But the Covenant for Health Care is not just a plan to insure our bodies. It is a promise that we will adequately care for our whole being. A national health insurance plan will guarantee that each of us will receive both physical and psychological care. While advocating for a transformed health system, spiritual progressives also emphasize personal responsibility for our own health. We all know that healthy diet, exercise, and other lifestyle issues are critical to our health and that we must take personal responsibility to do our part rather than relying on expensive technologies to cure us. And we also need to do the spiritual work as we grow older to accept the inevitability of death rather than acting as though aging and death could be avoided if only we had better technology. The enormous emotional, spiritual, and financial cost of trying to hang on to life as long as possible (and to make ourselves look as though we were not aging) is fostered by a marketplace that tries to sell us endless youth. It is also fostered by our cultural failure to honor our elders, provide them with real opportunities to share their wisdom, and combat the pervasive ageism with its willingness to discard people long before their creative juices have dried up, to stigmatize the sexuality of the elderly ("dirty old man" or "dried up old woman," as though cross-generational sex among adults were dishonorable because old people should not have sexual energy or the emotional and intellectual wealth to offer younger people in a sexual relationship), and to provide little in the way of adequately funded and beautifully conceived long-term care facilities. If we were to provide for our seniors a good twenty years of satisfying life suffused with meaningful ways for them to contribute to the common good, they might be less obsessed with hanging on at all costs when their bodies gave clear indications that it was ready to shut down. Learning to let go, to recognize that we can celebrate life and yet allow ourselves to pass to another stage in which we merge back with the unity of all being, is part of the teaching that spiritual traditions can bring to our society.

Caring about our health leads us inevitably to care about creating a healthy environment, a question that has particular urgency in an era in which the potential for environmental disaster hovers over the entire human enterprise.

Environmental Sanity

For the past several decades, ecologists have been warning about an impending environmental crisis, apologists for large corporations have been saying that the crisis is exaggerated, conservative politicians have warned that taking environmental reforms seriously could drive out jobs, and the rest of us—well, the rest of us have listened to all this and felt confused and powerless.

It's not that people don't care about the earth. We care powerfully. This earth is our only home, and our very lives are tied to its well-being. Many feel a deep reverence for the earth. But few people have found a way to connect their caring about the earth to actual life choices that would make a serious impact in saving the planet from destruction. When caring about the earth is made accessible, people do it. In some of our larger cities, many people started to recycle when city services provided special bins and offered to pick up recycled goods. A growing number of relatively well-to-do people buy organic foods, locally produced foods, and foods made with fewer poisonous additives—a luxury that most working-class people cannot afford on a regular basis. Even expensive hybrid cars are catching on, at least among those who have the money to spend.

These kinds of changes are good, but they are not enough to stop the onset of a real ecological crisis. The world's population has grown to 6.3 billion, approximately twice as many people as were alive on the planet just forty-five years ago. Though birthrates have declined in parts of Europe, there is an explosion of births in third-world countries, in large part because the lack of adequate birth control and reproductive health services makes it harder for many to engage in family planning. The opposition of the Vatican and of the Religious Right to providing this kind of information has contributed significantly to the rise in births, to the increasing rate of (often illegal) abortions, and to the number of women who die in childbirth.

As the demand for food grows, increases in land cultivation cannot keep up. Attempts to expand the land available for agriculture, as in the Amazon basin, destroy precious biosystems and put the rest of the world at risk. Simultaneously, fewer people are living in the same household as they were thirty-five years ago (down from 5.1 to 4.4 persons per household in developing countries and from 3.2 to 2.5 in industrial countries), and since each new household requires land and material, the decline in extended families or living units takes a significant toll on the environment.

Increased population combined with increased industry are creating a water shortage that in many parts of the world will soon reach catastrophic proportions. The damage to the health of the global environment caused by advanced industrial societies is more severe than that caused by developing countries. The United States, for example, releases 15.7 million tons of carbon dioxide into the atmosphere each year as compared with India, which, with four times the population, releases 4.9 million tons. The rise of carbon dioxide emissions has led to global warming. The rising temperatures, in turn, are causing rapid melting of the ice caps, thinning the ice at a pace that some scientists predict could make the Arctic Ocean ice free by 2100. In the past three decades, according to Christopher Flavin of the Worldwatch Institute, 13,500 square kilometers of Antarctic ice shelves have already disappeared. In essence, we are strip-mining the world's resources, leaving devastation and waste for future generations. Hurricane Katrina was a first taste of one of the many forms environmental disaster will take in the coming decades. Tragically, as always, it will be the poor and the powerless who will take the first brunt of the resulting suffering.

The environmental crisis is caused in part by pouring out into the environment poisons and environmentally destructive gases, in part by the overproduction and overconsumption of goods that have no redeeming social value. But the global corporations producing and selling these goods and polluting the environment have little incentive to stop. "We only produce what people will buy," they say. "We are in business to make profits, and our products respond to market demands. If people don't want these products, we'll know soon enough and produce what they do want." There's a fundamental dishonesty to that argument, because how can people buy what is unavailable and unaffordable—environmentally sound products? How can I show that I want nontoxic toys for my children if no such products are on the market? Or if they are available only at such a high price that I would have to sacrifice other necessities to buy them? How much of an impact any one of us has on what is being produced depends on our expendable income over and above the level of necessities—so people with lots of money have significantly more impact than many of us who have only enough to meet our basic requirements for food, clothing, and shelter. It's not one person, one vote, but one dollar, one vote, and we don't all have the same number of dollars. Still, the response of the corporations does raise an important point: reduced consumption of the earth's resources and cutbacks in fuels that are destructive will require the backing, whether active or passive, of the vast majority of the people of the world.

Environmental activists have been unsuccessful in convincing a majority of people to change the way we approach the earth's resources. Nor have they been successful in convincing government to play a decisive role in healing the earth from the destructive consequences of some one and a half centuries of environmental irresponsibility. It's true that these activists have been up against seemingly overwhelming odds. They stand alone against the power of corporations to threaten whole regions with economic devastation by moving their operations elsewhere should the people of that region dare to complain about environmental pollutants; a media that is slavishly subordinate to the interests of its corporate owners and hence unwilling to dramatize the level of catastrophe facing the human race until it actually happens; the irresponsibility of political leaders in both major parties who refuse to acknowledge, much less seriously contend with, the realities; and, frankly, the depth of denial among ordinary citizens like us that leads us to imagine that if we just do a little recycling and buy a few more hybrid cars all will be well.

At the same time, the environmental movement has often channeled the outrage and energy of ordinary citizens along paths that have proven extremely unproductive. Instead of demanding the fundamental restructuring of the global economy in ways that would guarantee a dramatic decrease in global warming, the environmental movements have often downplayed the seriousness of the challenges we face. They worry they will be called "Chicken Little." They work the power brokers in the nation's capital instead of mobilizing the public with a broad vision of what is needed. They get caught up in their own fundraising and buy into marketers' belief that fundraising does better when it delivers a positive message. As Peter Teague, the environmental program director at Nathan Cummings Foundation, put it: "So long as the siren call of denial is met with the drone of policy expertise— and the fantasy of technical fixes is left unchallenged—the public is not just being misled, it's also being misread. Until we address Americans honestly, and with the respect they deserve, they can be expected to remain largely disengaged from the global transformation we need them to be a part of."

Other critics agree. Michael Shallenberg has written a book he titled *The Death of Environmentalism* because he believes the environmentalists have killed their own movement by emphasizing technical policy fixes instead of a new set of core values. He writes, "In their public campaigns, not one of America's environmental leaders is articulating a vision for the future commensurate with the magnitude of the crisis. Instead, they are promoting technical policy fixes like pollution controls and higher vehicle mileage standards." Others agree that mainstream environmental groups spend too much time being "politically realistic" about what is really "environmentally catastrophic."

Environmentalists are not alone in being "realists." The "realism" they support is the "realism" we hear from all sides; it is the voice of the Right Hand of God. We live in a society in which the bottom line is money and power and the common sense is to look out for number one. In such a society, most people will reason: "If I cut back on my consumption, it won't really save the earth. I know how selfish everyone else is, how deeply materialistic, so I am sure that they won't cut back on their consumption either. So what I do won't really make that much of a difference because most other people are just going to keep on taking care of their own material needs as they please. Why should I end up being part of a small idealistic group that stops purchasing the ecologically destructive stuff while everyone else gets what they want? And for that matter, why should my country be put on the skids when I can see other countries, especially third-world countries like China and India, now rapidly industrializing and polluting so much that my own country's reduction in consumption won't have that much of an impact?" Even if we explained to such people that the United States leaves a much bigger footprint on the environment because of its levels of production and consumption, we are unlikely to convince them— not unless we can get the rest of the world on board.

The only way to counter this cynical realism is to recast the environmental movement as a spiritual movement aimed at building a new bottom line. That is the basis of our Covenant of Environmental Stewardship. Only a spiritual movement has the capacity to nurture an awareness of ourselves that transcends selfishness and lets us recognize our interdependence and oneness with all other life. The cynical realist worldview sees humans as independent little monads seeking to maximize self-interest and thus unlikely to sacrifice for some higher purpose. The spiritual politics advocated here supports that part of us that can recognize the generosity and capacities for self-transcendence in ourselves and in one another and hence our capacities to be genuinely motivated by a desire to care for the planet and to care for one another. Once we recognize this as a real potential in each of us, then it is possible to imagine a world that does wake up to itself and its own global environmental destructiveness, does *teshuva* (repentance), and reverses the path that it has been on. And if it is possible to save the planet, then our individual acts of consumption and environmental activism do matter, because they can arouse in others their own awareness of the need and desire to act as stewards for this incredible living entity on which and through which we live, the earth. So our belief in the possibility of environmental salvation becomes self-fulfilling. Yet no one can talk themselves into that perspective without some degree of spiritual foundation. The ability to see beyond what is, to recognize in ourselves and in one another a yearning for something that transcends the "getting and spending" that has become the dominant external behavior of the masses in capitalist society ever since Wordsworth noted it, requires a spiritual approach that eludes the social scientists and the talking heads and the sophisticated cynical realists of the Left and Right and center.

It is true that some religious and spiritual traditions have not been particularly environmentally sensitive. There are moments in the Bible when there is talk of human beings exercising dominion or rule over the earth. That is the language of the Right Hand of God.

And yet other biblical passages suggest a vision of stewardship—the idea that human beings have special capacities that give us special responsibilities to protect and take care of the earth. At least eighteen hundred years ago Rabbinic Judaism imagined God as deeply concerned about the survival of the planet:

> In the hour when the Holy One, Blessed be He, created the first man, he took him and let him pass before all the trees in the Garden of Eden and said to him: "See my works, how fine and excellent they are. Now all that I created I created for your benefit. Think upon this and do not corrupt or destroy my world. For if you destroy it, there is no one to restore it after you." (Ecclesiastes Rabbah 7:28)

From the standpoint of the ancient rabbis, affirming human specialness was not a license for destruction but rather an empowerment, a confirmation of our special responsibility toward the well-being of the planet.

Today, many religious and spiritual communities are affirming a new relationship to the planet, one that eschews domination and seeks instead to recontextualize human beings as just one member of the earth's family, affirming the worth and value of every type of life, supporting biological diversity and cultural diversity, and using our rational capacities for the good of all without claiming that those capacities make us fundamentally superior to and place us in a different ontological category from the rest of creation. To see ourselves as part of the Unity of All Being, made in the image of the One, reflecting God's caring for the All, is the religious answer from the Left Hand of God. But you don't have to believe in a supreme being or use religious language to grasp this spiritual insight. Many scientists have talked in a spiritual way about the amazing complexity of our earth's constantly changing open ecosystem with its intricate, interdependent parts. There are no scientific or empirical tests, experiments, or observations, however, that can prove that one ought to extend moral concerns to environmental issues. That is a faith position, whatever your faith may be, even if it is faith in secular ethics, and so should be at the center of the agenda of a progressive spiritual politics. What matters is to recognize that the earth includes the more-than-human. As environmental scientist Paul Wapner, writing in *Tikkun,* put it: "The earth is not the backdrop for our lives, but is part and parcel with them. . . . Rather than efficiency, system failure and the like, a Tikkun sense of things prods us to talk in terms of care, awe, appreciation, sacredness and love. The earth is not something we use but something we share our lives with—something we nurture, have fun with, are stunned by, respond to, empathize with, find nourishment from, and in turn, nourish" (September–October 2003).

Wapner's comments point to another deep teaching from the Left Hand of God: we insist that there *is* enough. It is only our spiritual emptiness that keeps us asking for more when we have all that we need. The earth's resources are enough to sustain us if we learn to respect and cherish them. It is our scarcity mentality that drives our rapacious consumption of the finite resources of the planet. To the always-hungry mind fostered by the capitalist marketplace and the globalization of selfishness, it seems counterintuitive, even the essence of irrationality, to be satisfied with what we have. What spiritual wisdom teaches us is that happiness cannot be obtained through the accumulation of goods and that therefore creating a society whose highest priority is to stimulate endless consumption is a spiritual error. The deep conviction that there is enough, that human life will not perish should we decide to forgo producing some goods in order to save the resources of the earth for future generations, is ultimately a spiritual lesson that cannot be taught solely through scientific experimentation. It is a dimension of understanding that emerges from spiritual practice.

The Torah commands that we take a sabbatical year once in every seven, in which the fields are not plowed and we live off the wealth of the land. The idea is for the entire society to shut down its production of things once every seven years and have a full year simply to concentrate on the celebration of all that is. If this practice were followed today, it would teach us to trust that there will always be enough; it would increase our humility and decrease our anxiety as a species, because we would no longer think that we've got no choice but to constantly be producing more in order to keep everything together.

In my own spiritual life as a Jew, I do engage in the ongoing practice of the Sabbath day. Each week, I take one day off in which I do not use money, do not spend time on any tasks related to my work as editor of *Tikkun,* and do not engage in any activity that would exert dominion or control over nature. This practice helps me foster and strengthen my understanding of the abundance that already is there.

It's actually quite an amazing experience to have a day each week when one is freed from worrying about holding everything together and making everything work, a day dedicated to celebration, joy, pleasure in one's inner life, food, sex, singing, dancing, being in nature, being with a community of others who similarly are committed to the joy of the celebration of the Sabbath.

I know that many other spiritual paths are available, that mine is only one of the ways to reach the point at which you no longer look at nature as something to sell or to turn into a commodity and no longer feel a yearning to own things you don't really need.

The Covenant of Environmental Stewardship recognizes that we receive the earth from the care of our ancestors and that we have a responsibility to leave it to future generations in good shape. We also have a responsibility to our fellow humans who happen to live downriver, as it were. A spiritual approach to the environment is about protecting the poor and powerless from suffering ecological devastation.

Caring about one another, from a planetary perspective, is the root of environmental concern.

Ultimately, though, the covenant extends our concern across species. We must see other living beings as deserving of our consideration. Aldo Leopold made this point forcefully when he said that the history of moral progress has been one of enlarging the moral community. At first this community included only free, white, property-owning men, but then our understanding grew to view slaves as people and then to see women and people of color as also part of the moral community. Leopold sees the species of life as the next frontier for that community.

The time to start acting with environmental consciousness is now. We don't have to wait until someone has figured out a solution to global warming or water scarcity before we can act.

Judaism has developed the notion of foods that are acceptable for eating (*kosher*) and those that are not (*treyf*). Some foods were designated kosher because of ethical concerns. For example, if you were a landowner, it was not kosher to eat food from the corners of your fields because the Torah mandates that those corners must be left open for the poor. Not all the rules have clear ethical purposes, but abiding by such dietary guidelines makes eating an intentional, spiritual act. With every bite, followers of the kosher laws (*kashrut*) are reminded that food is not simply theirs for the taking but has generously been given them.

Today, the Jewish renewal movement advocates extending this practice of intentional eating (they call it eco-*kashrut*) so that foods whose production harms the environment or is unjust to workers are *treyf*. The notion of ethical consumption already has a powerful foothold in the "fair trade" movement regarding coffee, teas, and chocolates. By encouraging people to buy only those products that can be certified as having been produced in ways that are both ecologically sound and fair to the workers who pick the crops and bring them to market, this movement has already made an important contribution to improving the quality of life of workers in the countries in which the food was grown.

Spiritual progressives need to take this same concept and expand it beyond food to cover all products. Imagine if all the religious and spiritual communities of the world, working in close cooperation with environmentalists, experts on toxins, and labor-movement organizers, were to develop criteria for a wide array of products so that we could certify that particular goods had been developed, grown, picked, or manufactured in ways that were respectful of the environment and of the needs of the working people involved. Governments could participate in this process by creating a labeling system and by providing funding to regulate these products. One of the projects of the Network of Spiritual Progressives is to encourage religious and spiritual communities to take the lead in creating the apparatus for a cooperative global effort to identify and publicize those products that are eco-kosher and hence legitimate to buy.

Imagine how much more powerful and credible the Democratic Party, or even the Greens, would be if its energies were directed as much toward establishing this system of ethical consumption as toward seeking electoral victories for itself. Breaking out of the mold of what a political party should do and be by showing this concern for the earth would demonstrate precisely the kind of transcendence of selfishness needed to model the possibilities for transformation and energize people into believing that a different kind of world really could be brought about. In so doing, it would allow them to reconnect with their own most hopeful self, which in turn would make them more likely to want to help those parties that embodied this idealism and hopefulness.

The push to create guidelines for ethical consumption brings us back to the idea that all of us share the benefits of our common resources. For much of human history, people in a given community usually held resources such as water wells and pasturelands in common, often in trust for what they perceived as the spiritual power of the universe. In the Torah, God explains an injunction concerning environmental justice by saying, "Because the whole earth is Mine." From the divine perspective, there is no such thing as a right to private property. We have a right to benefit from the earth, but only if we treat it as a gift from God that must be used in ethically and ecologically healthy ways.

The earth is our common wealth, on loan from God. Instead of trying to find new ways to patent it and make a profit from it, we need to put our energies into preserving it as the shared inheritance of humanity, our commons. Many commons still exist. The air, oceans, and flowing waters are not owned, nor is the continent of Antarctica or outer space. We need to voice our ethical outrage at attempts to privatize or environmentally soil these elements of the common wealth of humanity. And we need a strategy for rebuilding the common wealth.

We have both a wonderful opportunity and a serious responsibility to save this planet from environmental disaster. To rise to this challenge, however, we are going to have to get over what Paul Wapner describes as the biggest obstacle to our creating a powerful environmental movement: the deep cynicism we all share about whether we can have any impact on such a large-scale global problem. A spiritual consciousness that allows us to get off the consumption treadmill and become conscious of what we eat and what products we consume can show us how to reduce the size of our environmental footprint. But only a new spiritual consciousness will enable people to understand that reducing our level of consumption can actually enhance the quality of our lives—that it can raise the standard of living provided that standard is defined not in terms of money and material possessions but in terms of the new bottom line.

I've talked about changes in education, health care, and the environment primarily from the standpoint of the impact they would have on those of us in the United States. But the spiritual consciousness that is called for is one that links us to the unity of all being and insists upon our interconnectedness with all others. If we fully understand that we and the rest of humanity and the global environment are fundamentally interdependent, then it will be necessary to radically rethink foreign policy, defense, and homeland security, all of which are addressed in the final chapter.

TWELVE

We Will Make You Safer: The Strategy of Generosity for Foreign Policy

The past is prophetic in that it asserts that wars are poor chisels for carving out peaceful tomorrows. One day we must come to see that peace is not merely a distant goal that we seek, but a means by which we arrive at that goal. We must pursue peaceful ends through peaceful means. How much longer must we play at deadly war games before we heed the plaintive pleas of the unnumbered dead and maimed of past wars?
—Martin Luther King Jr.

The starting point of a spiritual approach to foreign policy and defense is acknowledging humankind's mutual interdependence and building policies and programs that reflect that understanding.

Interdependence

The well-being and safety of ourselves, our families, our communities, and our world depends on the well-being of every other human being on the planet. This is not just sweet sentiment—it is cold political reality. When we act from the standpoint of the best interests of the entire

322 THE LEFT HAND OF GOD

planet, we will in fact be more successful in protecting our own interests. But it is also deep spiritual truth, expressed by Buddhists when they talk about the unity of all being and expressed by Talmudic rabbis, who explained that Genesis emphasizes that human beings come from one original family (Adam and Eve) precisely to prevent anyone from saying that their origin is higher than someone else's and they are therefore entitled to different treatment. It is a theme repeated frequently in Torah: there should be a single standard for us and for the stranger, or Other. If we simply took this biblical injunction seriously and applied it to how we treat people on this planet, we'd have a fundamentally different approach to the world.

Right now, the United States has adopted a me-first policy, assuming that whatever is good for our country is good for the world. Trapped in the supposedly commonsense assumptions of cynical realism and the theology of the Right Hand of God, many public opinion shapers and political leaders have managed to convince Americans to believe that we must dominate the other before they dominate us. It's not surprising that many other countries aren't eager to go along with us. They are guided by a similar cynical realism and so want to put their own interests first. The end result is that the Bush administration's policies in Iraq and elsewhere have not solved our problems but have instead exacerbated the kinds of struggles for domination and power that lead to violence and war.

When we bomb cities, virtually leveling them and killing thousands in the process, as the U.S. Army did to the Iraqi city of Fallujah, or when we support dictatorships and economic policies that are literally destroying people's lives, we create swamps of anger and hatred. That anger fuels terrorists, who can succeed only when they can recruit people who hate us so much they are willing to die to express their anger. It's pure fantasy to think that we can keep these people from obtaining weapons or turning other materials into weapons in order to satisfy their desire to hurt us. They will find a way. The only protection you can give your family and your community is to undermine the anger. And that's what a strategy of generosity is all about.

A strategy of generosity means moving society from fear to hope. We must shift our foreign policy from one wholly identified with the Right Hand of God to one founded on the more generous spirit of the Left Hand of God.

We do not dispute that there is evil in the world. Nor do we want to just tend our own gardens. We want to act decisively to make the world a better and safer place. But attempting to right the wrongs of the world through violence and domination only encourages the view that violence is the only legitimate way to achieve one's ends. What really decides peace or war is not successfully winning places or things but winning the hearts and minds of people. Peace only comes through trust. The best foreign policy is not driven by defense departments or even by state departments but by policies that follow through to build a world based on mutual caring and mutual respect.

The Alienating Policies of the United States

There are real threats to Americans and to our homeland security. We do need to strengthen processes for protecting our borders. We will commit more energy and money to inspecting the cargo and containers that come into the country. We will strengthen global protections for existing nuclear stockpiles and put more attention toward preventing nuclear weapons from falling into the hands of terrorists. We believe that taking strong steps in this regard deserves a full commitment of America's resources and energy.

Foreign policy discussions in the past years, however, have too often centered on which ruler is in power where, and how friendly this ruler is to American interests. Friendliness is usually defined first and foremost by how much freedom a country gives American corporations to sell American goods in its markets and to buy up the raw materials it possesses on the cheap. We know now that the Bush administration attacked Saddam Hussein not because those in the government really thought he had weapons of mass destruction, but because they believed the world would be safer (and perhaps oil more plentiful) if Saddam were gone. Many of us in the progressive world rejoiced at the overthrow of Saddam Hussein—he was, after all, a cruel dictator who massacred and brutalized his own people. The vast majority of the countries of the world also and most of us spiritual progressives were happy to see Saddam go. What many of us opposed was the way in which the overthrow of this dictatorship was achieved and the continuing cost to human lives that has resulted.

I don't mean to equate George Bush with Saddam Hussein, but we all know that there are tens of millions of people who believe that the world would be far safer were George Bush removed from office. Does the United States really want to swagger around the world, giving people the message that it is okay to assassinate leaders and invade other countries if you believe their policies are immoral and murderous, which is the opinion many people now hold about Bush's America? This is the problem with using violence to achieve our ends. It is a slippery slope to more violence.

The United States will not always be the most powerful force in the world. Other countries are quickly modernizing their economies and may soon play a major role in global politics. Thirty or forty years from now China and India could be the world's leaders, with the most advanced military technologies, and there will be many members of their elites who will point to the unilateral action of the United States in Iraq as proof that the powerful can and do have a moral right to act with impunity to defend their own interests as they perceive them to be, using violence when that will bring quick results. The voices of moderation and respect for others in those societies will be correspondingly weakened because of what our country is doing today. Not only has the United States set a bad precedent, but our strategy of domination is not even working. Violence in Iraq persists, and there is no end in sight. Attempts to push the government to set a clear deadline or develop a coherent plan to bring all the troops home have consistently been resisted by the Bush administration. Meanwhile, the murderous regime in North Korea has learned the very lesson that the Bushites were worried about concerning weapons of mass destruction and so has accelerated development of those weapons in the hopes that having them (or appearing to have them) will prevent an American invasion. The United States pushes for smaller countries to end nuclear proliferation but refuses to significantly reduce its own nuclear program. People are not blind to the hypocrisy, and so many countries see no reason not to develop their own weapons of mass destruction, to the detriment of world peace.

In fact, following the path of the Right Hand of God has only made the world a more dangerous place for most Americans. The United States has a long way to go to win back the world's trust.

And then there is the issue of selfishness. We are the richest nation in a world in which one out of every three people lives on less than $2 a day, and 1.3 billion live on less than $1 a day. Many of these people are near starvation. That was not the case a hundred and fifty years ago, before the Western powers managed to create a global economy and impose their will on the rest of the world.

Most Americans simply will not let this information sink into their consciousness. We momentarily hear it, even acknowledge it, but it is hard for us to really take in these facts. While we are living in the richest society in the history of humanity, every single day somewhere between 20,000 and 30,000 children under the age of five die of starvation and inadequate health care, deaths that could have been avoided had we shared just a fraction of our resources with the poor.

My teacher at the Jewish Theological Seminary, Abraham Joshua Heschel, taught me that "while our eyes are witness to the callousness and cruelty of man, our heart tries to obliterate the memories, to calm the nerves, and to silence our conscience." Heschel went on to declare that "morally speaking there is no limit to the concern one must feel for the suffering of human beings. . . . In regard to cruelties committed in the name of a free society, some are guilty, while all are responsible." Heschel roots his view in the Torah command: "Thou shalt not stand idly by the blood of thy neighbor" (Leviticus 19:15). On this basis he taught that while Jewish tradition enjoins Jews to obey the decrees issued by the government, whenever a decree is unambiguously immoral or supportive of immoral policies, one has a duty to disobey.

I am constantly amazed at the capacity of our leaders and the media to ignore the suffering caused by the policies of our government. I've watched as brilliant minds have been harnessed to the cause of denial—denial that our military interventions in the name of democracy have killed tens of thousands of innocent civilians, denial that our military bases around the world could legitimately be considered outposts of imperial rule, denial that we are systematically engaged in torture, denial that our demands that Iran or North Korea halt development of nuclear weapons seem hypocritical when we ourselves are upgrading our own nuclear capacities. Defenders of U.S. policy counter these charges with other truths: there are other countries that have imperial desires and defend their own corporations as they seek markets, Europeans are hypocritical when they critique imperialism yet seek to benefit from it economically, communist countries have played a major role in polluting the planet as well, corporations are not all bad but sometimes do very good and helpful things, and some of the regimes the United States has toppled were terrible and oppressive. Why should anyone have to deny any of these truths? And why should they mitigate our moral outrage and shame at the way our society does stand idly by at the massive suffering and death caused by the unequal distribution of the world's resources?

Ask yourself, when was the last time the media reported on the actual number of civilians killed, maimed, or wounded in Iraq since the beginning of the war or, for that matter, the number of people around the globe who have starved to death or died from inadequate health care? These aren't issues that concern our media, politicians, and military leaders because the unnecessary suffering of others is a cost that they are willing to pay for the sake of maintaining what an increasing number of conservative commentators are willing to openly acknowledge is the "American empire."

Those who supported war in Vietnam or Iraq often present themselves as wishing to extend democracy by making the world more like America. They are challenged by self-described "realists" who believe, in the words of Henry Kissinger, that the United States "must temper its missionary spirit with a concept of the national interest." Spiritual progressives take a third path: we do not believe it is accurate to think that American interventions in the past fifty years have been motivated by a commitment to democracy, but by crass self-interest and desire of those who run the country to serve the interests of America's economic elites and corporate powers (though they honestly, albeit in my view mistakenly, believe that in serving those interests they are ultimately serving the best interests of all Americans). A moral foreign policy such as that described in this chapter would actually be far more realistic about our country's long-term self-interest than the policies suggested by Kissinger and his ilk who brought us disgrace in Vietnam and in Chile. It is in our self-interest to be and to be perceived to be a moral force.

Economic Globalization and Its Problems

The message that we must dominate others so we are not dominated ourselves may be anathema to some Democrats when it comes to warfare, but it often gets touted as truth when it comes to economics, an area in which many traditional Democrats join Republicans in an enthusiastic embrace of the notion that America needs to dominate the world economically.

A more sophisticated view recognizes that the tendency toward greater global economic integration has set corporations into greater competition with one another, thereby dividing American society into those who have developed the skills that corporations need if they hope to be more effective in global competition and those who have not developed those skills. In this view, the special advantages that the United States and Europe currently derive from a global empire may soon fade, as economic success becomes less and less restricted to those of a particular country and becomes a feature not of nations but of multinational corporations.

One leader in this discussion is *New York Times* columnist Thomas Friedman. In his recent book *The World Is Flat: A Brief History of the Twenty-First Century* (Farrar, Strauss and Giroux, 2005), Friedman argues that the United States must prepare immediately for this world or else it will no longer be able to guarantee that its corporations will be successful in the emerging global marketplace of the future and so will sacrifice its current economic hegemony.

Friedman tells a compelling story about the way new technology has enabled people and corporations to compete or collaborate across countries and continents. The world has become "flatter," Friedman says, because rapidly advancing electronic technology has dramatically reduced the obstacles to global integration of the capitalist marketplace. Consumer goods can be produced more cheaply in third-world countries and then brought back to the United States to be sold in chain stores that can offer their products at prices so low that they drive local merchants out of business. And services that were traditionally delivered locally can now be farmed out to lower-paid but highly trained personnel in the third world. For example, chances are good that some of your banking, your use of credit cards, and your ordering of goods on the telephone or online are already being carried out by someone sitting in an office in India. More and more aspects of the U.S. economy are being outsourced by corporations that rely on the savings they get from using globally dispersed technicians and production units.

Friedman is as happy as a clam in announcing that the flattening of the world is already happening. He waxes eloquent, almost breathless in his excitement about what these corporations can do, using Wal-Mart as one of his examples. He marvels at Wal-Mart's ability to move 2.3 billion cartons of merchandise each year down its supply chain into stores. "Supply-chaining is a method of collaborating horizontally— among suppliers, retailers and customers, to create value. Supply-chaining is both enabled by the flattening of the world and a hugely important flattener itself, because the more these supply chains grow and proliferate, the more they force the adoption of common standards between companies (so that every link of every supply chain can interface with the next), the more they eliminate points of friction at borders, the more the efficiencies of one company get adopted by the others, and the more they encourage global collaboration."

Of course, what benefits corporations does not necessarily benefit everyone. Friedman points out, "As consumers, we love supply chains, because they deliver us all sorts of goods . . . at lower and lower prices," but he goes on to admit that as workers, we are sometimes ambivalent or hostile to these supply chains, because they expose us to higher and higher pressures to compete, cut costs, and also, at times, cut wages and benefits.

Although Friedman notes that problem, he doesn't let that distract him from his awe at corporate globalization. Wide-eyed, he describes the process by which every move of Wal-Mart's employees is monitored. "A computer tracks how many pallets each employee is plucking every hour to put onto trucks for different stores, and a computerized voice tells each of them whether he is ahead of schedule or behind schedule." Wal-Mart's executive vice president explained that the headphones with a soothing computer voice to instruct them gives Wal-Mart a boost in productivity. "It is a million tiny operational innovations like this that differentiate Wal-Mart's supply chain," Friedman tells us. Now, Wal-Mart has also introduced RFID, radio frequency identification microchips, which are attached to each pallet and merchandise box that comes into their stores. With RFID you can tell more quickly which stories are selling which items. During hurricanes, for example, Wal-Mart knows that people eat more things like Pop-Tarts, need kids' games that don't require electricity, and drink more beer; it rushed to supply these items to its stores during Florida's hurricane season in 2004. This is what Friedman calls Wal-Mart's "collaborating with its customers."

Friedman's notion of collaboration is rather expansive, including every extension of the power of the boss over the workers. He is excited that your boss "can give you instructions day or night. So you are never out. You are always in. Therefore, you are always on. Bosses, if they are inclined, can collaborate more directly with more of their staff than ever before—no matter who they are or where they are in the hierarchy. But staffers will also have to work much harder to be better informed than their bosses."

But it's not only workers who will have to work harder. Friedman tells us that our kids need a bit of tough love so that they will get the message about the world we are entering. We need to stop making them feel entitled and instead give them a sense of the insecurity that the world will actually bring them. We have to push kids beyond their comfort zones and "be ready to suffer some short-run pain for longer gain."

Friedman wants us to prepare for this new world, recognizing its inevitability and then shaping our lives so as to maximize our potential for success within the emerging globalized economy. For those who do prepare appropriately, Friedman promises not only economic security but also the pleasurable prospect of endless consumption of the innovative products of the future.

My main response to Friedman and the "salvation through globalization" crowd is that their version of globalization is not inevitable and that it describes a world that is powerfully immoral. It simply puts the wrong thing on the top of the hierarchy of goods: making it financially.

There are at least two other ways in which "salvation through globalization" misses the boat, however. First, Friedman massively downplays the amount of pain that most people will experience as this process accelerates. It's not too hard to envision hundreds of millions of people joining the ranks of the unemployed or underemployed in the globalized world of the twenty-first century but without any of the benefits to which workers in the United States were previously accustomed (victims of the Republicans' tough love, perhaps). Friedman himself acknowledges that the old Marxist fantasy may be coming true: as capitalism knocks down the wall of China, everything that is solid melts into air. We may actually see on a global scale the emergence of an international proletariat in struggle with an international ruling elite. Nationalist versions of economic domination may be replaced by an international class struggle.

I don't imagine that as a happy prospect. I am too well aware of how some of the most insensitive elements rise to the top in such struggles. But I worry as much about a more likely scenario in response to the economic dislocations Friedman predicts, namely, a repeat of what happened in Germany after the First World War: immiseration followed by popular support for fascist forms of nationalism. Today, fascism would play to the resentments of a population that perceives itself as betrayed and abandoned by the liberals, who appear to be among the major cheerleaders for corporate globalization. Liberals have in fact done little to protect working-class Americans from the worst effects of this globalization beyond exhorting them, Friedman-style, to get a better education and be prepared to learn new job skills every few years as old job skills get quickly outdated or are outsourced. In that situation, fascist dictators who accommodated to corporate power would provide diversion by channeling the anger of the impoverished into ever more destructive nationalist wars, but by using weaponry far more dangerous than anything available in the first half of the twentieth century.

Neither Friedman nor the political elites who cheer him on have any serious plan for building the social supports needed to make the transition to the coming global economy a process that is sensitive to human needs. Indeed, for many of the cheerleaders of corporate globalization, the attempt to make life more secure for working people, as has occurred in Europe, is the very culprit they identify as making people soft. In their view, giving workers some security only makes them less likely to develop the willingness to be exploited in order to meet the requirements of the coming global competition for jobs.

It would be silly to imagine that the process of integrating economies and communication systems and transportation networks among the countries of the world could or should be stopped. But when apologists for this process say "there is no alternative" to globalization, they miss the obvious point that there are many different paths to globalization and that the one currently being followed by Western countries has had results that can be challenged. The United States—urged on by liberal Democrats like Friedman as well as by most corporate Republicans—has organized global trade agreements that further enrich the wealthy and further impoverish the poor, weakening the bargaining power of workers and farmers while increasing the power of merchants, traders, and corporations. Millions of people around the world have demonstrated against these global pacts, correctly noting that the poor have faced deepened misery as a result of the particular way globalization has been imposed. Anger at this form of globalization contributed to the defeat in France and the Netherlands of the proposed constitution for the European Union. In third-world countries, however, few people have the power to effectively challenge the impact of American corporate power allied with local elites and a small middle class who actually do benefit from the globalization. And the impact on the lives of the impoverished majority in the third world is often unambiguously destructive.

The 2004 report of the International Labor Organization of the United Nations offers some important statistics that reveal how corporate-dominated globalization is actually working:

Since 1980, the growth of world gross domestic products (GDP) has decreased in comparison with the growth in preceding decades. This decline calls into question the optimistic prognoses regarding the effects that globalization will have on growth. It's true that the GDP of poorer countries is rising, but that does not mean that the poor within those countries are benefiting. Globalization aids the richest in poor countries while making the poor poorer.

The income gap between the richest and the poorest countries has widened enormously. The average annual per capita income in the world's poorest countries between 1960 and 1962 was $212, as opposed to $11,417 in the richest. Between 2000 and 2002, the average per capita income in the poorest countries had risen only to $267, while that in the richest countries had risen to $32,339.

The United States is not the only culprit in this global economic imbalance. To understand its source, we'd have to look back at the cumulative history of Western colonialism and Western control of the world economy over the past several hundred years, taking into account the distorting impact of the cold war. But the United States gets the brunt of the anger today because it is the leader of the Western world and because its corporations have been most successful in using American military and global economic power to advance their own interests in third-world countries. Of course, American corporations don't set out with an agenda to hurt the poor; they simply seek out new markets, cheap labor, and cheap raw materials, and they compete for these with other international corporations from other advanced industrial societies.

The effect of modern international trade arrangements, however, has been to destroy the market for many locally produced agricultural goods or handcrafted products. The poor lose out when international companies come in and buy up or enclose land, making it impossible to move animals to traditional grazing and watering lands, and when multinational corporations privatize essential natural resources such as water and sell them back to the people of the country at what are prohibitive rates for those who live at subsistence levels. Some villages are literally uprooted physically to accommodate corporate projects. In the case of other villages, integration into the global marketplace destroys the market for their products, making village life impossible to sustain economically. So people are forced off their lands and into the huge slums surrounding major cities, where they live in horrific conditions, often witnessing their children being forced to choose between starvation, crime, and prostitution. Clearly, these are not the people who will be "saved" by globalization. Yet it is the poor who are being urged to understand that there will be "necessary sacrifices" for the sake of "progress"—and they and their children are the sacrifices.

The second gaping flaw in the "salvation through globalization" strategy is that it is based on an Enlightenment fantasy that the world has unlimited resources and that therefore growth has no limits. Friedman quotes Marc Andreessen, the cofounder of Netscape, who blithely declares that "the pie keeps growing because things that look like wants today are needs tomorrow." Google is cited as an example. We have always needed to search for things, but now a technology has been created that in turn produces jobs for people with PhDs in math. "If you believe human wants and needs are infinite," Andreessen says, "then there are infinite industries to be created, infinite businesses to be started, and infinite jobs to be done, and the only limiting factor is human imagination."

It is not much of a surprise that very few of the flag-wavers for corporate globalization appear to have any in-depth understanding of the environmental crisis that has been intensifying over the course of the past half century. Though Friedman sheds half a tear for disappearing species, he takes little account of global warming or the destruction of the air and waterways of the planet.

Introducing the Worldwatch Institute's latest annual report, *State of the World 2005,* Mikhail Gorbachev describes the global situation this way:

> "We need to recognize that Earth's resources are finite. To waste our limited resources is to lose them in the foreseeable future, with potentially dire consequences for all regions and the world. Forests, for example, are increasingly being destroyed in the poorest countries. Even in Kenya, where Wangari Maathai has helped plant over 30 million trees, forested acreage has decreased. The global water crisis is also one of the single biggest threats facing humankind."

You probably know the facts—and you can keep up with the latest developments by reading the reports from the Worldwatch Institute at www.worldwatch.org. The forests are shrinking rapidly, the topsoil for cropland is being lost, deserts are growing, waterways are being polluted, and increasing numbers of the earth's population can no longer find clean drinking water. Many species of fish are no longer safe to eat because they have absorbed toxics poured into the waterways. Rising temperatures confirm predictions of global warming and the melting of the polar ice caps, with growing likelihood of flooding particularly in the poorest parts of the world. Poisons are seeping into food supplies and waterways as the rate of environmentally linked deaths correspondingly increases.

As China enters the world in "catch-up" mode, emulating the materialism and selfishness of the West, the demand on resources will grow exponentially. And if China is able to begin to build cars at a rate comparable to that in advanced industrial societies, the impact on energy and air quality will be devastating. Perhaps there is a way that all this could be regulated, but, as the proponents of a global economy are well aware, the very corporate forces that are the engine for globalization are the forces that will resist most forms of global regulations. That's why even the very inadequate Kyoto accords, which sought minimum reductions in global warming, were treated as "radical" by a Congress whose election costs are largely funded by the very corporations that would pay the price of a more rational policy.

By way of a typical example, a June 17, 2005, report by *Washington Post* correspondent Juliet Eilperin informs us, "Bush administration officials working behind the scenes have succeeded in weakening key sections of a proposal for joint action by the eight major industrialized nations to curb climate change. Under U.S. pressure, negotiators agreed in the past month to delete language that would detail how rising temperatures are affecting the globe, set ambitious targets to cut carbon dioxide emissions, and set stricter environmental standards for World Bank–funded poverty projects."

It is possible that the globalizers will remain willfully ignorant of the impact of their policies for several decades. The worst impact of global environmental collapse will first hit indigenous peoples and those least able to defend themselves, and people in the advanced industrial societies will simply accommodate to the various "inconveniences" of this collapse, such as changing weather patterns, rising cancer rates, and the disappearance of certain varieties of food. But eventually, and in our lifetime, the consequences will be too horrendous to ignore. By that time, the kinds of changes needed to save life on the planet may be equally extreme. Yet facing such extremes is almost a certainty if the world continues to dance on the decks of the environmental *Titanic,* cheerfully focused on who will come up with the next exciting video game or engineer the next electronic miracle, on how to open up new markets to sell new goods (produced, of course, with the world's ever-diminishing supply of raw materials), and on who will be most successful in creating "new needs" so that people across the globe can experience themselves as desperately needing what a decade earlier didn't even exist, which will in turn allow corporate interests to continue recklessly depleting the world's resources and increasing the chances of environmental disaster.

Fundamentalism

Faced with the undermining of their social life and daily attacks on their human and natural environment, many in the third world already resent the West. What most Westerners do not understand is that this global resentment is not just economic but also cultural and spiritual. People worldwide increasingly resent the culture of selfishness and materialism that globalized capital brings with it, even as they sometimes accede to it, purchase its products, dance to its music, and watch its movies and videos (just like many of us do in the United States).

To some extent, the attack on Western culture is not entirely fair. Western societies are rightly proud of having developed democratic institutions. In particular, the institutionalization of human rights stands as a contribution that will remain a major advance in the history of humanity. For that alone, the people of the world owe a lasting debt to Westerners and in particular to some "dead white men" who played a major role in putting these ideas on the agenda of the human race. We who live in the West have good reason to rejoice in these accomplishments of our society and to want to do all we can to preserve and extend them and to offer them to the rest of the world as well, because they rest upon universal values that are appropriate for the entire human race.

We spiritual Democrats who rightly critique George Bush's militarist methods for advancing democracy must nevertheless agree with him that the ideal of global democracy is one important component of the advance of human rights and should be championed and applauded.

Unfortunately, however, most people living in the third world don't associate the United States with democracy. In many countries, the only knowledge people have of the United States is that we have sent military aid to their dictators or oligarchs (as we continue to do in Saudi Arabia, Kuwait, Egypt, Pakistan, and many other countries), loaned money to these dictators or oligarchs (which they then siphoned into their personal bank accounts while sticking their countrymen with the burden of paying back those loans, a major component of "third world debt"), and vigorously promoted Western corporations and Western economic arrangements that have had little, if any, benefit to most people in the underdeveloped countries. Some pundits argue that these people embrace fundamentalism because they are jealous of Western democracy. I ask, how could members of these societies resent democracy when they've never seen any such democracy being exported by the United States?

The face of the West that most people see is not our democratic liberalism but our market-based economy. That economy champions a narrow notion of rationality: institutions are judged efficient, rational, and productive when they generate lots of money and power for those at the top. Anyone working in these institutions quickly learns that the most important thing they can do is to focus on the bottom line (that is, the amount of money or power being generated). People quickly learn to see others primarily within a utilitarian framework: to ask whether these others can be "useful" in advancing their own individual goals and to determine how best to use others to maximize their own advantage, or what is called "looking out for number one." In the first part of this book, I detailed many of the ethical and societal dysfunctions and personal human suffering created by this old bottom line.

In advanced industrial societies, some of that individual suffering is buffered by the reality that global economic arrangements allow for an expanding wealth in the West that gets divided, albeit unequally, in ways that provide material satisfactions that can momentarily distract people from the spiritual crisis surrounding them. But there is no such buffer in much of the third world. The entrance of global capital into those societies provides a set of opportunities for a small domestic elite, who are perhaps able to convince themselves that their society as a whole will be better off if they can make deals with international cap-

ital to bring the marvels of Western corporate life to the underdeveloped areas in their country. The small middle classes that emerge in
these countries benefit mightily from the infusion of Western capital,
and this can produce a rise in the average income level or the collective
wealth of the society—although it is a rise that is never seen by and
does not work for the benefit of many people in those countries. For
most third-world people, the impact is quite different: the market-
based bottom-line consciousness erodes traditional tribal, communal,
and familial sources of support that have kept these societies functioning for hundreds of years. Increasingly, people are left to fend for
themselves. In contrast to the situation in the industrialized societies of
the West, for these people there is no "safety net" funded by the third
world, because they *are* the third world.

Dictators and oligarchic leaders have often manipulated the anger at
global capital as a way of shoring up their own repressive rule. Fundamentalists, sometimes aligned with repressive oligarchs and sometimes
fighting against them, also manipulate this anger. Some fundamentalists
genuinely oppose a culture of selfishness and materialism, and not surprisingly they see that culture as coming from the influence of the West
in their own societies. In reaction, they romanticize the past, particularly village life and old-time religious systems—what they see as the
"fundamentals" of their former, better life. Many decent and humane
people turn to fundamentalism after contact with corporate "modernization" because fundamentalism promises its followers a caring
community based on higher values than the Western- and corporate-
dominated marketplace.

As outsiders, we can see that fundamentalism often creates a community of caring at the expense of some Other who is then demonized.
Fundamentalist societies are often patriarchal, xenophobic, and homophobic. Fundamentalists often counterpose their religious truths to
Western forms of rationality, denying the value of scientific inquiry, the
value of bodily pleasure, and any attempt of individuals to control their
own lives. Under the guise of providing protection for women against
the marketplace, women's freedom and rights in these male-dominated
societies are usually severely restricted. Stories of women being kid-
napped into forced marriages in Afghanistan, like ongoing reports of
forced clitorectomies in African patriarchal societies, may be news in

the West, but they are only the most dramatic symptoms of societies that routinely abuse women in the name of cultural tradition and for the sake of male power.

Yet people throughout the world—yes, even some women who have lived in liberated, Western-style societies—have voluntarily chosen to align themselves with fundamentalist religious communities and leaders. It is hard for most Americans to believe, but people are willing to give up their rights in order to feel they are really cared for. As I've argued throughout this book, fundamentalism succeeds because it tries to satisfy people's hunger for a framework of meaning and a sense of purpose that can transcend the thinking of the competitive marketplace. Fundamentalism affirms community and social solidarity. It becomes a form of resistance to the worst aspects of the globalization of selfishness that has been the public face of the international capitalist marketplace.

When we in the West see the very real abuses that happen in these supposedly caring societies, it is hard for us to understand how people can continue to support them. Just imagine, however, how hard it was for people in these societies to imagine how we could call ourselves "democratic" and pride ourselves on exporting freedom when we were funding the Shah of Iran or the Pinochet government, in the past, or when we support dictatorships in Saudi Arabia, Egypt, and Pakistan, as we do today. Imagine how people of color around the world react when they see the way blacks and poor people become most vulnerable and least cared for in American society, as was dramatized yet again in the aftermath of Hurricane Katrina. We may begin to understand how intelligent, sophisticated people might choose to join with fundamentalists to express their anger at the excesses of the competitive marketplace, even though this understanding is not meant to be a code word for approval.

Apologists for Western power like to whine about the irrationality of third-world peoples that leads them to hate America out of jealousy over our wealth and power or out of blind adherence to religions like Islam that are purported to teach little more than hatred. "They hate us," this argument goes, "because it's in the nature of their fundamentalist religion to hate us, and nothing we can do will ever have the slightest impact in changing that. To think otherwise is to be naive about the degree to which their religious culture has created a group of hate-filled individuals who simply want to destroy the West because of historic resentments at the way the West's very success has made them feel left behind and humiliated." It is an argument that appeals to all those who are unwilling to look at the actual role of Western societies in the Islamic world. If you ignore the way Britain and France took over the Middle East after World War I, carving out a set of countries from what had previously been a single Arab world and backing local elites who agreed to sell oil to the West at cheap rates in exchange for being allowed to run dictatorial regimes at home and whose leaders pocketed vast wealth while largely ignoring the economic and educational needs of their own populations and brutally repressing all dissent, if you ignore how the United States took over major responsibility for maintaining this kind of relationship after World War II and overthrew the democratically elected government in Iran to set up the Shah in 1954, how Israel was supported in giving inadequate support to the 800,000 Palestinian refugees produced by its creation in 1948, how the United States funded Saddam Hussein and encouraged his war against Iran in the 1980s, and how in the meanwhile American culture's valuation of money and individualism was fostering a breakdown of traditional families and communal support systems, leaving many people without any safety net to protect them against the vicissitudes of the capitalist marketplace, then it becomes easy to accept a story of American and Western innocence versus Islamic irrationality. But once you become aware of the history and understand the current role of Western societies and the dictatorial regimes they continue to fund and back militarily, once you recognize that Israel's role in the Middle East as a surrogate for Western power has not always been constructive and innocent and that its insistence on holding on to much of the West Bank and thwarting the aspirations to self-determination of the two million Palestinians who live there has not been helpful in reducing tensions, once you appreciate that while the breakdown of traditional social and gender roles has a huge positive side, it also causes huge pain, then it becomes harder to dismiss rage at the West as nothing more than fundamentalist religion gone bad. To understand these complexities is to recognize that at least some of those who seek to fight U.S. global domination are not simply power trippers (though many are) but are motivated by genuine outrage at the destructive role of the G-8 countries in global politics.

None of this should lead us to think that the fundamentalists have righteousness on their side. I can understand why the breakdown of patriarchal families causes pain, but that doesn't lead me to want to support the retention of a system that has been immensely painful to women and children. I can understand why the unbridled capitalist marketplace causes huge resentment, but that doesn't make me want to support a return to feudal economic arrangements. I have the same interest in understanding Islamic fundamentalism as in understanding the Jewish fundamentalists who have distorted the political life of Israel and the Christian fundamentalists who are increasingly shaping American policy—namely, an interest in recognizing and respecting their humanity and also in acknowledging what is legitimate in their worldviews in order to find effective ways to address real needs in a nonfundamentalist and nonviolent way that will not be demeaning of others. Just as I do not seek to understand the Religious Right in the United States in order to soften opposition to its actual policies, so I do not want us to soften opposition to the radical fundamentalists and hatemongers in other parts of the world. But once we do understand the underlying history and dynamics, we can also see that the policies we have been pursuing are not the most successful way to protect ourselves or to prevent those who hate from mobilizing hate so effectively.

The Strategy of Generosity

And the work of generosity shall be peace; and the effect of generosity will be quietness and security forever.
—Isaiah 32:17

To explain the anger fundamentalists have at the United States is not to suggest that the actions of terrorists are therefore acceptable. They are not. But the only way to develop a strategy to make the United States safer is to understand the basis of their appeal.

Once we understand that fundamentalism provides its adherents with an effective weapon against selfishness and materialism and the role the West has played in the world, we can create what I call a Strategy of Generosity to counter it. Such a strategy will affirm altruistic motives as a legitimate and essential part of foreign policy, while acknowledging that those motives also abet our own long-term self-interest. Once we truly understand the nature of the shrinking world and the functioning of our global environment, the interconnection of our well-being with the well-being of everyone else on the planet will become the central guidepost for all of our policies, domestic and foreign.

This is what Martin Luther King Jr. was trying to teach us when he wrote: "All life is interrelated. All men [sic] are caught in an inescapable network of mutuality, tied in a single garment of destiny. Whatever affects one directly affects all indirectly. I can never be what I ought to be until you are what you ought to be, and you can never be what you ought to be until I am what I ought to be. This is the interrelated structure of reality" (*The Strength to Love,* Fortress Press, 1981, p. 75).

There are some who argue that America's role in creating and sustaining current global economic arrangements should be praised. After all, they argue, two-thirds of the people in the world are doing fine. In other words, if it is true that one out of three people is living on less than $2 a day, don't forget that the other two out of those three must be doing much better than that. And many in the advanced industrial societies, including many people in working-class jobs, have a higher standard of living than most people have ever had throughout human history.

This argument only seems plausible because of the hidden premise that we are not really connected to, nor do we need to care about, the fate of these others, including the estimated 20,000 to 30,000 children who die every day (yes, every day) of starvation or of diseases related to malnutrition—diseases that could have been prevented had there been a global system that distributed food, shelter, and health care equitably. If instead we saw the world as the spiritual and religious communities urge us to see it—as one family united through a common embodiment of Spirit or as equally created in God's image—we would be outraged at this kind of a global arrangement.

Imagine that you lived in a family in which there were five children. One of those children had been given 40 percent of the resources of the family, a second had 32 percent, a third had 20 percent, a fourth was struggling with 6 percent of the resources, and one was starving to death with only 2 percent of the resources. Surely you would reject the argument of the richest child who praised the arrangements and pointed to the way that it was good for the family because a majority of the children were thriving. You'd say: "No, it is unacceptable to see one of these children starving and another struggling so hard to survive. This is a crazy and immoral arrangement, and it must immediately be changed. I will not be part of any arrangement that has these consequences." The only reason we don't say that about the world we live in today is because we refuse to acknowledge these others as actually part of our family.

A spiritual sensitivity challenges this denial of our interconnectedness and hence demands a different kind of foreign policy. That's why many spiritual progressives today call for something like what I refer to as the Strategy of Generosity.

This strategy has as its goal to create a world in which the United States would be:

The world's leading force in supporting an end to global poverty, homelessness, hunger, inadequate education, and inadequate health care

The world's leading force in repairing the damage done to the global environment

The articulator and embodiment of an economic new bottom line and a country willing to embrace the Left Hand of God and to rely on love and kindness, and hence a country unwilling to support dictatorships and oppressive regimes around the world no matter how friendly they may be to American corporations

A Global Marshall Plan

He that pursues acts of generosity and speaks uprightly, he that despises the gain of oppression, that shakes his hands from holding of bribes, that stops his ears from hearing of blood and shuts his eyes from seeing evil; he shall dwell on high, his place of de-

fense shall be a fortress of rocks; bread shall be given to him; his
water shall be sure.

—Isaiah 33:15–16

Execute true judgment, and show loyal love and mercy every man
to his brother; and do not oppress the widow, or the fatherless,
the stranger, or the poor; and let none of you devise evil against
his brother in your heart.

—Zechariah 7: 9–10

Because so many of our foreign policy problems are rooted in our market-based economy, the first step of the Strategy of Generosity is a
Global Marshall Plan. Our plan would have the United States take the
lead in creating an international consortium of the G8 countries, who
together would dedicate hundreds of billions of dollars each year for
the next thirty years to the cause of eliminating hunger, homelessness,
inadequate education, and inadequate health care in underdeveloped
countries. Let the United States set up an international body of internationally recognized spiritual leaders, academics, health care workers,
educators, and community organizers to supervise the expenditures—
to guarantee that they are not siphoned off by selfish national (or religious) leaders but instead are used in creative ways to achieve the goals
cited. A somewhat more modest plan, including how to fund it, is fully
described by Franz-Josef Radermacher (in his book, *Global Marshall
Plan: A Planetary Contract,* and online at www.globalmarshallplan.org).
I cite that version to show that detailed thinking about how to create a
Global Marshall Plan is well under way and that a more generous version of a Global Marshall Plan could easily be built on those foundations.

Renowned economist Jeffrey Sachs, author of *The End of Poverty*
and director of the Earth Institute at Columbia University, has also detailed a plan for ending global poverty in the worst-hit countries. He
suggests that the United States provide $60 to $90 billion per year between now and 2015 to end poverty. Sachs points out that development assistance is only 0.14% of our GNP compared to the
international goal of 0.7% of GNP, a goal that several countries have
already reached or exceeded. "How hard should it be to raise that

money?" Sachs asks, and then answers: "Our Congress quickly approved $87 billion for military operations in Iraq and gave away $250 billion of tax cuts a year. We raised military spending by an annual rate of $150 billion over the last three years. President Bush proposed his Millennium Challenge Account of only $1 billion, and it has not disbursed a penny yet. Right now, we give just $16 billion in development assistance, but our defense budget gets nearly $450 billion each year. We must increase public awareness of how little we currently dedicate to developing countries."

I believe that Sachs's goals are too modest. They restrict caring to the immediate emergency of mass starvation. They do not reflect what the Western countries truly need to spend on a sustained basis for the next twenty to thirty years to create a planet without hunger, homelessness, and inadequate health care, education, or employment. When it comes to political possibility, it often takes the same amount of energy to get less as to get more—so we should aim for a solution that is really a solution, not for a global version of the kind of ameliorating of suffering that welfare programs aimed for in the United States, often with somewhat destructive, albeit unintended, consequences.

I propose that we fund the Global Marshall Plan at a much more significant level. Funding for this initiative could be based on a worldwide tax on financial transactions at an initial level of 0.1% of the value traded and a worldwide tax on trade of 0.5% of the value of internationally traded goods. The goal of these taxes would not be to penalize trade (and they would not do so) but to promote worldwide development. The essential elements of a Global Marshall Plan (although not my proposed taxes) have been endorsed by Britain's chancellor of the exchequer, Gordon Brown, by the former foreign minister of Germany, Hans-Dietrich Genscher, and by the Eco-Social Forum of Europe, as well as by a sufficient number of other powerful voices that, if the United States were to take the lead, there is a reasonable chance that other advanced industrial societies would buy in. The plan will avoid the vulgar approach of dropping money into the laps of local elites. It will seek not to obliterate but to work with market mechanisms, not to impose a command-and-control economy but to modify market forces by supporting measures to increase equality, focusing first and foremost on permanently eliminating poverty and creating the economic infrastructure for a global economy that will be able to provide adequate education, health care, and employment for everyone on the planet.

Meanwhile, as this is getting in place, there is much more we can do:

1. Let the United States take steps immediately to eliminate the multilateral debt of the world's poorest countries. Currently the world's poorest countries spend more on debt repayments than they do on health care. An important first step was taken by the G-8 countries at their meeting in July 2005, but those steps were partial and did not fully eliminate debt repayments.

2. Let the United States initiate a program of global ecological repair to undo the damage done by well over a century of environmental irresponsibility on the part of advanced industrial societies, both capitalist and socialist.

3. Let the United States require that every citizen spend at least two years in national service, administering aid and health care, providing education and skills training, or otherwise assisting in the implementation of the Global Marshall Plan—but only for that purpose and only after the plan has actually begun to function, not to bolster the sagging enlistment rate into the military.

4. Let the United States use the full weight of its resources and power to convince Israel to end the occupation of the West Bank and provide security for both Israel and Palestine. Let the United States seek an end to the occupation of Chechnya by Russia and of Tibet by China. Let the United States lead efforts to end the genocide in Darfur. Let the United States cooperate in efforts to extend the power and field of operations for the International Court of Justice.

5. Let the United States bring all of its troops home from Iraq immediately, replacing them with an international force so the United Nations could conduct a plebiscite to determine whether the Sunnis, Kurds, and Shia wish to stay together in one state or break into three separate states, and under what terms (remembering that Iraq itself was created by Western

powers putting together communities that did not democratically choose to create a state). If the U.S. troops were no longer
a target, if the United States gave the international community
full assurances that it would exercise no control over Iraqi oil,
would withdraw from all military bases, and would provide tens
of billions of dollars each year in reconstruction aid to help an
international force rebuild what the U.S.-initiated war had destroyed, it would no longer be the obstacle to the international
community's attempting to aid Iraqis in avoiding civil war. Done
in a spirit of generosity, U.S. withdrawal could also be catalytic
for splitting the Iraqi insurgency between those who fight for
an independent Iraq and those who use the Iraqi struggle to
foster support for the destructive global terrorist aims of Al
Queda.

6. Let the United States demonstrate in word and deed that wherever it sends money, it is not trying to "buy influence" but to
   genuinely respond to a new set of priorities, embodying a new
   bottom line of generosity and kindness. That does not mean
   sinking money into corrupt local elites but instead establishing
   mechanisms of transparency and accountability that are overseen
   not by the United States or by the recipients or by the United
   Nations, but by an international agency set up for this purpose.
   This agency will be supervised by the religious, academic, cultural, and moral leadership of the countries throughout the
   globe rather than by their current political and economic leaders. Not only are the former unlikely to do a worse job than the
   latter have already, but they are more likely to be free of the self-
   interest that has corrupted political and economic leadership in
   guiding international investment and aid.

7. Let the United States develop a new set of guidelines for international trade that promote and reward ecological safety
   and sustainability, workers' rights, respect for indigenous
   peoples and for the world's multicultural realities, and a clear
   commitment to promoting the well-being of the least powerful
   people on the planet.

8. Let the United States adopt the Social Responsibility Amendment as described earlier and extend its concerns to supervise the impact of U.S. corporations on all other countries in which they operate, sell goods or services, or otherwise exercise and impact on people's lives and the environment. Meanwhile, let communities around the world develop the questions and categories for an Ethical Impact Report that juries could use in focusing attention on what issues to assess and how to assess them when engaged in their deliberations about whether a given company should be allowed to continue to operate.

9. Let the United States take immediate steps to ensure that the democratic principles it preaches abroad are actually functioning at home. The United States must dramatically reduce the role of money in elections (if necessary, by constitutional amendment) and provide free and equal access to media time for all major candidates in a given election and prohibit any other use of electronic or print media to publicize one candidate without providing equal time to others. The Electoral College should be eliminated. Voters, as they cast their ballots, should also be enabled to indicate the five most important issues that led them to support the candidate they selected, thereby giving the candidate and the country an idea of precisely what matters most to them.

10. Let us in the United States implement this strategy in a new spirit, with a willingness to atone for past misdeeds, to approach other countries in a spirit of cooperation and repentance, and to commit to learning from the histories and traditions of these countries lessons that might be valuable for us as we attempt to build a society based on generosity and openheartedness. Without this kind of a spirit, all the rest will be perceived as little more than bribery and will not work.

Sounds visionary? Well, yes. But it often turns out that the visionary approach is far more practical than the approaches of the pragmatists, who have led us into the world at which terrorists struck on 9/11. If you are satisfied with the level of homeland and global security brought to us by trillions of dollars of defense spending and support of dictators around the world, you won't find this approach attractive. But if you realize how ineffective it has been, then give the idea of approaching the world with kindness and generosity a chance. A Strategy of Generosity has worked in the past. During the cold war, hawks advocated preemptive actions designed to provoke the Soviet Union into conflict. It took the combined action of tens of millions of ordinary Americans, plus the decency and intelligence of people in both major parties, to restrain these hawks and insist on a policy of peaceful coexistence. In the end, those who argued that the Soviet Union could never be brought down or communism eradicated except through military intervention were proved wrong. And yet they were just as "certain" later on that Saddam Hussein could never be overthrown in any other way. The militarists-realists never learn.

Terrorists draw their recruits from cesspools of anger at the United States the world over. It will be much harder to sustain that anger against an America that is actively engaged, along with other Western countries, in a major and visible effort to end hunger and homelessness and to build the clinics and schools, the roads and communication technologies and electronics capacities, that will enable third-world countries to modernize and provide vital social services to their own population.

A Nonviolent Peace Force

Even with the Global Marshall Plan, there will still be some in these countries who will remain resentful at the developed countries, no matter how sensitively we train the messengers of generosity to be. We should not expect a total and immediate end to violence against the United States—not after the United States has been responsible for the deaths of tens of thousands of Iraqis, for example, and the wounding and maiming of tens of thousands more. Not when it has engaged in systematic torture of prisoners, when it has treated Islam's holy book with disrespect, and when it has empowered oppressive regimes for decades.

We will be paying the price for these actions for many more decades, and the outrage at these polices will continue to lead others to respond to our violence with violence of their own, often aimed at innocent American civilians who did not know about and would not have supported the vicious and hateful policies currently being pursued in our name. For this reason, we will need to have strong and efficient protection on our borders. Nor can we expect that wars will end and world peace magically ensue when we start truly living according to the Left Hand of God. Sadly, there may be more Saddam Husseins out there, and the enslavement of millions by the oppressive regime in North Korea already demands a global response. Even as we adopt a new bottom line, then, we are going to need a way to address international violence.

We recognize these realities, and that is why I am *not* calling for unilateral disarmament and the end to our military. As we move toward the Left Hand of God, we will transition gradually from a society that depends upon its military might to enforce its will to a society that fully commits its resources to ending poverty, homelessness, hunger, inadequate health care, and inadequate education. The use of the American military in December of 2004 to help victims of the devastating tsunami that hit Southeast Asia is an important model for how we can begin to take steps to use our power to reflect our generosity. Military power need not be a zero-sum game. We can have enough credible strength to prevent countries from taking aggressive actions against their neighbors and still channel massive resources into the path of generosity. Our aim, however, should be to trust in our Strategy of Generosity and move toward a nonviolent peace force. Imagine today if we could mobilize even five million people in such a nonviolent army to separate and protect Israelis and Palestinians or to stop the bloodshed in Darfur.

Are there millions of people around the world who would join such a force? Absolutely. Don't ever let the sneering cynicism of the pundits obscure the powerful generosity of spirit of the American people and of many other people on this planet once their attention gets focused on a global problem. In fact, a small nonprofit calling itself the Nonviolent Peace Force, without any of the resources needed to do this on a grand scale, has already recruited thousands of people to do precisely this kind of peaceful intervention in Sri Lanka.

I know many people will believe a Strategy of Generosity alone would never work and that we will always need a military force. These people will argue, "How would a strategy of generosity and a nonviolent peace force have deterred a Hitler?" Well, by the time Hitler was ready to invade Czechoslovakia in 1938, no amount of generosity would have made much difference. But that is not true about the period from 1919 to 1932, in which a generous Western program to rebuild the countries they had defeated in the First World War might very well have strengthened democratic forces sufficiently to have prevented Hitler from ever reaching power, particularly if that generosity had been tied to a politics of meaning that consciously articulated an ethos of global solidarity.

Similarly, had U.S. policy in the 1970s not supported the Shah of Iran and had instead given real assistance to democratic forces seeking to topple him, and had it then offered those forces an aid program to help them rebuild the educational and health care infrastructure of Iran, it would have won support from many Arabs and Muslims and perhaps prevented the subsequent rise of Shia fundamentalism in that country.

Sometimes the realists say, "Sure you are right to have your hopeful principles, but now that we are in the real world situation with all its messiness, we have to act in light of these realities." My point is that this logic is self-perpetuating. We will always be in some horrendous immediate situation as long as we rely upon force and violence. The time to make the switch is now, right now, and by way of a down payment on this commitment, we should take all the funds that are currently being expended on the war in Iraq and use them instead to jump-start our Strategy of Generosity.

But how can this possibly work when we are up against implacable and seemingly irrational dictators?

What the cynical realists never seem to understand is that the critical vulnerability of all governments, even dictatorships like Saddam Hussein's, is that they rely on human beings and their loyalty. When a few people around a dictator or a repressive regime start to defect, they can be jailed or killed. But when there is a massive defection, when the very people expected to carry out orders no longer believe in the legitimacy of the regime that they serve, the whole powerful structure can collapse in the course of months or even weeks. It is this human dimension, and particularly the recurring call from the Left Hand of God into our consciousness, that, despite the best efforts of political scientists and economists to ignore it, repeatedly overthrows the plans of the powerful. This is exactly what the Bible meant when it said that the powerful can make all their plans and use all their shrewd counsel, but it will eventually falter if the spirit of God is not with them (Isaiah 8:10).

I'm always surprised when people on the Religious Right argue so vehemently in favor of spending money on the military. I want to ask them, "What exactly do you think Jesus meant when he said, 'Turn the other cheek'?" Do you think he meant, "and also wipe out your enemy?" Even the most frightened and frightening champions of the Right Hand of God have a part in them that knows that Jesus did not instruct his followers to commit acts of violence. The reason that those on the Religious Right are not confronted with the nonviolent vision of Jesus is that liberals and progressives have never fully embraced the Left Hand of God and insisted that, yes, love and generosity and non-violence actually are the path to peace and security. It's time to take that plunge now and state our insistence unequivocally—even though this will mean a ferocious battle with others in the Democratic Party and other parts of the Left whose cynical realism will trump their commitment to nonviolence as the path to peace.

Our goal must be to replace military might with the power that comes from speaking to and rallying into action the part of each human being that really wants a world based on kindness, not on violence. Jonathan Schell's powerful *The Unconquerable World: Power, Nonviolence, and the Will of the People* (Metropolitan Books, 2003) provides a systematic study of how the Left Hand of God, manifested as nonviolent social movements, has managed to play a major role in some of the most important social and political transformations in history. When cynical realists say that states don't behave in the way that humans do and can be persuaded only by material self-interest or power, we can answer, Then how did the communist regimes collapse? Would anyone have believed that the people of East Berlin would tear down the Berlin Wall or that a largely nonviolent movement would bring down apartheid in South Africa? Read Schell's book and you will find a detailed argument for why it was nonviolent power, not Reaganesque military expenditures or the African National Congress's acts of terror, that brought about these monumental transformations.

So yes, we should be seeking to create an international nonviolent peace force of tens of millions of people who will be funded by the countries of the world and whose work will consist in bringing massive numbers of nonviolent people to places on the globe where violence is threatened, people trained in reconciliation and people willing to die for the principle of creating a world based on nonviolence, just as today there are millions who are willing to die for the sake of fulfilling the militaristic goals set for them by their own country's ideology. As it begins to win international recognition as a morally coherent force— not a representative of one country or one group of powerful countries but a force committed to nonviolence as its guiding and most fundamental principle—it will be harder and harder for tyrants, oppressors, or even just your ordinary racist hate monger to feel comfortable obeying an order to kill members of this nonviolent force.

Ultimately we will need an international body with the legitimacy to deploy such a force. I'm sorry to have to acknowledge that the United Nations as currently structured is unlikely to achieve that legitimacy. Created to represent nation states and their interests, the U.N. provides little opportunity to give voice to the moral aspirations of the peoples of the world to see humanity evolve toward a world of peace. The calls for peace and justice and the denunciations of Western imperialism one hears from some countries ring hollow when their own elites continue to deny democratic and human rights. Whereas right-wingers use the hypocrisy of some as a reason to reject any form of international cooperation, I utter this criticism not in the name of preserving U.S. power or to weaken the United Nations but rather to suggest that we need a new conception of international governance and coordination that places moral and spiritual sensibilities, ecological sustainability, human rights and economic justice, nonviolence, and respect for the accumulated wisdom of the human race at the center of the enterprise. Working out that alternative vision in detail should be one of the principal goals of spiritual progressives.

Important first steps in this direction should include revitalizing the International Court of Justice and extending its authority and developing the resources needed to establish an international nonviolent peace force.

The transition from a militarized world to a nonviolent world proposed by spiritual progressives will necessarily be gradual, acknowledging people's fears and working to alleviate them. But it must begin today, and it must also be sufficiently dramatic, taking place over twenty or thirty years in which each year there will be measurable transfers of funds from military budgets to the nonviolent peace force and the Strategy of Generosity. There's a great danger in gradualism— that things never actually happen. That was the problem with past nuclear disarmament agreements, and that remains the problem with plans to phase in such agreements, namely, that militarist interests will find new ways to subvert the intent of any disarmament process unless we plunge in fully. That's why it is not enough to talk about a world of peace and justice in political speeches. We need to see the budgets of the advanced industrial societies reshaped immediately to begin phasing in a whole new conception of how to build peace and homeland security.

It is likely that spiritual progressives will be in the forefront of the struggle for a strategy of generosity and for a societal commitment to nonviolence. Less shackled to the "realism" that has created the violent world and the ecological disasters of the past century and today, spiritual progressives are already willing to think creatively about how to turn eternal spiritual truths into contemporary political policies.

And that is precisely what the Democrats need to do as well. Yes, they will surely be attacked for being unrealistic if they begin to endorse the Strategy of Generosity and the commitment to move from a violent to a nonviolent stance as the centerpiece of our vision of the defense forces of the future. Yet it is precisely by having this kind of a vision that the Democrats will awaken the idealism and hopefulness capable of inspiring people across the old Left-Right dichotomies and across the boundaries of class, race, and gender. If the Democratic Party can stand up and declare, "Yes, we actually take the teachings of Moses, Jesus, Buddha, and other spiritual and religious traditions seriously, and we are going to implement them in the real world because we see ourselves as part of one united human family," it will be able to win majority support and hold it for many decades to come.

This becomes one of the central challenges of a spiritual politics: to actually believe in the possibility of nonviolence and to begin now, not in some far-off messianic period, to build the kind of world everybody says they truly believe in. Taking spiritual vision seriously will have a transformative impact on the peoples of the world as well, making them far more open to rethinking their own fears about the United States and its role in the world.

Isaiah foretold a transformative possibility: "They shall beat their swords into ploughshares, and their spears into pruning hooks. Nation shall not lift up sword against nation, neither shall they learn war any more" (Isaiah 2:4). It's a beautiful vision, but ever since we Jews were exiled from our land by Roman imperialism some two thousand years ago, many of the rabbis have counseled a more cautious approach, teaching that what we need for the *tikkun* (healing) of the world are several small steps. Unfortunately, the small-steps approach has not usually proved viable. But then neither has the apocalyptic grab-for-the-future-in-one-fell-swoop approach had much success. So it is time to make the several-small-steps approach viable by making them much bigger steps. And the first, absolutely essential step is the transition from violence to nonviolence as the only acceptable method of pursuing the world we want to achieve.

Isaiah predicts that "they will neither harm nor destroy on my holy mountain, for the earth will be full of the knowledge of the Lord as the waters cover the sea" (11:9). Well, now is the time for us to stop harming and destroying.

The Talmudic rabbis understood, of course, that peace was deeply connected to social justice, and so they outlined paths of peace for daily life that fundamentally follow the argument of the Covenant for Building a Safer World. As they put it in the ancient Jewish text called Mishnah: "For the sake of peace, the poor of the nations should be supported as we support the poor of Israel, the sick of the nations should be visited as we visit the sick of Israel, and the dead of the nations should be buried as we bury the dead of Israel." This notion of caring for others as the path to peace is at the heart of the Strategy of Generosity.

Progressive Christians see the call to nonviolence and social justice as central to Jesus's teachings. Faced with the certainty that his challenge to Roman authority would lead the occupiers of Judea, in alliance with local Jewish elites whom they had put in power, to seek his death, Jesus refused to use power or self-defensive violence to counter the violence of the state, and he insists on the same nonviolence from his followers. Even on the cross and in immense pain, he called not for retribution against the perpetrators of this evil but prayed to God "to forgive them, for they know not what they do." From the perspective of believing Christians, it was not that Jesus lacked the power to come down from the cross and overthrow the evildoers by force but that he chose not to do so in order to model the path of nonviolence, namely, by demonstrating that even in such extreme circumstances those who have physical power must not use it.

In this spirit, many Christians have adopted the path of nonviolence. Martin Luther King Jr. saw this path as more than a momentary tactic to beat segregation. "Nonviolence," he wrote, "is the answer to the crucial political and moral questions of our time—the need for people to overcome oppression and violence without resorting to violence and oppression.... Nonviolence is not sterile passivity but a powerful moral force which makes for social transformation. Sooner or later, all the people of the world will have to discover a way to live together in peace.... If this is to be achieved, people must evolve for all human conflict a method which rejects revenge, aggression, and retaliation. The foundation for such a method is love" (*A Testament of Hope: The Essential Writings of Martin Luther King, Jr.,* ed. James Washington, Harper & Row, 1986, pp. 224–25).

America's Catholic bishops made an important statement on behalf of these values in 1983 in a pastoral letter on peace: "The whole world must summon the moral courage and technical means to say 'no' to nuclear conflict; 'no' to weapons of mass destruction; 'no' to an arms race which robs the poor and the vulnerable, and 'no' to the moral danger of a nuclear age which places before humankind indefensible choices of constant terror or surrender. Peacemaking is not an optional commitment. It is a requirement of our faith. We are called to be peacemakers, not by some movement of the moment, but by our Lord Jesus" (*The Challenge of Peace: God's Promise and Our Response,* National Conference of Catholic Bishops, 1983, no. 333—and for a more comprehensive discussion of the many Christian sources that advocate nonviolence, please read John Dear's important book *The God of Peace,* Wipf and Stock Publishers, 1994).

Mahatma Gandhi's pioneering of nonviolence against British colonialism showed that nonviolence was as powerful in international affairs as any army might be. "Nonviolence," said Gandhi, "is a power which can be wielded equally by all—children, young men and women, or grown-up people—provided they have a living faith in the God of Love and have therefore equal love for all humanity. When nonviolence is accepted as the law of life it must pervade the whole being" (*All Men Are Brothers,* Continuum, 1982, p. 83). Humanity can be released from violence only through nonviolence, and hatred can only be overcome by love. As Gandhi also stated: "The force generated by non-violence is infinitely greater than the force of all the arms invented by humanity's ingenuity" (*The Words of Gandhi,* ed. Richard Attenborough, Newmarket Press, 1982, p. 55).

The Dalai Lama teaches, as Gandhi also taught, followers to "be the peace that you wish to see in the world." I recently had the honor of being the speaker at a Sunday service at the Riverside Church in New York and sat in the presence of a great spiritual teacher, the Reverend James Forbes. At that service I heard a hymn whose refrain was, "Let there be peace on earth, and let it begin with me." These words are not just personal instruction; they are instructions for an entire society. We must learn to embody the values we wish to see in the world: "Be the peace that you wish to see." It's time to turn our ideals into actions, both as individuals and as a society, to break the illusion that one can be a "moral person" in an "immoral society."

The Left Hand of God is not merely a symbolic vision, a sweet idea for church and synagogue and mosque that has no connection to what we are trying to accomplish in "the real world." We have the ability right now to follow the prophets and bring peace to the world in our lifetime or in our children's lifetime. But we can't accomplish this without making peace the explicit and overriding goal of our foreign policy, along with a commitment to nonviolence as the primary means to achieving that peace.

Conclusion

Someday, after mastering the wind, the rains, the tides and gravity, we shall harness for God the energies of love, and then for a second time in the history of the world, humanity will have discovered fire.
—Teilhard de Chardin

There is an enormous spiritual hunger in America. It is a yearning for a new way to think and a new way to live.

We have been trapped into thinking that fulfillment comes from achieving material success. But as the globalized economy makes accessible more and more material goods at prices that can be afforded, and more Americans have more commodities—more computers, cell phones, DVDs, cars, boats, televisions, and other gadgets—than anyone else on earth, we find ourselves reaching for something else, something that cannot be satisfied by a new purchase.

We want meaning to our lives, a way of connecting our own path to a higher purpose. And when we can't find that higher purpose, when our lives are stuck in a kind of endless struggle to just get by and get through, we often feel dispirited, depressed, or just plain unhappy.

One reason why the Religious Right has been so successful is that it has been able to speak to this hunger for meaning and to provide a context in which this need for a higher purpose becomes the central unifying concern of a community. It has developed spiritual communities that pray together, provide one another with mutual support, and engage in political activity to advance a right-wing political agenda.

To achieve this end, the Right has embraced the Right Hand of God, a way of understanding the sacred that emphasizes the need to wipe out the evil forces in the world through war, domination, and the control of evil impulses. This is a view of God that has roots in the Bible and gains plausibility whenever people face an overwhelmingly oppressive reality—as did the Jews held as slaves in ancient Egypt or Jesus and his disciples under Roman imperialism—and can see no way to transform that reality short of a divine intervention to overpower the evil force.

But when the Right Hand of God is embraced by the powerful, it has a whole different meaning. In contemporary America, the most militarily and economically powerful force the world has ever known, the embrace of the Right Hand of God has been used to provide legitimacy to an American empire and a competitive and unjust economic marketplace.

There is another view of God that also has roots in the Bible, as well as in the sacred stories and visions of most of the world's spiritual and religious traditions. The Left Hand of God emphasizes the need to build a world based on love, kindness, compassion, generosity, mutual cooperation, recognition of the spirit of God in every other human being and an awareness of our interdependence with others, responsibility to the well-being of the planet, and a powerful sense of awe and wonder at the grandeur of creation.

Throughout history, and within each of us, there are elements in our experience that encourage us to see the world through the vision of the Right Hand of God and elements that encourage us to see the world through the vision of the Left Hand of God. The more we are in a state of fear, the more that the Right Hand of God seems intuitively correct, whereas the more we feel hopeful and trusting, the more that the Left Hand of God speaks to us.

At any given moment, we are somewhere on a continuum between these two voices, and our political, economic, and social arrangements reflect that positioning. When social energy flows more toward hope, we find ourselves supporting policies that are more generous, more oriented toward establishing peace and justice; when social energy flows toward fear, we find ourselves supporting policies that seek to dominate others before they dominate us and to build institutions based on the supposition that there is not enough in the way of material goods to go around. And so we feel that we can't afford to share and that we need to protect ourselves. Similarly, when we are in fear, we think that caring for others will undermine or deplete the caring we have to offer our own families and communities, so we narrow the range of our caring and shut ourselves off from concerns about the well-being of others around the globe.

The political Right has been powerful because it has played on our fears and built spiritual communities that find meaning and purpose in life through the vision of reality based on the Right Hand of God. Moreover, the economic and political realities of globalized capital have created a social reality in which our fears are massively reinforced by the daily experience of the world of work. Every day billions of people interact through a set of economic and social institutions that teach us that our own welfare depends on using others to advance ourselves, teaches us that there is not enough to go around and that the bottom line of our world is money and power.

Living in that world, however, is very unfulfilling. Human beings have a need for lives of loving connection and for a sense of some higher purpose than money and power. So the world that is built on the assumptions of the Right Hand of God is very unstable. It is a world that cannot provide ultimate satisfaction. Even the moments of community and solidarity that can be achieved in the churches, synagogues, mosques, and ashrams of a Religious Right cannot offset the massive spiritually and psychologically destructive impact of the daily grind of life in a competitive market society, with its ethos of materialism and selfishness.

The good news is that American politics can be fundamentally transformed if we can create a spiritual Left that embraces hope and builds spiritual communities that find meaning and purpose to life through a vision of reality based on the Left Hand of God. Most people yearn for a world in which peace, social justice, ecological sanity, caring relationships, solidarity among humans that transcends race, class, gender, and national boundaries, and a spirit of openheartedness and generosity prevail.

But most of us have to deal with inner demons, including the psychological and social conditioning we have received that teaches us that we don't deserve to have this yearning fulfilled, that this yearning for a world of kindness and generosity is utopian and fundamentally impossible to achieve, and that nothing significant can be changed in our social world because the world of domination and power is somehow more real. Men have a particularly difficult time here, because male conditioning has made them feel that yearning for a world of love and kindness shows that they haven't become "real men"—and to be a real man is to fully sublimate impulse toward a world of generosity and trust in favor of a world of domination and power.

We need each other if we are to overcome these demons of despair. It is only when we begin to build loving families, communities, and social movements that can embody the Left Hand of God that we find the encouragement and support necessary to allow us to feel that we can really begin to trust in the possibility of a different kind of world. But families, communities, and social movements are themselves composed of human beings who have these demons inside them, and so they are always deeply imperfect, often reflecting internally the struggle that goes on inside each of us over how much to fear and how much to trust. So even as we seek to build a different kind of world, we need massive amounts of compassion for each other's weaknesses, fears, and tendencies to revert to the values of patriarchal societies of the past, with their emphasis on judgment and subordination, rather than uphold the cooperative values that a more equalitarian society seeks to validate.

Actually, thousands of projects already exist, both in the United States and around the world, that embrace the logic of the Left Hand of God. Hundreds of millions of people have rallied to support movements for environmental sanity, the reduction of poverty, human rights, an end to the oppression of women, an end to family and societal violence, and a commitment to nonviolence and world peace. Even within explicitly right-wing communities many of these values are embraced, although they are often applied only to those who share that community's particular religious or ethnic or national orientation. But the desire for a world of love and generosity is present even among those who do not affirm the possibility of building a world based on these values.

There is a huge, global yearning for the Left Hand of God. At the same time, most people do not know that hundreds of millions of others share this desire for a very different kind of world. All too often we give up on our highest aspirations and instead settle for deeply compromised versions of what we really believe in, telling ourselves that we must be "realistic." But the truth is that when we become realistic in these ways, we obscure for others the fact that we share their aspirations. And then they feel that they, too, must compromise and accept "reality" as it is.

This is why it is so important for people to come out of the closet as spiritual beings and become visible to one another. The more we can publicly embrace the Left Hand of God, the more we will support that part of every other person on the planet who also wants to live in a world of love, kindness, and generosity. Eventually, we will reach a critical mass, a number large enough that this desire can no longer be kept from public view. And once it becomes evident that there are so very many people yearning for a world of peace, justice, kindness, love, compassion, generosity, and cooperation, the momentum will be unstoppable.

We've already seen how this can happen. Over the past fifty years we've witnessed historic breakthroughs in which the patriarchal and racist assumptions and social practices that have governed human societies for thousands of years have been successfully challenged. When movements emerged that questioned these arrangements and assumptions, they were told that they were being naive, that they lacked an understanding of history and human nature and were trying to change things that would never change. Yet these voices of cynical realism were wrong.

Today we must challenge the powerful voice of fear embedded in the Right Hand of God. That challenge will be successful. We will build the Network of Spiritual Progressives composed of secular, "spiritual but not religious," and progressive religious people who will give one another the strength and support to affirm a vision of a world of love and generosity, nonviolence, social justice, and ecological sanity. There are tens of millions of Americans who would respond to a progressive spiritual movement if they really heard its message in a clear and undistorted fashion and encountered people who were already giving their full life energies to this project and having a good time doing so.

Such a movement will eventually deeply influence the Democratic Party or create a party of its own to reflect the values of the Left Hand of God. And it will speak to human needs in ways that overcome the contemporary split between Left and Right and forge a progressive politics of meaning that addresses our desires for a life of higher purpose. The sooner this happens, the sooner the Democrats can start winning elections in a way that will give them a mandate for real change.

Together we will transform American economic and political institutions so that instead of each of us having to struggle to maintain our highest values despite our daily experience in the world of work and despite the values of the culture, we will build an economy and culture that support us to be the most generous, loving, and compassionate beings we can be.

There is a huge urgency to this project. The world cannot afford to waste more of its time in wars and other struggles for political and economic domination. While the attention of our media and our politics gets diverted by these insane struggles for power, the population of the world keeps growing, the profligate waste of our earth's resources continues, and the polluting of the environment threatens to destroy the life-support systems of the planet within the next fifty to seventy years or even, as some environmental scientists argue, the next twenty to thirty years.

We, the people of the world, need to get a grip, take control of our own destiny, and protect ourselves from this coming disaster by reorganizing the planet in ways that will make all our activities ecologically sustainable. If we in the advanced industrial societies manage to create a successful model for placing caring relationships above endless material consumption, we will have some basis for influencing the form of modernization that China, India, and other underdeveloped countries adopt before they accelerate environmental destructiveness to levels that eventually will exceed the destructiveness of the West. If, on the other hand, we continue to pursue our current environmental irresponsibility by remaining committed to the old bottom line, we have little chance of influencing other countries to place the well-being of the entire planet ahead of their desire to "catch up" with Western consumer society. We are in the final decades of American hegemony in politics, economics, science, communication, and culture. If we use our power for the sake of the well-being of all people on the planet, we could make a huge impact on the consciousness of everyone else on the planet and reverse the current plunge into irreversible environmental damage.

But that won't happen as long as the most powerful country on the planet is in the hands of people who actually look forward to the destruction of the earth, imagining that to be part of a divine plan that will produce the Second Coming of Jesus and an ultimate redemption of those who have been saved in the eyes of their religious tradition. Nor will it happen as long as we have people in both parties whose primary commitment is to preserve our current economic and political power arrangements.

Responding to the pressing needs to reconstruct our global economic and political life in rational ways to prevent ecological disaster cannot happen until there is a fundamental change in the way that we in the West, and particularly in the United States, organize our own societies and control our multinational corporations. And that won't happen until we have a powerful spiritual movement that can speak to the hunger for meaning and purpose and win people over to a progressive spiritual perspective.

To build such a movement will require sensitivity, smarts, compassion for each other's weaknesses and distortions, and a willingness to use our talents and our money and our life energies and our precious time on this planet.

This is an amazing moment to be alive. We have the possibility in our own time to take a major step toward the fulfillment of ancient prophecies that brought us tidings of comfort and joy about a world in which war and injustice would be replaced by love and peace and kindness. We can embrace the Left Hand of God and build on the loving energies of the human race.

Let's do this together.

As for me, I want to end this book by thanking God for giving me the opportunity to be alive at this moment, to experience the awesome grandeur of creation, to take in all that I can take in given all my limitations, and to share with others this message of radical hope. How very great are Your works, God, and how very deep Your thoughts. What a blessing to be able to connect to this world at this time and to give what I can give to the process of healing and transformation.

—*Rabbi Michael Lerner*
RabbiLerner@tikkun.org

Next Steps

Imagine that you'd like to see the Democratic Party, the Greens, and the liberal and progressive social change movements begin to articulate a spiritual politics and to promote the Spiritual Covenant with America. You can't do this alone. You need a community of spiritual progressives who can work with you.

Please use this book to begin the process of building such a community. Create a study group. Invite friends, coworkers, members of your church, synagogue, mosque, or temple, students, professional colleagues, and other people you know. Allow the study group to go on for many weeks, encourage open debate and dissent, chew on the ideas, accept those that you can, reject those that don't work for you. Using your own intelligence and creativity, work out your own ideas, adopting those that make sense to you, refining them, developing them, and transforming them until they are your own. Role-play conversations with people who are going to disagree with the vision you've come up with. See whether you can form out of this study group a core of people who feel confident talking about these kinds of ideas.

Okay, now you and your group have finished reading the book together, and you want to do something. We at *Tikkun* magazine have formed an interfaith Network of Spiritual Progressives (NSP), and I'd like to invite you to join it. You can read about our core vision at www.tikkun.org and join the NSP online, or you can e-mail us at NSP@tikkun.org or write to the NSP/*Tikkun* at 2342 Shattuck

Avenue, Suite 1200, Berkeley, CA 94704. That will put you in touch with others who share your perspective and are working together to implement these ideas.

After you've joined the organization, write me a self-revealing personal letter, telling me about your path, your current situation, the talents and skills you think you could bring to the table in building the Network of Spiritual Progressives, the parts of this book that speak most deeply to you, the parts of the covenant that you most want to promote in the public sphere, and the projects listed below that most excite you, and I'll try to connect you with others who have similar interests and skills. I can't do this for every person who reads the book, but if you are someone who feels committed enough to become a dues-paying member of the Network of Spiritual Progressives, I want to know you. Let's be allies. So e-mail me at RabbiLerner@tikkun.org or send regular mail to the NSP/*Tikkun* address above. If you would, send me your photo so I can have the pleasure of seeing how God manifests through your physical being!

Still, you'd like to know what you could actually do as part of such a network. What concrete steps can be taken to bring the Left Hand of God back into public consciousness and into our communal and political life?

Here are a few specific projects for spiritual activism:

1. *Organize a movement of spiritual Democrats or spiritual Greens.* Form a spiritual caucus within the Democratic Party, the Greens, or any other political party with which you are affiliated. Ask them to adopt the Spiritual Covenant with America as a central focus of their political campaigns. Call up the local office of your political party and find out when they will be selecting representatives from your legislative and congressional districts to attend the party's state and national conventions. Ask them whether there is any way you can send an announcement to the members of the party in your area to invite them to a meeting of a caucus of spiritual progressives. If there isn't, go to the party's local meetings and hand out a leaflet announcing your meeting.

Meanwhile, put yourself forward as a potential representative to the party's state and national conventions (well, who else do you know who is going to do it?). When you present yourself, call for a new focus to the party—the Spiritual Covenant with America and a new bottom line for American society. Even if you don't get selected the first time, chances are that you will meet some new people who are interested in working with your local Network of Spiritual Progressives and in building a spiritual caucus. Let's aim to have a caucus of Spiritual Democrats and Spiritual Greens at their national conventions in 2008 and at statewide conventions by 2007. Let's seek to persuade both the Democrats and the Greens to endorse the Spiritual Covenant with America and the concept of the new bottom line and the SRA (Spiritual Republicans? Sure, try it). If you keep at this, if you build a local Network of Spiritual Progressives and promote its ideas by running for office in the primaries of the various political parties in your area (and this can include every political party), by 2010 we could be a significant force at statewide conventions and by 2012 a really significant presence at the national conventions.

2. *Create a "new bottom line" caucus within your professional organization, union, or workplace.* Get a conference room reserved at the next national, regional, or local meeting of your professional organization or union or set up a meeting in your workplace. Announce that you are inviting people who might be interested in the new bottom line and describe what that is. At the meeting, explain the goal of this caucus: to develop a coherent picture of how your profession, union, or workplace might function if there really was a new bottom line. The task is to work out in detail what would have to change and precisely what it could look like if at every point of decision in your professional life or your daily work the main criteria for decision making were really not about how to make more money or gain more power but about how to maximize caring, generous, and peace-loving behavior, how to increase ethical and ecological sensitivity and a sense of moral responsibility, and how to foster a nonutilitarian way of viewing other human beings and nature and encourage a sense of awe, wonder, and radical amazement.

Only one rule must govern this discussion: "Keep the reality police out of the room." The reality police are the voices of cynical realism that tell you there is no point in engaging in this discussion because, after all, no one is ever going to take these ideas seriously. Instead, the idea is that this is a place where one's highest ethical and spiritual aspirations can shape the outcome of the discussion.

When you've completed this process (it will likely take at least a year or two before you've got a group of people who have really thought through all the ramifications of a new bottom line and how to make this approach really work), send us your plan and we will put you in touch with others who are thinking along similar lines. The NSP will disseminate the ideas, and before you know it, you'll have a group within your profession or union or workplace that is ready to move forward: to propose specific, first-step changes to those in charge or even incorporating those first steps into your next contract or next round of bargaining.

3. *Become a consultant on spiritual politics or a trainer for councils on the common good.* Over the course of the next twenty years there will be increasing numbers of institutions that will want assistance in conceptualizing how they might embody a new bottom line, political candidates who will need assistance integrating a spiritual politics into their campaigns and into the decisions they make once elected, governmental institutions that will want to change how they function in accord with a spiritual politics, and workplaces that will want to establish councils for the common good. They will need people who can help in the creation and supervision of these projects—people who are not simply self-interested promoters but rather people who are deeply interested in serving the Left Hand of God. Similarly, if you are a candidate for public office, you might find this training invaluable to prepare you for the array of assaults on your ideas that the cynical realists may throw your way. If you are interested in receiving this kind of certification and training, please contact the Network of Spiritual Progressives at NSP@tikkun.org.

4. *Develop a spiritual politics agenda for your local school board.* The most effective way to challenge the Right's assault on the separation of church and state in education is to put forward a program that speaks to parents' legitimate desire for spiritual values that do not impose a specific religious perspective to form part of their children's schooling. Take the ideas about education presented in the Spiritual Covenant with America and make them your platform. In liberal districts, you may find a surprising resonance among people who want the Democrats to be more effective nationally and can see how your local school district could become an example of how to set up a values-based curriculum.

In conservative districts you may find that many right-wingers have no effective way to challenge this progressive spiritual program.

5. *Create an ethical consumption project in your area.* Help alert consumers to stop purchasing food and consumer goods that have been produced in ways that are harmful to the environment or unjust to the workers and communities in which these goods are produced, distributed, and advertised. Then extend that concept to include a broader notion of what is morally acceptable. While it will take the cooperation of hundreds of millions of people around the globe to work out a full-blown system of ethical consumption, we can build upon current efforts to promote the ethical and ecological labeling of products and can also encourage people to buy products that meet international fair-trade standards.

6. *Get the Social Responsibility Amendment to the Constitution onto local and statewide ballots as an initiative.* Persuade your local city council to endorse the SRA and allocate some funds to help with an initiative campaign. Or put the amendment on the ballot yourself by organizing supporters to collect the needed signatures, if this is the official process in your state. Insist that anyone running for public office seeking your financial support endorse the SRA. (If they say, "Well, I agree with the objectives, but there are better ways to achieve it," ask them to show you what concrete steps they have taken or will now take to achieve those objectives.) Meet with representatives of professional organizations, unions, and religious institutions, and ask them to sign endorsements for the SRA, then list those on your fliers. A consistent campaign on behalf of the amendment will eventually allow the idea to break through into public consciousness and receive tremendous support. Much like the Equal Rights Amendment, which never passed yet stimulated major changes, the SRA will no doubt face huge opposition. Nevertheless, it is bound to provoke a national discussion that will have lasting value and may make state-by-state efforts to require corporate responsibility far more likely to succeed.

Meanwhile, organize a nonviolent pray-in or sing-in in front of the homes or the churches or synagogues of corporate executives and members of the boards of directors of corporations that are destroying the environment, are insensitive to workers' needs, or are polluting the airwaves with cynicism and hatred.

7. *Challenge the cynicism of the media.* Many of the commentators and reporters working for local or national news outlets are perfectly decent people, but they operate within the confines of the mainstream definition of what it is to be "savvy" and skeptical, according to which we should assume that everyone is out to manipulate us. Try to approach them individually, through personal encounters or letters, to explain why their cynicism is neither justified nor ethically responsible, and detail the instances in which you've noticed it. Send them a copy of *The Left Hand of God,* and ask them to meet with you after they've read it. We have a list of columnists and media people on our Web site whom it is important to contact and challenge.

National entertainment and advertising are harder nuts to crack. There are groups who monitor political balance or sexuality or violence, but no one yet monitors the various ways in which the entertainment industry fosters cynicism and unconsciously but consistently weighs in on the side of the Right Hand of God (by assuming, for example, that it's natural for people to look out for number one at the expense of everything else or to use power to achieve domination over others). Pick a particular show and monitor it through the year, or do the same with a particular advertiser. Keep careful notes about what you see, including which programs you are referring to and shown on which days. Then send me these details so that I can work with you to bring this challenge into the public sphere.

What we really need is our own spiritually progressive media institutions, television networks, movies, newspapers, and video games. We have the creativity but lack the funding, but eventually that will come. Meantime, ask liberal and progressive media to become more open to the voice of spiritual progressives.

8. *Develop rituals to put progressive meaning back into America's most significant holidays.* Compile a progressive Haggadah, or storybook, and create a ritual meal like a Passover seder for the Fourth of July, to celebrate all the incredible victories for democracy and human rights that ordinary people have struggled to win, often in the face of enormous opposition from America's ruling elites and the media they control. Turn July 4 from Independence Day into Interdependence Day by celebrating our connection to the rest of humanity and affirming the equal worth of people all over the world and by telling stories

of contemporary struggles for independence. Teach this tradition to your children by making the ritual meal a time for them to participate in telling these stories and by dedicating each round of fireworks to one such past victory or one such current struggle in need of support.

Create an "Honor Labor" day in your community. Assemble political and religious leaders along with popular entertainers and sports figures to listen to and honor the stories of ordinary working people and the contributions they make to the well-being of the rest of us. Ask the local media to do a feature each week about a different profession or workplace that will allow workers to tell their stories. Then, at the annual celebration, pick five of these to receive special attention and honor from the community.

Create a Family Day to honor families and explore the difficulties people have in building and sustaining relationships within the context of the old bottom line. Be sure to provide equal honor to single-parent families, blended families, and gay and lesbian families. Affirm the right of people to choose to remain single. Use this day for public education about the various ways that communities and friends can provide support for families along the lines suggested in the Spiritual Covenant with America.

9. *Build a spiritual progressives caucus in your church, synagogue, mosque, or temple.* Believe it or not, some of the places that most need a strong spiritual politics caucus are liberal churches, synagogues, and the like. Often these institutions are led by senior members of the clergy or board members who are afraid of the loss of membership and the disunity that might ensue should the institution openly advocate the Spiritual Covenant with America and a new bottom line. We need to help the leaders of the liberal religious communities understand that in the long run their institutions will be far more robust and far more likely to attract large numbers of people if they become less wishy-washy and more explicitly committed to the Left Hand of God.

A spiritual progressives caucus in your church or synagogue can strengthen the backbone of the leadership provided it takes the time to work in a compassionate yet firm way to insist that the religious values being taught inside the community must be taken seriously in the larger world. Right-wing religious institutions have no compunctions about taking a stand on a wide variety of public issues. Your religious institution can and should do so as well, without officially advocating on behalf of any particular political party or candidate. But it can become a passionate advocate for a vision like the Spiritual Covenant with America and can officially affiliate with the Network of Spiritual Progressives.

Don't let your community of worship back away from this challenge by focusing only on one issue: insist on the covenant and the new bottom line as a foundation for a whole new approach. Single-issue politics leads to a dead end because, while people may become knowledgeable about that specific issue, they rarely get the larger picture. Insist that your community teach support for the Left Hand of God as an intrinsic part of religious education, preparing both children and adults to meet the onslaught of cynical realism they will face the moment they say they intend to take the commandments "Love thy neighbor" and "Do not oppress the stranger" to heart.

10. *Develop "We Care" support groups and activities in your community.* While our primary focus must be on changing economic and political institutions so that they can provide the services needed for everyone, a spiritual politics movement should also encourage a high level of volunteerism in projects designed to alleviate the worst suffering caused by the old bottom line. So local chapters of the Network of Spiritual Progressives should seek to cooperate with religious groups and progressive social change movements to create a network of volunteer "We Care" support activities that can address:

The plight of seniors and, particularly, the loneliness faced by many people who are aging and alone, sometimes barely able to do their own shopping or to afford life's necessities

The realities of subsistence living for several million homeless people

The fear suffered by people facing severe health problems

The challenges that confront people leaving oppressive marriages

The difficulties singles experience in finding appropriate partners without having to participate in a rat race of competition and endure demeaning comparisons with media-generated ideals of attractiveness

The terrible strain on parents who cannot afford adequate child care and for whom the demands of work often conflict with the need to ensure the safety of their children who must walk home from school and then fend for themselves until their parents arrive

The problems with self-esteem as well as the financial problems facing people who cannot find new employment after having been laid off from work

Nothing can substitute for the social transformations outlined in the Spiritual Covenant with America, but we are nevertheless obligated in the meantime to do what we can to mitigate some of the suffering in our society caused by the continuing triumph of the ethos of selfishness and materialism.

Here we must bear in mind two important caveats. First, spiritual progressives must organize these support activities without seeking political gain other than that accrued simply by letting recipients of these services know about the idea of the Left Hand of God and the existence of a Network of Spiritual Progressives. Attempts to manipulate people while they are vulnerable are morally despicable and correctly condemned.

Second, if we are to be truly helpful, we must understand that people facing difficult circumstances require special levels of sensitivity. Not everyone who shares a spiritually progressive orientation is necessarily well suited to do this kind of support work, so such efforts must be preceded by careful training. In addition, people who do not appear to have the appropriate people-skills and communication-skills should be discouraged from participating in We Care support activities. Remember: don't try to do everything. Burnout of caregivers is no real service to the world!

11. *Use nonviolent direct action to challenge the institutions of social injustice, militarism, and environmental destructiveness.* Spiritual progressives should not limit their activities to those organized by established peace, social justice, and environmental movements. Too often, for example, antiwar demonstrators have little in the way of a vision of what kind of world they want to see other than one in which a specific

war has ended. Nor is it sufficient to have our alternative vision of the world listed as the thirty-fifth item on a laundry list of demands.

If a progressive spiritual politics is to be heard, we will need to create our own public demonstrations, sit-ins, pray-ins, and other activities that directly challenge the war machine, corporate irresponsibility, and governmental injustice. These actions can take the form of trailing and leafleting candidates for office (of whatever party—Democrats are often as likely to be offenders as Republicans) whose policies have a detrimental impact that may not be understood by their supporters. They can take the form of challenging donors to political candidates who support policies destructive to peace or environmental sustainability. Yet these confrontations must be conducted in a spirit of respect for the humanity of the people who are nonetheless engaged in morally unacceptable activities and with a clear commitment to affirming their worth as human beings and even as potential allies in healing the planet and building peace and social justice.

12. *Contribute your ideas to the Tikkun think tank.* The think tank seeks ways to apply the vision of the Left Hand of God to the specific policy issues that face us as a country and as a global community. We'd love to hear your ideas about how to apply this perspective. So once you've joined the Network of Spiritual Progressives, we'll give you a way of interacting directly with the people in the Tikkun think tank so that you can share your ideas. Some of that thinking will be published in *Tikkun* magazine.

13. *Reach out to people who disagree with our ideas, listen to their concerns, and engage in respectful dialogue.* We have much to learn from others, so the point of these sessions should be less to convince them than to share ideas and perspectives. This ongoing dialogue is very different from the familiar practice of showing up once every four years to "get out the vote." The goal here is to introduce others to the ideas of the Left Hand of God while hearing from them their own views on the best way to heal and transform our world. Do not use guilt as a motivator. Simply share information and perspectives. You'll be amazed to find that many people who identify with the Right actually support many of our goals, particularly in regard to ecological sanity and ending poverty. Many of them don't want to be part of a nation that tortures people. Many simply do not know the story of how the

global economy works to generate poverty in the third world, do not know about the realities of torture that the United States supports both directly and indirectly, do not know about the role of this country in overthrowing democratic governments over the past fifty years, or do not know the pain the United States has inflicted upon the people of Vietnam and Iraq. Sharing information can be a very powerful way to begin a conversation. Most important, many of these people will never have heard a coherent presentation of the Left Hand of God or met anyone who was serious about creating a world of love and nonviolence. Be that person for them, and you may open for them a set of questions that may eventually lead some of them to join your local Network of Spiritual Progressives.

14. *Develop your own inner life.* Do not let your involvement in political activity, even spiritual political activity, eat up so much of your life that you no longer have time for daily nourishing of your soul. For some people, this will mean taking time each morning to pray, meditate, walk in nature. For others, it will mean taking time to listen to or create beautiful music, art, or literature. For still others, it will mean engaging in some of the "We Care" activities suggested above. For still others, it will mean making a weekly commitment to a full-day Sabbath observance. Stay honest with yourself, and if a given spiritual practice or path no longer seems to be working, try another.

If you engage in these activities and do so with an attitude of love and generosity and forgiveness toward those who have offended you or who fail to act in ways that you believe they ought, you can make a major contribution to saving America from the Religious Right and building a world of social justice, peace, environmental sanity, and loving-kindness. Let's do it together!

APPENDIX TWO

How to Do Politics with Spirit:
Building the Culture of
a Spiritual Politics Movement

There is never going to be a simple formula that will tell us how to embody the life energy of the universe, the spirit of God, or the love of humanity when we engage in politics. No matter how wonderful the ideas that we put forward, they are unlikely to draw a strong and lasting following unless we ourselves exemplify those ideas in the way we treat each other and treat those with whom we disagree. So, to the extent that we are committed to the Democratic Party (whether because it comes close to representing our ideas or whether because it is the party most likely to win power that still has something vaguely in common with our ideas) or the Greens or whatever other political party we believe will be able to advocate effectively for the Spiritual Covenant with America, we are going to have to give some real energy to changing the culture within that party to make it less prone to a "whatever it takes to win" orientation and more receptive to a "let's embody our highest ideals and articulate them fully and honestly" approach to the world.

I grew sick to my stomach when I attended the last Democratic Party Convention in 2004. The militarism on the floor of the convention was bad enough, but what was equally sickening were the parties, caucuses, and other gatherings surrounding the event. Huge corporations had spent hundreds of thousands of dollars on various entertainments in an effort to curry or retain favor with the powerful. And the delegates seemed mesmerized by the combination of high technology, glitterati, and loud music. There was not a touch of spiritual awareness, no moment of higher purpose, no sense that one was part of a community that stood for anything more than consumption and money and a love of show business.

Perhaps this kind of thing was appropriate for the Republicans—after all, their convention was mostly about celebrating all that they had been able to pour into the coffers of the rich from the hands of poor and middle-income people. But what about the culture of a party that was supposedly protesting against the enrichment of the rich and presenting alternative values? To be credible, a political party must have a culture that at least in some manner represents the values it claims to support.

Not that I'm objecting to having fun as part of a social change movement. The social change movements of the past forty years have always combined fun and music with protest and moral seriousness. Nor, of course, would I want to see a particular spiritual practice imposed on us by government. No government should ever seek to mandate a particular religion or set of religious practices for all the people in a society. While people will always bring their spiritual, religious, and ideological assumptions into the political arena to argue for specific social policies, those policies have to be justifiable on universal rational grounds and not simply because they fit the moral preferences of a particular religious community.

There is, moreover, another reason why we don't want to see government beginning to use its vast power to push people to adhere to a particular set of spiritual practices: the critical need of human beings for privacy, for a space in their lives in which the government has no power to intervene. So, when I talk about spiritual practices, I am not talking about practices that a political party or movement should seek to have implemented by the government.

The Republicans already have a cultural and spiritual context for their politics: the churches of the Religious Right, along with a growing number of Orthodox and Conservative synagogues. The Right Hand of God is celebrated and woven into the psyches of tens of millions of children and adults each week in these assemblies. But in the churches of the mainstream denominations of Protestantism and in many Reform, Reconstructionist, and Renewal synagogues there is a great reluctance to "impose" a particular political character or to preach unambiguously in favor of the Left Hand of God. Liberal ministers and rabbis will tell you that they don't want to be seen as forcing any particular position on their congregants because they wish to be "inclusive" and because they know of some members of their congregations who would be offended and possibly leave the community were they, for example, to be consistent in opposing war as an instrument of American foreign policy or were they to introduce into the religious instruction of the young information about the connection between America's patterns of consumption and the destruction of the global environment, much less about the ways in which their own religious tradition is being used today to justify wars and oppression.

While some of the Protestant denominations, and also Reform Judaism, do pass liberal resolutions at their national conventions and maintain lobbyists in Washington who present those positions to Congress, few of their congregants know much about the content of those resolutions. Fewer still feel that they could expect that their churches and synagogues would be the place to turn to discuss how to successfully combat the growing power of the Religious Right or how to prevent the government from starting a war with Iran or from packing the courts with right-wing judges. These conversations would be judged far too "political" by most of the liberal synagogues and churches—since they are liberal about their liberalism. You would find no similar hesitation in most right-wing churches to, for example, mix into their Sunday services explicit prayers and rituals supporting the war in Iraq or, in Orthodox synagogues, to pray for "victory" for the state of Israel and protection for its soldiers "in the air, on the ground, and in the sea."

The Left Hand of God needs a more secure context in which spiritual consciousness and a shared commitment to a spiritual politics can flourish. A spiritual culture in the Democratic Party would first have to try to create some reality for the Democratic Party as an entity that actually exists rather than a collective hallucination that comes into being in the months before each election. To accomplish this, the Democrats would have to take some of the tens of millions of dollars that it currently pours into election campaigns and channel it into paid organizers, whose task would be to help with what MoveOn.org and other organizations have already proven to be possible—the mobilization of millions of ordinary citizens to attend local meetings to discuss pressing national issues.

Imagine, for instance, if the Democrats set for themselves the modest goal of bringing together people in every community in the country once a month to attend a meeting at someone's house, meetings at which they watched the network evening news together, and then turned to a cable station where some of the more insightful and provocative Democrats around provided half an hour of commentary on the news and its significance when seen through the framework of a consistent progressive spiritual politics, and then were encouraged to discuss what they had seen and their reactions to it, and then shared some spiritual inspiration in the form of music, singing, poetry, or meditation, and then heard reports from representatives of local projects in which the Democrats were engaging in acts of kindness and generosity and learned about opportunities to join those projects, and finally shared a potluck meal, before ending with a blessing after the meal on the food and a shared commitment to reorganizing the world so that everyone on the planet would have enough to eat.

At first, most Democrats would probably not participate, suspecting that this would just be another event dreamed up by the slick public relations firms hired by the Democratic Party in hopes of manipulating people into going door-to-door to "get out the vote." But if these meetings were run in a way that encouraged genuine discussion about politics in a respectful tone, if the national party commentators on cable TV did not simply repeat whatever the party line was at the moment but instead talked about an array of perspectives, including those critical of the current party lines, if the religious and spiritual practices introduced each month always remained sensitive to the diversity of backgrounds and spiritual proclivities of those in attendance, if there was a chairperson at each household gathering who made sure that no one person spoke for too long and that none of the evening's events exceeded its allotted time, and if there was someone empowered to exclude from the meeting anyone who was abusive or disruptive (in the way that the president or minister in a congregation ultimately has the authority to exclude such people from religious gatherings), and if, on top of all that, the food was good, the word would spread, and these meetings would soon flourish. Meetings such as these would create a concrete culture for the Democratic Party that could only enhance its success when election season did roll around.

I imagine that, for each of these gatherings, we would want to have local committees who would select the musical offerings, poetry, prayers, and songs with two criteria in mind: a commitment to include various sectors of the population in each evening's cultural offerings and a commitment to a high-enough quality that people could feel they were getting the very best of the cultures included in that evening's program. But, of course, a culture is more than a performance. It is a way of thinking and being together.

There is much that we can learn from movements of the past and from the wisdom of the world's religious and spiritual communities. First, we could learn a lesson taught by the Quakers and Buddhists, namely, that we need to be less focused on immediate outcomes and more focused on maintaining the integrity of our vision and the lives we live in attempting to embody that vision. We can give our fullest attention to developing the best possible strategy for change and pursue it with all our energies, but we should let go of our attachment to the notion that we are failing unless we have already won. Or, as one Rabbi Tarfon put it in the Mishnah: "It is not incumbent upon you to finish the work, but neither are you free to desist from it." Religious communities have been able to sustain themselves without despair when they kept this in mind.

Second, we could learn that the path to change must embody the values that we seek in the future. We can't build a world of love and generosity and integrity with a movement that is unloving, ungenerous, and opportunistic. Above all, we can't build a world of compassion without being compassionate—so we can't be excessively judgmental about either ourselves or others. We must avoid the tendency prevalent in many social change movements to allow our desire to be living examples of our values to be turned into a club we use to beat up each other for sometimes not being loving, generous, or principled enough.

Third, we need to have balance in our politics as in our lives. There is no easy formula for this. Spiritual balance is achieved through a long life of spiritual practice. Meditation, prayer, walks in nature, immersion in poetry and fiction and philosophy and the study of sacred texts, dance, exercise, art—all these can be important sources of energy for promoting balance. Such activities need to be encouraged among those who are engaged in social change movements.

Fourth, we need to find spiritual technologies to help us pass on from generation to generation the wisdom and the values that we embrace. For example, we in the Jewish world have placed a huge emphasis on telling the story of the liberation of the Israelites from bondage in Egypt, especially to our children. Every week a portion of that story is read from the Torah in synagogues around the world. The Sabbath celebration is intended in part as a way of reliving the experience of being free from the demands of work to which we were enslaved in Egypt. And once a year, at a family or community dinner, the Passover seder, dedicated fully to celebrating that liberation, Jews gather to retell and rejoice in that story.

Wouldn't it be wonderful if all the various movements committed to social change agreed on one day a year when everyone collaborated to celebrate the great victories of human liberation throughout the millennia, developed a shared storybook that recounted some of these stories in a way that could be understood by children as well as adults, held family and community dinners at which stories from the book were read and people could add their own special stories and at which people sang songs, danced, ate delicious food, and joyously conveyed to the next generation how, despite overwhelming obstacles, the human race has made progress toward building a world of love, generosity, and kindness? Let that annual celebration also be a moment to conceive new visions of the future and even to debate ideas about how to make them real.

A Democratic Party or a social change movement that allowed itself to learn from the accumulated spiritual wisdom of the human race would have an immense potential to engage the most creative energies of the American people, liberating us from fear and supporting us in building the world we really want. If we encourage that culture to flourish, rather than seek to imitate the worst of the consumer culture, pretty soon we will have a movement that people want to be part of not only because it is morally right but also because it is fun, exciting, and deeply engaging to both the heart and the head.

Acknowledgments and Resources

I've long ago given up trying to fully acknowledge all the people who contributed to my thinking—the list is too long and goes beyond my capacities. I know that 99.9 percent of everything I think derives from the contributions of previous generations, starting with the Torah, the prophets, the holy writings, the Talmud, the great rabbinical teachers through the centuries, and the shapers of the kabbalah and Hasidism, and of the most creative thinkers in my own generation, including my own teachers, particularly Abraham Joshua Heschel and Zalman Schachter-Shalomi. They also have benefited from the important contributions to thought made by the women's movement over the past forty years, particularly the work of Carol Gilligan, Nancy Chodorow, Simone de Beauvoir, Shulamith Firestone, and Judith Plaskow.

The specific formulations of my ideas developed over thirty years of dialogue with Peter Gabel, my deepest friend and the source of many of the ideas in this book. I say this to encourage you to learn from Gabel, who serves as chair of the Institute for Spirituality and Politics at the New College of California, in San Francisco, as well as being the associate editor of *Tikkun* magazine.

There are many who have directly contributed to this work by giving it a careful reading and critique or by sharing their wisdom with me. I want to thank Dr. Michael Bader, Rabbi Debora Kohn Lerner, Estelle Frankel, Steve Goldbart, Michael Ziegler, Deborah Kory, Paul Wapner, Lisa Garrigues, Tony Campolo, Jordan Pearlstein, Joe Fischel, and Hal

Sampson. I want to give special thanks to my literary agent, Candice Furhman, my in-house editor at *Tikkun,* Jo Ellen Green Kaiser, and my editor at Harper San Francisco, Gideon Weil, whose extraordinary efforts on behalf of this book are tremendously appreciated.

It took all of my energies to restrain myself from heavily footnoting this book. But after my early years as a college professor, I came to the conclusion that most readers get distracted from the main themes when they find each page linked to a footnote. In this book I have not sought to prove my points so much as to present a worldview, a way of thinking, a framework that can be brought to bear on experience. But at the end of almost every paragraph I wanted to add an attribution, mostly to Peter Gabel, but then also to many others whose ideas permeate this book. Instead, what I decided to do is to list the books they have written in hopes that if you have been moved by the approach to a spiritual politics I outline here, you'll read them as well. The ancient rabbi Hillel was asked to teach the entire Torah while his challenger stood on one foot. His answer: "Do not do to another what would be hateful to you. This is the entire Torah. Now, go and study." Well, my book is not quite as pithy as that, but I do want to end it with the same advice: "Now, go and study"—to which I would append the request: "and join us in making it happen."

It's easy to use study as a substitute for action. At the same time, I've seen too many people jump into action without having developed a sufficient base of thought and spiritual practice to be able to sustain that action.

There are, of course, a wide variety of spiritual practices and communities that teach them. Start with your own church or synagogue, mosque, or temple, and seek the guidance of your local religious leader or spiritual practitioners to find out where you can go to learn how to deepen your personal spiritual practice. Personally I've benefited from the teachings at Spirit Rock Meditation Center, in Woodacre, California; the Omega Institute, in Rhinebeck, New York; Elat Chayyim, in Accord, New York; and the Esalen Institute, in Big Sur, California, as well as from the rigorous study I pursued at the Shalom Hartmann Institute in Jerusalem. I also have great respect for the learning that is available at Union Theological Seminary in New York and the various colleges of the Graduate Theological Union in Berkeley, particularly the Pacific School of Religion. And I am inspired by the work of Matthew Fox and believe that his new Wisdom University, in Oakland, California, has a wonderful program. Any way that you can study with Peter Gabel, at the Institute for Spirituality and Politics at the New College of California, will be very worth your time as well.

Here are some of the authors and books from which I have drawn ideas and inspiration:

Allen Aftermam. *Kabbalah and Consciousness.* Sheep Meadow Press, 1992.

Gar Alperovitz. *America Beyond Capitalism: Reclaiming Our Wealth, Our Liberty, and Our Democracy.* John Wiley & Sons, 2005.

Leonard Angel. *The Book of Miriam.* Mosaic Press, 1997.

Marc D. Angel. *Loving Truth and Peace: The Grand Religious Worldview of Rabbi Benzion Uziel.* Jason Aronson Publishers, 1999.

Karen Armstrong. *A History of God: The 4,000-Year Quest of Judaism, Christianity and Islam.* Knopf, 1993.

Marc Ian Barasch. *Field Notes on the Compassionate Life: A Search for the Soul of Kindness.* Rodale, 2005.

Nigel Barber. *Kindness in a Cruel World: The Evolution of Altruism.* Prometheus Books, 2004.

Zygmunt Bauman. *Wasted Lives: Modernity and Its Outcasts.* Blackwell, 2004.

Morris Berman. *Coming to Our Senses: Body and Spirit in the Hidden History of the West.* Simon & Schuster, 1989.

Brad Blanton. *Radical Parenting.* Hampton Roads, 2002.

Marcus J. Borg and N. T. Wright. *The Meaning of Jesus: Two Visions.* HarperSanFrancisco, 1989.

C. A. Bowers. *Mindful Conservatism.* Rowman & Littlefield, 2003.

Denise Breton and Stephen Lehman. *The Mystic Heart of Justice.* Chrysalis Books, 2001.

Walter Brueggemann. *The Book That Breathes New Life.* Fortress Press, 2005.

———. *The Land.* Fortress Press, 1977.

———. *Living Toward a Vision.* United Church Press, 1982.

———. *The Prophetic Imagination.* Fortress Press, 1978.

Martin Buber. *I and Thou.* Charles Scribner's Sons, 1958.

Yitzhak Buxbaum. *Jewish Spiritual Practice.* Jason Aronson Publishers, 1990.

Tony Campolo. *Speaking My Mind: The Radical Evangelical Prophet Tackles the Tough Issues Christians Are Afraid to Face.* W Publishing Group, 2004.

Deepak Chopra. *Peace Is the Way.* Harmony Books, 2005.

Robert Coles. *The Spiritual Life of Children.* Houghton Mifflin, 1990.

Rabbi David A. Cooper. *God Is a Verb.* Riverhead Books, 1997.

Harvey Cox. *When Jesus Came to Harvard: Making Moral Choices Today.* Houghton Mifflin, 2004.

John Dominic Crossan. *The Birth of Christianity: Discovering What Happened in the Years Immediately After the Execution of Jesus.* HarperSanFrancisco, 1968.

Lama Surya Das. *Awakening the Buddha Within.* Broadway Books, 1997.

John Dear. *The Question of Jesus: Challenging Ourselves to Discover Life's Great Answers.* Doubleday, 2004.

Dave DeLuca. *Vivekananda: Lessons in Classical Yoga.* Namaste Books, 2003.

Sara Diamond. *Roads to Dominion: Right-Wing Movements and Political Power in the United States.* Guilford Press, 1995.

David Domke. *God Willing?: Political Fundamentalism in the White House, the "War on Terror," and the Echoing Press.* Pluto Press, 2004.

Geroge Eberle. *Sacred Time and the Search for Meaning.* Shambhala, 2003.

Riane Eisler. *The Power of Partnership.* New World Library, 2002.

Mark Epstein, M.D. *Open to Desire: Embracing a Lust for Life Insights from Buddhism and Psychotherapy.* Gotham Books, 2005.

Ralph Estes. *Tyranny of the Bottom Line: Why Corporations Make Good People Do Bad Things.* Berrett-Koehler Publishers, 1995.

Amitai Etzioni. *Civic Repentance.* Rowman & Littlefield, 1999.

Leonard Felder. *The Ten Challenges: Spiritual Lessons from the Ten Commandments.* Harmony Books, 1997.

Matthew Fox. *Signs of the Spirit, Blessings of the Flesh.* Harmony Books, 1999.

Michael Allen Fox. *Deep Vegetarianism.* Temple University Press, 1999.

Thomas Frank. *What's the Matter with Kansas? How Conservatives Won the Heart of America.* Metropolitan Books, 2004.

Estelle Frankel. *Sacred Therapy.* Shambhala, 2003.

Marc Gafni. *The Mystery of Love.* Atria Books, 2003.

Nan Fink Gefen. *Discovering Jewish Meditation.* Jewish Lights Publishing, 1999.

David W. Gill. *Doing Right: Practicing Ethical Principles.* InterVarsity Press, 2004.

Daniel Goleman. *Emotional Intelligence.* Bantam Books, 1995.

Chris Goodrich. *Faith Is a Verb.* Gimlet Eye Books, 2005.

Marc Gopin. *Healing the Heart of Conflict.* Rodale, 2004.

Roger S. Gottlieb. *Joining Hands: Politics and Religion Together for Social Change.* Westview Press, 2002.

———. *A Spirituality of Resistance.* Crossroad, 1999.

Norman K. Gottwald. *The Bible and Liberation.* Orbis Books, 1983.

Marion Grau. *Of Divine Economy: Refinancing Redemption.* T & T Clark International, 2004.

Arthur Green. *Seek My Face: A Jewish Mystical Theology.* Jewish Lights Publishing, 2003.

Mary C. Grey. *Sacred Longings: The Ecological Spirit and Global Culture.* Fortress Press, 2004.

David Ray Griffin, ed. *Deep Religious Pluralism.* Westminster John Knox Press, 2005.

Douglas Gwyn. *The Covenant Crucified: Quakers and the Rise of Capitalism.* Pendle Hill Publications, 1995.

Dean Hamer. *The God Gene: How Faith Is Hardwired into Our Genes.* Doubleday, 2004.

Thich Nhat Hanh. *Finding Our True Home: Living in the Pure Land Here and Now.* Parallax Press, 2003.

Tom Harpur. *Would You Believe: Finding God Without Losing Your Mind.* McClelland and Stewart, 1996.

Tobin Hart. *The Secret Spiritual World of Children.* Inner Ocean Publishing, 2003.

Stephen R. Haynes and John K. Roth, eds. *The Death of God Movement and the Holocaust.* Greenwood Press, 1999.

Kabir Helminski. *The Knowing Heart: A Sufi Path of Transformation.* Shambhala, 1999.

Abraham Joshua Heschel. *God in Search of Man.* Farrar, Straus & Cudahy, 1955.

———. *Moral Grandeur and Spiritual Audacity.* HarperCollins, 1996.

———. *The Prophets.* Burning Bush Press, 1962.

Dieter T. Hessel and Rosemary Radford Ruether, eds. *Christianity and Ecology.* Harvard University Center for the Study of World Religions Publications, 2000.

Suzanne Holland, Karen Lebacqz, and Laurie Zoloth, eds. *The Human Embryonic Stem-Cell Debate.* MIT Press, 2001.

Mark Hulsether. *Building a Protestant Left: Christianity and Crisis Magazine, 1941–1993.* University of Tennessee Press, 1999.

Robert Inchausti. *Subversive Orthodoxy: Outlaws, Revolutionaries, and Other Christians in Disguise.* Brazos Press, 2005.

Christopher J. Insole. *The Politics of Human Frailty: A Theological Defense of Political Liberalism.* University of Notre Dame Press, 2004.

Robbie Pfeufer Kahn. *Bearing Meaning: The Language of Birth.* University of Illinois Press, 1995.

Rabbi Aryeh Kaplan. *Inner Space.* Moznaim Publishing, 1990.

Sam Keen. *Apology for Wonder.* Harper & Row, 1969.

Catherine Keller. *God and Power: Counter-Apocalyptic Journeys.* Fortress Press, 2005.

Marjorie Kelly. *The Divine Right of Capital.* Berrett-Koehler Publishers, 2001.

Abraham Isaac Kook. *The Lights of Penitence, The Moral Principles, Lights of Holiness, Essays, Letters, and Poems.* Paulist Press, 1978.

Joel Kovel. *History and Spirit.* Beacon Press, 1991.

Jeffrey J. Kripal. *Kali's Child.* University of Chicago Press, 1995.

Hans Kung. *Does God Exist?* Vintage Books, 1981.

George Lakoff. *Metaphors We Live By.* University of Chicago Press, 2003.

———. *Don't Think of an Elephant.* Chelsea Green Publishing Co., 2004.

Rabbi Michael Lerner. *Healing Israel/Palestine: A Path to Peace and Reconciliation.* Tikkun Books, 2003.

————. *Jewish Renewal: A Path to Healing and Transformation.* G. P Putnam's Sons, 1994.

————. *Surplus Powerlessness: The Psychodynamics of Everyday Life and the Psychology of Individual and Social Transformation.* Humanities Press International, 1986.

Rabbi Michael Lerner and Cornel West. *Jews and Blacks: A Dialogue on Race, Religion, and Culture in America.* Plume Books, 1996.

Rabbi Robert N. Levine. *There Is No Messiah and You're It: The Stunning Transformation of Judaism's Most Proactive Idea.* Jewish Lights Publishing, 2003.

Richard Lichtman. *The Production of Desire.* Free Press, 1982.

Sara Maitland. *A Joyful Theology.* Augsburg Books, 2002.

Herbert Marcuse. *One-Dimensional Man.* Beacon Press, 1964.

Martin E. Marty. *The One and the Many: America's Struggle for the Common Good.* Harvard University Press, 1997.

Richard Mason. *The God of Spinoza.* Cambridge University Press, 1997.

Daniel C. Matt. *God and the Big Bang.* Jewish Lights Publishing, 1996.

Alastair McIntosh. *Soil and Soul: People Versus Corporate Power.* Aurum Press, 2004.

Corinne McLaughlin and Gordon Davidson. *Spiritual Politics: Changing the World from the Inside Out.* Ballantine Books, 1994.

Thomas Merton. *The New Man.* Farrar Strauss Giroux, 1961.

Alice Miller. *The Body Never Lies: The Lingering Effects of Cruel Parenting.* Norton, 2005.

John (Jack) Miller and Yoshiharu Nakagawa, eds. *Nurturing Our Wholeness: Perspectives on Spirituality in Education.* Foundation for Educational Renewal, 2002.

Don Mitchell. *The Right to the City.* Guilford, 2003.

Ian Mitroff and Elizabeth Denton. *A Spiritual Audit of Corporate America.* Jossey-Bass, 1999.

Thomas Moore. *The Re-enchantment of Everyday Life.* HarperPerennial, 1996.

Alan Morinis. *Climbing Jacob's Ladder.* Broadway Books, 2002.

Seyyed Hossein Nasr. *Islam: Religion, History, and Civilization.* HarperSanFrancisco, 2003.

————. *The Heart of Islam.* HarperSanFrancisco, 2002.

Samuel P. Oliner. *Do Unto Others: Extraordinary Acts of Ordinary People.* Westview Press, 2003.

Dean Ornish. *Love and Survival.* HarperCollins, 1998.

Edmund V. O'Sullivan. *Transformative Learning.* Zed Books, 1999.

Edmund V. O'Sullivan, Amish Morrell, and Mary Ann O'Connor, eds. *Expanding the Boundaries of Transformative Learning.* Palgrave, 2001.

Glenn D. Paige. *Nonkilling Global Political Science.* Xlibris Corporation, 2002.

Parker J. Palmer. *The Courage to Teach.* Jossey-Bass, 1998.

Alex Pattakos. *Prisoners of Our Thoughts.* Berrett-Koehler Publishers, 2004.

Rodney L. Petersen. *Christianity and Civil Society.* Orbis Books, 1995.

Salvatore Puledda. *On Being Human: Interpretations of Humanism: Western Humanisms from the Renaissance to the Present.* Latitude Press, 1997.

Robert D. Putnam and Lewis Feldstein, with Don Cohen. *Better Together: Restoring the American Community.* Simon & Schuster, 2003.

Franz Josef Radermacher. *Balance or Destruction: Ecosocial Market Economy as the Key to Global Sustainable Development.* Oeksoziales Forum Europa, 2004.

Robert B. Reich. *Reason: Why Liberals Will Win the Battle for America.* Knopf, 2004.

Rabbi Zalman Schachter-Shalomi. *Paradigm Shift.* Jason Aronson Publishers, 1993.

————, with Joel Segel. *Jewish with Feeling: A Guide to Meaningful Jewish Practice.* Penguin Books, 2005.

Rabbi Zalman Schachter-Shalomi and Ronald S. Miller. *From Age-ing to Sage-ing.* Warner Books, 1995.

Naomi Schaefer. *God on the Quad: How Religious Colleges and the Missionary Generation Are Changing America.* St. Martin's Press, 2005.

Richard H. Schwartz. *Judaism and Global Survival.* Atara Publishing, 1987.

Jonathan Schell. *The Unconquerable World.* Henry Holt, 2003.

Kirk J. Schneider. *The Rediscovery of Awe: Splendor, Mystery, and the Fluid Center of Life.* Paragon House, 2004.

Rabbi Kalonymus Kalman Shapira. *Conscious Community.* Jason Aronson Publishers, 1996.

Rabbi Rami M. Shapiro. *Minyan: Ten Principles for Living a Life of Integrity.* Bell Tower, 1997.

————, ed. and tran. *The Hebrew Prophets: Selections Annotated and Explained.* Skylights Paths Publishing, 2004.

Jason Shulman. *Kabbalistic Healing: A Path to an Awakened Soul.* Inner Traditions, 2004.

Peter Sloterdijk. *Critique of Cynical Reason.* University of Minnesota Press, 1987.

Daniel L. Smith. *The Religion of the Landless.* Meyer-Stone Books, 1989.

Robert C. Solomon. *Spirituality for the Skeptic: The Thoughtful Love of Life.* Oxford University Press, 2002.

Rabbi Joseph B. Soloveitchik. *Out of the Whirlwind: Essays on Mourning, Suffering, and the Human Condition.* KTAV Publishing, 2003.

Charlene Spretnak. *The Resurgence of the Real: Body, Nature, and Place in a Hypermodern World.* Routledge, 1999.

John Stoltenberg. *Refusing to Be a Man: Essays on Sex and Justice.* UCL Press, 2000.

Brian Swimme. *The Hidden Heart of the Cosmos.* Orbis Books, 1996.

Kathryn Tanner. *Economy of Grace.* Fortress Press, 2005.

Charles Taylor. *Sources of the Self.* Harvard University Press, 1989.

Robert Thurman. *The Jewel Tree of Tibet.* Free Press, 2005.

Geza Vermes. *The Religion of Jesus the Jew.* Fortress Press, 1993.

Jim Wallis. *God's Politics: Why the Rights Gets It Wrong and the Left Doesn't Get It.* HarperSanFrancisco, 2005.

Rabbi Arthur Waskow. *Down-to-Earth Judaism.* William Morrow, 1995.

Zoe Weil. *Above All Be Kind: Raising a Humane Child in Challenging Times.* New Society Publishers, 2003.

Cornel West. *Democracy Matters.* Penguin Group, 2005.

Marianne Williamson. *The Gift of Change.* HarperSanFrancisco, 2004.

Paul Woodruff. *Reverence.* Oxford University Press, 2001.

Worldwatch Institute. *Vital Signs 2005.* Norton, 2005.

Robert Wuthnow. *Growing Up Religious.* Beacon Press, 1999.

John Howard Yoder. *The Politics of Jesus.* Eerdmans, 1972.
Danah Zohar and Ian Marshall. *Spiritual Capital: Wealth We Can Live By.* Berrett-Koehler, 2004.
Laurie Zoloth. *Health Care and the Ethics of Encounter: A Jewish Discussion of Social Justice.* University of North Carolina Press, 1999.

Index